Missed Opportunities?

Also by New Academia Publishing

SOCIAL PROPRIETIES: Social Relations in Early-Modern England (1500-1680), by David A. Postles

SOCIAL GEOGRAPHIES IN ENGLAND 1200-1640, by David A. Postles

NATIONALISM, HISTORIOGRAPHY, AND THE (RE)CONSTRUCTION OF THE PAST, Claire Norton, ed.

SHAKESPEARE'S THEATER OF LIKENESS, by R. Allen Shoaf

www.newacademia.com

Missed Opportunities?

Religious Houses and the Laity in the English "High Middle Ages"

David A. Postles

New Academia Publishing
Washington, DC

Copyright © 2009 by David A. Postles

New Academia Publishing, 2009

All rights reserved. No part of this book may be reproduced or transmitted in any form or by any means, electronic or mechanical, including photocopying, recording, or by any information storage and retrieval system.

Printed in the United States of America

Library of Congress Control Number: 2009935179
ISBN 978-0-9823867-5-0 paperback (alk. paper)

New Academia Publishing, LLC
P.O. Box 27420
Washington, DC 20038-7420
www.newacademia.com - info@newacademia.com

Contents

Acknowledgments vii
Abbreviations xi
List of Illustrations xxiv

Introduction 1

Part I

1. Religious Houses and the Laity in Eleventh- to Thirteenth-Century England: An Overview 19
2. Lamps, Lights and Layfolk: "Popular" Devotion Before the Black Death 35
3. Monastic Burials of Non-patronal Lay Benefactors 61
4. Small Gifts, but Big Rewards: The Symbolism of Some Gifts to the Religious 85
5. Pittances and Pittancers 113
6. The Austin Canons in English Towns, ca.1100-1350 131
7. Heads of Religious Houses as Administrators 159

Part II

8. Gifts in Frankalmoign, Warranty of Land, and Feudal Society 177
9. Seeking the Language of Warranty of Land in Twelfth-Century England 199
10. Tenure in Frankalmoign and Knight Service in Twelfth-Century England: Interpretation of the Charters 221
11. Choosing Witnesses in Twelfth-Century England 241

Acknowledgments

An immense debt is owed to all those editors of journals and their anonymous referees and readers who made innumerable kind and helpful suggestions for the improvement of these papers. The following publishing houses have kindly allowed reproduction of the papers here: Boydell (Chapters 1, 5); Elsevier (Chapters 2, 4); Cambridge University Press (Chapters 3, 8); Blackwell (Chapter 6); and Shaun Tyas Publishing (Chapter 7).

Chapter 1 was published as "Religious Houses and the Laity in Eleventh- to Thirteenth-century England: An Overview" in *Haskins Society Journal* 12 (2003): 1-13, and was presented at the Haskins Society Conference at Cornell University in 2001. I am grateful to Paul Hyams for yet more kindness.

Chapter 2 "Lamps, Lights and Layfolk: 'Popular' Devotion Before the Black Death" is reprinted from *Journal of Medieval History* 25 (1999): 97-114. Malcolm Barber kindly guided this paper through the press.

Chapter 3 reproduces "Monastic Burials of Non-patronal Lay Benefactors", *Journal of Ecclesiastical History* 47 (1996): 620-37 and was much improved by the comments of Martin Brett and Christopher Harper-Bill.

Chapter 4 ("Small Gifts, but Big Rewards: The Symbolism of Some Gifts to the Religious") first appeared in *Journal of Medieval History* 27 (2001): 23-42, and again benefited from the attention of Malcolm Barber as Editor.

Chapter 5 was originally presented at the "Thirteenth Century Conference" at the University of Durham in 2001 and was subsequently published as "Pittances and Pittancers" in

Thirteenth Century England IX, edited by Michael Prestwich et al. (Woodbridge: Boydell, 2003), 175-86. Participants at the conference kindly made helpful suggestions, in particular Paul Brand, Michael Clanchy, Nicola Coldstream, Henry Summerson, and Jocelyn Wogan-Browne. The paper was subsequently (28 November 2001) read at the Cambridge "Medieval Economy and Society Seminar" at Corpus Christi College and I am grateful to John Hatcher for that invitation. Thoughtful comments were made there by Dominic Alexander, John Hatcher, Miri Rubin and Richard Smith. I have not been able respond to some of the ideas since pittancers' accounts tend not to be "diet" accounts, and for associations between food and gender (Wogan-Browne) my data are insufficient. Barbara Harvey commented on the published paper and some changes have been introduced in the light of her points.

Chapter 6 "The Austin Canons in English Towns, c.1100-1350" was included in *Historical Research* 66 (1993): 1-20, and had previously been read at the Centre for Urban History, University of Leicester, in November 1991. The late Babette Evans made many important points at and after that seminar. Earlier obligations had been incurred to the late Geoffrey Martin for much discussion about these matters.

Chapter 7 "Heads of Religious Houses as Administrators" appeared in *England in the Thirteenth Century,* edited by Mark Ormrod (Stamford: Paul Watkins Publishing, 1991), 37-50. When the paper was read at the "Harlaxton Medieval Symposium", Michael Clanchy and Mark Ormrod made important suggestions.

Chapter 8 "Gifts in Frankalmoign, Warranty of Land, and Feudal Society" is reprinted from *Cambridge Law Journal* 50 (1991): 330-46, and benefited from comments by S. F. C. (Toby) Milsom.

Chapter 9 "Seeking the Language of Warranty of Land in Twelfth-century England" appeared first in *The Journal of the Society of Archivists* 20 (1999): 209-22, and was kindly read in draft by Paul Hyams.

Chapter 10 "Tenure in Frankalmoign and Knight Service in Twelfth-century England: Interpretation of the Charters", *Journal of the Society of Archivists* 13 (1992): 18-28, benefited from conversations with Benjamin Thompson.

Chapter 11 "Choosing Witnesses in Twelfth-century England", *The Irish Jurist* n.s. xxiii (1988): 330-46, was improved by the comments of Paul Brand and Michael Clanchy.

The papers reproduced here were composed over a long period from 1990 (the *Irish Jurist* included, despite that volume's date of publication) and 2003. During that time, considerable literature appeared which had implications for the papers. That secondary work as been integrated into the later papers, but is missing from the earlier papers which have not been revised in the light of later literature. In the last six years, of course, research into these issues has been even more refined. No attempt has been made to introduce that more recent work; the articles re-published here are exactly as they first appeared. The reason for not revising the papers is that the introduction of the later secondary material would be awkward. Instead, some recapitulation of and comments on some of that more recent literature is offered below.

Some of the obligations must be further recollected and emphasized. Discussion with Benjamin Thompson in the early 1990s about many matters relating to free alms helped to clarify many points. More generally, the whole of Part II engages within the highly significant suggestions of Michael Clanchy, Paul Hyams, Emily Tabuteau, and Stephen White, which explains the constant references to their publications. The debts to Michael Clanchy and Paul Hyams extend to personal communication and discussion too. Barbara Harvey has been a constant source of advice and perspicacious criticism. Janet Burton has often given sound advice to temper my precipitate ideas.

Those are the formal academic acknowledgements, although the blemishes which remain are entirely my own responsibility. The support of many others in various ways has been extremely valuable. Close colleagues at the University of Leicester, especially Greg Walker and Elaine Treharne who have now moved to pastures new, have been not only friends, but thought-provoking acquaintances. The Medieval Research Centre there has provided collegiality and rich stimulation, directed at various stages by Elaine, Greg, Jo Story and Anne Marie D'Arcy. A convivial and congenial environment has been necessary over the years for casual reflection and the tedious process of reading through drafts. Four venues have been especially important in that respect: the Senior Common Room and the Piazza at the University of Leicester (so inordinate thanks to Catherine, Charlotte, Gaz, Jackie, Jo, Liz, Odette, Rose, and Sue); Costa in Loughborough (so warm thanks to Danielle, Jo, Lauren, Paul, Richard, Rob, Sam, and the amazing bunch of young people studying for their A2s who have worked there at the weekends); and Costa (formerly Ritazza) at Donington Park Services, to whose various staff I am grateful for their kindness.

I came to the world of research into medieval history by mistake. As an undergraduate, my fascination and primary interest was in all matters early-modern. I was diverted in my final year to medieval economy and manorial society because the early-modern Special Subjects did not attract my interest. My engagement with medieval matters continued through my contract as archive trainee at the Bodleian Library in 1970-1, where I had the opportunity to peruse the manorial accounts of Osney Abbey in the evenings and the great attraction of seminars in diplomatics with Pierre Chaplais. So it was that during my archival career of eighteen years, I maintained an interest in medieval matters, although the archival profession demands much wider competence. Much of my working life was thus concerned with the records of local government and urban development and with the rescue of the records of businesses. Two conferences allowed contact with the world of medieval research: the triennial Anglo-American Symposia on the Medieval Economy and Society (in Exeter in 1983 and Norwich in 1986) organized by Bruce Campbell and the annual Harlaxton Medieval Symposium. Those two events sustained my contact with medieval research until I acquired an academic post in 1988.

Abbreviations

"Abstract ... Burton Chartulary"	George Wrottesley, "An Abstract of the Contents of the Burton Chartulary", Collections for a History of Staffordshire vol. I, part, v, Stafford, 1884
Account-book ... Beaulieu	S. F. Hockey, ed., *Account-book of Beaulieu Abbey*, Camden 4th ser., vol. 16, London, 1975
Accounts of the Obedientiars of Abingdon Abbey	R. E. G. Kirk, ed., *Accounts of the Obedientiars of Abingdon Abbey*, Camden n.s., vol. 51, London, 1892
Annales Monastici	H. R. Luard, ed., *Annales Monastici*, Rolls Series, 5 vols., London, 1864-9
Basset Charters	W. T. Reedy, ed., *Basset Charters c.1120 to 1250*, P.R.S. n.s., vol. 50, London, 1995 for 1989-91
Beauchamp Cartulary	Emma Mason, ed., *The Beauchamp Cartulary and Charters 1100-1268*, PRS n.s., vol. 43, London, 1980
BL	British Library, London
Blythburgh Priory Cartulary	Christopher Harper-Bill, ed., *Blythburgh Priory Cartulary*, Suffolk Record Society Suffolk Charters vol. 3, Ipswich, 1981
Bodl.	Bodleian Library, Oxford

Bracton on the Laws and Customs of England	Samuel E. Thorne, ed. and trans., *Bracton On the Laws and Customs of England*, 4 vols. (Cambridge, Mass.: Harvard University Press, 1968-77)
Calendar of the Manuscripts of the Dean and Chapter of Wells	*Calendar of the Manuscripts of the Dean and Chapter of Wells*, HMC Report no. 12, 2 vols., London, 1907 and 1914
Cartularium ... Gyseburne	[William Brown, ed.] *Cartularium Prioratus de Gyseburne ...*, Surtees Society, vols. 86, 89, 2 vols., Durham, 1889-91
Cartulary of Beaulieu Abbey	S. F. Hockey, ed., *The Cartulary of Beaulieu Abbey*, Southampton Record Society vol. 17, Southampton, 1974
Cartulary of Blyth Priory	R. T. Timson, ed., *The Cartulary of Blyth Priory*, HMC JP17, London, 1973
Cartulary of Bradenstoke	Vera C. M. London, ed., *The Cartulary of Bradenstoke Priory*, Wiltshire Record Society, vol. 35, Trowbridge, 1979
Cartulary of Burscough	N. Webb, ed., *An Edition of the Cartulary of Burscough Priory*, Chetham Society 3ᵈ ser., vol. 18, Manchester, 1970
Cartulary of Bushmead Priory	G. H. Fowler and J. Godber, eds., *The Cartulary of Bushmead Priory*, Bedfordshire Historical Record Society, vol. 22, Bedford, 1940.
Cartulary of Canonsleigh Abbey	Vera C. M. London, ed., *The Cartulary of Canonsleigh Abbey*, Devon and Cornwall Record Society, n.s., vol. 8, Exeter, 1965

Abbreviations xiii

Cartulary of Cirencester Abbey	C. D. Ross and M. Devine, eds. *Cartulary of Cirencester Abbey Gloucestershire*, 3 vols. (London: Athlone, 1964-77)
Cartulary … Clare	Christopher Harper-Bill, ed., *The Cartulary of the Augustinian Friars of Clare*, Suffolk Record Society, Suffolk Charters 11, Ipswich, 1991
Cartulary of Cockersand	William Farrer, ed., *The Cartulary of Cockersand Abbey*, Chetham Society 2^d ser., vols. 28-40, 43, 56-7, Manchester, 1898-1905
Cartulary of Dale Abbey	Avrom Saltman, ed., *The Cartulary of Dale Abbey*, HMC JP11, London, 1967
Cartulary of Darley Abbey	R. R. Darlington, ed., *The Cartulary of Darley Abbey*, 2 vols. (Kendal: Titus Wilson, 1945)
Cartulary of Daventry Priory	Michael J. Franklin, ed., *The Cartulary of Daventry Priory*, Northamptonshire Record Society vol. 35, Northampton, 1988
Cartulary of God's House	J. M. Kaye, ed., *The Cartulary of God's House, Southampton*, Southampton Record Society, vols. 19-20, 2 vols., Southampton, 1976
Cartulary of Holy Trinity, Aldgate	J. M. Kaye, ed., *The Cartulary of God's House, Southampton*, Southampton Record Society, vols. 19-20, 2 vols., Southampton, 1976
Cartulary of Missenden Abbey	J. G. Jenkins, ed. *The Cartulary of Missenden Abbey Part III* HMC JP1, London, 1962

"Cartulary ... Old Wardon"	H. G. Fowler, "The Cartulary of the Cistercian Abbey of Old Wardon, Bedfordshire", Bedfordshire Historical Record Society vol. 13, Bedford, 1930
Cartulary of Oseney Abbey	Herbert E. Salter, ed., *The Cartulary of Oseney Abbey*, Oxford Historical Society 89-91, 97-8, 101, 6 vols., Oxford, 1929-36
Cartulary ... Park of Helaugh	J. S. Purvis, ed., *The Chartulary of the Augustinian Priory of St John the Evangelist of the Park of Helaugh*, Yorkshire Archaeological Society Record Series, vol. 92, Wakefield, 1936 for 1935
Cartulary of the Priory of St Gregory	Audrey M. Woodcock, ed., *Cartulary of the Priory of St Gregory, Canterbury*, Camden 3^d ser., vol. 88, London, 1956
Cartulary of St Augustine's, Bristol	David Walker, ed., *The Cartulary of St Augustine's Abbey, Bristol*, Gloucestershire Record Series, vol. 10, Bristol, 1998
Cartulary of St Denys	E. O. Blake, ed., *The Cartulary of St Denys*, Southampton Record Series vols. 24-5, 2 vols., Southampton, 1981
Cartulary of St Frideswide's	S. F. Wigram, ed., *The Cartulary of St Frideswide's Priory*, Oxford Historical Society vols. 28 and 31, 2 vols., Oxford, 1895-6
Cartulary of St Mary Clerkenwell	William O. Hassell, ed., *The Cartulary of St Mary Clerkenwell*, Camden 3^d ser., vol. 71, London, 1949
Cartulary of Shrewsbury Abbey	Una Rees, ed., *The Cartulary of Shrewsbury Abbey*, 2 vols. (Aberystwyth: University of Wales Press, 1975)

Cartularies of Southwick Priory	K. Ann Hanna, ed., *Cartularies of Southwick Priory*, Hampshire Record Society vols. 9-10, 2 vols., Winchester, 1989
Cartulary of Tutbury Priory	Avrom Saltman, ed. *The Cartulary of Tutbury Priory*, HMC JP2, London, 1962
Cartulary Wakebridge Chantry	Avrom Saltman, ed., *The Cartulary of the Wakebridge Chantries at Crich*, Derbyshire Archaeological Society Record Series, vol. 6, Derby, 1976 for 1971
Cartulary ... Worcester	R. R. Darlington, ed., *The Cartulary of Worcester Cathedral Priory (Register I)*, P.R.S. n.s., vol. 38, London, 1962-3
Cellarers' Rolls of Battle Abbey	Eleanor Searle and Barbara Ross, eds.,*The Cellarers' Rolls of Battle Abbey 1275-1513*, Sussex Record Society, vol. 65, Lewis, 1967
Charters of the ... Earls of Chester	Geoffrey Barraclough, ed., *The Charters of the Anglo-Norman Earls of Chester c.1071-1237*, Record Society of Lancashire and Cheshire vol. 126, Manchester, 1988
"*Charters ... Earldom Hereford*"	W. W. Capes, ed., *Charters and Records of Hereford Cathedral* (Hereford, 1908)
Charters of the Honour of Mowbray	Diana Greenway, ed., *Charters of the Honour of Mowbray 1107-1191*, British Academy Records of Social and Economic History n.s., vol. 1, London, 1972
Charters ... Norwich	Barbara Dodwell, ed., *The Charters of Norwich Cathedral Priory Part Two*, P.R.S. n.s., 46, London, 1985 for 1978-80

Charters ... Redvers Family	Robert Bearman, ed., *Charters of the Redvers Family and the Earldom of Devon 1090-1217*, Devon and Cornwall Record Society n.s., vol. 37, Exeter, 1994
Charters ... St Bartholomew's	Richard Mortimer, ed., *Charters of St Bartholomew's Priory Sudbury*, Suffolk Record Society Suffolk Charters, vol. 15, Ipswich, 1996
Chartulary ... Pontefract	R. Holmes, ed., *The Chartulary of St John of Pontefract*, Yorkshire Archaeological Society Record Series, vol. 30, Wakefield, 1902
Chronicon Monasterii de Abingdon	J. Stephenson, ed., *Chronicon Monasterii de Abingdon*, 2 vols. Rolls Series, London, 1858
Compotus Roll ... Worcester	S. C. Hamilton, ed., *Compotus Roll of the Priory of Worcester of the XIVth and XVth Centuries*, Worcestershire Historical Society, Worcester, 1910
Compotus Rolls ... Winchester	G. W. Kitchin, ed., *Compotus Rolls of the Obedientiaries of St Swithun's Priory Winchester*, Hampshire Record Society, Winchester, 1892
Coucher Book of Selby Abbey	J. T. Fowler, ed., *The Coucher Book of Selby Abbey*, Yorkshire Archaeological Society Record Series, vols. 10-11, 2 vols., Wakefield, 1890
Councils and Synods, I	Dorothy Whitelock, Martin Brett and Christopher N. L. Brooke, eds., *Councils and Synods and Other Documents Relating to the English Church I AD 871-1204 Part I 871-1066* (Oxford: Oxford University Press, 1981)

Councils and Synods, II	Frederick M. Powicke and Christopher R. Cheney, eds. *Councils and Synods with Other Documents Relating to the English Church* volume II *AD1205-1313* (Oxford: Oxford University Press, 1964)
Customary ... Bury St Edmunds	Antonia Gransden, ed., *The Customary of the Benedictine Abbey of Bury St Edmunds in Suffolk*, Henry Bradshaw Society vol. 99, London, 1973
Customary Rents	Nelly Neilson, *Customary Rents*, Oxford Studies in Social and Legal History vol. 2, Oxford, 1910
Danelaw Documents	Frank M. Stenton, ed., *Documents Illustrative of the Economic and Social History of the Northern Danelaw*, British Academy Records of Social and Economic History vol. 5, London, 1920
Digest of the Charters ... Dunstable	H. G. Fowler, ed., *A Digest of the Charters Preserved in the Cartulary of Dunstable Priory*, Bedfordshire Historical Record Society, vol. 10, Bedford, 1926
Documents ... English Black Monks	William A. Pantin, ed., *Documents Illustrating the Activities of the General and Provincial Chapters of the English Black Monks 1215-1540*, Camden 3^d ser., vol. 45, London, 1931
Documents ... Wenlok	Barbara F. Harvey, ed., *Documents Illustrative of the Rule of Walter of Wenlok, Abbot of Westminster, 1283-1307*, Camden 4th ser., vol. 2, London, 1965

Earldom of Gloucester Charters	Robert B. Patterson, ed., *Earldom of Gloucester Charters* (Oxford: Oxford University Press, 1973)
Early Charters ... St Paul	Marion Gibbs, ed., *Early Charters of the Cathedral Church of St Paul, London*, Camden 3^d ser., vol. 58, London, 1939
Early Charters of Waltham Abbey	Rosalind Ransford, ed., *The Early Charters of Waltham Abbey 1062-1230* (Woodbridge: Boydell, 1989)
Early Compotus Rolls ... Worcester	J. M. Wilson and C. Gosden, eds., *Early Compotus Rolls of the Priory of Worcester*, Worcestershire Historical Society, Worcester, 1908
Early Yorkshire Charters (IV-XII)	Charles T. Clay et al., eds., *Early Yorkshire Charters*, Yorkshire Archaeological Society Record Series Extra Series vols. I-VII, 7 vols., Wakefield, 1935-65
EcHR	*Economic History Review*
EEA I	David M. Smith, ed., *English Episcopal Acta. I, Lincoln 1067- 1185*, British Academy, London, 1980
EEA II	Christopher R. Cheney and B. E. A. Jones, eds., *English Episcopal Acta. II, Canterbury 1162-1190*, British Academy, London, 1986
EEA IV	David M. Smith, ed., *EEA. IV, Lincoln 1186-1206*, British Academy, London, 1986
EEA VII	Christopher Harper-Bill, ed., *EEA. VII, Norwich*, British Academy, Oxford: Oxford University Press, 1990
EHR	*English Historical Review*

English Lawsuits	R. C. Van Caenigem, ed., *English Lawsuits from William I to Richard I*, Selden Society, vols. 106-7, 2 vols., London, 1990
Cartulary of Eynsham	Herbert E. Salter, ed., *Cartulary of Eynsham Abbey*, Oxford Historical Society vols. 49 and 51, 2 vols., Oxford, 1907-8
Facsimiles ... Early Northamptonshire Charters	Frank M. Stenton, ed., *Facsimiles of Early Northamptonshire Charters*, Northamptonshire Record Society vol. 4, Northampton, 1930
Facsimiles of Royal and Other Charters	G. F. Warner and H. J. Ellis, eds., *Facsimiles of Royal and Other Charters in the British Museum I William I-Richard I* (London: British Museum, 1903)
Feudal Documents ... Bury St Edmunds	David C. Douglas, ed., *Feudal Documents from the Abbey of Bury St Edmunds*, British Academy Records of Social and Economic History, Oxford, 1932
"Glapwell Charters"	R. R. Darlington, "The Glapwell Charters", *Transactions of the Derbyshire Archaeological and Natural History Society* 76 (1957-8 for 1956)
Historia et Cartularium ... Gloucestriae	W. H. Hart, ed., *Historia et Cartularium Monasterii Sancti Petri Gloucestriae*, Rolls Series, 2 vols., London, 1863
HMC	Historical Manuscripts Commission
JEH	*Journal of Ecclesiastical History*
JP	Joint Publication

Landboc ... Winchelcumba	D. Royce, ed., *Landboc sive Registrum Monasterii Beatae Mariae Virginis et Sancti Cenhelmi de Winchelcumba* (Exeter, 1892)
Liber Memorandum ... Bernewell	J. W. Clark, ed., *Liber Memorandum Ecclesie de Bernewell* (Cambridge: Cambridge University Press, 1907)
Liber Albus ... Oxoniensis	W. P. Ellis and Herbert E. Salter, eds., *Liber Albus Civitatis Oxoniensis* (Oxford: 1909)
Luffield Priory Charters	Geoffrey R. Elvey, ed., *Luffield Priory Charters*, Northamptonshire Record Society vols. 25-6, 2 vols., Northampton, 1974-5
Magnum Registrum Album	H. E. Savage, ed., *The Great Register of Lichfield Cathedral Known as Magnum Registrum Album*, Collections for a History of Staffordshire [William Salt Archaeological Society], Stafford, 1926 for 1924
Manorial Records of Cuxham	Paul D. A. Harvey, ed., *Manorial Records of Cuxham, Oxfordshire, circa 1200-1359*, HMC JP 23, London, 1976
Munimenta Civitatis Oxonie	Herbert E. Salter, ed., *Munimenta Civitatis Oxonie*, Oxford Historical Society vol. 71, Oxford, 1920
Newington Longeville Charters	Herbert E. Salter, ed., *Newington Longeville Charters*, Oxfordshire Record Society vol. 3, Oxford, 1921
n. s.	new series
Pipe Roll ... Winchester	Mark Page, ed., *The Pipe Roll of the Bishopric of Winchester 1301-2*, Hampshire Record Society vol. 14, Winchester, 1996

PRS.	Pipe Roll Society
Reading Abbey Cartularies	Brian R. Kemp, ed., *The Reading Abbey Cartularies*, Camden 4th ser., 31 and 33, 2 vols., London, 1986-7
Records ... Norwich	William Hudson and J. C. Tingey, eds., *The Records of the City of Norwich*, 2 vols. (London and Norwich, 1906 and 1910)
Register ... St Bees	J. Wilson, ed., *The Register of the Priory of St Bees*, Surtees Society vol. 126, Durham, 1915
Registrum Antiquissimum	C. W. Foster and Kathleen Major, eds., *Registrum Antiquissimum of the Cathedral Church of Lincoln*, Lincoln Record Society vols. 27-9, 32, 34, 41-2, 46, 51, 62, 67-8, 12 vols., Lincoln and Horncastle, 1931-73
Rolls and Register ... Sutton	Rosalind M. T. Hill, ed., *The Rolls and Register of Oliver de Sutton, Bishop of Lincoln*, Lincoln Record Society 39, 44, 48, 52, 60, 64, 69, 76, 8 vols., Lincoln and Horncastle, 1948-86
Rufford Charters	Christopher J. Holdsworth, ed., *Rufford Charters*, Thoroton Society Record Series vols. 29-30, 2 vols., Nottingham, 1972-4
Rutland MSS IV	[John H. Round, ed.,] *Rutland Manuscripts IV*, HMC Report, London, 1906
Select Cases ... Eccles. Courts	Naomi Adams and Charles Donohue, eds., *Select Cases from the Ecclesiastical Courts of the Province of Canterbury c.1200-1301*, Selden Society vol. 95, London, 1981
ser.	series

St Benet of Holme	J. R. West, ed., *St Benet of Holme 1020-1210*, Norfolk Record Society vol. 2, 2 vols., Norwich, 1932
Sandford Cartulary	A. M. Lees, ed., *The Sandford Cartulary*, Oxfordshire Record Society, vols. 21-2, 2 vols., Oxford, 1941
Sibton Abbey Cartularies	Patricia Brown, ed., *Sibton Abbey Cartularies and Charters*, 4 vols., Suffolk Record Society Suffolk Charters vols. 6, 8-10, Ipswich, 1985-8
Select Documents ... Bec	Marjorie Chibnall, ed., *Select Documents of the English Lands of the Abbey of Bec*, Camden 3^d ser., vol. 73, London, 1951
Statuta Capitulorum ... Ordinis Cisterciensis	D. J-M. Canivez, ed., *Statuta Capitulorum Generalium Ordinis Cisterciensis* tome 1 *1116-1220* (Louvain, 1933)
Stoke by Clare Cartulary	Christopher Harper-Bill and Richard Mortimer, eds., *The Stoke by Clare Cartulary*, Suffolk Record Society Suffolk Charters vol. 5, 2 vols., Ipswich, 1983
Testamenta Eboracensia	J. Raine, ed., *Testamenta Eboracensia*, Surtees Society vol. 4, Durham, 1836
Thame Cartulary	Herbert E. Salter, ed., *The Thame Cartulary*, Oxfordshire Record Society vols. 24-5, 2 vols., Oxford, 1947
Thurgarton Cartulary	Trevor Foulds, ed., *The Thurgarton Cartulary* (Stamford: Paul Watkins, 1994)

Transcripts ... Charters of Gilbertine Houses	Frank M. Stenton, ed., *Transcripts of the Charters of Gilbertine Houses*, Lincoln Record Society vol. 18, Horncastle and Lincoln, 1922
Triennial Chapters ... Augustinian Canons	Herbert E. Salter, ed., *Triennial Chapters of the Augustinian Canons*, Oxford Historical Society vol. 74, Oxford, 1922
TRHS	*Transactions of the Royal Historical Society*
"Visitations of churches ... St Paul's Cathedral"	W. S. Simpson, "Visitations of Churches Belonging to St Paul's Cathedral, 1249-1252", Camden Miscellany 9, Camden Society n.s., vol. 53, London, 1895, 1-33
Walter of Henley	Dorothea Oschinsky, ed., *Walter of Henley and Other Treatises on Estate Management and Accountancy* (Oxford: Oxford University Press, 1971)
Westminster Abbey Charters	Emma Mason et al., eds., *Westminster Abbey Charters 1066-c.1214*, London Record Society vol. 25, London, 1988

List of Illustrations

Figure 1 Principal Religious Houses Mentioned in the Text — 8

Table 1 Provision for Lights at Thorpe, Walton and Kirkby, 1249x1252 — 47

Table 2 Burials of Non-patronal Benefactors in Religious Houses — 64

Table 3 Characteristics of Austin Canon Houses Founded Before 1135 — 151

Table 4 Valor of Houses of Austin Canons 1535 — 152

Table 5 Rank-order of Houses in the 1535 Valor Above £500 — 153

Table 6 Descriptive Statistics of Fines and Aids Levied on Religious Houses (Including Those Which Were Not Ecclesiastical Tenants in Chief) Towards the Fifth Scutage of John in 1204 — 231

Table 7 Length of Some Lists of Witnesses in the Twelfth Century — 254

Introduction

Since religion involves confession, a useful starting point is perhaps to admit some of the difficulties in formulating a title for this book. One possibility considered was "the age of monasticism: the impact of religious houses on English society in the twelfth and thirteenth centuries". The rationale here was that the twelfth century, but more particularly its first half, constituted the period of the most intensive foundation of religious houses in England. Accordingly, the existence of these proliferating religious houses had a profound impact on society, particularly at the local level, as indicated in Part I of this collection of papers, but also, as examined in Part II, on wider social norms and customs. A second candidate was "before parochialism" with the same subtitle. By "parochialism" here is meant simply a deep attachment to the parish and the parish church. The idea behind that potential title was that these religious houses were introduced in part because of a perceived failure of the secular clergy in the prior century: an inability to respond to efforts to reform the clergy in the face of monumental new social changes. In fact, the parochial "system" was developing in parallel with the expansion of religious houses. The reforms of the early thirteenth century combined with the full evolution of parishes abrogated the impact of the religious houses. The religious houses were eclipsed by a reformed, celibate, sacramental clergy whose role was invigorated by the emphasis placed on communication (the mass) and confession. Finally, the title "missed opportunities" was selected because the new religious orders were despatched as part of a movement for religious reform, in the case of some Orders (such as the Austin Canons) as missionaries. In this objective, they ultimately failed, but not without having attracted significant interest amongst the laity and influenced lay social and cultural organization.

Whilst the book thus concentrates on the twelfth and thirteenth centuries, it does so in a wider context of what might be described as "phases" of religious devotion. The term "phases" is employed without any implication of stages, or ineluctable linear movement from one stage of development to another. The "phases" are, moreover, not entirely discrete; characteristics of some phases existed in others. The "phases" are perhaps no more than heuristic devices for detecting large-scale changes.

The twelfth and early thirteenth centuries ("Phase I" for our purposes here) are thus regarded as a phase of expansion of the religious Orders and religious houses in England, probably at the expense materially of parishes and parish churches. The tardy reform of the parochial clergy contributed to their relative eclipse. That "dissatisfaction" applied to colleges of secular canons too. The spiritual services of the professed religious offered a more effective alternative for salvation.

By the early thirteenth century ("Phase 2"), however, the position was beginning to be reversed, as the character of the secular clergy was transformed, with the emphasis on the parish church and the parish clergy as sacramental centers and sacramental intermediaries, formally instituted by the Fourth Lateran Council of 1215 and disseminated in England through the Council of Oxford of 1222 and diocesan synods. Religious houses, nonetheless, retained the affection of some of lay society. In particular this "phase" was characterized by lower levels of secular society, who had not the means to found their own religious houses or make large donations to them, attempting through smaller benefactions to participate in the spiritual benefits afforded by religious houses. In this context too, the supervision of chantries and the foundation of chantries within religious houses signified this continued belief in the greater efficacy of the regular Orders.[1]

From the early to mid fourteenth centuries through the later middle ages ("Phase 3"), the religious Orders were superseded in the affections of the laity by the the secular clergy and the local attachment to the parish (and also by the mendicant Orders, particularly in urban places). Any effervescence of late-medieval devotion was channelled through the parish and the "parish community". It should be clarified that the general effacement of religious houses by the secular clergy does not assume a complete eclipse of religious houses, but their relative demise. That outline is the bald schema which is adapted here, but it is not uncontentious.

If we take a rather crude approach, chantries can be perceived as an intermediate phenomenon in the transition from phase 2 to phase 3. As Wood-Legh indicated, chantries were predominantly (although not exclusively) established first either in religious houses employing the regular clergy in priests' Orders in the houses or, if the cantarist was a secular cleric, under the supervision of a religious house.[2] During the later middle ages, chantries became much more the preserve of the secular clergy.

The paradigm promoted by David Knowles contended that the significance of religious houses, with the exception of the mendicant establishments, declined in the later middle ages.[3] It appeared that Benjamin Thompson's exploration of the severance of the relationship between families of patrons and founders from "their" religious houses during the later middle ages added some grist to this argument.[4] Partly, the dissolution of ties resulted from the changing fortunes and genealogies of the families and partly from an indifference to religious houses. More recently, however, a substantial body of research has questioned the decline propounded by Knowles. Pioneering examination of houses of the female religious in Norfolk by Marilyn Oliva maintained that these houses continued to have a strong association with local society, in particular with "middling" social groups.[5] Martin Heale and Karen Stöber both effectively challenged the dismal deterioration suggested by Knowles.[6] The vitality at St Albans Abbey has been expounded by James Clark who has advanced some conclusions about a more general continuation of the contribution of monastic life in the later middle ages.[7]

If we can then no longer adhere strictly to the thesis of Knowles, how far has his depiction been revised? If we dissect and digest the revisionist research, does it amount to a wholesale rebuttal of Knowles? The following comments are predicated as devil's advocate, as a lowest level of acceptance. Much revisionist research has illustrated that late-medieval devotion in East Anglia remained eclectic. There too individual female devotional fervour flourished. Whilst we must not be dogmatic, there is still some mileage in the association of religious piety with women. So there is the possibility that what Oliva's research has detected is an association of a local laity with female devotional practices in a geographically-specific environment. It is quite possible that her conclusions have a much wider application, but the argument above is deliberately a reductive one. How typical was St Albans? How does it compare with Westminster?[8] Are either representative of the generality of very large Black Monk houses? How does the position of these large Benedictine houses reflect on the fortunes of houses of medium and lesser size of that and other Orders? In other words, is St Albans, with its immense resources and liberties, a special case of vitality? More generally, have Clark, Heale, and Stöber discerned a wide pattern of resilience? Or have they discovered: examples of establishments which had a different experience; and relationships between some specific social affinities with religious houses? The problem is that the picture is still provisional. We might at this point conclude that either Knowles was incorrect to the extent that there was no more than a relative decline or that he completely misjudged the impact of religious houses in the later middle ages.

Whilst this debate about the fortunes of religious houses in the later middle ages is important on its own terms, why should these propositions matter for the following text which is almost exclusively concerned with the development of religious houses in the twelfth and thirteenth centuries? The pragmatic reason is that overviews of the contribution of religious houses still tend to conform to a chronological division around 1300 (although in the case of this present work, the *terminus ad quem* is extended to about 1350). Although no historian may thus accept Knowles unreservedly, his paradigm may still influence general treatments of monastic development. In those works, historians are attempting to discern some cohesion–and their effort is important.[9]

It is in the same spirit that the text which follows is circumscribed by a boundary about 1350. The text acknowledges that there is something qualitatively different between the period of the proliferation of foundations in the twelfth century, but extending into the thirteenth, and the later middle ages. The differences examined here revolve around the relationships between the laity and the religious house rather than the internal condition of religious houses.

We can define those particular issues from two perspectives. First is the question of the association between the laity and religious houses. In the later middle ages, the parish became increasingly a focus of lay devotion and spiritual awareness, perhaps, in the perception of some, eclipsing the position of religious houses.[10] In the twelfth and thirteenth centuries, that distinction was less clear cut. The formation of the parish was yet in its evolutionary stages. Whilst the impetus of the enunciations of the Fourth Lateran Council in 1215, disseminated in England through the Council of Oxford in 1222 and synodal and diocesan decrees thereafter, may have simply recognized the developing importance of the parish for lay participation in religion, plenty of scope existed in the twelfth and thirteenth century for lay people to seek another association. In their minds, those different attachments may not have been exclusive, of course. It was sagacious to make all arrangements possible for salvation. On the other hand, there is a sense that the professed religious offered a more efficacious option than the secular clergy: a hierarchy of recourse.

The problem, of course, was one of accessibility. Although everyone engaged on a regular basis with the parish church, association with a religious house might involve more discretion. It required the capacity to make an additional benefaction. It equally required that the religious house be prepared to accept the association. The element of social emulation was an influence, containing all those elements of honor, status, marking off, and distinction.

Those issues of association and relationship are addressed in the first part of the text. By and large, the focus is on the new foundations of the twelfth century which radically increased the numbers of religious houses and reflected the devotional interest in the religious Orders. The concentration is on the newer, smaller religious houses which had more local significance and which did not have the cachet or prestige of the great Benedictine houses of the *Regularis Concordia* and tenth-century reform. The attempt is also made to assess how far these lesser houses made an impact on their local society, and how far the active participation of the local laity was attracted.

What cannot be neglected, however, is the impact of religious houses through the very acquisition of benefactions. The proliferation of religious houses in the twelfth century had immense consequences for the tenure of land–in particular the perception, if no more, of the balance of land in the hands of religious houses and the laity. So contained within the affection for religious houses in the twelfth century was the seed of its own destruction. The endowment at foundation of the smaller religious houses was, as is well know, often parsimonious, sometimes a deliberate policy, often as a consequence of the immaterial status of the founder. There was a stimulus then to attempt to increase the resources of the religious house, from two perspectives: for survival, but also for the glorification of the patronal saint of the house (and God). Those motives cannot really be separated, although there is a temptation to emphasize the aspect of materiality. Religious houses became the beneficiaries of innumerable gifts and grants which detracted from the resources of the laity. Equally, religious houses entered into the land market, at varying levels, occasionally acquiring manors and larger holdings, more frequently smaller amounts of land, rents or services. At different points, the political and social consequences were reversed. By the late twelfth century, concerns were expressed about the balance of land removed from the hands of the significant laity. Benefactions from the lower laity, nonetheless, continued to be directed to religious houses as the lower laity attempted to obtain the same spiritual benefits that the higher laity had obtained, if at a lower material cost. Through the thirteenth century, however, those lesser benefactions diminished too.

Through their acquisitions–and, indeed, acquisitiveness–in the twelfth century, religious houses had a profound effect on the genesis of ideas about tenure and the proper and appropriate conditions for land held for spiritual purposes. The second part of the text accordingly investigates these implications.

If, as above, it has been explained that even the benefactions from the lower laity declined during the thirteenth century, why, then, does the examination here continue down to about 1350? The explanation is that a residual sentiment may have existed which regarded the professed religious as still more efficacious than the secular clergy. That confidence is manifested through the foundation of *cantarie* in religious houses or under their supervision. The laity continued to solicit regular clergy as soul priests or, where secular clergy were instituted, to request a religious house to oversee the secular priest. It was only in the later middle ages that trust was unreservedly invested in the secular clergy for this purpose.

Inevitably, in approaching all these issues, there is a tendency to dichotomize, to produce distinctions which appear too hard and fast. The differences import many nuances, confusion, and lack of clarity. Much overlapped. So it should finally be clarified that the distinctions are indeed heuristic ones, designed to make some sense and provide some cohesion. Those dichotomies may indeed become more blurred as more detailed research is conducted into the condition of late-medieval religious houses. For the moment, however, it makes sense to concentrate on the relationship between the laity and religious house from the twelfth century through to about 1350 as a coherent discussion.

Within the overall context of religious houses and the laity in the twelfth and thirteenth centuries, a number of particular issues are important. One is the sentiment for "association" on the parts of both the religious house and local lay society. That concern is especially important in the situation of relationships between the lesser laity and religious houses. It is a notion (somewhat ashamedly) derived from Megan McLaughlin's exploration of relationships between people of higher status and larger religious houses at a much earlier time.[11] It strikes me, however, that it is a persistent influence. Somewhat allied is the idea that donations by the local laity consolidated local networks of the laity which promoted or confirmed local sentiments (although not as concrete as "identities"). That notion was promulgated at a higher and lower level by the considerations of Cassandra Potts on Normandy and C. J. Wales on north Lincolnshire (the relationship between knightly families and the abbey of Wellow in particular).[12] Again, it seems to me that the same force operated in the context of the lesser laity and local religious houses.

8   *Introduction*

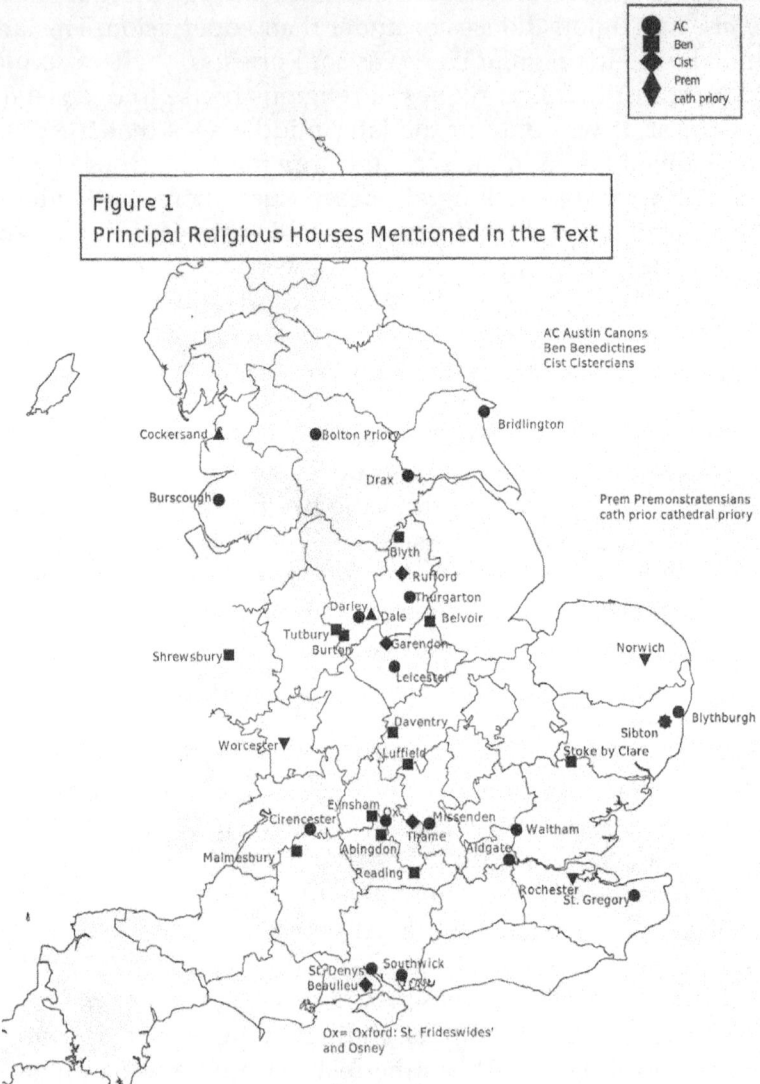

Figure 1
Principal Religious Houses Mentioned in the Text

Two subjects in particular require addressing further: gift-exchange and the gift; and ritual. Some of the papers published here made an effort to engage more widely with anthropological and sociological notions, in particular those two aspects of symbolic economies. Both themes have been elaborated and understanding advanced since my papers were written.

The significance of the gift was, indeed, well established in considerations of medieval relationships, perhaps best expressed in Stephen White's research into western "France". The stimulus remained, of course, the reflections of Mauss as they were made available to an English audience. An additional impetus was provided by the contributions of Ilana Silber which had a profound influence, for she demonstrated how gift-exchange applied to western monasticism.[13] Discussion of gift-exchange specifically in the context of medieval society was then advanced further by Arnoud-Jan Bijsterveld.[14] In the last twenty years, there has been a profusion of writing about gift and exchange in pre-modern English society, consolidated recently by Ilana Ben-Amos.[15] Whilst Mauss had relied principally on anthropological information from other societies (especially Malinowski on the Trobriand islanders and Boas on the Kwakiutl tribe), the importance of gift-exchange in pre-modern western culture has thus been confirmed. Mauss had implied as much, but the exact operation of gift-exchange has only recently been more concretely explained by historians of the European past.

One of the most cogent dissections of the notion has, however, largely been ignored in the historical literature, Lewis Hyde's expansive reflections.[16] The reason for this omission is perhaps because Hyde is not concerned with the full repertoire of what the gift does, but only with that gift which "speaks commandingly to the soul and irresistibly moves us." Whilst recognizing the multiple motives and expectations which inspire any single gift, Hyde attempts to extract the beneficent. Again, however, he concedes the "limits of altruism". So, for his main purpose Hyde sets aside the "gifts that leave an oppressive sense of obligation, gifts that manipulate or humiliate, gifts that establish and maintain hierarchies ..."[17] Before addressing the altruistic, nonetheless, his book contains an interesting exploration of the the whole notion of gifts: the "Indian" gift anticipating a return; the necessity for circulation of some gifts (either to reinforce notions of the small "community" or to confirm that acquisition is only purposeful for redistribution); the demand for consumption of gifts (to use them up as conspicuous consumption); reciprocity, but the return of the gift as equivalence, although without any regulation or complaint that it be so; the status exhibited by the capacity to give; the ritual activity involved in the process of some giving; the emotional content of the gift, on both sides, "enriched with social feeling, with generosity, liberality, goodwill".[18]

For the context of gifts to the religious examined in this present book, there are some succinct and felicitous expressions in Hyde's writing.

> ... as a natural fact (when gifts are actually alive); as a natural-spiritual fact (when gifts are the agents of a spirit that survives the consumption of its individual embodiments); and as a social fact (when a circulation of gifts creates community out of individual expressions of goodwill).[19]

Inherent in gifts then is the possibility of "the gifts of incorporation", which produce solidarity through emotional bonds.[20] It remains, nonetheless, only the possibility: the gift can go wrong if there is unaccustomed emphasis on the obligation or on the status of the "giver". Indebtedness can "create an inexorable tension." The "giver" may be disappointed if the recipient does not express the expected level of gratitude, even whilst exclaiming that nothing is owed.[21] The acceptance of the "gift" may be regarded by the recipient as coercive, and so may be resented. So, whilst we must return to Mauss, who contemplated all these issues in small societies, Hyde is an accessible, but also profound, introduction.

The gift is then a multi-faceted social event and process. In the discussion of the relationship between religious houses and laity, the attempt has been made to acknowledge all these variations which may operate simultaneously. Maurice Godelier has explained how the process of the gift produces and reproduces social relationships, extending the considerations of Mauss.[22] Problems arise, however, because the gifts with which we are concerned, are not exchanges confined to the secular world, between lay people. The relationship is between inferiors and superiors, the latter comprising the saints and God.[23] Whilst the saints might have been coerced or manipulated in the earlier middle ages, tempting God was anathema. The gift could have no more effect than anticipate a change in the course of events through the mediation of the religious and the intercession of saints. At canon law, these gifts sailed close to the wind of simony: the performance of spiritual services in return for material reward.

Godelier has made the distinction between the non-agonistic gift and the antagonistic gift, the latter as an elaboration of Mauss's description of the potlatch. The antagonistic gift is explicitly deployed to gain the acknowledgement of the superiority of the giver: competitive giving.[24] Non-agonistic gifts, whilst expecting some ultimate reciprocity, were extended with the purpose of social harmony, since the anticipation is for a counter-gift, in due course, of an equivalent level or amount.[25] The intention is not to embarrass. How that differentiation might apply to gift-giving and religious houses involves a number of issues. Theoretically, one might conceive of the foundation of a religious house as involving some aspects of the antagonistic gift. It is an assertion and display of superior status. The act represents the importance of the founder and represents the founder to the outside world. In particular, the foundation of religious houses in the later years of Henry I's reign and during the "Anarchy" as an exhibition of "territorial lordship" contained elements of antagonistic giving, although it does not equate with the potlatch since the endowments of these houses were slender rather than conforming to the extreme consumption and waste of the potlatch.[26] The question remains open whether gifts from lower social groups contained any element of the antagonistic or remained purely non-agonistic. One suspects that, to some extent or another, most gifts comprehended some element of the "antagonistic" broadly defined in that they exhibited the ability to expend.

One final aspect of the gift calls for consideration. Again, it involves an aspect which Mauss perceptively implied, but which was only elaborated by later anthropological investigation: revisiting the *kula* of the Trobriand islanders. Annette Wiener noticed the separation of goods into those which can (and should) circulate as gifts and those which are "inalienable".[27] "Inalienable" goods perform a number of roles. Confirming individual identity is one, but in the collective social world obligations to kin and wider social interests are others. Godelier invested them with the quality of "sacred", in the widest sense.[28] The ability to detain them from circulation also marked social status, so we have the paradox of social position acknowledged in giving, but also confirmed by reserving to oneself.

> Reciprocity only provides the outer manifestation of social interaction. Such acts appear to disguise difference, but in reality they proclaim the variation between participants in status and rank authenticated by the inalienable possessions a person is able to retain.[29]

Inalienable possessions impact on the present discussion in several ways, one of which is to demonstrate the complexity of motives which may obtain behind any gift. Another aspect is the restraint on the alienation of land, an obligation defined by the various interests in the land: lord and kinship. That latter complication has been much considered in the relationships between the laity and religious houses, whether from anthropological, legal or normative perceptions. This complication is a recurrent theme in part two of this book, inevitably owing much to the prior and perspicacious research of Stephen D. White, Barbara Rosenwein, Emily Tabuteau, Paul Hyams, and latterly John Hudson.

Whilst there has been a return to the discussion of the gift in historical contexts, the problem of ritual has never disappeared. It remains, advisedly, a problem, because of the various nuances, emphases, interpretations and expectations of what ritual is, means and does. Below, the coercive intention and outcome of ritual has been explored, but ritual could simultaneously have several different impacts. To another extent, then, the cautions of Humphrey and Laidlaw have been assimilated, that ritual can become an empty vessel for the imposition of meaning. I have avoided the structural-functionalist interpretations of ritual, despite the frequent recourse by historians to such as the Turners (Victor and Edith). Partly, the omission is precisely because that understanding is so well known

Introduction   13

and recited, but also because it seems too tidy, insufficiently ambiguous.

The ambivalences of ritual are very well addressed in two detailed examinations of ritual by Catherine Bell.[30] Where my text below is inadequate, perhaps, is in not acknowledging the contribution of Roy Rappaport. Whilst I discovered Rappaport's book shortly after its publication, it has not been integrated into the papers reproduced here.[31] On the other hand, there does not seem to be too much point in entering on a grand excursus about ritual here, what it means or what it does. It is the subject of a continuing debate in early medieval history.[32] Whilst Rappaport's book is immensely welcome, there are some points of discussion for the present context.[33]

First, he emphasized, like many others, the invariance of ritual.[34] In fact, he constantly qualifies this constancy and iteration, allowing some change. Deviation from the established code, however, may also cause calamity, so we return to the invariance and the mystical circumstances when change is accepted. One of the problems of ritual is that it is often observed only in its "mature" and "perfected" state. How did it originally occur and how was its text produced? A deeper reading than I originally gave to the material below may illustrate some incremental development of ritual, from inchoate to substantial text.

The second point of Rappaport's to address is the close association of ritual with religion. Whilst he intended religion as a broad concept, it still retains the air of transcendence. Ritual performances usual depend on some element of the transcendent, perhaps the "sacred", through oaths or ultimate belief, but for what must be construed as *secular* circumstances, as are involved in the second part of this present book, in matters of land tenure.

Notes

[1] Since the references are recited in the chapters below, I deliberately keep them to a minimum here.

[2] Kathleen L. Wood-Legh, *Perpetual Chantries in Britain* (Cambridge: Cambridge University Press, 1965). See also Chapter 1 below.

³ David Knowles, *The Religious Orders in England: Volume 2 The End of the Middle Ages* (Cambridge: Cambridge University Press, 1955); Joan Greatrex, "After Knowles: Recent Perspectives in Monastic History", in *The Religious Orders in Pre-Reformation England*, ed. James G. Clark (Woodbridge: Boydell, 2002), 35-47.

⁴ Benjamin Thompson, "Monasteries and their Patrons at Foundation and Dissolution", *TRHS* 6th ser., 4 (1994): 103-25.

⁵ Marilyn Oliva, *The Convent and the Community in Late Medieval England: Female Monasticism in the Diocese of Norwich, 1350-1540* (Woodbridge: Boydell, 1998).

⁶ Karen Stöber, *Late Medieval Monasteries and their Patrons: England and Wales, c.1300-1540* (Woodbridge: Boydell, 2007); Heale in various places.

⁷ James G. Clark, *A Monastic Renaissance at St Albans: Thomas Walsingham and his Circle, c.1350-1440* (Oxford: Oxford University Press, 2004) and elsewhere.

⁸ Barbara F. Harvey, *Living and Dying in Medieval England 1100-1540: The Monastic Experience* (Oxford: Oxford University Press, 1993).

⁹ Janet Burton, *Monastic and Religious Orders in Britain 1000-1300* (Cambridge: Cambridge University Press, 1994).

¹⁰ The vast literature is encapsulated by Katherine L. French, *The Good Women of the Parish: Gender and Religion after the Black Death* (Philadelphia, Pa.: University of Pennsylvania Press, 2007).

¹¹ Megan McLaughlin, *Consorting with Saints: Prayer for the Dead in Early Medieval France* (Ithaca, N. Y.: Cornell University Press, 1994).

¹² Cassandra Potts, *Monastic Revival and Regional Identity in Early Normandy* (Woodbridge: Boydell, 1997), but see also Chapter 1 below; C. J. Wales, "The Knight in Twelfth-century Lincolnshire", PhD dissertation (Cambridge, 1983), 235-60.

¹³ Ilana Silber, "Gift-giving in the Great Traditions: The Case of Donations to Monasteries in the Medieval West," *Archives Européennes de Sociologie* 36 (1995): 209-43; Silber, Jeffrey C. Alexander, and Steven Seidman, *Virtuosity, Charisma and Social Order: A Comparative Sociological Study of Monasticism in Thereveda Buddhism and Medieval Catholicism* (Cambridge: Cambridge University Press, 1995).

¹⁴ Arnoud-Jan Bijsterveld, "The Medieval Gift as Agent of Social Bonding and Political Power: A Comparative Approach", in *Medieval Transformations: Texts, Power, and Gifts in Context*, ed. Esther Cohen and Mayke B. de Jong (Leiden: Brill, 2001), 123-56.

¹⁵ Ilana K. Ben-Amos, *The Culture of Giving: Informal Support and Gift-Exchange in Early Modern England* (Cambridge: Cambridge University Press, 2008), 1-14, recapitulates the historiographical contexts.

[16] Lewis Hyde, *The Gift: How the Creative Spirit Transforms the World* (Edinburgh: Canongate Books, 2006, but first published in the USA and Canada in 1983).

[17] Hyde, *The Gift*, xix.

[18] Hyde, *The Gift*, 35, for the expression of social emotions.

[19] Hyde, *The Gift*, 38.

[20] Hyde, *The Gift*, 59.

[21] Hyde, *The Gift*, 71.

[22] Maurice Godelier, *The Enigma of the Gift*, translated by Nora Scott (Cambridge: Polity, 1999), 104-5.

[23] Godelier, *Enigma of the Gift*, 186.

[24] An important context for this issue is Paul R. Hyams, *Rancor and Reconciliation in Medieval England* (Ithaca, N. Y.: Cornell University Press, 2003).

[25] Godelier, *Enigma of the Gift*, 92-3.

[26] This well-known phenomenon is briefly described in Chapter 1.

[27] Annette B. Wiener, *Inalienable Possessions: The Paradox of Keeping While Giving* (Berkeley: University of California Press, 1992) (which is also a critique of Lévi-Strauss on the circulation of women as exchange).

[28] Godelier, *Enigma of the Gift*, 111-38: "sacred" from multiple perspectives, the one concerning us here their detention from circulation.

[29] Wiener, *Inalienable Possessions*, 64.

[30] Catherine Bell, *Ritual Theory, Ritual Practice* (Oxford: Oxford University Press, 1992); Bell, *Ritual: Perspectives and Dimensions* (Oxford: Oxford University Press, 1997), reflects on the previous literature.

[31] Roy Rappaport, *Ritual and Religion in the Making of Humanity* (Oxford: Oxford University Press, 1999).

[32] Centered on the varying perceptions of Geoffrey Koziol, *Begging Pardon and Favor: Ritual and Political Order in France* (Ithaca, N. Y.: Cornell University Press, 1992) and Philippe Buc, *The Dangers of Ritual: Between Early Medieval Texts and Social Scientific Theory*, English edn. (Princeton: Princeton University Press, 2009).

[33] References to other anthropological discussions of ritual occur in the chapters below.

[34] Rappaport, *Ritual and Religion*, 36-7 introduces it as the "third feature" of ritual.

Part I

1
Religious Houses and the Laity in Eleventh- to Thirteenth-Century England: An Overview

> *R. de Gant omnibus ecclesie filiis salutem. Notum sit vobis me presentem fuisse ubi Gilbertus comes frater meus fecit diuisam suam in extrema egritudine sua coram hominibus suis qui presentes fuerunt et dedit Ecclesie Brid' cum corpore suo in liberam et perpetuam elemosinam Burtonam cum omnibus suis pertinenciis …*
>
> *Hec omnia confirmauit eidem ecclesie cum libertatibus que sunt in Carta sua et precepit mihi sicut fratri suo et homini ut ego ad scribendum et ad sigillandum presens essem cum hominibus suis qui tunc erant cum eo et cum lecte essent carte de hiis coram nobis per consilium et assensum eorundem hominum suorum de manu mea accepit. Johannes Camerarius sigillum et sub testimonio nostro sigillauit eas de hac re testis sum ego et si aliquis contradicere uoluerit paratus sum ego de hoc facere quicquid pertinet ad testem legittimum. Valete.*[1]

A benefaction to a religious house, even by a lay magnate such as de Gant, and even to the family's foundation whose inmates had been described in proprietary fashion by Gilbert de Gant, earl of Lincoln, as *canonici mei*, was thus a momentous occasion, inscribed in local memory.[2] In this case, the event was heightened by the death-bed anxiety and the congregation of the lord's followers. Exceptional it certainly was, therefore, in the context of the multitudinous benefactions to religious houses. With few exceptions, English charters of this time notifying benefactions to religious houses are cursory, indeed often little more than notifications.[3]

What motivated the laity, then, to continue to make benefactions to English religious houses as they did through the twelfth and into the late thirteenth centuries, but more particularly, what were the consequences for that relationship between local laity and local religious house? Although there have recently been published several general discussions of the context of the foundations and development of English religious houses in the eleventh through to the thirteenth century, some scope remains for exploring further the relationship between the local laity and their local houses.[4] It has for some time been evident that the motives of the laity were informed by a variety of perspectives. For, from those examinations, it is clear that, although spiritual motives were present, sometimes even paramount, other impulses were also influential. At the beginning, then, it is necessary to recapitulate some of the diversity of those motives, but the substance of the analysis here will be of some unintended outcomes and experiences.

At the ultimate level–foundation of a religious house, particularly by the baronage of the early twelfth century–political imperatives were an integral part of some decisions behind foundations, to promote "territorial lordship".[5] Indeed, it would seem that the earl of Leicester engaged in successive foundations primarily related to ritual events in his life-course, frequently motivated by political purposes, and culminating in the foundation of a daughter house of Fontrevault at Nuneaton to mark his reconciliation with the Angevin empire and Henry II.[6] Occasionally, religious houses were established as acts of contrition and certainly numerous ostensible benefactions to religious houses in the mid twelfth century were restitutions for depredation of their lands, whether overtly or implicitly.[7] In the twelfth century, motives for both new foundations and benefactions to religious houses remained ambiguous and complex.

In terms of other motivations, however, it might be suggested that there was a continuation of the desire of the laity at all levels of freedom for an association with religious houses.[8] Conversely, the difficult conditions of the late twelfth century, when benefactions of any significant size became increasingly rare, also induced the religious to endeavor to maintain this association with the local laity at all levels. It perhaps follows that the association of the local lay elite with and around a religious house consolidated local identities, social networks of knightly families being constituted in one respect around local religious houses. Perhaps more contentiously, another perception maintains the continuation of gift-exchange through benefactions moving down the social scale to the free peasantry and burgesses.[9] No doubt all these phenomena were aspects of the relationship between the laity and religious houses in the twelfth and thirteenth centuries.

In terms of unintended outcomes, there has been a concentration on the impact on the laity of the more concerted entry into the land market by religious houses, particularly large Benedictine houses, in the twelfth century, which engendered something of a debate which is now more or less exhausted.[10] By contrast, discussion of the advent of the houses of the new religious Orders revealed the relatively difficult circumstances of property accumulation and the non-manorial elements in their estates. Furthermore, encroachment of religious houses into the local land market, particularly for smaller acquisitions of rents and small amounts of land, may have been disruptive, not least in the urban land market. Concentration on the terms of the land market in the late twelfth and early thirteenth century thus illuminates one–but only one–aspect of the relationship between the laity and the religious.

Two other aspects of contingent outcomes, however, will be explored here in more detail: the formation of local lay social relationships through and around religious houses; and the appropriation by the laity of monastic culture and liturgy. The first concerns the change in the relationship between religious houses and local society. The suggestion is well known that in the late eleventh and early twelfth century benefactors of religious houses tended–although not exclusively–to conform to a vertical organization: that benefactors were quite often based on the honor. Mesne tenants of honorial founders of religious houses tended to make benefactions to the religious house founded by their superior lord and, indeed, were encouraged to do so.[11] Despite the debate over the nature of tenurial organization in the twelfth century, that pattern of giving is still visible into the middle of the twelfth century.[12] By the late twelfth century, that pattern had broken down, whether it had implications for honorial organization or not.[13] Knightly benefactors to a local religious house derived from several different honors in the late twelfth century, so that in this respect—if in this respect only—neighborhood had become more important than the honor. What was more important was that they belonged to a local neighborhood of knightly families. So religious houses influenced or assisted in the formation of local neighborhoods of knightly families. By the early thirteenth century, continuing benefactions to religious houses were largely derived from free tenants and burgesses and were on an individual basis remarkably small in size. To some extent, there might then have been a reversal of motives. Bearing in mind that motives are always mixed, having both spiritual and instrumental purposes, in the early twelfth century gift-giving was partly governed by belonging to the honor. By the late twelfth century, being a benefactor of knightly status involved belonging to a local neighborhood society of significant actors. By the early thirteenth century, religious houses were actively encouraging association with local lay society across the social spectrum, for, since individual benefactions were so small and insignificant, the motive of the religious house must have been even more than hitherto the benefits of association with local lay society in general rather than the merits of the particular gift.

Some aspects of this transition are well illustrated through the foundation and development of Garendon Abbey.[14] It is clear that many founders and their families quickly lost interest in their foundations and the development, even proper establishment, of small, religious houses depended very much on local lay society rather than the founder and the founder's family, and Garendon distinctly belongs to that category. The circumstances of the abbey's foundation are well known. Colonized from the first English Cistercian house, Waverley, in 1133, some five years after the introduction of the Order into England, Garendon was the fifth foundation of English White Monks, if one excludes the Savignacs for this purpose. Garendon belonged to two sequences of foundations: first, the foundations of the earls of Leicester, symbols of stages in his life-course; and second, foundations of Cistercian houses to confirm territorial lordship in the later years of Henry I and the "Anarchy". The earl's foundation of the house involved a rather slender endowment, principally located in the poorer, western part of Leicestershire. It was the benefactions of the local knightly families in the late twelfth century which allowed a firmer financial establishment of Garendon and the expansion of its estates into the more valuable Soar and Wreake valleys and up into the Wolds of east Leicestershire. These accretions derived from several honors, from Leicester, Chester and Mowbray fees. It thus appears that the knightly families of north and north-east Leicestershire adopted Garendon as the primary religious institution in their neighborhood. The strength of this association of knightly families and Garendon is perhaps best symbolized by the sentiment inserted into a charter from Robert Putrel. At issue was the confirmation of a carucate previously given and confirmed by his *auus*, Henry Putrel, and his father, Robert Putrel. In its confirmation, Robert's charter included the warranty clause *defensor astabo*, but that was not unusual in charters in favor of the house. More significant was the charter's inclusion of the term *aduocatus*. Whether the charter was compiled on behalf of Robert or written by the beneficiaries, it was, presumably, at least informed by his wishes. By the employment of this term, Putrel was either represented as a special protector of the house for this purpose or the monks were making a special appeal for his support (and perhaps by implication to local knightly society more widely).

> *Si quis predictos monachos inde uexare uoluerit ego .R. Putrel sicut aduocatus eiusdem elemosine cum eis defensor astabo saluo forinsi seruicio*[15]

Whilst it is possible that the isolated inclusion of the term *aduocatus* derived from the house's idiosyncratic search for the diplomatics of warranty in its charters, the inclusion of the term was unique, and so the assumption might reasonably be made that reflected here is the affection between local lay society, especially at the knightly stratum, and the house.[16] More certainly, the economic viability of the house was assured only by the accumulation of benefactions from the local knighthood, since its founder lost interest after the initial slender endowment at the foundation of the house.

How local religious houses contributed to the formation of local neighborhoods can be illustrated by some further case studies.[17]

Of course, there were other institutions which assisted with that development, such as county courts.[18] Importantly, Wales has, for example, suggested the cohesion of a local neighborhood of knightly families in north-east Lincolnshire through, in part, relationship with religious houses such as Wellow.[19] In the case of witnessing of charters to religious houses, the argument is not unambiguous and is certainly complex.[20] To be inserted in the attestion list, witnesses needed perhaps already to be of some standing. Nevertheless, their inclusion confirmed their social status. The position is thus less a circular argument than a reinforcement of their social status. Of course, charters were invoked not only for benefactions to religious houses, but for transactions between lay parties as well. Significantly, however, before the middle of the thirteenth century, charters did predominantly concern religious houses, so that these written instruments in favor of religious houses provided the greatest opportunity for confirmation and communication of social position. No doubt there were some existing relationships between these families, through personal (such as marriage) or institutional contacts, but witnessing charters to religious houses provided another occasion for lay association through the auspices of the religious house. The event was also a ritual and ceremonial forum which made a substantial impression on local society and local memory.

Of course, objections to the role of witnessing can be advanced. First, the witnesses might not actually have been in attendance–the real presence of witnesses? Moreover, charters were written instruments. They were, however, read out and their details "published" in that way, so that inclusion in the witness clause was known to local society.[21] So also the dignity of the person was confirmed by inclusion in the witness list as read out. Insertion in the witness list meant the opportunity for the confirmation of social position by title: the employment of the titles *dominus* or *miles* which were introduced into charters in the early thirteenth century.[22] Attesting a charter in particular to a religious house may have also accrued other advantages, for it is possible that witnesses expected to participate in some spiritual benefits through their act of witnessing, perhaps construed, in the case of witnessing charters to the religious, as a good work, deserving of divine reward, extending the notion of gift-exchange.

How is all this manifest? It is ostensible in the repetitive witnessing of charters to religious houses by particular witnesses. Examine first the case of Bridlington Priory.[23] It has not been possible to analyse all witnesses, so a purposive sample is presented. Arnold de Bucton' senior and junior attested some 121 charters to the priory during the thirteenth century, in eight of which the style *dominus* was affected, *miles* twice. The two Arnolds witnessed charters for lands acquired by the priory in numerous places in the East Riding, particularly Willerby, Fraisthorpe, Rudston, Sewerby, Burton Fleming, and Buckton, but they were also benefactors to the house, including a conveyance of half a carucate. Now, it may well have been that the inclusion of the Arnolds in many of these charters was simply replication of a witness list from an earlier charter relating to the same land, but the association of the Arnolds with Bridlington and other "repetitive" witnesses was evident. Other recurrent witnesses for Bridlington comprised Arnold de Marton', senior and junior, who together attested eighty-seven charters for the priory during the thirteenth century, concentrated in the same places, particularly Willerby, Sewerby, Burton Fleming, and Fraisthorpe.

Another example is the Silver family, burgesses of Bridlington, but also *quondam* free tenants of rural land in Sewerby, Marton and Fraisthorpe, later generations becoming concentrated in the urban center. It was Henry (*floruit* 1175x1191) who seemingly initiated the association with the priory, of which he had also been a tenant (*homo noster*).[24] Henry witnesed thirty-three charters for the house, only one of which related to property in Bridlington. One of his sons, Gregory, attested only three charters for the convent, but the other, Luke, constantly witnessed charters for the house, more than 175 in all, only three of which related to urban property. Between ca.1211 and ca.1236, Luke witnessed charters concerned with a multitude of places in the East Riding, but also in Lincolnshire, not least over a dozen relating to Skillington. Again, however, the concentration of attestations occurred in charters relating to Willerby, Sewerby, and Fraisthorpe.[25] In succession, Luke's son, Gilbert, and Gilbert's son, Gilbert, were witnesses in fifty-two further charters in favor of the priory between 1228 and 1301, with a similar geographical concentration.

An equivalent pattern of witnessing is exhibited by the case of Robert de Redenesse, a free tenant, in the first half of the thirteenth century, his total attestations amounting to 121 instances in charters concerning numerous vills in the same part of the East Riding, most particularly Willerby, Sewerby, Lebberton, and Fraisthorpe. John de Sywardby witnessed forty-one charters in favor of the priory, relating to eighteen different vills, in the same vicinity, whilst Walter de Spetona attested forty-three such charters, although twenty-seven were concentrated on Willerby. Gilbert de Spetona attested eighty-one charters for the priory, relating to lands located in twenty vills in this area, fourteen concerning Willerby, twelve Fraisthorpe, nine Buckton, seven Sewerby, and only five the eponymous Speeton. Replication of such examples could be extended. The predominant feature of charters for the priory relating to lands in this delimited area of the East Riding was thus repeated attestation by this caucus of witnesses.

To take another example, the important actors in local society were closely involved in the attestation of charters to Saint Bees Priory.[26] Examining two fairly representative frequent witnesses from the late twelfth and early thirteenth century, Hugh de Moriceby witnessed almost fifty charters in favor of Saint Bees, concerning lands in twenty-three vills in north-west England. In some instruments, he was accorded the title *dominus*. Subsequently, Nicholas and Hugh II de Moriceby continued this tradition of attestation of the priory's charters. Similarly, Robert de Haveringtona witnessed eighteen of the charters to the priory between 1185 and 1234, described occasionally as a *miles*, a heritage continued by Michael, John and Robert II de Haveringtona through the later thirteenth and early fourteenth century, attributed the titles of both *dominus* and *miles*. In a similar manner, Robert de Lamplogh and John de Langliver continuously witnessed charters for the house in the middle of the thirteenth century, both accorded the titles of *dominus* and *miles*.

To introduce the second element which is associated with benefactions by the lesser laity from the late twelfth century, the notion of gift-exchange was especially significant. Transactions in land between the laity and religious houses resulted in the appropriation of monastic culture by some of the laity. No doubt the difficulty of attracting benefactions in the twelfth and thirteenth century contributed to the development from the monks' and canons' part, but it is interesting to approach the matter from the perspective of the laity. What may be observed here is the adaptation of monastic culture and liturgy as the laity negotiated for those spiritual benefits previously reserved to the regular clergy. The monastic culture was not at this stage taken outside the religious house, but, in contrast, the laity penetrated the liturgy in the conventual church.[27]

The laity wished to participate in the benefits of the spiritual elements of monastic culture enclosed within religious houses in the twelfth and thirteenth centuries, whereas in the later middle ages the laity's adoption of monastic culture expropriated the culture from the houses, taking it outside. In some cases, such as chantries, this transformation of the locus or space of the culture was significant: for, whereas some of the earliest chantries were located within religious houses, chantries were frequently established in the later middle ages outside them and out of their control. Not all aspects of monastic culture adopted in the twelfth and thirteenth century were expropriated in the later middle ages, but several were, so that it was the whole culture which was at issue. The intention here, then, is to consider briefly several aspects of monastic culture adopted in the twelfth and thirteenth centuries as indicative of a general tendency: pittances, chantries, burial, confraternity, the eucharist and mass, chantries and lights. In other words, benefactions for specific purposes more emphatically than gifts for unspecified spiritual purposes represent the adoption of monastic culture by the laity. Since much has already been elicited about these individual elements, the argument here will concentrate on the general aspect of appropriation rather than closely on particular cultural items.

Illustrative of this overall process are the foundation and early benefactions to Bushmead Priory, which, although a tiny house, inspired extraordinary affection and devotion in its locality. Founded as a group of secular canons without a rule before 1198 and possibly ca.1195 by Hugh son of Oliver de Beauchamp, the house was reorganized as a convent of Austin Canons by 1215x1233. In the thirteenth century, the complement of the house probably never exceeded half a dozen regular canons. Despite the late date of its late foundation and smallness, the house attracted the benefactions of a nexus of local families: Bretville, Pertesoil, le Daneys, le Moyne, Weldeboef, and Braibroc. Two contexts are important: first, the original endowment by the founder was minimal and concentrated entirely at Bushmead; and second, the non-patronal benefactors of the house originated almost exclusively from outside Bushmead in a spread of parishes in Bedfordshire, Huntingdonshire, and Cambridgeshire. A large proportion of these benefactors participated in specific spiritual benefits at the priory: at least twenty-four were interred at the priory; at least ten established *cantarie* in the house; seventeen made provisions for lights in the conventual church; three acquired fraternity; two furnished benefactions towards the fabric; and six established pittances. Additionally, desiring a closer association with the liturgy and divine office celebrated in the conventual church, Henry son of William *filius Nigilli* [sic] in 1215x1242 made provision for the annual delivery of three *hope* (heaped bushels) of "pure" wheat for wafers, a benefaction which was expanded by Nigel son and heir of Henry *ate Wode* after 1242-3 through his furnishing of five bushels of "pure" wheat for making wafers. These benefactions for specific purposes reflect the desire of local lay society for association with the liturgy of this local house, even though that house was insignificant in size. The converse of this image of local society is the intention of the regular canons of Bushmead to have an affiliation with local lay society, for the lay benefactions were almost exclusively of small amounts, whilst the expectation of at least ten *cantarie* on such a small number of regular canons must have been burdensome.[28]

Paradoxically, perhaps, the most definite reflection of this appropriation concerned the smallest material benefactions to the religious. Pittances had been established within religious houses as special dishes.[29] In many cases of benefactions towards pittances, the laity desired a commemorative dish on an anniversary. In some of the earlier instances of benefactions for pittances, however, no lay anniversary was involved; the donation was an increment to pittances on holy days. These benefactions too reflect a lay desire for some association with liturgical observances within religious houses. Peter de Brus provided for Guisborough Priory *ad pitancias suas in refectorio* all the fish which was usually caught by his own seven boats and men, reserving to himself initially one hundred haddock from each boat once a year which he subsequently transferred as well. The same priory benefited from the provision by William de Tamerton of thirteen common pittances annually of salmon, sea-fish, and herring on specified feast-days: Saint Thomas Archbishop and Martyr, the Conversion of Saint Paul, the Purification, Saint Peter *in Cathedra*, and the Vigil of the Ascension.[30] What had thus in its origins comprised an internal commemorative commensality for the religious on specified holy days became appropriated by the laity for secular anniversaries.

In furnishing elements for the mass, some of the laity intimated more strongly their desire for an association with the liturgy inside religious houses. Nor were such benefactions confined to the higher nobility. Indeed, it seems that more frequently the benefactors belonged to knightly society or the upper free peasantry.[31]

Although some religious houses were intended by founders as private mausolea, Belvoir priory constituting a prime example, there were few long-term dynastic attachments to religious houses.[32] In contrast, the significant local laity of the late twelfth and early thirteenth century actively sought that privilege of burial within the enclave of religious houses, most usually in the cemeteries of the monks or canons. Frequently that privilege was achieved at minimal expense for the laity. For example, Geoffrey *Parmentarius* transferred to Drax Priory merely one selion *cum corpore meo humando*, whilst Walter *filius Morgani de Draxburgh'* furnished only three acres towards the fabric *cum corpore meo ibidem humando*.[33] Benefactions *cum corpore* for burial abound in the cartularies of some religious houses, at least eighteen, for example, in the cartulary of Guisborough Priory.[34]

Those religious houses whose foundation had effectively been intended as private mausolea furnished also the characteristics of chantries for their founders. Lacking the means of the option of founding a religious house, many of the local laity by the early thirteenth century began to establish chantries inside religious houses as a lesser option, not having the resources for the more expensive option of their own house. Robert *filius Johannis de Syuuardeby* quitclaimed to Bridlington Priory land and a capital messuage so that the canons *inuenient et sustinebunt unum capellanum pro animabus* [of three named individuals and two couples] *ad altare sancti Johannis baptiste in ecclesia sancte Marie de Brid' celebrantem imperpetuum Pro quo autem seruicio Cantarie ...*[35] As Howard Colvin has demonstrated, the fairly immediate consequences of the popularity of this option was to overwhelm religious houses which rapidly became unable to perform all the obligations desired by the local laity, even when employing secular clergy under the supervision of the religious house.[36]

The extent to which these transformations represented an appropriation by the laity of a culture and liturgy previously limited to the professed religious is illustrated by some grants of fraternity. When William *Nigelli* [sic] transferred the advowson of the parish church of Flamborough to Bridlington Priory, he requested for himself the liturgical provisions and spiritual benefits reserved to one of the house's canons.

> ... *in elemosinam* [sic] *pro anima uxoris mee Adeliz et pro me et pro liberis meis ea condicione ut ipsa ecclesia de Burch' ad minus ab uno deseruiatur Canonico Pro hac ergo elemosina recepi in capitulo eiusdem ecclesie sancte marie hanc fraternitatem ut ipsi Canonici qui modo sunt et qui futuri sint pro me et pro uxore mea iam defuncta sicut pro canonico professo totum seruicium faceant et liberi mei commune beneficium habeant* ...[37]

Rather than a simple association with the liturgy in the conventual church, this request–demand, even–extended much further; it effectively signified an appropriation of a liturgical arrangement usually appropriate only to the dignity of those who had assumed the habit. Association was exceeded and appropriation enacted.

All the indications are therefore for the continuation of those relationships between religious houses and the laity which have been observed in, for example, western France by White, Potts, Rosenwein, and McLaughlin at an earlier time.[38] What had changed was the social milieu. Gift-exchange persisted between religious house and the *lesser* laity. The lesser local laity was concerned to form an association with local religious houses which confirmed and further promoted local neighborhoods of, for example, knightly families–reinforced a local identity, if you will. In pursuing benefactions for specific purposes, the local laity defined closely the association which it was seeking with the monastic liturgy, through burial, cantarists, the elements of the eucharist in the conventual church, and anniversaries through pittances. To that extent, what occurred was an appropriation of monastic culture and liturgy. For, what had previously been reserved for the monks and canons was now desired and achieved by the local laity. Whilst not appropriating that liturgy and culture outside the religious house, the penetration of the monastic liturgy and culture brought the laity more than an association, more an appropriation of something previously confined to those in religious Orders. Conversely, of course, in the difficult circumstances of the late twelfth and early thirteenth century, as significant benefactions of land declined, religious houses, particularly those of the new Orders of the twelfth century, also prosecuted this association with the local laity, not for the material benefits–which were minuscule–but for support. It was, amongst other matters and to some extent, the further change of that relationship in the later middle ages which caused some problems and dislocation.[39]

Notes

[1] BL Add. MS 40,008, fol. 41v.

[2] BL Add. MS 40,008, fol. 55r: *Hanc elemosinam feci Canonicis meis pro anima mea et omnium parentum meorum et hominum meorum qui sunt mortui uel sint morituri* (benefaction of pasture for five hundred sheep and the site of a bercary [sheep-cote] of two acres in size in Hundmanby).

[3] Paul R. Hyams, "The Charter as a Source for the Early Common Law", *The Journal of Legal History* 12 (1991): 173-89. A useful exercise is to compare the charters respectively to the "French" and English houses in *Charters of the Redvers Family*; see also Emily Z. Tabuteau, *Transfers of Property in Eleventh Century Norman Law* (Chapel Hill, N. C.: University of North Carolina Press, 1988).

[4] Janet Burton, *Monastic and Religious Orders in Britain 1000-1300* (Cambridge: Cambridge University Press, 1994) and *The Monastic Order in Yorkshire, 1069-1215* (Cambridge: Cambridge University Press, 1999); Benjamin Thompson, ed., *Monasteries and Society in Medieval Britain*, Harlaxton Medieval Studies, vol. VI (Stamford: Paul Watkins Publishing, 1999); Emma Cownie, *Religious Patronage in Anglo-Norman England 1066-1135* (Woodbridge: Boydell, 1998), the last of which is influenced by interpretations by North American scholars such as Stephen White and Barbara Rosenwein on the relationship between the religious and the laity in "France." For a

specific house in its locality, Joan Wardrop, *Fountains Abbey and its Benefactors 1132-1300* (Kalamazoo, Mich.: Medieval Institute Publications, 1987).

[5] Edmund King, "Mountsorrel and its Region in King Stephen's Reign", *Huntington Library Quarterly* 44 (1980-1): 1-10; Marjorie Chibnall, "The Empress Matilda and Church Reform", *TRHS* 5th ser., 38 (1988), 107-30; Peter Golob, "The Ferrers Earls of Derby: A Study of the Honour of Tutbury (1066-1279)", PhD dissertation, University of Cambridge (1984): 70, 140-2.

[6] David Crouch, *The Beaumont Twins: The Roots and Branches of Power in the Twelfth Century* (Cambridge: Cambridge University Press, 1986), 196-204; Marjorie Chibnall, "L'Ordre de Fontrevault en Angleterre au xiiie S.", *Cahiers de Civilisation Médiévale* 29 (1986): 41-7.

[7] Examples from the "Anarchy" are: *EEA* I, 125 (no. 200); "Charters ... Earldom of Hereford", 23-4 (no. 25).

[8] Megan McLaughlin, *Consorting with Saints: Prayer for the Dead in Early Medieval France* (Ithaca, N. Y.: Cornell University Press, 1994), for the suggestion that at an earlier time the principal relationship was a desire for associative bonds between laity and religious to form a liturgical *communitas*. It is argued below that this consideration extended into the thirteenth century, centered on the monastic liturgy. My argument is, however, stronger, contending that there was as much appropriation of the liturgy as association.

[9] Arnoud-Jan Bijsterveld, "The Medieval Gift as Agent of Social Bonding and Political Power: A Comparative Approach" in *Medieval Transformations: Texts, Power, and Gifts in Context*, ed. Esther Cohen and Mayke B. de Jong (Leiden: Brill, 2001), 123-56, which inserts into a new context the argument of Ilana Silber that gift-exchange was formative in Western monasticism: Silber, *Virtuosity, Charisma, and Social Order: A Comparative Sociological Study of Monasticism in Therevada Buddhism and Medieval Catholicism* (Cambridge: Cambridge University Press, 1995).

[10] Perhaps concluded by David Carpenter, "Was There a Crisis of the Knightly Class in the Thirteenth Century? The Case of Oxfordshire", *EHR* 95 (1980): 721-52.

[11] Christopher Harper-Bill, "The Piety of the Anglo-Norman Knightly Class", in *Anglo-Norman Studies 2*, ed. R. Allen Brown (Woodbridge: Boydell, 1979), 63-77.

[12] David Crouch and Peter R. Coss, "Debate: Bastard Feudalism Revisited", *Past and Present* 131 (1991): 165-203.

[13] Peter R. Coss, *Lordship, Knighthood and Locality: A Study in English Society c.1180-c.1280* (Cambridge: Cambridge University Press, 1991); Hugh Thomas, *Vassals, Heiresses, Crusaders, and Thugs: The Gentry of Angevin Yorkshire, 1154-1216* (Philadelphia, Pa.: University of Pennsylvania Press,

1993); David A. Carpenter, "The Second Century of English Feudalism", *Past and Present* 168 (2000): 30-71.

[14] The following is based on BL Lansdowne MS 415, the abbey's cartulary.

[15] BL Lansdowne MS 415, fol. 9v. The point about the appeal from the monks was made to me by Benjamin Thompson. See also Chapter 9.

[16] More usually, founders and patrons adopted this term *advocatus*: Bodl. Fairfax MS 9, fol. 13v.: *Omnibus &c Robertus de Ros Dominus de Beuuer salutem &c Nouerit uniuersitas uestra quod Ego predictus Robertus aduocatus prioratus de Wartria ...*; Susan Wood, *English Monasteries and Their Patrons in the Thirteenth Century* (Oxford: Oxford University Press, 1955).

[17] Note here, however, that the scale is not the "regional society" discussed by Cassandra Potts, *Monastic Revival and Regional Identity in Early Normandy* (Woodbridge: Boydell, 1997).

[18] Peter R. Coss, "Knighthood and the Early Thirteenth-century County Court", in *Thirteenth Century England II*, ed. Coss and Simon D. Lloyd (Woodbridge: Boydell, 1988), 45-58.

[19] C. J. Wales, "The Knight in Twelfth-century Lincolnshire", PhD dissertation (University of Cambridge, 1983), 235-60, in the specific context of houses of the new religious Orders giving an opportunity for such consolidation in the neighborhood.

[20] Emilia Jamroziak and I had a useful discussion of this issue at a conference in Nottingham.

[21] Some examples to illustrate this argument include: *Coram omnibus lecta est hec cartula et ab hominibus Malgeri ipsa concessa et confirmata* (*Rufford Charters* II, 162-3 (no. 293)); *Notum sit omnibus audituris litteras istas* [named witnesses] *coram parochianis* (*Cartularium ... Gyseburne* II, 195 (no. dcclix)); *Sciant legentes et audientes litteras istas* (*Cartularium ... Gyseburne*, I, 192 (no. ccclxxxvii)). Such flexible formulae are indicative of actual proclamation.

[22] Donald Fleming, "*Milites* as Attestors to Charters in England, 1101-1300", *Albion* 32 (1990): 185-98; David Crouch, *The Image of the Aristocracy in Britain 1000-1300* (London: Routledge, 1992), 150-2.

[23] BL Add. MS 40,008, fols. 1r-291r (the later parts comprise only Lincolnshire and, indeed, up to fol. 291r include latterly significant parts of that county as well).

[24] BL Add. MS 40,008, fol. 13r.

[25] For his role in the prior's court, BL Add. MS 40,008, fol. 27r.

[26] *Register ... St Bees*.

[27] Janet Burton, *The Monastic Order in Yorkshire*, 210; my thesis is perhaps slightly more emphatic. Celia Chazelle, Robin Fleming and Chris Lewis reminded me that some appropriation had occurred earlier too.

[28] *Cartulary of Bushmead Priory*; on the implications of the excessive

burden of *cantarie*, Howard M. Colvin, "The Origin of Chantries", *Journal of Medieval History* 26 (2000): 163-73, modified by David Crouch, "The Origins of Chantries: Some Further Anglo-Norman Evidence", *Journal of Medieval History* 27 (2001): 159-80.

[29] See Chapter 5 below.

[30] *Cartularium ... Gyseburne*, I, 34 (no. dclxviia), 119-20 (no. dccxcviii).

[31] See Chapter 4 below.

[32] See Chapter 3 below for details and bibliographical references.

[33] Bodl. MS Top. Yorks. c72, fols. 16v and 17r.

[34] *Cartularium ... Gyesburne*, I, 50, 70, 158, 226, 240, 257, 265; II, 18, 42, 96, 121, 132, 144, 147, 169, 239, and 243. See also Christopher J. Holdsworth, *The Piper and the Tune: Medieval Patrons and Monks* (Reading: University of Reading Stenton Lecture 1990, 1991), 12-14.

[35] BL Add. MS 40,008, fol. 44v.

[36] Colvin, "Origin of Chantries".

[37] BL Add. MS 40,008, fol. 135r.

[38] Stephen D. White, *Custom, Kinship and Gifts to Saints: The* Laudatio Parentum *in Western France 1050-1150* (Chapel Hill, N. C.: University of North Carolina Press, 1988); Potts, *Monastic Revival and Regional Identity*; Barbara H. Rosenwein, *To Be the Neighbor of St Peter: The Social Meaning of Cluny's Property 909-1049* (Ithaca, N. Y.: Cornell University Press, 1989); McLaughlin, *Consorting with Saints*.

[39] Eamon Duffy, *The Stripping of the Altars: Traditional Religion in England 1400-1580* (New Haven, Conn., and London: Yale University Press, 1992), 210.

2
Lamps, Lights and Layfolk:
"Popular" Devotion Before the Black Death

> Before the altars and images lights were set, and the maintenance of these lights, especially during times of service, became the single most popular expression of piety in wills of the late medieval laity.[1]

Long, however, might that have been so. In 1109x1114, Nigel d'Aubigny gave to Selby abbey a carucate of land in Amcotts for the provision of light in the abbey church.[2] Many of the strategies for personal salvation which were associated with popular piety in the English late middle ages have a longer history, and it is by no means clear that there was a greater efflorescence to this recourse in the late middle ages. What is probably true is that the higher disposable income of many people in the later medieval period combined with the relative emancipation of the peasantry might have brought such strategies within the compass of more people.[3] Lighting had an immense practical and symbolic importance for the medieval church and its congregations even before the late middle ages.[4]

Scope thus exists for an extended consideration of the laity's contribution to lighting before the middle of the fourteenth century. Benefactions for lights reveal much about lay piety in the twelfth and thirteenth centuries, and the extent to which personal religious observance had become focused on the parish church or whether religious houses continued to be as, if not more, attractive at a time when parochial organization and parochial obligations on the laity were still evolving. Lights are significant because quite modest endowments could be made for their maintenance, which allowed the participation of wide social groups in this form of association with the liturgy, including burgesses and even the free peasantry. Whilst the first part below explores the symbolic importance of lights, the second section considers the involvement of the laity in their provision, both through ecclesiastical compulsion and as part of voluntary religious observance. It is clear that lights were a continuous focus of lay piety in the middle ages, but that some differences existed between the twelfth and thirteenth centuries and the later middle ages in the nature and direction of the benefactions as, in the later middle ages, the parish stood increasingly at the center of lay devotion.

Before the construction of clerestories and large windows in the nave and the use of grisaille glass to allow reading of texts by at least some parishioners, churches were darker, which made the contrast between light(ing) and dark even more significant, both practically and symbolically, especially in, for example, ceremonies such as the *tenebrae*.[5] In the dark, and before the introduction of seating, so that congregations were assembled standing, the raising and positioning of lights at the elevation of the host in masses, presented the contrast again.[6] By 1226, the cathedral church at Wells was consuming at least 450 lbs. of wax every year for its lighting, whilst, when the lighting was increased at Salisbury cathedral church in the early thirteenth century, the treasurer was allowed another 200 lbs. of wax.[7]

This close association of lights and the mass confirmed their symbolic and ritual importance.[8] In ca.1200, for example, William *filius Herberti* of Derby donated to Darley Abbey half an acre of land in his borough to help to maintain a light *coram corpore dominico* (before the host).[9] The statutes of English dioceses in the early thirteenth century elaborate on this point. A lamp must burn continuously day and night before the host.[10] Diocesan statutes required two candles or at least one candle and a lantern for the solemnization of the mass.[11] The statutes for the diocese of Winchester (1247?) specified that the candles should not only be large but made *ad modum torticeorum*; when the priest began the communication, with the *incipit* of the *Te igitur*, two assistants should move the two candles to the right and left of the altar.¹² Similarly, when the eucharist was taken to the sick, it was to be preceded by a light, sometimes as in the statutes for the diocese of Salisbury defined as a candelabrum or lantern, and churches in that diocese were reputed in 1238x1244 to have two candelabra and two processional candles.¹³ The host was also blessed with candles.¹⁴

In keeping with the ritual significance of the liturgical lights, their use had to be demarcated from normal life–marking off both the substance and its use.¹⁵ The ritual demarcation was most pronounced afterwards, as by the statutes of Salisbury of 1217x1219 which required that after Holy Trinity small candles should be made from Easter wax which could be employed in the burials of the poor–reserving the use of the wax to its ritual occasions.¹⁶ Similar promulgations for the diocese of Worcester (1229 and 1240) allowed use of Easter wax after Holy Trinity for the lesser altars as well as for burials for the poor.¹⁷ Even more emphatically, however, the statute of 1229 prohibited any other use (common use) of the candles blessed for Purification unless the wax was first melted down.¹⁸

Quotidian material was thus marked off symbolically from normal consumption both in time and use. Liturgical time and use were separated from the rest of life, although the material was in common daily use, for candles remained a common assistance to the pursuit of normal life. The author of the *Seneschaucy* (compiled before or not much after 1276), for example, ordered that the cowherd should not take fire or candle into the cowshed except under controlled manner. For the ploughmen, he proscribed the use of naked flame for warmth nor should the ploughmen use candles unless in a lantern. The carter, furthermore, required to sleep every night with his horses, should take no flame or candle into the stables except in a lantern.¹⁹ Consequently, the manorial accounts of Cuxham, a manor of Merton College in Oxfordshire, recorded the purchase of tallow for candles; in 1290-1, twelve lbs. of tallow were bought for candles for harvest and winter, an amount adjusted upwards to twenty-two lbs. in 1293-4, although still at 1d. per lb. In 1288-9, the account recorded that the tallow was bought for candles for the use of the *famuli* in winter, but in some years the costs of the visits to the manor were also included. The purchase of fourteen lbs. of tallow in 1297-8 was defined as for all expenses of the *familia*, which must mean the body of the *famuli* in this case.[20] Some of the peasants on the manors of the Bishopric of Winchester contributed wax as their annual recognition (chevage) in 1301-2; more than thirty found half a pound each and four a full pound.[21]

The itinerant household of Abbot Walter of Wenlock, head of Westminster Abbey, purchased twenty-seven lbs. of Paris candles at Pitford for 2s. 10½d. In 1289-90, several quantities of wax were also bought from Thomas Romain, pepperer and later Mayor of London.[22] Tallow was purchased for the guesthouse of Beaulieu Abbey in 1269-70; the same commodity was forestalled outside the market at Norwich leading to presentment at the leet in 1289.[23] Beaulieu, however, was assiduous in producing its own wax from swarms in all its manors and workshops in Hampshire. By a centralized organization, the wax was delivered from the points of production to the lesser chamber, whence it was redistributed. The lesser chamber thus received 215½ lbs. of wax, 140 lbs. of which were directed to the sacristan, all to be consumed in churches and chapels in his care. The abbot's chamber received eighteen lbs. (fourteen from the lesser chamber and four from the sacristan) and the abbot's notary 3½ lbs., the keeper of the works six lbs., the refectory a small amount, the cellarer three lbs., and the guesthouse ten lbs.[24] Additionally, the larder produced two stones of tallow which was sold, and the tanner substantial quantities of tallow; large amounts of oil were also purchased for the churches, the monks' dormitory, the dormitory of the *conversi*, and both of their infirmaries.[25] At least some of the wax, most of the tallow, and some of the oil was thus used for lighting for non-liturgical purposes. It is estimated that sixteen candles for this purpose might be derived from one lb. of material.[26] Even in an ecclesiastical context, then, candles retained a practical purpose which was not liturgical, and the three officials of the treasury of Lincoln cathedral received in the late middle ages an allowance each week of thirteen or fourteen candles through winter and seven in summer to search the cathedral twice each night for the security of valuables.[27] A further way in which liturgical candles were marked off from daily use, however, was by material, size and complexity. At the lowest social levels, candles for daily use consisted of fat dipped in rush, at the higher level tallow, with some wax and a maximum weight considerably less than 1 lb. Liturgical candles were uniformly of wax, heavy and decorated (such as torches), although candles used by penitents at their penance were slight, as might have been the candles used by parishioners at Candlemas processions.[28]

Candles were thus familiar from daily life but also separated off for ritual use. In certain circumstances, wax assumed a heightened significance and symbolism.[29] The penance of Walter *filius Simonis* for insulting the Priory of Daventry was, in 1239, to keep a light constantly burning before the high altar of Daventry.[30] The appropriation of some parish churches by religious houses in the twelfth century was only allowed on the condition that the revenues be employed in maintaining the lights and ornaments of the monastic church.[31] In the early twelfth century, William Gifford, bishop of Winchester, allowed his cathedral priory the Pentecostal oblations to be used for their lights and other necessities, perhaps mindful of the *cerae deneratae* provided by parishioners to mother churches at such processions in Normandy.[32] Rents of lay fee between clerics involved these symbolically-invested materials as rent, different from secular services in some sense (although enforceable at common law). Thus when Mr William de Bening[worth] received a toft and croft from the Dean and Chapter of Lincoln in 1241x1243, the rent consisted of a wax candle weighing one lb. to burn on the high altar of the cathedral church and when Daventry Priory was forced to distrain for a rent, the distraint consisted of the forfeiture of 2d. to provide a candle for the daily Lady Mass.[33] When, before Papal judges-delegate, agreement was reached between the priory of Saint Gregory, Canterbury, and Roger, rector of Lenham, about the tithes of Lenham in 1240, the priory was obliged to make an annual payment of a candle weighing two lbs. to the parish church on the feast of the Nativity of the Blessed Virgin Mary (BVM) *pro bono perpetue pacis*.[34] Similarly, an agreement with the consent of Reading Abbey between the rector of the parish church of Rowington and Pinley Priory about the lesser tithes due to Rowington was concluded by the nuns providing a small pension of wax for the lesser tithes, in 1195x1213.[35] In compensation for their accommodation in the house on the east side of the cathedral close at Lincoln, poor clerks contributed a lighted candle in a silver candlestick to burn before the high altar on specific days.[36]

Candles were symbolically employed in excommunication, as well as restitution of penitents, but perhaps more illuminating is the incensed reaction of Bishop Oliver Sutton to the desecration of the church and altars at Thame. For this profanity, Sutton, in 1294, excommunicated the occupiers of the church by taking up a candle (*sumens candelam*) and then, with the words *fiat, fiat, amen* on completion of the excommunication, dashed the candle to the ground (*et proiecit candelam ad terram*).[37] Ritual and everyday use commingled and became confused, however, in "popular" religion when candles were constructed to take to shrines to aid the sick. The wick was measured against the body of the sick person and then folded and coated in wax, the candle, thus representing the sick body, being then placed before the shrine.[38]

The symbolic, ritual and liturgical importance of lights thus existed from an early time and was profound by the twelfth century. The discussion now concentrates on the involvement of the laity in the provision and maintenance of lights in the variety of religious institutions, including the parish, which attracted lay devotion before the late middle ages. It begins by considering the compulsory obligations imposed on the laity from an early time, but progresses by way of an example, the provision for lighting in the parish church of Tytherley, to explore voluntary benefactions by the laity for lighting. Described then are the comparative levels of benefactions for lights in religious houses and parish churches in the twelfth and thirteenth centuries, attempting to locate the focus of lay devotion. These two forms of institution were, in a sense, competitors for lay grants for lights, but more complexity obtained. Religious houses were appropriators of parish churches. Since many advowsons were in the hands of the religious, it is not always clear whether, in grants for lights in some parish churches, the parish church was the primary focus and the religious simply acted in a supervisory capacity, or whether donors had mixed motives. It is, however, possible to discern that in many cases the benefaction was exclusively intended for parish church and illustrative examples are collected together. Finally, some of the wider implications of benefactions for specific purposes such as lights are considered again.

Originally, it was the obligation of all the laity to provide for lights in churches, whether monastic or parochial. The early pastoral role of the large Benedictine religious houses is reflected in the scot for lights levied on their tenantry. The *Regularis Concordia* of ca.970 "assumes a regular presence of lay parishioners at mass in a monastery", with the consequence that some houses, such as Crowland, continued through the later middle ages to entertain worship by the laity.[39] Minsters too continued as "primary centres of lay attraction".[40] As a result, the large Benedictine houses imposed the obligation to provide some of the lighting of their churches on their tenantry. Thus Ramsey Abbey exacted lightscot in the early twelfth century at the rate of 1d. from married and ½d. from unmarried cottars on its manors of Abbot's Ripton and Broughton, whilst on another manor, Wistow, each house contributed ½d. at Easter for lighting the church; the abbey required 1d. from every plough of the *curia* on its manor of Brancaster for Easter wax. In ca.1125, Peterborough Abbey received 1d. from every plough on its manor of Glinton for Easter wax. On the manors of the Bishop of Ely waursilver or waresilver was levied, a comparable scot. The tenants of the secular cathedral chapter of Saint Paul's, London, contributed 2s. each year for *candlewekesilver*, the name also of the levy raised from the manors of the Bishop of Durham.[41]

Slightly different, however, was the provision of wax for parochial churches, to which all parishioners contributed through the payment of lightscot. In the Old English law, *leohgesceot* was mentioned in 1002x1008; slightly later, the "Canons of Edgar" (1005x1008) commented on the levy of light dues three times each year, as did the Code of Æthelred although this enunciation allowed the laity to contribute more regularly than three times a year voluntarily.[42] Cnut's laws maintained the three feasts, Easter, All Saints and Candlemas, establishing the rate of payment at ½d. on every hide.[43] The statutes of the diocese of Salisbury (1228x1256) confirmed that parishioners should contribute Easter wax and sufficient lighting throughout the whole year for matins, vespers and mass.[44] A list of 1230x1240 for waxscot (*De ciragio*) for the villages of Haddenham, Linden, Hill, Hinton and Aldreth in the Isle of Ely denominated 213 persons (or households) who should contribute.[45]

By the early thirteenth century, nevertheless, individual grants and gifts to maintain lighting in churches were widely anticipated, so that diocesan statutes repeatedly made provision that rents assigned by the devotion of lay persons to lights should not be diverted by rectors of vicars to other purposes.[46] Encouragement was extended by statutes for Winchester and Wells dioceses in respectively 1247(?) and 1258(?), with the grant of an indulgence of ten days to those contributing to lighting.[47]

In the mid-thirteenth century Matthew *de Columbariis* attorned to the parish church of Tytherley all the service and rent of Philip *de Querco*, that is twelve candles yearly burning every day at all masses, each candle weighing one lb. Two candles were to be delivered on Christmas eve and to burn until 1st March, two from the 1st March to the 1st May, two from 1st May to 1st July, two from 1st July to 1st September, two from 1st September until the eve of All Saints, and two from then until Christmas eve. Additionally, he prescribed that half of the residue of the candles should burn before the cross and the other half of the residue before the Lady altar for the antiphony after mass.[48] Unusually, this donor was of a relatively high social status and his definition of the use of the candles was exceptional, as also was their quantity. On the other hand, illustrated well is the association of this sort of grant with the assignment of rents and with the mass and Lady altar.

The assignment or attornment of rents also allowed the participation of the free peasantry in such gift-exchange, but more particularly townspeople. Religious houses, however, offered a symbol of social and religious association different from the parish church, again especially in towns, but also amongst the rural free peasantry. The further benefit which accrued from the granting of rents to maintain lamps was flexibility of association and private devotion. Grantors selected altars dedicated to a wider range of saints than merely the dedication of the religious house or parochial church. Popular piety was thus expressed through benefactions to lights for a wide range of altars rather than restricted to the patronal saint of the church's dedication.[49]

Whilst donors or grantors of high social status had a range of strategies for salvation–place of burial, (con)fraternity, chantry, pittances in expectation of response–the exchange of rents for lights in expectation of salvation was much more accessible to lesser benefactors.[50] Perhaps only the fabric fund of religious houses and pittances allowed a similar opportunity.[51] There remain, nevertheless, complexities for any analysis, not least hidden purchase even for such purposeful benefactions. It is possible that the circumstance of some, at least, of the acquisitions was purchase by the religious house. For example, when Southwick Priory received a house in Southwick from William *de* [sic] *Lardenir* in ca.1250, the priory paid a consideration of 18s. although a light would be maintained at the high altar of the priory church (which acted also as the parish church). What appears to have happened here is that in recompense for its acquisition the priory undertook to provide the light.[52] So also when Arnold son of Roger *Niger* transferred to Shrewsbury Abbey a messuage in that borough to increase the light before the high altar by providing a candle at high mass, the abbey gave in consideration two marks and 10s. 4d. *in urgentissima necessitate mea*.[53]

A second complication occurred when the church of the religious house also contained the parish church, if the professed religious used the chancel and the parishioners the nave, or if the two congregations had different naves, since it is difficult to differentiate whether the benefaction was intended primarily for the conventual or parochial parts of the church. For example, both Daventry and Southwick Priories had been founded within parish churches. Cathedral priories and churches present a similar confusion of interests, although the cartulary of Worcester cathedral priory apparently contains few charters with benefits for the lights and Brown refers to only a few such grants to the lights at Salisbury.[54]

Although, as we shall see, predilection for the high and Lady altars was paramount, those making grants for lights could exercise a wider personal choice from a range of altars dedicated to a variety of saints.[55] In 1323, John *Launcelevey* requested that wax candles annually valued at 4s. 5½d. burn on the altar of Saint Nicholas on the feast of that saint in the chapel of Saint James in Southwick Priory, the reason for his choice being obscure.[56] Roger son of William de Houton' gave two tofts (1218x1231) to Thurgarton Priory, a house dedicated to Saint Peter, for the maintenance of three lamps in the priory, one for the Lady mass, one before the altar of Saint Nicholas for masses, and one in the Lady chapel of the infirmary for masses.[57] The same priory received from Henry *Ruffus* three selions partly to maintain lamps, one to provide a lamp before the high altar of the house, one for its fabric fund, and the final one to provide two lamps before the altar of Saint Margaret the Virgin in Owthorpe church.[58] Muriel de Langetoft selected the altar of Saint Nicholas in the parish church of Saint Peter, Shiplake, granting lands and villeins for two candles at that altar at the altar's patronal feast day and a lamp before the same altar burning *festiuis diebus ad uesperas et ad missam*.[59] More unusual was the choice of William *Juvenis* who in ca.1275 assigned a rent of 4s. from property in Derby to Dale Abbey to maintain a lamp day and night before the altar of Saint Werburgh in the house.[60] Rents of 12d. were assigned by Henry Inge to Saint Frideswide's Priory, Oxford, in 1230x1240 for a lamp in the chapel of Saint Lucy the Virgin *que sita est in curia dictorum Prioris et Conuentus*.[61] Saint Catherine the Virgin was the beneficiary of a rent of 9d. granted in the early thirteenth century to Blyth Priory to sustain a candle before her altar in the house on her feast day.[62] On receipt of a messuage and plot of land from Adam Bat in ca.1230, Beaulieu Abbey agreed to contribute 2s. annually to maintain lights before the altars of Saint Thomas and Saint Catherine in the parish church of Saint Laurence, Hungerford.[63] At the instance of his wife, Eustacia Basset, Richard de Camville conveyed to Robert *clericus* a virgate in Bicester with the condition of providing a lamp before the altar of Saint Nicholas in Bicester Priory, which was dedicated to Saints Mary and Edburga, every day and night when divine office was celebrated and during canonical hours (1206x1216).[64] Ralph de Cornehell elected to sustain lights before the altars of Saints Erkenwald and James in Saint Paul's cathedral some time before 1211.[65]

Despite this variety, however, provision was mainly directed to the high altar and more particularly the Lady altar and their masses. More typical was Thomas *la* [sic] *Wayte* who assigned a messuage in Southwick to the priory there for a light before the altar on the north side of the priory church when Lady mass was solemnly sung.[66] William de Hoo, a townsman of Portsmouth, requested a light on the altar of the BVM in the priory.[67] Indeed, six of the ten grants for lights to Southwick Priory, mostly from townspeople of Southwick, were associated with the Lady mass, so that a keeper before the lights of the altar was necessary.[68] Similarly the keeper of the Lady altar at Shrewsbury Abbey received twenty-five of twenty-nine grants of rents, mainly in the borough, to maintain lights in the first half of the thirteenth century.[69] At Westminster Abbey as early as 1200x1214, provision was made for all those who had contributed towards lights at the Lady altar to be entered in the martyrology.[70] Indeed, townspeople in Westminster and London were involved in twenty-one charters in 1198x1216 granting rents for lights for the Lady altar in the abbey, totalling £2 10s. 0d., at a mean rent of 2s. 4d. The lowest amount was a rent of 4d. and the highest 7s. 8d., the median lying at 2s.[71] By this time, the light had been assigned to the precentor.[72] In Oxford, William Vincent contributed a rent of 6d. in ca.1230 for the Lady light in Osney Abbey, whilst the light at the Lady altar in Norwich cathedral benefited from a gift of 4d. of rent from Alice *filia Egidie*.[73] Attested once again in this phenomenon is the strength of Marian devotion by the early thirteenth century.[74]

In the tenor of most of the grants for the Lady lights in the borough of Shrewsbury, the size of rents varied widely, but fell in the lower levels. Thus Adam son of Andrew *le Turner* gave a rent of a mere ½d. there towards the lights for the Lady altar in 1260x1280, whilst Reiner *filius Godwini* assigned only 1d. rent.[75] Eighteen of the rents did not exceed 1s. The size-distribution is complicated, however, by the actions of Hugh *filius Ricardi* who contributed a sequence of rents of 3d., 3½d., 4½d., 1s., 5s. 10d., 8d. and 1s. 2d. with no ostensible consideration or counter-gift, but finally 1s. for a consideration of 10s. *in magna necessitate mea*.[76] Nevertheless, the donations to Shrewsbury by townspeople illustrate both how accessible this form of salvific benefaction was to townspeople and their predilection for the BVM.

The same preference was exhibited in benefactions for the lights to Daventry Priory, the church of which also contained the parochial church, a former minster. In 1148x1166, Simon *filius Roberti* confirmed the advowsons of five parish churches granted by his father to the priory, to which Simon added a virgate of the glebe of Foxton to provide a light for the Lady altar and to fund a weekly Lady mass on Saturday or any other day.[77] His gift was complemented about the same time by Philip de Daventre whose benefaction had the purpose of providing two candles on the Lady altar at all Lady masses.[78] Six of the nine subsequent benefactions for lights before 1320 were directed to Lady altar or mass.[79] At least two townspeople in Lichfield favored with rents the lights before the Lady altar in the cathedral church, but another respected the high altar.[80]

The most complete description of the funding of parish lights involving a range of saints, however, derives from the visitations of churches in the gift of Saint Paul's cathedral, 1249x1252.[81] All the lighting in the church of Barling was provided by the leasing out of sixty-one ewes to eight of the tenants, contributing wax for the altar of Saint Giles, before the cross, before the images of Saint Nicholas and the Lady, and the rowel light. Many, if not all, of these leased sheep were accumulated through legacies or benefactions; for example, Reginald Wile rented fourteen ewes, twelve of which had accrued under the will of Walter Pavery. Additionally, Brice had to find wax for candles before the altar of Saint Giles. It was fortuitous indeed that these provisions had been made, for the great tithes of the demesne and parish had been appropriated to support the lighting of Saint Paul's.[82] At Heybridge, seventeen ewes and two cows were leased out to provide lights for the altar of Saint Andrew (the dedication of the church), the Lady altar, three other altars and before the cross. Pain *de Boscho* had taken on a lease of a cow and three ewes bequeathed by the will of John de Araz for maintaining a lamp in perpetuity before the cross to burn on four feast nights each year.[83] To provision the lights at Tillingham, including the Lady light and in front of the cross, fifty-four tenants had received on lease 103 ewes, a lamb, three cows and a horse.[84] Less well endowed, however, was Alderbury, where three lamps before the high altar were enumerated in the inventory, one of which was maintained by the parishioners. The parish had, however, no stock for leasing and relied for Easter wax and the rowel light for levies on houses and households, whilst the support for other lights depended on offerings.[85] A similar situation obtained at Pelham Forness, with its four candelabra listed, where no rents had been assigned for lights; Easter wax was collected at the rate of ½d. on holdings of eighteen acres and proportionately for smaller tenements. The rest of the wax and lamps before the crosses and altars depended on offerings.[86] So too at Pelham Arsa, where two candelabra were listed, *ad luminare ejusdem ecclesie nichil est certum* since there were no assigned rents, for a gift of two acres by Geoffrey Sarvors to provide two candles for the high altar had been absorbed into the demesne of the treasurer of Saint Paul's and at the time nothing had been allocated to the parish church. Whilst Easter wax was gathered on the basis of a farthing from each messuage by custom, the remainder of the lighting derived from offerings.[87] Entirely consistent was the pattern of provision at Navestock where the rowel resulted from a levy of ½d. on each messuage, as did Easter wax, two candles before the Lady altar being supported only by rents of 2s.[88]

By contrast, lights in the churches of Thorpe, Walton and Kirkby were amply supported by the stock of animals leased to the tenantry (Table 1). Perhaps most significantly, most of these collections for different lights of the church of Kirby had been assigned by the middle of the thirteenth century to specific keepers (*custodes*), selected from amongst the parishioners.[89]

During the twelfth and early thirteenth century, religious houses competed with parish churches for the allegiances of parishioners in terms of benefactions, including those for lights.[90] Parochial organization was still developing into the early thirteenth century, so that, in some places, and perhaps in towns, local religious affiliations were expressed through religious houses as much as parish

Table 1 Provision for Lights at Thorpe, Walton and Kirkby, 1249x1252

Manor	Animals leased	No. of lessees	Rents	Purpose (lighting)
Thorpe (a)	28 ewes	14	2d. each	rowel
	20 *pecora*	12	2d. each	before the cross
	6 *pecora*	5	2d. each	St Margaret's chapel
	5 *pecora*	5	2d. each	Lady chapel
	20 *pecora*	9	2d. each	BVM next to high altar
Walton (b)	26 ewes	11	Total: 4s. 8d.	rowel
	5½ ewes (sic)	6	Total: 10d.	before the cross
	63½ ewes (sic)	30	Total: 11s. 4½d.	Lady light
	20 ewes	10	Total: 3s. 3d.	St Michael's light
	37 ewes	11	Total: 5s. 5d.	high altar
Kirkby	7 sheep	7		Easter wax
	41 sheep	18		Lady light
	6 sheep	3		before the cross
	9 sheep	4		St Peter's light
	18 sheep	5		rowel
	22 sheep	14		St Michael's light
	7 sheep	6		two lights in the chancel
	11 sheep	5		before the cross

Notes to Table 1 (a) there was a small number of additional legacies of cows and ewes; (b) the total rents comprised 25s. 6½d., but *non est aliquis redditus ad cereum paschalem* ("Visitations of the churches of St Paul's cathedral", 30)
Source: "Visitations of the churches of St Paul's cathedral", 24-6, 28-30, 32-3.

churches. The extent of benefactions of this kind for lights in parish churches is more difficult to establish by comparison with those to religious houses and, paradoxically, some of the best evidence derives from the charters and cartularies of religious houses, in many cases where the advowson was held by the house. Where the religious had an interest in the parish church–through advowson, portion or pension–some confusion is inevitable. Was the benefaction only to the parish church or by association to the religious house as well? That complexity was exacerbated when, for example, in 1227, John son of John Cordewaner conveyed to Ralph *molendinarius* a messuage with a rent reserved to the altar of Saint John in the parish church of Hertford when the canons of Waltham celebrate mass for the parishioners.[91]

In many cases, however, although recorded in the cartularies of religious houses which held the advowson, the benefaction was clearly to the parish church or to a chapelry. The charter of benefaction was registered in the cartulary simply because the religious house had the supervisory role, but the benefaction was from the lay grantor to the parish church. In ca.1180, Emma de Langetoft attorned a rent of 16d. for the provision of a lamp in the chapel of Saint Mary at Shiplake.[92] In the middle of the thirteenth century, Nicholas *Iuuenis* transferred a rent of 6d. in Derby towards the lights before the high altar in the parish church of Saint Peter in the borough.[93] Recorded in the cartulary of Darley Abbey are numerous grants of rents for the provision of lights at the altar in the parish church of Saint Mary, Scarcliffe, including ½d. from Roger son of William de Somerford ca.1250 at the low end and 4s. 4d. from Hubert FitzRalf at the top end.[94] In 1190x1200, Hugh de Pluggenait conveyed a rent of 2s. to provide a lamp in Saint Andrew, Headington.[95] Shortly afterwards, (1200x1219), land which yielded a rent of 2s. was conveyed to the priory of Saint Gregory, Canterbury, for the perpetual maintenance of the lights in the parish church of Saint James, Elmstead.[96] In the early thirteenth century, some eighteen grants of rents for lights and lamps (and oil) were directed to the chapel of Saint Mary at Bures, but recorded in the cartulary of Stoke by Clare Priory.[97] A very significant gift, of a virgate in Rushton, was made to Cirencester Abbey for the maintenance of a lamp before the Lady altar in her chapel in the parish church of Rothwell in the early thirteenth century, to burn *omnibus noctis seculi*.⁹⁸ Parish churches in Oxford received rents from townspeople, such as the 12d. for lights in Saint Mary's, 5s. for the Lady light in Saint Peter le Bailey, and 2d. for lights in the chapel of Saint Thomas.⁹⁹

In Derbyshire, the chapelry of Glapwell, and in particular the Lady altar, benefited from several gifts of assigned rents in transactions in land between the local free peasantry. Thus, when in ca.1250, John *filius Hugonis* sold land there to Robert de Sumerford', provision was made for a rent of 1d. to sustain a light before the Lady altar in the chapel. The acquisition of 1½ acres by the same Roger involved a rent of ½d. for the same light, just as William Haranc's acquisitions of land produced rents of ½d. and ¼d. for the same light. A further ¼d. of rent resulted from another transaction, but when Roger de Bollisouer passed *inter vivos* to his two sons two tofts, a croft, lands and meadow, he required 8d. in rent to accrue annually towards a lamp burning in the chapel. The obligation to furnish oil for a lamp before the Lady altar in the chapel ensued from a conveyance of an acre. Reflected here, then, is not only the strength of Marian devotion, as noted above, but also the participation of the local free peasantry in the maintenance of lights in the chapel in the thirteenth century.¹⁰⁰

Many charters in the cartulary of Thurgarton Priory record benefactions for lights to the parish churches of Tithby, Loudham, Kirkby Green and especially Scopwick.¹⁰¹ In the early thirteenth century, Adam Burel, John *filius Willelmi filii Tice de Roueston* and Reginald de Cubington all directed rents of ½d. to maintain lamps or lights at the altar of Saint Andrew in the parish church of Scopwick.¹⁰²

As a consequence of these benefactions, both to religious houses and parish churches, rents became reserved from tenements and burgage property; the rent thus became a service attached to and owed from the holding. In some cases, the new tenants might have regarded the assigned rent as simply that and as having no greater significance or its meaning might have been lost. For example, it is recorded in the cartulary of Daventry Priory for 1427 that John Brygge had withheld for twelve years 12d. rent due from a virgate to support a candle in the Lady chapel of the priory (which contained also the parish church).¹⁰³ Probably shortly after a benefaction, William *filius Egidii* acknowledged that he owed a reserved rent of 9s. for lights for the Lady altar at Lincoln cathedral where mass was celebrated daily at prime, although this recognizance in 1250x1255 might simply have been a precautionary action by the Dean and Chapter.[104] In similar vein, Henry *carnifex* of Winchester issued a notification in the late thirteenth century that he should remit one lb. of incense yearly for the Lady altar of Saint Denys, Southampton, for land in Winchester.[105]

In the twelfth and thirteenth century, the terms of gifts to the religious were not always specific. In particular, gifts of land were most frequently effected for the welfare of souls, although assignment of revenues for specific purposes in gifts to religious houses composed a large proportion of gifts to the religious.[106] The expectation of return in gift-exchange for salvific purposes was often unspecified, if generally understood: prayers for the benefactor and her or his kinship. Sometimes that anticipation was expanded, although in the vaguest of manners: *ut orationibus eorum apud dominum adiuuemur* (ca.1190); *preter participationem missarum et orationum que fiunt in eadem ecclesia* (late twelfth-early thirteenth century); and *preter missas et orationes et cetera beneficia spiritualia que fiunt in prefata ecclesia* (mid-twelfth century).[107] Specific provision for the purpose of gifts was often directed towards remembrance and before ca.1300 some of the smaller forms of remembrance–pittances and lights–allowed the greater participation in spiritual benefits of a larger number of lay benefactors, extending to the free peasantry and townspeople.[108] The provisions of the Fourth Lateran Council of 1215, such as annual communication and confession, were a stimulus to internal piety which was expressed through voluntary lay benefactions for lights. One of the consequences of these individual benefactions for lights might have been from the early thirteenth century the development of lay offices in the parish and over the later middle ages more "lay control" over the contributions of the laity to the parish.[109] Individual lay provision for lighting was already associated with the mass and Marian devotion, but there is no need to attribute an integrative or communitarian impulse or response. Individual benefactions for lights were received from only part of the "community", a small select part, so that social status was further defined by such benefactions. Indeed, social differentiation was visible in the material used, the size and weight of candles and the extent of decoration.[110]

Since the circumstances between late medieval piety and the twelfth and thirteenth centuries were somewhat different, so some changes also occurred. By the later middle ages, local social and religious allegiances had generally been transferred from religious houses to parish churches. Whilst a case might be made for a communitarian motive in the late middle ages by augmenting divine service in the parish, the direction in the earlier period of grants for lights in religious houses, to the enclosed religious, cannot be associated with that influence. Except where a religious house functioned also as parish church, parishioners were unlikely to be able to participate in the benefits of the lights.[111] If the origins of grants for lights in the later middle ages were located in the earlier grants, then the primary motivation must have been internal devotion, personal salvation, and definition of social status, rather than any wider sentiment.

A transformation occurred in the nature of grantors and their instruments for allocating grants for lights. In the twelfth and thirteenth century, at least some part of the grants consisted in charters, with the implication that, even if the contribution to the lights continued after the death of the grantor, the association was between the living and the religious institution. Since grants by charters were not usually ambulatory–that is, the grant had to be immediately effective rather than deferred until some future date, such as death–support for the lights occurred in the grantor's lifetime as well as afterwards. By the later middle ages, the patronage of lights was largely effected through testaments, so that the grant was made only after the grantor's death, by bequest. Fundamentally, the later medieval relationship was between the dead and the religious institution. Despite these differences, however, what is clear is the essential continuity of many aspects of late medieval popular piety, not least in lay provision for lights.[112]

Lights, consequently, had continuous symbolic importance in the liturgy. Through benefactions to their support, the laity hoped to be more closely associated with the liturgical rites and, before the later middle ages, lay piety was expressed through such grants. This sort of benefaction was inclusive since the cost could be small, so that participation extended to burgesses and even the free peasantry. The earlier circumstances differed, however, since the parish church had not yet become the primary focus of lay piety, as religious houses offered an alternative.

Notes

[1] Eamon Duffy, *The Stripping of the Altars: Traditional Religion in England 1400-1580* (New Haven, Conn., and London: Yale University Press, 1992), 134. For the association of gilds and the provision of lights, Duffy, *Stripping of the* Altars, 146-7; on this note that, whilst the maintenance of lights and lamps during the later middle ages was achieved by small groups of people and individuals as well as parochial and rectorial responsibilities, at an earlier time groups were not so in evidence, for which, see below, and also Gervase Rosser, "Communities of Parish and Guild in the Late Middle Ages" in *Parish, Church and People. Local Studies in Lay Religion 1350-1750*, ed. Susan J. Wright (London: HarperCollins, 1988): 29-55; Barbara A. Hanawalt, "Keepers of the Lights: Late Medieval English Parish Gilds", *Journal of Medieval and Renaissance Studies* 14 (1984): 21-37; Virginia Bainbridge, *Gilds in the Medieval Countryside: Social and Religious Change in Cambridgeshire c.1350-1558* (Woodbridge: Boydell, 1996), 68-9, 87.

[2] *Charters of the Honour of Mowbray*, 14 (no. 9). Of similar status was the gift of Abberton by Ranulph Peverel to Saint Paul, London, before 1142, for the lights in the cathedral church, Peverel having elected to be buried there: *Early Charters ... St Paul*, 173-4.

[3] Christopher C. Dyer, *Standards of Living in the Middle Ages: Social Change in England c.1200-1520*, new edn. (Cambridge: Cambridge University Press, 1994).

[4] See generally D. R. Dendy, *The Use of Lights in Christian Worship*, Alcuin Club Collections vol. 41 (SPCK, London, 1959).

[5] For the later use of grisaille glass for reading, H. Leith Spencer, *English Preaching in the Late Middle Ages* (Oxford: Oxford University Press, 1993), 38-9. About the contrast of light and dark, I hesitate to assume too much of a structuralist interpretation of binary opposition, but see the prayers for light dispelling darkness at Candlemas: Mary C. Mansfield, *The Humiliation of Sinners: Public Penance in Thirteenth-century France* (Ithaca, N.Y.: Cornell University Press, 1995), 136 and 136 n. 19, but note that Mansfield concludes that Candlemas was "resolutely unpenitential". For the Paschal candle as a metaphor for the Light and the contrast of light and dark in contemporary Franciscan theology, Robert Brentano, *Two Churches: England and Italy in the Thirteenth Century*, pb. edn. (Berkeley and Los Angeles, Calif.: University of California Press, 1988), 184-5. For the

ceremonial "creation of light" at Siena cathedral when the clergy processed into the church to cense the altars and light the candles after sunset, B. Kempers, "Icons, Altarpieces and Civic Ritual in Siena Cathedral, 1100-1530", in *City and Spectacle in Medieval Europe*, ed. Barbara A. Hanawalt and Kathryn Reyerson (Minneapolis, Minn., University of Minnesota Press, 1994), 95; see there also for the contrast of light and dark in processions with candles: 112. The *tenebrae* were described by Guillaume Durand (for thirteenth-century "France") as the repeated lighting and extinction of candles: Dendy, *Use of Lights*, 145. *Micrologus*, slightly earlier, made it clear that light at mass symbolized the Light: Dendy, *Use of Lights*, 25.

[6] For the raising of candles during priests' communication, Robert N. Swanson, *Religion and Devotion in Europe, c.1215-1515* (Cambridge: Cambridge University Press, 1995), 100 and 141. As early as the "Canons of Edgar" (1005x1008) it was required that a light should constantly burn when mass was sung: *Councils and Synods* I, I, 328; Dendy, *Use of Lights*, 89 (including the grant by Hugh de Westwode to Bushmead Priory of 6d. rent for the two torches which were lit at the consecration and elevation of the host). For the use of light at the elevation of the host, *Calendar of the Manuscripts of the Dean and Chapter of Wells*, II, 587 (no. 179).

[7] *Calendar of the Manuscripts of the Dean and Chapter of Wells*, I, 36-7, and II, 570; Kathleen Edwards, *The English Secular Cathedrals in the Middle Ages*, 2d. ed. (Manchester: Manchester University Press, 1967), 225 and 225 n. 4.

[8] For the development of the mass as a rite of incorporation and as "posthumous rituals of expiation" and purgation, requiring some sense of purgatory, from the eighth century and thus antedating LeGoff's notion of purgatory, Frederick S. Paxton, *Christianizing Death: The Creation of a Ritual Process in Early Medieval Europe* (Ithaca, N.Y., and London: Cornell University Press, 1990). 66-8. Paxton, however, also perceived the mass as an integral part of the culture of gift-exchange in early medieval society, a gift expecting or anticipating a return (that God should or would reciprocate) following Mauss (although not Mauss's account of the more extreme and competitive potlatch). I return to this aspect below in terms of the gift defining social honor and social status as well as being salvific. Marcel Mauss, *The Gift: The Form and Reason for Exchange in Archaic Societies* trans. W. D. Halls (London: Routledge, 1990), 33-43.

[9] *Cartulary of Darley Abbey*, I, 126 (no. B37).

[10] Statutes of Worcester 1240, c. 16: *Councils and Synods* II, 296.

[11] *Councils and Synods* II, 144 (an unidentified diocese 1222x1225) and 522 (Ely statutes 1239x1256, c.36); Dendy, *Use of Lights*, 26-36.

[12] *Councils and Synods* II, 404 (c.4). Torches might consist of wax weighing up to 24 lbs.: Barbara F. Harvey, *Living and Dying in England 1100-1540: The Monastic Experience*, pb. edn. (Oxford: Oxford University Press, 1995),

26. For lights at mass, Dendy, *Use of Lights*, 72-91.

[13] *Councils and Synods* II, 296 (Worcester 1240, c.2–one candelabrum and one lantern only; c. 15 for the eucharist taken to the sick), 379 (Salisbury 1238x1244, c.29), and 512-13 (Salisbury 1228x1256 c.8–the eucharist to the sick). See also Swanson, *Religion and Devotion*, 141; Dendy, *Use of Lights*, 68, suggests this arrangement had occurred by 1195.

[14] *Councils and Synods* II, 512-13 (Salisbury 1228x1256, c.8).

[15] For boundary-marking rules–in this case in the *puja* of the Jains– Caroline Humphrey and James Laidlaw, *The Archetypal Actions of Ritual: A Theory of Ritual Illustrated by the Jain Rite of Worship* (Oxford: Oxford University Press, 1994), 105, 116. For a more general discussion about the differentiation of ritual from social life, but using the same materials, Catherine Bell, *Ritual Theory, Ritual Practice* (Oxford: Oxford University Press, 1992), 90-1. For another view, relating to the imposition of ordering, Mary Douglas, *Purity and Danger: An Analysis of the Concepts of Pollution and Taboo* (London: Routledge, repr. 1995), 4.

[16] *Councils and Synods* II, 56 (c.10).

[17] *Councils and Synods* II, 178, 318.

[18] *Councils and Synods* II, 174 (c.21). For the marking off of communion, Joseph H. Lynch, *The Medieval Church: A Brief History* (London and New York: Longman, 1992), 282 (similar to the Jain marking off of the *puja*).

[19] *Walter of Henley*, 282-5 (cc. 52, 54, 56); for the date, 72.

[20] *Manorial Records of Cuxham*, 173, 185, 201, 235, 253, 270, 286.

[21] *Pipe Roll ... Winchester*, 16, 21-2, 24-5, 29, 32, 34, 38, 297. There may be a further significance, however, in that the payment recognized a dependency and submission to lordship, although many others paid in cash.

[22] *Documents ... Wenlok*, 167, 169, 173, 184; since the materials were acquired by the steward of the household, it is assumed that they were not for liturgical use, which is confirmed by the commodity being Paris candles, that is, made from tallow, a less expensive option: Heather Swanson, *Medieval Artisans: An Urban Class in Late Medieval England* (Oxford: WileyBlackwell, 1989), 16-17, 98-100. For Romain, Pamela Nightingale, *A Medieval Mercantile Community: The Grocer's Company and the Politics and Trade of London 1000-1485* (New Haven, Conn., and London: Yale University Press, 1995), 94-5, 123-7.

[23] *Account-book ... Beaulieu*, 277; *Records ... Norwich*, II, 367.

[24] *Account-book ... Beaulieu*, 54, 86, 108, 119, 124, 135, 145, 151, 157, 162, 169, 184, 188, 194, 212, 214, 227-8, 237, 239, 241, 242, 243, 253, 256, 269, 277, 281, 298.

[25] *Account-book ... Beaulieu*, 188, 212, 243.

[26] Harvey, *Living and Dying*, 202.

[27] Edwards, *English Secular Cathedrals*, 230.

[28] For the use of candles at submission in penance, Mansfield, *Humiliation of Sinners*, 187 and 187 n. 90, alluding to a symbolic ritual of submission through candles as reported by Guillaume Durand for parts of "France" ("complicated choreography with candles'"–Mansfield); Richard M. Wunderli, *London Church Courts and Society on the Eve of the Reformation* (Cambridge, Mass.: Medieval Academy of America, 1981), 50-1. One of the duties of the parish priest in the early twelfth century was to bless the candles at Purification: Martin Brett, *The English Church under Henry I* (Oxford: Oxford University Press, 1975), 222. The Paschal candle at Salisbury cathedral weighed seven pounds: Edwards, *English Secular Cathedrals*, 225.

[29] It is not certain in the following examples whether wax (*cera*) referred to wax for candles, but their occurrence is worth consideration: arbitration by the precentor and chancellor of York between the Dean and Chapter of Lincoln and the Prior and Convent of Sixwould was concluded by the last paying to Lincoln, *pro bono pacis*, two pounds of wax every year (1248); from 1295 the Abbess of Saint Clare contributed to the census of exclusive religious houses exempt from the Ordinary and Metropolitan directly subject to the Papacy, the only house to provide wax; Lunt suggested that the commodity was "a sign of liberty", but as well as signifying exemption it might also have communicated subservience to the Pope (it was in any case commuted): *Registrum Antiquissimum*, VII, 166-7 (no. 2142); William E. Lunt, *Financial Relations of the Papacy with England to 1327* (Cambridge, Mass.: Medieval Academy of America, 1939), 118.

[30] *Cartulary of Daventry Priory*, 13 (no. 24).

[31] *EEA* II, 243-4 (no. 284) (Leeds Priory and the parish church of Bearsted, 1185x1190); *EEA* IV, 107 (no. 161) (appropriation of the church of Haddenham by Rochester Cathedral, 1194x1200). An element of subjection might be involved also, as in the case of the stone of wax due from the church of Saint Andrew, Huntingdon, as a pension to Ramsey Abbey for lights (1189): *EEA* IV, 104-5 (no. 157). An alternative symbolic payment in religious situations was incense, as to be provided to the church of Winwick (1 lb.) before Christmas by Daventry Priory as a token; Daventry had been permitted to appropriate the churches of West Haddon and Cold Ashby, saving the rights of the church of Winwick held by the Prior of Coventry (1150): *Cartulary of Daventry Priory*, 228-9 (no. 697).

[32] Brett, *English Church under Henry I*, 162.

[33] *Registrum Antiquissimum* V, 57 (no. 1536); *Cartulary of Daventry Priory*, 105-6.

[34] *Cartulary of the Priory of St Gregory*, 159 (no. 220).

[35] *Reading Abbey Cartularies*, 463 (no. 625).

[36] Edwards, *English Secular Cathedral Chapters*, 313.

[37] *Select Cases ... Eccles. Courts*, 585; for excommunication with the ringing of bells and lighted candles (*accensisque candelis*) at mass on Sundays or feast days, 685 (1299).

[38] Ronald W. Finucane, *Miracles and Pilgrims: Popular Belief in Medieval England* (London: Palgrave Macmillan, repr. 1995), 95-6. For light as a mark of honor, Dendy, *Use of Lights*, 74. See the agreement about the wax candles deposited at the shrine of Saint Thomas Cantilupe in Hereford cathedral in 1293: *Charters ... Hereford*, 167.

[39] Gervase Rosser, "The Cure of Souls in English Towns before 1000", in *Pastoral Care before the Parish*, ed. John Blair and Richard Sharpe (Leicester: Leicester University Press, 1992), 270-1; Christopher N. L. Brooke, "The Missionary at Home: The Church in the Towns, 1000-1250", in *Studies in Church History* vol. 6 (Oxford: Blackwell, 1970), 59-83. Other examples of continuous lay congregations are Westminster, Hereford and Beverley: Rosser, "Cure of Souls", 271-2. On the pastoral role of monks in the twelfth century, Marjorie Chibnall, "Monks and Pastoral Work: A Problem in Anglo-Norman History", *JEH* 18 (1967): 165-72, and Brett, *English Church under Henry I*, 221-2.

[40] Rosser, "Cure of Souls", 275.

[41] *Customary Rents*, 42, 112, 192; note that all were cathedral chapters and/or older Benedictine religious houses.

[42] *Councils and Synods* I, I, 303, 332, 351, 393.

[43] *Councils and Synods* I, I, 477. A deponent in a cause in 1286 remembered the day of the event recalled because his father was ill at Brackley and was brought to the deponent's house at Steane, lying ill there until Purification, so that the deponent sent his mother the candle for the feast: *Select Cases ... Eccles. Courts*, 541.

[44] *Councils and Synods* II, 512-13 (c.8).

[45] Dorothy M. Owen, "Two Manorial Parish Books from the Diocese of Ely: New College MS 98 and Wisbech Museum MS 1", in *East Anglian and Other Studies Presented to Barbara Dodwell*, ed. Malcolm Barber, P. McNulty and P. Noble, Reading Medieval Studies vol. 11 (Reading, 1985), 125-6.

[46] *Councils and Synods* II, 271, 310, 348, 407 (Lincoln, 1293?, c.21; Worcester 1240, c.59; Norwich 1240x1243, c. 22; Winchester 1247?, c.27).

[47] *Councils and Synods* II, 404, 592-3.

[48] *Cartulary of St Denys*, 244 (no. 436). This gift constituted one amongst many from the family which held the advowson of the church: 258-9 (no. 463, 1171x1184).

[49] Gervase Rosser, "Parochial Conformity and Popular Religion in Late Medieval England", *TRHS* 6th ser., 1 (1991): 173-90, for the inflexibility of parochial organization and attempts to circumvent it.

[50] For chantries, Kathleen L. Wood-Legh, *Perpetual Chantries in Britain*

(Cambridge: Cambridge University Press, 1965).

[51] In this case less gift-exchange than a declared remission of sins: see, for example, the thirty-three masses in the cathedral each week for the brothers and sisters of the fraternity of the fabric: *EEA* IV, 166 (no. 258). Many grants to Thurgarton Priory were assigned to the fabric fund: *Thurgarton Cartulary*, for example 84-9 (nos 134-46–broken series). Some houses and chapters were particularly adept at receiving rents for pittances, whether on the anniversary of the grantor's death or not: *Cartulary of Holy Trinity, Aldgate*, 90, 109, 137, 158, 205, 210 (nos 449, 546, 701a, 812, 1013, 1028) and *Magnum Registrum Album*, 264-8 (nos 554-65). Elias Porter gave a toft to Blyth Priory in the late twelfth century to allow a pittance on the anniversary of his death *nulla festiuitate obstante*: *Cartulary of Blyth Priory*, 34-5 (no. 26).

[52] *Cartularies of Southwick Priory*, 104 (III, 297).

[53] *Cartulary of Shrewsbury Abbey*, 156 (no. 179, 1232x1252).

[54] *Cartulary ...Worcester*, 80-1, 181 (nos 143, 340) (1189x1196, 1219); Andrew Brown, *Popular Piety in Late Medieval England: The Diocese of Salisbury 1250-1550* (Oxford: Oxford University Press, 1995), 52 (provision of a candle of 1 lb. to burn before the Lady altar on the eve of the Assumption of the BVM). For the general configuration of the lights at Salisbury, Dendy, *Use of Lights*, 28. See also M. J. Franklin, "The Cathedral as Parish Church: The Case of Southern England", in *Church and City 1000-1250: Essays in Honour of Christopher Brooke*, ed. David Abulafia, Franklin and Miri Rubin (Cambridge: Cambridge University Press, 1992), 173-98.

[55] Dendy, *Use of Lights*, 108-19, for lights and the "cult" of saints, and 17-71 for lights around the altar, with the suggestion (19 and 69) that the accretion of lights *on* the altar was only permitted by the remodelling of parochial churches from the twelfth century, allowing the replacement of smaller, square altars by larger, rectangular ones.

[56] *Cartularies of Southwick Priory*, II, 378 (no. II, 923).

[57] *Thurgarton Cartulary*, 188-9 (no. 320).

[58] *Thurgarton Cartulary*, 386-7 (no. 630, 1202x1235, alluding to the blessed Margaret).

[59] *Cartulary of Missenden Abbey*, 101-2 (no. 691).

[60] *Cartulary of Dale Abbey*, 304-5 (no. 445).

[61] *Cartulary of St Frideswide's Priory*, I, 291-2 (no. 387).

[62] *Cartulary of Blyth Priory*, 64-5 (no. 76).

[63] *Cartulary ... Beaulieu*, 29-30 (no. 28).

[64] *Basset Charters*, 130-1 (no. 195).

[65] *Early Charters ... St Paul*, 187 (no. 237).

[66] *Cartularies of Southwick Priory*, 411 (no. III, 997, 1235x1266).

[67] *Cartularies of Southwick Priory*, 262 (no. III, 682, ca.1230).

58   Missed Opportunities?

⁶⁸ *Cartularies of Southwick Priory*, 104-5, 262, 378, 411-17 (nos. III, 297-8, 682, 923, 997-8, 1003, 1006, 1010-11). Excluded for this purpose are the lights established by William *de Humeto*, king's constable, not only because of his status, but also because the location of his lights was determined by the burial place of his wife, Lucy, before the cross: 24 and 43 (nos. I, 39, 76, 1170x1190); the gift of a tenement in Berkeley, Gloucestershire, by Robert de Berkeley in 1190x1215 had the simple purpose *ad emendacionem luminaris* (62, no. III, 200).

⁶⁹ *Cartulary of Shrewsbury Abbey*, 98-9, 156, 167-8, 178-80, 183-216, 287, 386-7, 388-9, 392-8, 401. Other grants were made simply to the altar rather than for its lights. The twenty-five grants involved no consideration and do not appear to be concealed sales although it is evident that the keeper was also purchasing rents in the borough for the altar: 392-402 (nos. 426-8, 436, 436c, 438, 442).

⁷⁰ *Westminster Abbey Charters*, 177 (no. 329).

⁷¹ *Westminster Abbey Charters*, 191-2, 202, 205-8, 229-32, 247-64, 266, 269, 271, 277-82, 288-9 (nos. 356, 362, 364, 387, 390, 407, 411-12, 415, 417-18, 420, 423, 425-7, 429, 432, 435, 441, 443-5, 451). See also Gervase Rosser, *Medieval Westminster 1200-1540* (Oxford: Oxford University Press, 1989), 46-50, 256-7.

⁷² I owe this point to Barbara Harvey.

⁷³ *Cartulary of Oseney Abbey*, II, 169-70 (no. 719); *Charters ... Norwich*, 178 (no. 329).

⁷⁴ Nigel Morgan, "Texts and Images of Marian Devotion", in *England in the Thirteenth Century*, ed. W. Mark Ormrod, Harlaxton Medieval Studies I (Stamford 1991), 69-103.

⁷⁵ *Cartulary of Shrewsbury Abbey*, 193, 200 (nos. 225, 234b).

⁷⁶ *Cartulary of Shrewsbury Abbey*, 208-14 (nos. 240-3, 245-7); Saint Paul's bought a rent of 5s. for the lights before its Lady altar for four marks in 1241x1242: *Early Charters ... St Paul*, 114-15 (no. 148).

⁷⁷ *Cartulary of Daventry Priory*, 291-2 (no. 885).

⁷⁸ *Cartulary of Daventry Priory*, 25 (no. 64, mid-twelfth century).

⁷⁹ *Cartulary of Daventry Priory*, 11, 13, 48, 93, 99, 105-6, 129, 148, 188-9, 196-7, 225, 228-9, 277, 285-6, 288-9 (nos. 19, 24, 139, 309, 325, 461, 580, 689, 853, 881).

⁸⁰ *Magnum Registrum Album*, 219, 265 (nos. 459, 556-7; rents of 2d., 1s., and 10s.).

⁸¹ "Visitations of the Churches ... St Paul's Cathedral", 1-33.

⁸² "Visitations of the Churches ... St Paul's Cathedral", 10.

⁸³ "Visitations of the Churches ... St Paul's Cathedral", 11-12.

⁸⁴ "Visitations of the Churches ... St Paul's Cathedral", 15-16.

⁸⁵ "Visitations of the Churches ... St Paul's Cathedral", 17-18.

[86] "Visitations of the Churches ... St Paul's Cathedral", 19-20.

[87] "Visitations of the Churches ... St Paul's Cathedral", 21.

[88] "Visitations of the Churches ... St Paul's Cathedral", 23; see the collection of ½d. from each house at *Chesewith* at 7.

[89] "Visitations of the Churches ... St Paul's Cathedral", 32-3.

[90] The exception was perhaps the Cistercians, who were austere in their use of lights, but also remote and less accessible for patronage of this kind: Dendy, *Use of Lights*, 12, 25, 37-8 (for their sparing use of, especially, candles). Few such grants are contained in *Rufford Charters* or *Cartulary ... Beaulieu*. Apparently there was a single grant (half a mark) for a light before the host at Kirkstall Abbey, but it was significantly received from Henry de Lacy and perhaps thus difficult to refuse: G. D. Barnes, *Kirkstall Abbey 1147-1539: A Historical Survey*, Thoresby Society vol. 58 (Leeds, 1984), 21. The Garendon cartulary (BL, Lansdowne MS 415) also contains little of such content, although Thomas *Dispensator* arranged for a pittance on the anniversary of his son's death (fols. 8v. and 32r.), but pittances were not unusual in Cistercian houses.

[91] *Early Charters of Waltham Abbey*, 218-19 (no. 327).

[92] *Cartulary of Missenden Abbey*, 84 (no. 870).

[93] *Cartulary of Darley Abbey*, I, 202 (no. E1).

[94] *Cartulary of Darley Abbey* II, 379-80, 395-7 (nos. H58, H85-89, late twelfth century to ca.1250).

[95] *Cartulary of St Frideswide's*, II, 26 (no. 715).

[96] *Cartulary of the Priory of St Gregory*, 25-6 (nos. 29, 31).

[97] *Stoke by Clare Cartulary*, I, 264-86 (nos. 393-428 intermittently).

[98] *Cartulary of Cirencester Abbey*, 568-9 (no. 680).

[99] *Cartulary of Oseney Abbey*, I, 201; II, 104-5, 366-7 (nos. 635, 942).

[100] "Glapwell Charters", 71-9, 111-12, 119-20 (nos. 83-7, 89, 123, 130).

[101] *Thurgarton Cartulary*, 158, 317, 495-6 (nos. 258, 525, 846, 1218x1231 and mid thirteenth century) for Tithby, Loudham and Kirkby Green; for Scopwick, see below.

[102] *Thurgarton Cartulary*, 507, 525, 527, 530, 534-5 (nos. 874, 923, 930, 936, 946-9) comprise all such grants to Scopwick, including those by clerical benefactors who favoured the Lady altar.

[103] *Cartulary of Daventry Priory*, 325 (no. 985).

[104] *Registrum Antiquissimum*, IX, 59-60 (no. 2453).

[105] *Cartulary of St Denys* II, 275 (no. 496).

[106] R. H. Snape, *English Monastic Finance* (Oxford: Oxford University Press, 1926); R. A. L. Smith, "The *Regimen Scaccarii* in English Monasteries", in *Collected Papers of R. A. L. Smith* (London: Longman, Green & Co., 1947), 54-73.

[107] *Thame Cartulary*, I, 59 (no. 71); *Blythburgh Priory Cartulary*, II, 141,

189 (nos. 247, 359). For a résumé of free alms, Benjamin Thompson, "Free Alms Tenure in the Twelfth Century" in *Anglo-Norman Studies XVI. Proceedings of the Battle Conference*, ed. Marjorie Chibnall (Woodbridge: Boydell, 1994), 221-43.

[108] Grants for lights to some religious houses in Suffolk, however, seem to have been more exclusive, conferred by people of higher social status, sometimes knightly: *Sibton Abbey Cartularies*, II, 284-5, 316-17 (nos. 390, 436) (Hugh II Bigod and Cecily de Herford, 1217x1230); *Blythburgh Priory Cartulary*, 114 (no. 196) (Roger de Mainwaring, 1244).

[109] Emma Mason, "The Role of the English Parishioner 1100-1500", *JEH* 27 (1976): 17-29; Beat A. Kümin, *The Shaping of a Community: The Rise and Reformation of the English Parish c.1400-1560* (Aldershot: Scolar Press, 1996), 17-42; Brown, *Popular Piety*, 77-91.

[110] For some examples of differentiation, Kempers, "Icons, Altarpieces, and Civic Ritual", 97, 112.

[111] See Clive Burgess, "'For the Increase of Divine Service': Chantries in the Parish in Late Medieval Bristol", *JEH* 36 (1985): 48-65.

[112] For the purposes of this chapter, I have consulted a number of other cartularies not previously cited in the text: *Cartulary of Burscough*; *Luffield Priory Charters*; *Cartulary of Tutbury Priory*; *St Benet of Holme*.

3
Monastic Burials of Non-patronal Lay Benefactors

Choice of place of burial in the middle ages was perhaps the most poignant indicator of belief in the efficacy of different sorts of religious intercession. Ariès concluded that the pre-modern response to death was public and communitarian, becoming only latterly private and individualistic.[1] Most recent considerations of notions of death and burial have concentrated on the early-modern period. For that time, the distinction made by Ariès between modern, private, individualistic burial practices and earlier public, communitarian rites, has been revised, both in the sense that the change occurred earlier than Ariès would allow and that other influences were at work, in particular the formative consequences of the Reformation.[2] Research into death and burial in the later middle ages has tended to confirm the communitarian nature of the rites surrounding death and burial.[3] Burial in the high middle ages has been reviewed from a much more pragmatic rather than theoretical perspective, as a consequence of which the wholly communitarian picture depicted by Ariès has hardly been challenged.[4] Presented here, however, is some modification to the Ariès thesis, supported by some very particular evidence, burials of lay persons who were not of patronal status, in religious houses, within the wider context of burial practices in the twelfth and thirteenth centuries in England.

The communitarian nature of burial rites was expressed in two ways: first, the dependence on intercession, both through particular saints and the whole community of saints and heaven, but also through the prayers of the living community of the laity; and secondly, in the later middle ages, through the location of burial and lay intercession in the community of the parish.[5] Nevertheless, rites, practices and beliefs were not static over the middle ages, and some differences existed in the twelfth and thirteenth centuries. Chantries, because of their foundation inside parish churches in the later middle ages, manifestly invoked not only the specialized intercession of the professionals, the secular clergy, chantry priests or chaplains, but also the parochial community as a whole. The placing of chantries within parish churches was a reminder to the whole congregation to intercede. Two other forms of burial before the general move towards chantries in the later middle ages imply a less public and more singularly specialized invocation of intercession.

From the middle of the thirteenth century, burial in friaries gained some popularity, particularly in urban centres, where these institutions were predominantly located.[6] Before then, burial in monastic houses was evidently a preferred option. That route to spiritual salvation was not exclusively reserved to founders and patrons and their families, but was extended to other lay persons. Interment among the religious has several important implications. Although the intercession of the community of heaven was the primary consideration, the community of the locality (lay persons) was less important. By contrast with the later middle ages, neither parish church nor community of the parish was considered the most efficacious for salvation. Burial in religious houses removed the corpse from both parish church and the community of the parish; intercession was placed in the hands of an extremely specialized group of people–the professed religious–and the body separated from the rest of the community. Salvation was entrusted only to the immediate and direct intervention of the enclosed religious. What seems to be thus signified, *pace* Ariès, is: private or at best semi-public rites of intercession rather than fully communitarian ideas; some degree of separation from the body of lay persons; and some rather personal and private sentiments about salvation, since the numbers of lay people actually buried in religious houses represented a select destiny (see Table 2).[7]

The following analysis considers the numbers of lay persons interred in religious houses; the motives of both lay person and religious house; the inchoate development of the parochial system, and in particular the under-development of cemeteries, which may have limited resistance to interment in religious houses; and two particular phases by which interment of lay persons in religious houses proceeded. The first of these phases, occurring in the early twelfth century, involved tenants and liege men of religious houses, but also some other persons, and the reserved part (usually a third) of their personal estate according to the rule of the *legitim*, which was to accrue to the religious house at death and burial, whilst the second phase, in the late twelfth and early thirteenth centuries, concerned a wider group of people who made small benefactions for burial, the *legitim* seemingly no longer a factor.[8] In all of this discussion, the burial of founders and patrons and their families is disregarded for two reasons: first, this group of people has been very cogently and recently considered by Brian Golding;[9] secondly, burial of patrons and founders, even amongst the Cistercians, was considered only right and proper, whilst the burial of other lay persons, in view of parochial rights as well as the rule of the religious, was more contentious.[10] Finally, the material considered here derives almost exclusively from the houses of the male religious, basically because evidence from nunneries is less plentiful. This dilemma has important implications: first, the twelfth century significantly acknowledged the spirituality of women;[11] secondly, it is impossible to consider the question of whether contemporaries regarded intercession by religious women as less efficacious than that by their male counterparts; and finally and following from that, no discussion can be given to notions of gendered space, in this instance in burial.[12]

Sometime before 1203, Richard *filius Gerardi* and his wife, Emma, gave to Stoke by Clare Priory two acres of land in the field called "Eight Acres" in free alms, and, on his death, Richard would give 5s. for his body to be carried to Stoke on his bed; Emma would similarly give 5s. and her body too would be carried to Stoke with her bed.[13] The priory had been founded and patronized by the earls of Clare with conventional "familial piety".[14] Originally founded by Gilbert de Clare at Clare by the appropriation of a college of secular canons to Bec Abbey ca.1090, but moved to Stoke in 1124, the priory was established on the anniversary of the death of his father,

Richard, and for the soul of his brother, Godfrey, buried in the cemetery at Clare.[15] "Whereas the twelfth-century earls had been buried at Stoke by Clare ... the mausoleum of their thirteenth-century successors was Tewkesbury."[16] That sort of changing relationship between founder's family and religious house has been illustrated by Brian Golding, but its significance here is that, since Stoke by Clare failed to persist as a private mausoleum, the burials of other lay persons were encouraged. Between 1173 and the 1230s, four male lay persons, two married couples and one female are known to have been interred at the priory (see Table 2).[17]

It is not clear, however, whether these lay people buried at Stoke by Clare between 1173 and the 1230s had any tenurial relationship

Table 2 Burials of Non-patronal Benefactors in Religious Houses

House	Order	Date range	Male	Couple	Female
Blythburgh	Austin Canon	Mid 12th-ca1258	3	0	0
Burscough	Austin Canon	1200x1250	2	0	0
Darley	Austin Canon	1198x1250	14	0	6
Leicester	Austin Canon	Not known	14	1	1
St Denys	Austin Canon	1150x1276	7	0	2
Southwick	Austin Canon	1153x1250	16	6	7
Thurgarton	Austin Canon	1131x1253	6	0	1
Daventry	Black monks	1148x1220	4	2	0
Luffield	Black monks	1220x1253	4	0	0
Reading	Black monks	1170x1248	10	0	0
Stoke by Clare	Black monks	1173x1230s	4	2	1
Tutbury	Black monks	ca1225	1	0	0
Beaulieu	Cistercian	1226x1250	2	0	1
Garendon	Cistercian	Before ca1220	6	0	0
Rufford	Cistercian	1146x1258	6	2	9
Sibton	Cistercian	1197x1252	13	1	1
Thame	Cistercian	1202x1242	3	0	0
Wardon	Cistercian	1180x1237	4	0	2
Cockersand	White Canons	1185x1272	10	0	4
Dale	White Canons	1200x1250	2	0	0

to the earls. In the case of this house and others, therefore, it is not always possible to demonstrate whether burials of non-patronal benefactors did or did not have an honorial connection. An inference can be made from some indicative cases that in the early twelfth century the honorial connection may have influenced choice of place of burial by non-patronal benefactors. For example, in their claim in 1107x1108 against Herbert de Losinga, bishop of Norwich, the monks of Thetford professed that Roger Bigod had given himself, his wife and his honorial barons (*barones*) to be buried at Thetford Priory.[18]

Intercession by the religious might be achieved by a variety of measures, of which simple gifts in free alms for unspecified spiritual purposes was the most common. The additional conferment of fraternity by the religious to a lay donor was less widespread, but not unusual. Being received into the house as a monk or canon was rather a drastic step, terminating the lay life, more usually in the form of a gift *ad succurrendum* later in life. An alternative to the finality of that sort of action was to provide an endowment to maintain a specific monk or canon, as when Ralph Basset provided for a monk at Eynsham Abbey in 1120 by conveying to the abbey a carucate, ten oxen and provision for clothing for the monk[19] In that case, the monk or canon may have been a substitute for the lay donor accepting the habit. Gifts *cum corpore meo/suo* for burial were thus just one of several options in the twelfth and thirteenth centuries. Burial elicited perhaps the most effective intercession, as the resting place of the corpse amongst those of the monks or canons was a constant reminder and a direct invocation to the religious for their intervention. Its zenith has been considered to have been the early thirteenth century, but its overall duration was longer, clearly evident already in the early twelfth century, expanding in the late twelfth, and declining about the middle of the thirteenth.[20]

Nevertheless, there remain considerable problems associated with the evidence. The interpretation of the development of the significance of burial in religious houses in the early twelfth century depends upon the evidence of the private charter, but this instrument had only recently evolved and become more widely used even amongst higher social groups. It is essentially an argument from silence, perhaps a reckless one. To the contrary, a considerable number of minor benefactions were made to Rochester cathedral priory in return for *societas* and confraternity before 1125, recorded only in the *Textus Roffensis*, with further such provisions made ca.1120-1140 in the *Registrum Roffense*.[21] Rochester was, however, a *matrix ecclesia* as well as a religious house, and the motive for burial there may have been its status as the mother church of the diocese. At Worcester cathedral priory charters for burial *cum corpore* do not seem to occur until the early thirteenth century.[22] Other evidence does suggest, however, that laymen were being buried at Worcester, for ca.1140 the cathedral priory agreed to a cemetery at Cotheridge on the understanding that freemen might still choose to be buried at Worcester.[23] Some minsters and religious houses which controlled urban parish churches also endeavoured to reserve their rights of burial against parochial rights declared at the Council of Westminster in 1102.[24] Indeed, burial in monastic houses had developed at a much earlier time in "France", although by the twelfth century restrictions had been placed on the choice of place of burial for lesser freemen.[25] It is likely therefore that charters for gifts for burial do not present a complete record of interments in monastic houses.

Further there is the problem of the numbers of persons buried in religious houses, a question critical to the perception of such burials as either removal from the great community of the dead (associated with the living community) in parochial cemeteries or as part of a large community of the laity interred amongst the religious. Episcopal and papal privileges permitting religious houses to bury lay persons who selected monastic burial may be one indicator of the extent of such interments.[26] It is not clear, however, what the motive was for these grants: whether they resulted from a strong demand for burial or from the monks' desire to extract maximum (social as well as material) benefit from a declining source in the face of canonical regularization of burial in parochial cemeteries.[27]

The issue whether burial in religious houses represented social separation from the larger body of the dead must also take into account the allocation of indulgences for prayers by the laity at the tombs and graves of deceased individuals.[28] Subject to the problems of the evidence, it seems that such indulgences came rather late on the scene and were predominantly associated only with the bodies of the deceased of high status. Nevertheless, these indulgences might be perceived as an attempt to attract a wider community of intercession than the monks alone. It is equally possible, however, to consider this action as an indicator of change away from monastic interment if earlier burials in monastic communities had not depended on the intercession of the laity.[29] Moreover, the indulgences were extended by the Ordinary and we have little evidence of the reasons for their grant. Considering the status of many of the deceased beneficiaries, it would seem probable that the bishop acted on his own discretion or at the petition of the family or dignitaries as that monks made the request. Indulgences for prayers conferred by Oliver de Sutton, bishop of Lincoln, mainly involved deceased persons of dignity and status, only some of whom had been interred in religious houses–his grants seem to be more *ad feminam* or *ad hominem* than for the benefit of the religious house.[30] Furthermore, bishops granted indulgences not only for prayers, but for a wide variety of causes–rebuilding of churches and roads, for example.

One origin of burial of non-patronal lay persons seems to derive from the prerogative insisted upon by some religious houses, holding *per baroniam*, that their mesne tenants or liege men should, on their death, be buried in the abbey and their *legitim* (the deceased's own or reserved part of his chattels and goods by comparison with the parts claimed by the heir, family or widow) returned to their lord.[31] In the terms of these charters, burial seems less a privilege of tenants than an insistence by their lords. The return of the *legitim*, however, is complicated; in part, it may have been a recognition of secular lordship, but it was also protected by canon law, in which case its exaction by a religious lord is ambivalent.[32] Control of the *legitim* in these cases might thus have ensued from either spiritual authority or the tenurial relationship.

When Abbot Geoffrey granted leases for lives of the manors of Burton Abbey to liege men (1114x1150), his charters specifically reserved the right of burial of the liege men and recovery of the *legitim*, ultimately revealed as one third of their chattels, by the abbey. In the light of restrictions on alienation of Church lands in the early twelfth century, it would seem that these grants were as close to subinfeudation as was possible.[33] The precursor of Geoffrey's grants was one from Abbot Nigel (1093x1113) to Orm, a lease for two lives (one heir) of the manor of Oakover; on Orm's death, his body was to be brought to the abbey for burial with all his chattels.[34] In the light of Abbot Geoffrey's charters, it seems clear that the chattels were restricted to Orm's *legitim*, his own part. A lease of Leigh to Andrew (1114x1150) referred to him specifically as the abbot's liege man; on his death he too was to be buried at the abbey *honorifice* and Andrew's own part of his chattels (implicitly his *legitim*) was to revert to the abbey.[35] Andrew also received a lease of the manor of Field as a liege man, with the same covenants.[36] In 1114x1150 (another?) Orm acquired from Abbot Geoffrey the lease of Darlaston, with the provision that on his death his body was to be transferred to the abbey for burial *multum honorifice* with all that part of his chattels; moreover, Orm's wife was to be buried there too *cum magno honore*, but her part of the chattels was also to be recovered by the abbey.[37] Similarly, a lease by the same abbot to Robert and his heir, for two lives, of the manor of Darlaston, had the same covenants.[38] A feefarm grant of the vill of Potter Heigham by the abbot of Saint Benet of Holme to Thomas *filius Turberni presbiteri* (1153x1168), although it stipulated the return of a third of the tenant's chattels on his death, does not have any specific provision for burial.[39]

Similar evidence can be garnered from the relationships between a few other religious houses and their tenants. For example, when Prior Herbert of Daventry Priory installed his man (*homo suus*) Chetelbern in half a virgate in Welton *hereditabiliter tenere* (1142x1170), which his uncle Serlo had held, provision was made that Chetelbern would be buried in the priory with the offering of his part of his chattels. Chetelbern, from the size of his tenement and his miscellaneous agricultural services, was not of the same stature as the tenants benefiting from the leases of Burton Abbey; this grant by Daventry may thus represent a widening of the benefit of burial to lesser persons. Another of Prior Herbert's charters, in favour of Gamel, concerned two virgates to which Gamel was admitted in Haddon; Gamel, who had not previously been the prior's man, became so by performing homage. When Gamel died his body too was to be brought to the priory with the third part (*tercia pars*) of his chattels. Later in the twelfth century, Robert de Costowe received a mill and lands from the priory and concurred that his body and that of his wife would come to the priory for burial along with their parts of their chattels.[40]

These relationships seem to suggest a widening of the conferment of burial in religious houses beyond important mesne tenants. That transition may also be visible in the benefaction made by Robert Pincent, knight, to Reading Abbey in the late twelfth or early thirteenth century. Although Robert gave only a meadow, the abbey would receive his body for burial on his death with one third (*tercia pars*) of his moveable and immoveable goods, grain and land.[41] When Geoffrey Malesours made gifts to Daventry Priory in ca.1210, his body was to be buried in the house and he was to leave half his chattels, the *legitim* of an unmarried man.[42] Some time after 1173, Hugh, son of William de Berdefeld, knight, gave to Stoke by Clare Priory all his fee (*totam hereditatem meam*) with the provision that on his deathbed he would be received as a monk in return for half his chattels (*cum catellorum medietate que tunc habuero*).[43] These arrangements are qualitatively different from those of the early twelfth century, in the following senses. First, the right of burial is one of election by the lay donors, rather than the prerogative of the religious house, even though the *legitim* was acquired by the house. Secondly, although some of the persons were still of knightly status, there is a decline in the overall social status of the buried. The late twelfth century thus encompassed a widening of the privilege of burial in religious houses. Such burials were usually elicited in the form of a gift *cum corpore* for burial.

Some important burials in the early twelfth century exhibited different characteristics, however, particularly those in the old Benedictine house of Abingdon. Geoffrey de Malchenceio procured burial in the abbey of Abingdon with the gift of one hide of land in Stoke (1100x1117); if he died in England as a layman, he was to be buried in the abbey, the house receiving one third of all his chattels which he held in England.[44] On his reconciliation with Abingdon, Robert I d'Oilly was buried in the north part of the chapter house of the abbey (*in capitulo*) and his wife laid to rest on his left side.[45] *Tempore* Henry I, Richard *filius Reinfridi*, approaching his day of death, gave rents of 19s. for the sake of his own soul, but also a further 6s. for that of his wife who had been buried in the abbey.[46]

Ansfrid, a concubine of Henry I before his accession to the throne, had also been buried in Abingdon in the cloister before the church door where the brethren entered and left the church–no doubt as a reminder to them to pray for her soul.[47] In 1108/9, Hugh son of Witgar de Bennaham, and his wife were received into the fraternity of the house in return for their tithes and they made an agreement (*convencio*) that their bodies would be laid to rest in the abbey.[48] An agreement more redolent of those of Burton Abbey was that between Abbot Vincent and Simon, the king's steward, by which Simon quitclaimed to the abbot all he had held from the house before Vincent's prelacy, in return for three-and-a-half hides in Garsington and the manor of Tadmarton, the former in fee and the latter in fee farm. Simon agreed not to be buried anywhere other than in the abbey if he died in England, with all his own part of his chattels; if he died outside England, the abbey was still to receive his *legitim*.[49] Ralph Basset, whilst he was ill at Northampton, agreed that he should be buried only at Abingdon; when his body was eventually brought there, the abbey received a substantial *legitim*.[50] At Abingdon, thus, burials of a diverse nature occurred in the early twelfth century, most of them seemingly resulting from the dignity and status of the lay person, but some still involving the acquisition of the *legitim*.[51]

Burials in religious houses had then substantial origins in the early twelfth century, when they principally concerned persons of status. Those in the late twelfth century embraced a much wider social group, although, since the evidence here is mainly drawn from lesser religious houses, there is an inherent element of self-fulfilling prophecy. Nevertheless, it is probable that the advent of the new religious Orders–in particular the regular canons, but also the Cistercians in practice–widened the opportunities for burial in religious houses and reduced the cost, especially the relinquishing of the *legitim* in favour of much more modest benefactions *cum corpore*. Until 1217 the Cistercian rule only allowed the burial of patrons and persons of high status, although after 1217 the houses were permitted to bury any seculars provided the parish priest agreed. The rule, however, does not seem to have been a restriction on some houses of the Order before 1217, nor is there much evidence of the seeking of parochial consent thereafter.[52] Houses of regular canons had a more legitimate interest in the burial of lay persons, because theirs were preaching orders with, in theory, cure of souls, a large number of their (smaller) houses had been established within parish churches, and they had appropriated many parochial livings.[53] For example, Archbishop Lanfranc founded the house of Saint Gregory, outside the north gate of Canterbury, in 1084x1085, then of regular canons of indeterminate status, but later Austin Canons; a foundation charter of 1086x1087 purports to show that he entrusted the house with the burial of priests, clerks and lay persons of both sexes without any fees or mortuaries.[54] The consequence was that in the late twelfth century, although the absolute numbers of lay persons buried in religious houses was rather small and select, yet some religious houses seem to have entered into a headlong rush to attract the burial of lay people of modest status within their precincts (see Table 2).

Since many charters are unspecific about the amount of land given *cum corpore*, it is impossible to provide descriptive statistics. Nevertheless, forty-eight benefactions involved less than five acres of arable and in two cases the bodies of married couples were given with respectively two and one acre only. Forty gifts transferred less than a virgate. A further twenty-six grants concerned only annual rents, excluding other forms of attornment, with the mean level at just over 9s., although the range ran from 1s. to six marks of silver. Only five grants returned advowsons to the religious. In the case of founders and their families "burial and choice of burial were of such great concern because burials brought endowments" and "in every case a grant, often a large one, would be expected in burial".[55] That motivation seems less clear in the case of these religious houses from the late twelfth century, since often only trifling amounts accrued from the burial of non-patronal seculars in the house.

Some of the larger benefactions *cum corpore* may, moreover, be explained by special circumstances, as the gift of seven bovates in Hawton by Roger son of William de Houton, knight, with his body for burial, in 1218x1231, for the gift was further to support a canon to celebrate mass every day.[56] Equally, the benefaction to Thurgarton by Richard de Wyverton', knight, was intended not only for his burial but to sustain a secular chaplain to celebrate at the altar of Saint Mary in the conventual church.[57] Sibton Abbey also benefited by such an arrangement when William (III) de Pirre, knight, gave a grove and rents with his body, for the monks were required to find a priest to celebrate mass in their church.[58] The acquisition of some lands with bodies for burial was occasionally less a benefaction than a purchase. The series of transactions between Robert Pincent and Reading Abbey, including his manor of Sulhampstead and culminating in a gift of meadow with his body for burial, was compelled by his becoming "necessitous".[59] Burial must therefore have held a different significance for these houses.

Importance may have been attached to their position within local and regional society, in which the symbolism of burials of seculars played an important role as a form of inverse patronage from religious houses to local society. In a sense it was a form of gift-exchange which enhanced the status of the house.[60] The economic benefit was thus less critical than the symbolic importance of burial within the house. Neither was the status of the buried essential; although a small proportion of the seculars buried were of knightly status, a great many more derived from just below that level.

Concomitantly, benefactions to these religious houses, including those *cum corpore*, may have provided one focus among several for neighborhood networks amongst the knightly families, based on geographical rather than honorial ties.[61] That phenomenon may have been partly consequence and partly motivation, but there were many other reasons why the laity might seek burial in religious houses. The emphasis on the direct intercession of the professed religious has been mentioned above. Not all selected this route to salvation. Burial in religious houses, however, was attractive to a select number of the laity. One of the attractions may have been the almost ambulatory nature of the gift *cum corpore*, since it might not be immediately effected–as in the case of Elias Gifford's gift of Cranham to the great Benedictine house of Gloucester Abbey, for a covenant allowed him to hold it for his life with reversion to the abbey with his body to be buried there.[62] In many cases, it was apparently made *in periculo mortis*, as the final act. Gifts *cum corpore* to lesser religious houses have nothing so demonstrative of an ambulatory nature, but the dispositive phrasing of some suggests either a final act or an ambulatory character as *post obitum* gifts: *legavit; legacio; legaui; Ut autem ista legacio rata ...; legasse; nomine testamenti;*

legauit in extremis.⁶³ Occasionally, however, gifts *cum corpore* were proffered at an early stage of life: Alice *de Chesneto* (Chesney) made benefactions *cum corpore* to Southwick Priory in ca.1220-7, but her charter of ca.1245 adding to the gift reveals that she was still alive very much later.⁶⁴

If gifts *cum corpore* were made *in extremis*, it is possible that they were the culmination of a sequence of gifts to the house, in which case the overall benefaction may have been more considerable.⁶⁵ For example, after 1173, Helewise de Croftuna made several separate benefactions to Southwick Priory: one and a half virgates; a furlong of demesne; a meadow; and two-and-half virgates.⁶⁶ Her *largesse*, however, was entirely singular. William *frankellanus* donated twenty selions to Luffield Priory in ca.1220-1230, although he had previously bestowed two acres, a tenement and five acres, rents and the reversion of three selions. Gifts made by the Baivel family, lords of Shalstone, to the same house from the middle of the twelfth century, culminated in Walter (III) Baivel presenting a messuage and virgate with his body for burial in 1220x1225.⁶⁷ In similar vein, Martin *filius Thoroldi de Ottendun'* benefited from the gifts made by his father to Thame Abbey, which had comprised two acres of meadow and a perch of land, three acres of arable and one of meadow, and one of arable and meadow, all in Oddington. To these, Martin added several separate benefactions, comprising small parcels of arable and meadow, and finally with his body a further perch of land and common of pasture in ca.1242.⁶⁸ Martin's is the most representative example of a sequence of gifts culminating in a charter *cum corpore*, although such series were not the norm. The vast preponderance of charters *cum corpore* were single donations by lay benefactors.

Similarly, decisions to be interred in religious houses seem to have been individualistic rather than "dynastic" or of the family. The precedent of an individual opting for burial in a particular religious house did not create an obligation on successors in the kinship. For example, William *Capra* gave a rent of 1s. with his body to Blythburgh Priory; whilst his son, Geoffrey, made several more gifts, all of small amounts, none was *cum corpore*.⁶⁹ Individual decisions did not become family commitment for burial, although there are some exceptions to this norm. One such was the gifts of the fitzGerald family to Reading Abbey, commencing with Henry *filius Geraldi* who conferred his body for burial with a rent of six marks of silver; his charter reveals that his father and brother had already been interred in the abbey, Henry specifying that he wished to be laid to rest at the feet of his father and next to his brother. That brother, Warin, who had died in July 1216, had provided the abbey with three marks of land in Sawbridgeworth so that his body might be placed at his father's feet.[70]

Ties of family and lordship are evident too in a succession of gifts to Southwick Priory in the late twelfth century. A charter of *Magister* John de Insula revealed that his uncle was buried in the house and his lady, Helewise de Croftuna, had decided to be interred there too. Her subsequent gifts show that her lord (husband), John Talebot, had been buried in the house, whilst confirmations by Geoffrey Talebot mentioned that his father, John Talebot, was indeed buried there and that his mother (Helewise) would be.[71] Comparable, and also relating to Southwick, are the burials of the family of de Windlesor', for the charter of Thomas of 1187x1195, electing burial there, discloses that his father, Gervase, had been buried there, and that his own corpse as well as those of his mother, wife and children, would also be placed there.[72] William *filius Henrici* who provided land in Winchester elected for his body to be buried next to his mother's in Southwick Priory.[73]

What non-patronal donors received in return in the late twelfth century was usually less than the benefits afforded patronal families. The latter were usually buried in honorific places within the conventual church, often in front of altars, as Henry de Ferrers was interred at the right side of the great altar of the conventual church of Tutbury Priory, the family's *Eigenkirche*.[74] Only a very select number of the later, non-patronal donors might expect a similar place of burial. Of the numerous benefactors to Rufford, John Burdon seems exceptional, for, in his charter of 1190x1196, which conferred a bovate, pasture, nineteen selions and assarts–a significant gesture by comparison with most gifts to the abbey–he requested burial *sub tecto*.[75] Most of the other charters have no specific details for the disposition of the body, but the implication is that they would be consigned to the cemetery of the house and that is occasionally explicitly stated: *in cimiterio dictorum monachorum*; *in cimiterio eorum*;

in atrio.⁷⁶ They essentially got something commensurate with the small amount they paid.

By the end of the thirteenth century, charters recording gifts for burials declined, but the question remains of how far this change reflects discontinuance of burials in religious houses and a new pattern of benefactions, or merely a transition to different means of providing interment in monastic cemeteries. Charters were replaced by the *ultima voluntas* as the means of making provision for spiritual welfare after death. Episcopal indulgences and *acta* also imply continued burial in religious houses in the later middle ages. Moreover, burial in friaries continued to have considerable popularity.

An indulgence of the bishop of Norwich in 1307, for example, was directed to those who prayed for the soul of Joan, late countess of Gloucester, wife of the earl of Clare and daughter of Edward I, whose body was interred in the church of the Austin Friars of Clare, where too her son, Sir Edward Monthemer was buried.⁷⁷ There also Edmund de Nortohft and his wife, Anne, were buried in return for 200 marks for re-leading the roof of the cloister.⁷⁸ Lionel, duke of Clarence made testamentary provision for burial at Clare, but on his deathbed in Italy stipulated that his heart and bones be carried to Clare and his flesh and entrails interred at Pavia.⁷⁹

Some important points emerge from these examples. These benefactors were of considerable status and their burial was associated with the mendicants, not with the older religious orders. Some families of higher status did continue to be associated with traditional religious houses, but the number seems smaller by comparison with an earlier time and the connection was the continuation of a family tradition.⁸⁰ The higher nobility in particular retained a stronger preference for burial in monastic houses.⁸¹ An example of this continuing allegiance for burial at gentry level was the Chaworth family and Beauchief Priory.⁸² With the exception of a lingering association between some notable families and monastic houses, however, the general movement was away from interment in religious houses to the benefit of parish churches. While social relationships with religious houses were represented by heraldry in conventual churches and gatehouses, the connection did not frequently extend to burial there.⁸³ Whilst Sir William Etchingham, his wife and daughter were buried at Robertsbridge Abbey according to the longstanding relationship between family and monks, from the 1330s the family diverted its allegiance to the parish church of Etchingham. So too the Berkeleys, patrons of Augustinian Saint Augustine, Bristol, and constantly buried there at an earlier time, developed the parish churches of Berkeley and Wootton-under-Edge as their mausolea.[84] The burial preferences of the gentry of Warwickshire, Kent and Yorkshire moved in the same direction. Of 148 wills of Yorkshire gentry between 1376 and 1482, some ninety specified burial in parish churches which were becoming "private mausoleums for the most prominent local family".[85] Over 76 per cent of the wills of knights in Kent elected burial in the parish church, and higher proportions of esquires and gentlemen, between 1422 and 1529, only some mendicant orders attracting the knights (just over ten per cent, mainly Observants and Carthusians).[86]

Burial of non-patronal benefactors in religious houses was a privilege bestowed not only by a particular house, but by the Church and the community of lay society. Interment there was essentially removal from the wider community of the deceased–in parochial cemeteries–and from general intercession by secular clergy and the laity, to an almost private and exclusive enclosure serviced by the professed religious, whose intercession was considered more efficacious. Whilst burial of patronal families in religious houses was approved, burial of non-patronal lay persons in cemeteries of religious houses need not have been easily condoned. One of the reasons why it might have met less resistance earlier was the inchoate nature of parochial development in the twelfth century, still not fully formed, which had profound repercussions on the location of cemeteries. Burial rights still pertained to–and were guarded by–minster and mother churches, so that cemeteries were not intimately local. Although rights to cemeteries were gradually conceded, both to parishes and chapelries, burial symbolized attachment to a wider place than the purely local.[87] To some extent, burial rights also ambivalently involved ties of lordship as well as ecclesiastical jurisdiction.[88] In this context of disputed rights over the burial of the laity in general, the smaller number buried in the cemeteries of religious houses might have seemed inconsequential and may indeed have been a result of the incoherence of parochial development.

Monastic Burials of Non-patronal Lay Benefactors

Although it never involved enormous numbers of the deceased and although its extent became further limited, burial of non-patronal lay persons in religious houses has a significance for the perceptions of death in the middle ages. By comparison with the multitude of bodies committed to parochial cemeteries, the number afforded burial in monastic cemeteries was select. It was an episode which diverged from the full communitarian beliefs of intercession which have been assumed to characterize the middle ages. Although still communitarian in its dependence on intercession by the community of heaven and the specialized religious community on earth, it was separatist since it removed bodies from the community of the dead in parochial burial grounds.

Its character also changed over the twelfth century. Some evidence suggests that even some minor benefactors were interred in the cemeteries of the regular cathedral priories in the early twelfth century, but it is difficult to disentangle the influences of monasticism and *matrix ecclesia* in the motives for seeking burial there. In many recorded instances of burial in other monastic houses, the privilege was reserved to benefactors of status, important tenants and liege men, to embrace a much wider social composition. Whilst in the case of tenants and liege men, burial with the recovery of the *legitim* was considered a prerogative of the religious house, by the late twelfth century the *legitim* was no longer involved and gifts for burial were predominantly inconsiderable. The proliferation of houses of new religious orders offered wider opportunities for burial amongst the religious at a smaller cost. Religious houses then offered burial not for its material benefits, nor for the obligation of good lordship, but for its symbolic value for the house within its locality. Subsequently, from the late thirteenth century, interment amongst the monastic orders continued to attract notables, especially when a traditional link was involved between family and convent, whilst the mendicants received for burial persons of a wider range of status. Nevertheless, a distinct preference developed for burial in parochial churches with a direct invocation of the parochial laity for intercession. Interment amongst the religious thus presents an interesting aspect of the provision for the dead in medieval England and illustrates changes in attitudes towards the means of salvation.

Notes

[1] Philippe Ariès, *Western Attitudes Towards Death: From the Middle Ages to the Present* (Baltimore: Johns Hopkins University Press, 1974), and Ariès, *The Hour of Our Death*, trans. Helen Weaver (Oxford: Oxford University Press, 1981).

[2] Ralph A. Houlbrooke's editorial introduction to *Death, Ritual and Bereavement* (London: Routledge, 1980) is perhaps the best exposition. Clare Gittings, *Death, Burial and the Individual in Early Modern England* (London: Routledge, 1984), preferred later changes with a different causation, following Laurence Stone. Joachim Whaley, ed., *Mirrors of Mortality: Studies in the Social History of Death* (London: Europa Publication Ltd., 1981), especially the "Introduction" (1-14) emphasizes rather the dynamics of ritual (especially at 2).

[3] Clive Burgess, "'For the Increase of Divine Service': Chantries in the Parish in Late Medieval Bristol," *JEH* 36 (1985): 48-65; Eamon Duffy, *The Stripping of the Altars: Traditional Religion in England c.1400-c.1580* (New Haven, Conn., and London: Yale University Press, 1992), 301-76, summarizes the extensive literature. Kathleen L. Wood-Legh, *Perpetual Chantries in Britain* (Cambridge: Cambridge University Press, 1965) emphasizes the late-medieval nature of this particular form of communitarian response to death. The ritual aspects of death and burial are interestingly elaborated by Ronald Finucane, "Sacred Corpse, Profane Carrion: Social Ideals and Death Rituals in the Later Middle Ages", in *Mirrors of Mortality*, 40-60. See also T. S. R. Boase, *Death in the Middle Ages: Mortality, Judgment and Remembrance* (London: Thames and Hudson, 1972).

[4] For a résumé of recent research, Janet Burton, *Monastic and Religious Orders in Britain, 1000-1300* (Cambridge: Cambridge University Press, 1994), 217-19. Research into burial in southern European religious houses has taken a less empirical approach. Thus Patrick J. Geary states that "The present abandonment of the dead is the end result of a gradual process in Western society. It began perhaps in the High Middle Ages, when specialists (monks and canonesses) were entrusted with the care and remembrance of the dead.": *Living with the Dead in the Middle Ages* (Ithaca, N.Y.: Cornell University Press, 1994), 2. The thesis presented here, whilst acknowledging the force of some of Geary's arguments, develops in a different direction. See also Geary, "Échanges et Relations Entre les Vivants et les Morts dans la Société au Haut Moyen Âge", *Droit et Cultures* 12 (1986): 3-17. For a further revision of Ariès, see Megan McLaughlin, *Consorting with Saints: Prayers for the Dead in Early Medieval France* (Ithaca, N.Y.: Cornell University Press, 1994), especially 44-54, 118-32, 147-8, for burials in religious houses in "France". Whilst Geary emphasizes the relationship of

gift-exchange between living and dead, McLaughlin promotes the notion of associative social bonds between laity and religious to form a liturgical community.

[5] Burgess, "'For the Increase of Divine Service'"; Robert Whiting, *The Blind Devotion of the People: Popular Religion and the English Reformation* (Cambridge: Cambridge University Press, 1989), 20; Susan Brigden, *London and the Reformation* (Oxford: Oxford University Press, 1989), 385-92; Jack J. Scarisbrick, *The Reformation and the English People* (Oxford: Oxford University Press, 1984), 3-18; A. Gervase Rosser, "Communities of Parish and Guild in the Late Middle Ages", in *Parish, Church and People: Local Studies in Lay Religion, 1350-1750*, ed. Susan Wright (London: HarperCollins, 1988), 29-55.

[6] The mandate of Pope Innocent IV to the bishop of Worcester in 1254 may have been concerned with the popularity of burials in friaries at the expense of parish churches: *Cartulary ... Worcester*, 241-2 (no. 464).

[7] The sources for Table 2 are cited within the paper, with additionally *Cartulary of Dale Abbey*; *Cartulary ... Beaulieu*; *Cartulary of ... St Denys*; *Cartulary of Blyth Priory*; "Cartulary ... Old Wardon".

[8] Richard H. Helmholz, "*Legitim* in English legal History", in his *Canon Law and the Law of England* (London: Hambledon, 1987), 247-62; the *legitim* involved here is the (third) part reserved to donors, over which they had full power of disposition, by contrast with the *legitim* or third part reserved for children and the third part (effectively dower) for widows.

[9] Brian Golding, "Burials and Benefactions: An Aspect of Monastic Patronage in Thirteenth-century England", in *England in the Thirteenth Century: Proceedings of the 1984 Harlaxton Symposium*, ed. W. M. Ormrod (Nottingham: Nottingham University Press, 1985), 64-75, and "Anglo-Norman Knightly Burials", in *The Ideals and Practice of Knighthood: Papers from the First and Second Strawberry Hill Conferences*, ed. Christopher Harper-Bill and Ruth Harvey (Woodbridge: Boydell, 1986), 35-48. Despite its title, the latter relates exclusively to burials of patrons or founders and their kin.

[10] D. H. Williams, "Layfolk within Cistercian Precincts", in *Monastic Studies II*, ed. Judith Loades (Bangor: Loades, 1991), 104-7.

[11] Sharon Elkins, *Holy Women of Twelfth-Century England* (Chapel Hill, N.C.: University of North Carolina Press, 1988); Sally Thompson, *Women Religious: The Founding of English Nunneries after the Norman Conquest* (Oxford: Oxford University Press, 1991).

[12] Christopher N. L. Brooke, *The Monastic World 1000-1300* (London: Thames and Hudson, 1974), 168; Roberta Gilchrist, *Gender and Material Culture: The Archaeology of Women Religious* (London: Routledge, 1994), 58-9, 61.

[13] *Stoke by Clare Cartulary*, 304-5 (no. 461).

¹⁴ *Stoke by Clare Cartulary*, III, 2.
¹⁵ *Stoke by Clare Cartulary*, III, 2.
¹⁶ *Stoke by Clare Cartulary*, III, 3.
¹⁷ But see, however, Christopher Harper-Bill, "The Piety of the Anglo-Norman Knightly Class", in *Proceedings of the Battle Conference II 1979*, ed. R. Allen Brown (Woodbridge: Boydell, 1980), 63-77, 173-6, where a case is made for Clare having been an honorial spiritual centre for some time, and perhaps by way of comparison, Janet Ward, "Fashions in Monastic Endowment", *JEH* 32 (1981): 427-51.
¹⁸ *Charters ... Norwich*, 12 (no. A20); *EEA* VII, 18-21 (no. 21). (I am grateful for this reference to Professor Harper-Bill who points out to me that although the *actum* of the bishop is spurious and although the bishop did not concede the claim of Thetford, the account represents what the monks of that house expected to happen–that the principal tenants of Bigod could be buried at Thetford in accordance with their honorial ties).
¹⁹ *Cartulary of Eynsham Abbey*, I, 91 (no. 100). See also the admission of a married couple into the fraternity of Norwich cathedral priory, 1107x1114, on their gift of the manor of Eaton, which involved a monk performing services on their behalf: *Charters ... Norwich*, II, 197 (no. 364).
²⁰ Burton, *Monastic and Religious Orders*, 138.
²¹ H. Tsurushima, "The Fraternity of Rochester Cathedral Priory about 1100", in *Anglo-Norman Studies XIV. Proceedings of the Battle Conference 1991*, ed. Marjorie Chibnall (Woodbridge: Boydell, 1992), 313-37; J. Thorpe, ed., *Registrum Roffense* (London, 1769), 370-1. I owe this reference to Dr Martin Brett. Tsurushima equates fraternity with burial, citing the evidence of the enlargement of the monks' cemetery (336), but there is no conclusive evidence that fraternity conferred burial; burial is mentioned only twice, in each case associated with the receipt of the deceased's part of his chattels.
²² *Cartulary ... Worcester*, 80-1, 128-9, 179, 207 (nos. 143, 243, 335, 394). Similarly, there appear to be no gifts for burial amongst the charters of Norwich cathedral priory: *Charters ... Norwich*, I-II.
²³ *Cartulary ... Worcester*, 81 (no. 144).
²⁴ Michael J. Franklin, "Bodies in Medieval Northampton: Legatine Intervention in the Twelfth Century", in *Medieval Ecclesiastical Studies in Honour of Dorothy Owen*, ed. Franklin and Christopher Harper-Bill (Woodbridge: Boydell, 1995), 57-81 at 68-79, and "The Cathedral as Parish Church: The Case of Southern England", in *Church and City 1000-1250: Essays in Honour of Christopher Brooke*, ed. David Abulafia, Franklin and Miri Rubin (Cambridge: Cambridge University Press, 1992), 173-98.
²⁵ McLaughlin, *Consorting with Saints*, 118-32. For burials in twelfth-century Burgundian and southern French religious houses, see Constance B. Bouchard, *Sword, Miter, and Cloister: Nobility and the Church in Burgundy,*

980-1198 (Ithaca, N.Y.: Cornell University Press, 1987), 190-3, and Marcus Bull, *Knightly Piety and the Lay Response to the First Crusade: The Limousin and Gascony, c.970-1130* (Oxford: Oxford University Press, 1993), 143-54.

[26] For example, Oliver de Sutton's permission to the Carmelites of Boston in 1293 to bury "others" in their conventual cemetery: *Rolls and Register ... Sutton*, IV, 127-8.

[27] I am grateful to Professor Harper-Bill for posing this question. In the case of the mendicants, it is probable that the permission was indeed used to meet demands for burial, but that explanation is less certain for the older religious Orders.

[28] See further below.

[29] Again, I am grateful to Professor Harper-Bill for posing this question. The primary objective at the earlier time of association with saints and the religious is promoted by McLaughlin, *Consorting with Saints*; equally, the anticipated association might have been with the relics of some houses at an earlier time: Stephen D. White, *Custom, Kinship and Gifts to Saints: The* Laudatio Parentum *in Western France, 1050-1150* (Chapel Hill, N.C.: University of North Carolina Press, 1988), 26. The evidence seems to suggest that the earlier motive for burial amongst the religious was not invited until later.

[30] *Rolls and Register ... Sutton*, III, 43, 54, 58-9, 81, 85, 145, 166-7, 180, 189, 191, 192-3; IV, 2, 7, 73, 81, 83, 87, 92, 101, 132, 146, 180, 191; V, 9, 10, 19, 31, 35, 107, 190, 195, 199, 212; VI, 8, 14, 20, 31, 99, 113, 116, 130, 149, 153, 204.

[31] For these houses, Helen M. Chew, *The Ecclesiastical Tenants in Chief and Knight Service* (Oxford: Oxford University Press, 1932).

[32] Helmholz, "*Legitim* in English Legal History".

[33] Mary Cheney, "Inalienability in Mid-twelfth Century England: Enforcement and Consequences", in *Proceedings of the Sixth International Congress on Medieval Canon Law*, ed. Stephen Kuttner and K. Pennington (Vatican City, 1985), 467-78; John Hudson, *Land, Law and Lordship in Anglo-Norman England* (Oxford: Oxford University Press, 1994), 231-46; Susan Reynolds, *Fiefs and Vassals: The Medieval Evidence Reinterpreted* (Oxford: Oxford University Press, 1994), 176-7.

[34] "Abstract ... Burton Chartulary", 30: *Cum autem mortuus fuerit deferre ad nos se faciet cum tota pecunia sua ad sepeliendum.*

[35] "Abstract ... Burton Chartulary", 34.

[36] "Abstract ... Burton Chartulary", 34-5.

[37] "Abstract ... Burton Chartulary", 35-6.

[38] "Abstract ... Burton Chartulary", 36.

[39] *St Benet of Holme*, 105-6 (no. 190).

[40] *Cartulary of Daventry Priory*, 172-3, 243-4.

[41] *Reading Abbey Cartularies*, II, 242 (no. 1079).
[42] *Cartulary of Daventry Priory*, 286-7 (nos. 875-8).
[43] *Stoke by Clare Cartulary*, II, 351 (no. 540).
[44] *Chronicon Monasterii de Abingdon*, II, 124.
[45] *Chronicon Monasterii de Abingdon*, II, 12-15.
[46] *Chronicon Monasterii de Abingdon*, II, 108.
[47] *Chronicon Monasterii de Abingdon*, II, 122-3.
[48] *Chronicon Monasterii de Abingdon*, II, 145.
[49] *Chronicon Monasterii de Abingdon*, II, 166-7.
[50] *Chronicon Monasterii de Abingdon*, II, 170.
[51] Compare the gift, 1100x1106, of the land of Stanmere by William, count of Mortain, to Saint Albans Abbey, where his sister, Mabilia, was buried: E. A. Levett, *Studies in Manorial History*, ed. Helen M. Cam, M. Coate and Lucy S. Sutherland (Oxford: Oxford University Press, 1963 ed.), 171.
[52] Williams, "Layfolk within Cistercian Precincts", 104-7.
[53] J. C. Dickinson, *The Origins of the Austin Canons and their Introduction into England* (London: SPCK, 1950); Howard M. Colvin, *The White Canons in England* (Oxford: Oxford University Press, 1951); Ian Kershaw, *Bolton Priory: The Economy of a Northern Monastery 1286-1325* (Oxford: Oxford University Press, 1973), 5-7.
[54] *Cartulary of the Priory of St Gregory, Canterbury*, 1 (no. 1). Dr Brett informs me that this document is a thirteenth-century composition, which may affect the authenticity of its details.
[55] Golding, "Anglo-Norman Knightly Burials", 36.
[56] *Thurgarton Cartulary*, 187-8 (no. 319).
[57] *Thurgarton Cartulary*, 342-4 (no. 561).
[58] *Sibton Abbey Cartularies*, II, 272-3 (no. 374).
[59] *Reading Abbey Cartularies*, 242-6 (nos. 1079-86).
[60] Marcel Mauss, *The Gift: The Form and Reason for Exchange in Archaic Societies*, trans. W. D. Halls (London: Routledge, 1990); Barbara H. Rosenwein, *To Be the Neighbor of St Peter: The Social Meaning of Cluny's Property, 909-1049* (Ithaca, N.Y.: Cornell University Press, 1989).
[61] C. J. Wales, "The Knight in Twelfth-century Lincolnshire", unpublished PhD (University of Cambridge, 1983), 235-60.
[62] *Historia et Cartularium ... Gloucestriae*, I, 244-5 (1148x1179).
[63] *Cartulary of Burscough*, 89 (no. 88); *Luffield Priory Charters*, II, 126-7 (no. 444); *Cartulary of Darley Abbey*, 125, 277, 287, 305 (nos. B35, F80, F104, G24); *Thurgarton Cartulary*, 39, 342-4 (nos. 61, 561); *Cartulary of Cockersand*, I/ii, 267-8 (no. 8); *Rufford Charters*, I, 33 (no. 50); *Blythburgh Priory Cartulary*, I, 84 (no. 128); Bodl., MS Laud Misc. 625, fols. iv-v at fo. vr (Leicester Abbey).

[64] *Cartularies of Southwick Priory*, II, 101-3 (no. III, 289-92).
[65] *Rufford Charters*, I, xl, but this example reveals that even cumulative gifts still amounted to inconsiderable totals–only two acres.
[66] *Cartularies of Southwick Priory*, I, 28-32 (nos. 1, 48, 50, 52, 54).
[67] *Luffield Priory Charters*, ii, liv-lvi, 126-9, 158-9 (nos. 444-7, 490).
[68] *Thame Cartulary*, I, 18 (no. 27).
[69] *Blythburgh Priory Cartulary*, I, 57-64 (nos. 65-82).
[70] *Reading Abbey Cartularies*, I, 244-5, 319 (nos. 295, 393).
[71] *Cartularies of Southwick Priory*, I, 28-32 (no. I, 47-54).
[72] *Cartularies of Southwick Priory*, I, 35 (no. I, 62).
[73] *Cartularies of Southwick Priory*, II, 219-20 (no. III, 568).
[74] *Cartulary of Tutbury Priory*, 66-7 (no. 53).
[75] *Rufford Charters*, I, 211 (no. 396).
[76] *Sibton Abbey Cartularies*, II, 117, 313 (nos. 148, 429).
[77] *Cartulary ... Clare*, 90-2 (nos. 158-9, 161-2).
[78] *Cartulary ... Clare*, 84 (no. 140; 1361).
[79] *Cartulary ... Clare*, 75 (no. 121; 1377).
[80] See, for example, the comments of Christine Carpenter, "The Religion of the Gentry of Fifteenth-century England", in *England in the Fifteenth Century: Proceedings of the 1986 Harlaxton Symposium*, ed. Daniel T. Williams (Woodbridge: Boydell, 1987), 67: "although some gentry and noble families were still remembering monastic institutions with which they had a particular link."
[81] Joel T. Rosenthal, *The Purchase of Paradise: Gift Giving and the Aristocracy 1307-1485* (London: Routledge and K. Paul, 1972), chap. V, esp. Table 7 at p. 82.
[82] *Testamenta Eboracensia*, I, 47 (will of Thomas de Chaworth, 1347). There are other instances from the 1340s through the late fourteenth century of burial in other houses: Sulby Abbey; Gisbourne Priory; Bretton Priory; Malton Priory; Whatton Priory; Cockersand Abbey; Saint Mary's, York; Worksop Priory; Helaugh Park; Rievaulx Abbey; Selby Abbey; but see further the comments below for the comparative context.
[83] Nigel Saul, *Scenes from Provincial Life: Knightly Families in Sussex, 1280-1400* (Oxford: Oxford University Press, 1986), 145, n. 18.
[84] Saul, *Scenes from Provincial Life*, 142-43, 145; Saul, "The Religious Sympathies of the Gentry of Gloucestershire, 1200-1500", *Transactions of the Bristol and Gloucestershire Archaeological Society* 98 (1981): 103-4.
[85] Malcolm G. A. Vale, *Piety, Charity and Literacy among the Yorkshire Gentry, 1370-1480* (York: Borthwick Papers, 1976), 5, 9 (quotation at 9); for Warwickshire, Carpenter, "Religion of the Gentry". See also Andrew D. Brown, *Popular Piety in Late Medieval England: The Diocese of Salisbury 1250-1550* (Oxford: Oxford University Press, 1995), 30-1, 35-6, 44, 47.

[86] Peter Fleming, "Charity, Faith and the Gentry of Kent, 1422-1529", in *Property and Politics: Essays in Later Medieval History*, ed. A. (Tony) J. Pollard (Gloucester: Sutton, 1984), 48-50. The reluctance for burial in religious houses was even more marked amongst townspeople; although they left bequests to the mendicants, burial amongst them was not extensive: Peter Heath, "Urban Piety in the Later Middle Ages: The Evidence of Hull Wills", in *The Church, Politics and Patronage in the Fifteenth Century*, ed. R. Barrie Dobson (Gloucester: Sutton, 1984), 215, 220-2; Norman Tanner, *The Church in Late Medieval Norwich, 1370-1532* (Toronto: University of Toronto Press, 1984), 119, 123-5, 189 (appendix 3), 222-3 (appendix 12).

[87] Brian Kemp, "Some Aspects of the *Parochia* of Leominster in the Twelfth Century", in *Minsters and Parish Churches: The Local Church in Transition 950-1200*, ed. John Blair (Oxford: Oxbow, 1988), 88-9; P. H. Hase, "The Mother Churches of Hampshire", in *Minsters and Parish Churches*, 54, 56; Julia Barrow, "Urban Cemetery Location in the High Middle Ages", in *Death in Towns: Urban Responses to the Dying and the Dead 100-1600*, ed. Steven Bassett (Leicester: Leicester University Press, 1992), 86 (burial rights of Worcester).

[88] Martin Brett, *The Church under Henry I* (Oxford: Oxford University Press, 1975), 93-4, 98, 221-2, 227; *Historia et Cartularium ... Gloucestriae*, I, lxxv-lxxviii.

4
Small Gifts, but Big Rewards:
The Symbolism of Some Gifts to the Religious

In the late twelfth century, Plympton Priory, a house of Austin Canons in Devon, received from the earl of Devon, a conduit of water from the spring, the source of which was under the earl's cross, for the specific purpose of providing pure water for celebrating mass.[1] Some time later, perhaps in the second decade of the thirteenth century, Robert de Berkeley attorned to Saint Augustine's Abbey, Bristol, Hugh *pistor* whom he had manumitted, with a virgate at Elmcote (attornment is basically the transfer of the services of a free tenant). Hugh and his heirs should thereafter furnish the canons with two bushels of *pure* wheat and 10s. for the purchase of wine for consecration as the body and blood of our Lord, Jesus Christ. Any challenger to the benefaction then or in the future would suffer excommunication.[2] Within the configuration of benefactions to religious houses by both families, such endowments were minuscule. Such is the problematic of gifts for specific purposes to religious houses, for materially they constituted only minor benefactions. Moreover, quantitatively, they were overwhelmed by the preponderance of benefactions for unspecified spiritual purposes, gifts in free alms, for which no *specific* reciprocity was requested except for the general requirements imputed in a salvific clause for the welfare of souls of both nominated and undefined kin and lineage, and occasionally for the rather loose reference to prayers. Compared to the vast numbers of such general benefactions for undefined spiritual purposes, benefactions for specific intentions remained rather insignificant.[3] The question, nevertheless, which might be asked is what was the significance of such a gift to the benefactor as well as the beneficiary?[4]

Such a question might assist in analysing some long-term questions about the nature of religious and devotional experience in England and about the social role of religion. It is clear that gifts in free alms to religious houses marked their donors off from the rest of society in terms of personal salvation and social honor and prestige. First, such an action was not achievable by all, for material reasons; as importantly, it was an action not accessible to all because the benefactor as well as the benefaction needed to be acceptable to the religious house. Whilst religious houses were acquisitive, it might be argued that one of their objectives by this process was to cultivate local social relationships as well as to enhance the wealth of the house and consequently the honor of the patronal saint. Donors for unspecified spiritual rewards were thus able to differentiate themselves from the remainder of local society and to form another network of the locality or the neighborhood associated with a religious house rather than *only* the parish church, and this association, because it was supplementary, must have been assumed a superior one.[5] Examining beyond gifts for unspecified spiritual benefits to those which defined the expected purpose of the gift allows a further insight into these motivations of separation and marking off, of self-fashioning and self-representation. Below, for example, will be considered the earlier foundation of *cantarie* by the laity inside religious houses, which has been regarded as a default option by those of a status not high enough to establish their own religious houses. Such a foundation (of a cantarist) might then be construed not merely as an institution for personal salvation, but clearly as a self-definition of honor and status and as a separating off. There are, moreover, other motivations.[6]

In the social and mental world of gift-exchange, in which social relationships were at some levels at least partly constituted around land, gifts to the religious expected some reciprocity.[7] In gifts in free alms, the element of reciprocity was left undefined, although it was still anticipated.[8] In the case of gifts for specific purposes, however, this norm, for such it was, was transgressed, for the benefactor defined what was expected, still in spiritual terms, of the use of the material gift; the spiritual conditions were precise. What motivated these donors to go beyond the norms of gifts in free alms to make more definitive demands on the religious house? It is in this motivation that the significance of gifts for spiritual purposes must reside, regardless of their numerical insignificance. The significance of the benefaction would seem to involve a closer association with the local professed religious and, further, at least in some cases, such an association with a symbolic ritual performed by those religious.

From both these associations ensue further important considerations, for participation in all these spiritual benefits was available in the lay community of believers, the parish. The decision to seek an alternative association was thus an exercise of voluntary religion and devotion at least to some extent away from the parish, for even if the donor continued to participate in the community of the parish, another association had also been desired. In the twelfth and thirteenth centuries the ability to make such a choice was obviously still circumscribed by social group; although gifts might be small, they were not achievable by all, not simply because of the material consequences, but also because of the discretion of the religious house about who it wished to participate in its spiritual benefits.

Such negotiations were not, however, free of further ambiguity, for the acquisition of some grants for specific purposes was exactly that: an acquisition, in the sense that the initiative for the transfer came from an obedientiary who was concerned to augment the resources of the obedience. Thus, for example, some acquisitions of material support for lights were in effect purchases by sacristans.[9] It is from this direction that gifts for special purposes have sometimes, although not exclusively, been perceived, as part of the assigned revenues to obedientiaries, and thus as an aspect of the financial organization of religious houses and, indeed, one which contained inherent problems.[10] It has, furthermore, been suggested that benefactions for specific purposes, although never numerically large, increased during the twelfth century as donors became more demanding.[11] With the decline in benefactions in general in the late twelfth century, small benefactions assumed a greater significance, so that religious houses were prepared to offer "incentives" for their acquisition, provided that the association with the lay donor was beneficial, that is honorific. The context also explains why obedientiaries were also prepared to purchase such smaller items. It should not be forgotten, however, that there was a symbolic value to both lay benefactors and religious house in such transactions, through which the religious house expanded its association with the local laity and the local laity established an association with the liturgy within a religious house. Finally, it was precisely at this time, the late twelfth century, that the parish was developing as the center of lay devotion for the preponderance of the laity.

The chronology of these relationships between laity and religious houses is even more interesting because at precisely this time there was some development of the importance of the parish for lay spirituality, which culminated in and was reinforced by the canons of the Fourth Lateran Council of 1215. That Council's provisions, not least for confession (*Anglice* shrift) and communication (*Anglice* housel), placed the parish firmly at the centre of lay religious observance for most people. The dissemination of this practice through the Council of Oxford in 1222 and diocesan synods, gave impulsion to that process. About the same time, parishioners were becoming more formally responsible for parochial financial obligations, within an evolving institutional structure and the development of the office of churchwarden.[12]

Another context of this conjuncture was the appropriation of parish churches by religious houses, particularly by houses of the new religious Orders, complicating the relationship between laity, parish and regulars. Officially conceived as the restitution of spiritualities and temporalities to the Church from lay hands, this transfer nevertheless had numerous other consequences, amongst which was competition, fragmented revenues, the failure of the regulars to be involved in pastoral provision, and the integration of parochial temporalities into the estates of the religious. The transfer of the spiritualities to the care of the regulars also reflects a current attitude towards the regulars on the part of the benefactors, invariably from the higher social echelons.[13]

Here, consequently, to define the extent of that preference for symbolic association with the lay religious in the locality, the emphasis will be directed to three forms of benefactions for specific purposes which were, by and large, less likely overall to have been purchased and which are likely to express a voluntary association: support for the elements of the mass as a general office; contributions to the fabric; and maintenance of the mass as a specific office, for specific souls, that is the early development of cantarists, if not chantries, in religious houses for the welfare of the laity.

Although unusual in its incidence, the most significant of benefactions for specific purposes to the religious involved supplying the elements of the mass. Seeking a closer association with divine office celebrated in the conventual church, Henry son of William *filius Nigilli* [sic] in 1215x1242 provided Bushmead Priory annually with three *hope* (heaped bushels) of "pure" wheat for wafers, a benefaction which was expanded by Nigel son and heir of Henry *atte Wode* after 1242-3 by his provision of five bushels of "pure" wheat for making wafers.[14] Amongst some of the laity there was a desire to be associated with the celebration of divine office in religious houses which was achieved through the provision of materials in both kinds for the mass. A significant example was the gift by Ralph II de Tilly of half a skep of "clean and pure" wheat annually to Blyth Priory in 1166x1200 for the making of the eucharist for the conventual church, which was confirmed by his daughter, Philippa, who additionally provided three *hoppae* of "clean and pure" wheat for making the eucharist.[15] Blyth had been founded by de Busli, so both Ralph and Philippa were seeking an intimate relationship with a house not of their foundation, by association with the most symbolically charged ritual within the house. A similar donation was made by William de Kaynes in 1208x1216 to Christchurch Priory, three quarters of wheat each year from his demesne grain at his manor of Tarrant Keynston to make their host.[16] Although the ritual was also performed in the parish church, the preference here was beyond the parish. Importantly, it was precisely at this time that the eucharist was being transformed as a devotional symbol and as a penitential instrument for the laity, with the expansion of its reception as a mystical act for the laity and in theological debate about the nature of the substance and accidents. The sacramentality, moreover, of the eucharist would become a "sacerdotal ritual action", sacramentally associated with the priesthood.[17] In the twelfth century, nonetheless, the parochial clergy might still have been considered unreformed, so that, although the miracle of the eucharist was effected *ex opere operato*, through the ministration of the priest despite his character, divine office celebrated by the parochial clergy might have carried a stigma of being less efficacious.[18] In contrast, the perceived purity of the enclosed and professed religious might, in the twelfth century, have been more attractive to the laity for the ministration of divine service. The definition of the wheat provided as "clean and pure" undoubtedly evoked the devotional and ritual symbolism of the host which, as concomitant with the body of Christ, had necessarily to be pure.[19] To the laity of the twelfth century, it might have been important that those in holy orders administering the host were also spiritually pure. Parochial churches might, furthermore, have remained in the twelfth century rather unprepossessing buildings, despite some rebuilding in the late eleventh and twelfth century, by comparison with the capacious and imposing conventual churches of both old and new religious houses.[20] The benefaction to the religious for the celebration of mass could only constitute association with, not participation in, the mass, but the desire for this identification affected some of the laity in the twelfth century; by acting in this manner, they were marking themselves off from the rest of the parochial laity, not satisfied with the parochial performance of the ritual, but seeking a closer association with a different performance of it.

The symbolic value of these materially small benefactions is thus partly to be explained by the involvement in the crucial point of the liturgy, but is further explicable by the social honor of marking off. Although the amount of grain provided was inconsiderable, the simple value of being in a position to dispose of grain of the highest value–with a high semiotic value–itself defined the status of the donor. Its description as pure reflected not only on this necessity and quality for the eucharist, but also on the virtue of the donor.[21]

As late as about 1250, Robert de Esseburn' assigned rents of 9s. 6d. in Wirksworth (Derbyshire) to Darley Abbey for the purchase of wine for divine service.[22] Much earlier, in the late twelfth century, William *filius Radulphi* had performed much the same action by donating a rent of half a mark (6s. 8d.) for the purchase of wine for the celebration of masses in the abbey church.[23] Missenden Abbey, of the same Order of Austin Canons, benefited in the same manner when William *filius Radulphi* provided a rent of 12d. to be paid at the feast of the Assumption (the dedication) to buy wine for masses, about 1200.[24] In 1189, Margaret de Cressy granted a rent of 40s. to Sibton Abbey for the purchase of wine and wax for the celebration of masses.[25] Perhaps unusual because the date is so late (1361), Roger Chamburlayne conveyed nine messuages, two bovates, eight acres and 7s. rent to Darley Abbey for the celebration of divine service.[26] Even one of baronial status, Roger, earl of Hereford, was motivated to this association when he gave land outside the gates of Hereford to the monks of Saint Guthlac, Hereford, in 1148x1155, specifically to make a vineyard for celebrating masses, apparently his only benefaction to the house.[27]

The intensity of this desire to be associated with the celebration of mass in a religious house is most aptly demonstrated by the action of William fitzAlan who, by his grant of a rent of one mark from the mill of Cound (until he could convey land from his demesne) in 1144x1155 to buy wine when masses were sung in Shrewsbury Abbey, hoped that by the virtue of this sacrament and through the merits of the patronal saint, Saint Peter, his soul might be propitiously delivered.[28]

In 1187x1189, Simon le Bret, of the knightly family of Lincolnshire, gave to Waltham Abbey twelve acres in Leake Newland in the parish of Wrangle, the income from which was directed to provide the necessaries for the altars at the abbey, for bread and wine for making the Lord's body and blood.[29] Of similar status was Richard *filius Roberti* who granted to Waltham the advowson of the parish church of Alphamstone not only for a light before Holy Cross at Waltham, the dedication of the abbey, but also for wine to celebrate all sacraments in that church (presumably Waltham rather than Alphamstone). Richard regarded Alphamstone as his proprietary church, even in 1186x1191, since it was founded in his patrimony and land. His actions seem to suggest a desire for an association with a religious house rather than with the administration of these sacraments in the parish church.[30] Through provision of the elements to the religious house, a closer association with the celebration of the mass was achieved, conceived as far more beneficial than the restricted role of the parishioner in providing towards the Holy Loaf (*eulogia*) partaken by the laity after the parochial mass.[31] Whilst the *eulogia* was merely blessed, not consecrated, and divided amongst the parishioners, the grain provided to the religious in these gifts was consecrated and underwent transubstantiation. Provision of the elements for the celebration of the mass by the religious might, in a sense, not merely have allowed a closer association, but may also have extended to some of the laity a surrogate for a more regular communion than the annual canonical communication prescribed for the laity.[32]

The assumption is made here that the initiative for directing the grant towards the sacraments came from the grantor; for an example, but to a large Benedictine and royal house, Westminster Abbey, there is the grant of 14s. rent to be assigned *per meam petitionem* of the grantor, William de Haverhulle, to the sacristy to buy wine and oblations at masses (1190x1212) (if this is the correct construction of this charter and its intention).[33]

Some other benefactions entreated association with the celebration of divine service by the religious in the twelfth century by provision not of the elements but of materials in the preparation of the host. Walter FitzHerbert furnished firewood for the sacristan of Daventry Priory in 1190x1200 for baking the host in the special conditions required. A gift to an old Benedictine house, Abingdon Abbey, comprised a paten for conveying the host for communion, in the early twelfth century (1100x1135).[34]

Even so, the motivation was sometimes more complex and distinction between religious house and parish church not precise, for some religious may have served churches within their cure, even if only on special occasions. For example, 4d. rent granted for a light before the altar of Saint John's church, Hertford, before September 1227, was reserved for when the regular canons of Waltham celebrated mass for the parishioners there.[35] When Saer de Quincy and his wife, Matilda de Senlis, gave land in Daventry to the priory there in 1148x1166 for the purchase of wine for celebrating masses, the motives might have been equally complicated, for Matilda descended from the patronal family, but the priory had been refounded in the parish church some forty or fifty years earlier.[36]

This situation is replicated by the benefaction of Iwen de Albineio to Belvoir Priory, when he gave five acres in Barkeston for the souls of his uncle, William de Albineio and William's wife, Cecily, their son, another William, and Iwen and his wife, Beatrice, and especially of his lord, William de Albineio (III) and his mother, Matilda, for Iwen was related to the founder's family. The five acres of the gift, however, were bestowed for the provision of hosts for the altar of the priory.[37]

Nor is it always certain who had the greatest advantage from the association, which can be illustrated by comparing two benefactions to Pontefract Priory. In ca.1160, Adam *filius Petri* furnished half a bovate for oblations and for wine for masses, but for merely a rent of 4s., ostensibly, 12d. of which was to be assigned for purchasing wine for masses. William *filius Herveij* was permitted on the day and anniversary of its procurement a mass by each priest for his kin and fifty psalms by monks not in priestly orders during his lifetime, and then, after his death, the same for an anniversary of his death.[38] It would seem then that the monks were as solicitous of William's loyalty as he was for an association in their masses.

The mystical significance of Christ's body was thus profound, sought by some of the laity, but perhaps confirming that the site of Christ's body was also socially ambiguous rather than "communitarian", for some had access to a higher form of association with it. Social unity was thus not guaranteed and the intense meanings of the eucharist were capable as much of confirming social differentiation through exclusive social acts, even if those acts were not conflictual or contested.[39]

Most of the benefactions recorded above involved quite insubstantial material costs; what was more important was the symbolic association of the laity with the elements and of the laity with the religious, in a local context. Occasionally, however, as has been seen in at least one case, the extent of the material benefaction was greater, and so it was with Henry *Siluer* of Bridlington, for Henry transferred to Bridlington Priory two bovates *ad vinum emendum ad missas in eadem ecclesia* [the priory church] *celebrandas*.[40] Nevertheless, although the benefactions were predominantly minor materially, yet the status of the donors was significant enough for the religious, from their part, to accept the association. The negotiations behind such acceptance by the religious might be revealed in the attornment of 11s. rent by Robert *filius Ricardi de Trouwelle* to Dale Abbey, for the assignment seems to have been stimulated by Sir Robert de Esseburne who gave the ostensible grantor seven marks of silver *in gersumma* so that by agreement (*de consensu*) of the abbot and canons the 11s. rent was to be delivered to the sacristan to buy wine for celebrating divine office in the priory church.[41] Whilst not of the highest status, and usually not of a status capable of founding their own religious house, the donors were of a suitably high free position.

Bridlington Priory also benefited from a few gifts towards the development of its fabric, as when Gilbert *filius Luce* of Bridlington conveyed *deo et ecclesie beate marie de Bridel' et sacriste qui pro tempore fuerit ad opus fabrice eiusdem ecclesie* meadow pertaining to half a carucate of arable in Bridlington. The sacristan was also to receive 6d. annual rent granted by Elias Pulain of Bridlington *ad opus fabrice eiusdem ecclesie*.[42] Surprisingly, however, Bridlington was apparently the beneficiary of only a small number of endowments towards the fabric in contrast with some, if smaller, houses of Austin Canons. The reasons for these more munificent benefactions for the fabric of local Austin Canon houses, at the period of their intensity of building in the late twelfth and early thirteenth century, are again ambivalent. It might well be that in the case of those houses principally in receipt of support for the fabric, the house had been established with the endowments of the local parish church and, indeed, the laity might have worshipped within some part of the monastic church.[43] Affiliations with the religious house and the parish were consequently inextricably combined.

Houses within this category included the three Austin Canon priories of Thurgarton, Drax and Guisborough. Thurgarton received twenty-one benefactions for the building of its fabric in the thirteenth century, from eighteen different donors, the lowest benefaction consisting of a rent of 2s. and the largest of, unusually, two bovates, but the norm was from one to three selions.[44] Not all the donors, however, were inhabitants of Thurgarton, for seven were described as of Goverton, an adjacent settlement; the rural location might explain that distribution. In that context, Drax Priory provides an interesting contrast, for its location was more urban and the benefactions which it received for the fabric were predominantly from local urban families, many described as burgesses.[45] Twenty-three different donors effected thirty-six gifts to the fabric of the house.[46] Although slightly larger than the individual gifts to Thurgarton, the benefactions for this purpose to Drax were still comparatively small, extending from a single perch to three and a half acres, with a mode around half an acre. Not every such acquisition, however, was unambiguous, for one or two transactions were evidently sales. Thus Agnes *quondam uxor Eustagii de Draxburgo* transferred half an acre in Drax to the fabric of the priory church, but she received a certain sum of money as consideration *in magna necessitate*.[47] The purchase from her was unusual, however, and few of these transactions were apparently purchases and, indeed, several of the donors requested burial in the priory through gifts to the fabric *cum corpore*.[48]

Benefactions to Guisborough Priory were comparable with those to Drax.[49] At least fifty-six benefactions were made for the construction of the fabric of the house, although a very small number of donors provided more than a single gift. Again, there is a slight complication in that some of the acquisitions were purchases. Thus, although William *Forestarius* made four benefactions to the house for the fabric, one acquisition from him was described as a purchase in his great need and, moreover, the acquisition from his son, Richard, was also a purchase. Indeed, the two acquisitions from William *filius Hervei* were also purchases in his great need. Otherwise, however, the remaining acquisitions were ostensibly real benefactions for spiritual purposes, preponderantly transfers of arable ranging from a single selion to ten acres. Predominantly the donors were of modest, free status, with the exception of Eustace *filius Eustachii de Gyseburne* whose father, Eustace, had been steward of Guisborough, and his six charters conveyed five acres and one rood of land, and "land".

Other religious houses attracted contributions to the development of the fabric by different methods. Osney Abbey, for example, established a *confraria novi operis* about or before 1230, to support the conventual building programme, in the cause of which itinerant collectors visited parish churches to elicit donations, and rolls of subscriptions were deposited in parish churches, perhaps as additions to the bede roll, and with spiritual benefits in the conventual church through masses, psalters and paternosters.[50] The strategy of Osney was inherently ambivalent, for, whilst depending on parochial collections (presumably largely from parishes of which it held the advowson), it also subtracted potential donations from parish churches. The sort of quantity of spiritual provisions in return for sustaining the fabric might be elicited from the grant of fraternity and participation in indulgences issued by the abbot of Westminster in the early thirteenth century for those who contributed to the repair of the abbey's cell, Saint Bartholomew's Priory at Sudbury.[51]

The same consequences of depriving parish churches of funds might be understood in the foundation of some early *cantarie* in religious houses, for several reasons. First, the foundation of a *cantaria* in the religious house has been interpreted as the default action of donors not of sufficient status to establish their own religious house; it was in the process a subtraction of potential benefactions to the parish church. Second, it might also be conceived that there was a dissatisfaction with the performance of the secular clergy at this time, so that the cantarist should be either one of the professed religious, a regular in priest's orders, or, at least, a secular under the supervision of the professed religious. It is possible, perhaps ambiguously, to detect such apprehension in the regulations for the appointment of the cantarists. Finally, as was as important in the later middle ages, the provision of a cantarist allowed the benefactor some control over the liturgy, through its specification in the charter of endowment. It can further be suggested that the endowment of a cantarist inside a religious house was not a communitarian devotional response and that it did not provide for "the increase of divine service" (as has been maintained for the later middle ages) since the cantarist in a religious house celebrated within a closed "community", not always accessible to the parochial congregation.[52] The motivation for such foundations must then have been almost entirely personal, both in terms of salvation and definition of status and honor.

Some of the foundations of *cantarie* inside Dale Abbey perhaps also reflect the desire of the laity to have some influence over the liturgy. For example, in the first half of the thirteenth century, Walter de S[n]eynton made the large benefaction of eight and a half bovates to Dale Abbey for cantarists, but was allowed to specify the two collects, the *Deus qui caritatis* and the *Inclina*.[53]

Again, in some cases, the action confirmed the social relationships of the laity around the religious house. Robert *filius Johannis de Sywardeby* made a quitclaim to Bridlington Priory on the understanding that the canons would provide a *capellanus* for the souls of himself and his wife, Juliana, but also those of Robert de Saint Paul, John de Syward', William *Bareu*, and Alice de Sywardeby, celebrating at the altar of Saint John in the priory church (Saint Mary) forever.[54] The *cantaria* established by William de Hurst in Bushmead Priory–at a cost of one and a half bovates–included the souls not only of the donor, but also of Christine Ledet (who had herself founded a chantry in the house before 1234), Gerard and Isabel de Furnival, and the donor's brother, Walter de Hurst. In similar manner, Reginald de Baa supported a *cantaria* in the same house–again for a high provision (twenty-six acres of land)–which incorporated the souls of Reginald de Stacheden' and Hugh de Weldebof.[55]

In 1252x1253 Richard III de Wyverton', knight, conveyed a toft and three bovates and two acres of meadow in Barnston and Wiverton to Thurgarton Priory to sustain a secular chaplain to celebrate daily at the Lady altar in the conventual church. If the chaplain acted *inhoneste* or *irregulariter* the prior would have discretion to remove and replace him.[56] Evidently Richard, of knightly status, had not the means to establish his own religious house; indeed, the major period of foundations of religious houses had largely passed, especially Austin Canon houses such as Thurgarton. His nearest approximation was to establish a cantarist inside his local religious house, but, perhaps recognizing the fallibility of the secular clergy, although the language employed might be a topos, to arrange for supervision of the cantarist's reputation.[57]

Many of the earliest chantries were established within religious houses or were supervised and regulated by the religious. Particularly was this the case for the earliest form of *cantarie*, the simple provision for "personal needs at private expense", by which "chantries" were merely an extension of anniversaries of deaths.[58] This development was influenced, perhaps, by at least two issues: first, the recognition of the rule that priests should not celebrate more than one mass each day might have re-directed *cantarie* away from the parish to religious houses which had a larger complement of priests in orders than the parish at that time; and second, the persistent suspicion of the secular clergy into the early thirteenth century diverted lay attraction to the professed religious.

Nevertheless, the arrangements were more complex. In some cases, the foundation of chantries in religious houses furnished no greater lay control over divine service or its order, since the provision of the liturgy remained in the hands of the religious. In some cases too, especially in earlier institutions, the provision of personnel was retained by the religious.[59] Even so, other foundations allowed the benefactors and their heirs to recruit or present to the house, thus removing from the religious house its own control over recruitment and selection of its own monks or canons.[60] In the later middle ages, the religious sometimes acted as supervisors of chantries, a role which may, in some cases, have developed out of their status as appropriators of parish churches.[61] Although the chantries were located within religious houses, some founders had a preference for the appointment of secular clergy to perform the duties of the office, so that, even with internal chantries, the role of the religious was still only supervisory.[62] Another point, which is intimated rather than elaborated by Wood-Legh, is that the coming of the mendicants subtracted the celebration of anniversaries from the religious, although by the later middle ages chantries were predominantly established either in a separate institution or within parish churches.[63] Related to all these points is the assertion that chantries did not effectively expand in numbers until the thirteenth century, although the problem of the sources is acknowledged.[64] There may then be some justification for re-examining the earlier foundations of chantries and proto-chantries in religious houses in the twelfth and thirteenth centuries, to establish more closely the nature and extent of their provision.[65]

Many of the earliest forms of *cantarie* are visible in donors' charters of the late twelfth century, even in small, newly founded houses. Several benefactors of the priory of Helaugh Park in its early years as an Augustinian priory in the late twelfth century, made gifts to support the canons, as cited below. By ca.1200, however, the religious had become involved in several different forms of chantry.

Thus in 1223x1232, Robert II de Vilers made a substantial benefaction to Thurgarton Priory of four bovates in Owthorpe for the maintenance of a canon of Thurgarton or a secular chaplain celebrating in Owthorpe church; when he relinquished this benefit shortly afterwards, the term *cantaria* was specifically employed.[66]

Such an arrangement illustrates directly the complicated questions of the relationship between regular canons–and, indeed, monks– and livings in their gift and the local pastoral role of the religious. In contrast, Richard III de Wyverton', knight, as well as electing for burial of his body at Thurgarton, in return for a toft, three bovates and two acres in Barnston and Wiverton, in 1252x1253 instituted a secular chaplain to celebrate divine service daily at the Lady altar in the conventual church, the priory's role to supervise the life of the chaplain.[67] In the London Aldgate in 1278, John son and heir of William Wylihale contributed three houses, shops, solars and cellars, a not insubstantial urban benefaction, to maintain three perpetual chaplains to celebrate mass for his soul in another house of Austin Canons, Holy Trinity, Aldgate.[68]

Another knight, William Sampson, transferred all his land to Thurgarton Priory in return for which the regular canons established an altar in their conventual church dedicated to Saint James, to whom William had previously made a vow.[69] Roger de Houton', of similar status, in 1218x1231 conveyed to the priory all his lands in Woodborough, consisting of one and a half bovates and three tofts with the three unfree tenants, for the augmentation of the daily Lady mass in the conventual church.[70] As Roger *filius Willelmi de Houton'*, he provided in 1218x1231 seven bovates in Hawton to Thurgarton to maintain a canon to celebrate the daily Lady mass in the conventual church for the souls of himself and his wife. Thurgarton thus benefited substantially by the foundation of early chantries and related arrangements by the local knightly families, perhaps to the detriment of parish churches, from which such benefactions might have detracted. In the later middle ages, chantry foundations of this kind were more frequently established within parish churches.

Dale Abbey (White Canons) benefited in particular from early arrangements for prototypes of chantries, which continued through the thirteenth century. One of the earliest provisions, about 1230, involved an association between a cleric, Hugh *decanus*, and Dale, by which Hugh conveyed to the house two bovates in Alvaston to maintain a canon to celebrate divine service in the conventual church.[71] Perhaps the implication here again is that there did not exist any *communitas* of the clergy and that the secular clergy themselves looked to religious houses in the thirteenth century for salvific purposes. Simon, a local rector, assigned the reversion of rents to Dunstable Priory for a chaplain for his anniversary for seven years, ca.1247, which perhaps confirms this reliance of the secular clergy on the regulars at this time.[72] Although Simon had the opportunity to select the secular cathedral chapter at Lincoln (the Commons), he sought an alternative solution, close to home, reflecting the problems of an enormous diocese like Lincoln.

About the same time, Simon son of Walter de Ver transferred fourteen bovates with the villein tenants in Little Hallam to provide for three canons at Dale to celebrate divine service as well as to improve hospitality in the house.[73] Shortly afterwards, Walter de S[n]eynton' furnished the house with four and a half bovates to maintain a canon to celebrate the Lady mass in perpetuity, in which the donor specified the order of the service (the collects), and a further four bovates to maintain another canon celebrating the office for the dead with special mention of Walter (1233x1253).[74] Another substantial benefaction ws received from Hugh fitzRalph who provided firstly ca.1250 eleven bovates to maintain a canon performing mass daily in the house and another two bovates, toft, seven acres and the unfree tenants to maintain another canon for the same purpose.[75] Two additional benefactions in 1272 completed the endowments for canons celebrating masses. Three bovates were provided by Sir Robert son of Walter de Stretleg', knight, to maintain one such canon (celebrating specifically for the soul of William de Dyve), whilst the other arrangement was slightly more complex.[76] At the instance of William *Juvenis* who paid Geoffrey Dethick fifty marks, Geoffrey alienated to Dale a tenement with its services and free and unfree tenants for the purposes of maintaining a canon at Dale to celebrate mass for William's soul.[77] Although a rather small house and founded rather late, Dale had thus attracted from the local knightly families an unusual degree of association through the support of canons celebrating mass in the conventual church. One of the implications is that at this social level there was as yet no permanent commitment to the parish church and salvation was sought elsewhere, through the efficacy of services of the religious rather than the secular clergy, even into the late thirteenth century in this part of Derbyshire and Nottinghamshire. Dale received substantial benefactions through this process. To some extent, knightly society focused on the abbey for local religious affiliation rather than on parish churches.[78]

As successful, perhaps, was the Priory of Helaugh Park, for it received superficially quite substantial benefactions to support chantries and *cantarie*. Whilst Theodore de Rieboc gave six bovates for the maintenance of a canon with no further defined purpose, William son of William *de Marisco* and his wife, in their endowment of five bovates and six tofts and crofts, required that the canon supported celebrate masses for their souls. A more considerable benefaction was provided by Walter de Percy, in the form of twelve and two-third bovates and a little wood, to support a canon to officiate at divine service. In contrast, Henry *Marescall* [sic] transferred to the priory only a rood of meadow in Tadcaster for a chaplain celebrating mass, although meadow was a valuable commodity.[79] Although the productivity of arable in some parts of the North continued to be low, the size of these benefactions remains impressive so that the maintenance of chantries by the priory attracted important accretions of land. If the canons were provided from within the existing complement of the house, the significance of these accumulations was even greater. Even more spectacularly, nearby Pontefract Priory acquired the entire vill of Barnsley in ca.1150 in return for providing monks for the donor, his sister and their mother, although the priory did also reciprocate with counter-gifts of ten marks to the donor's sister, three to the donor, and a palfrey and five marks to the donor's two sons.[80]

It was not only in houses of regular canons that such provisions were made, for John Lestrange, as late as 1269x1275, conveyed to Shrewsbury Abbey a mill, suits of mill, and land in Ruyton, so that a monk would celebrate divine service daily for the souls of the Lestranges.[81] Nor were the Cistercians more reluctant to have such contact with the laity, as Sibton Abbey, in 1246x1263, agreed to designate the services of one monk in their conventual church in return for the confirmation charter of Hugh II de Cressy acknowledging the benefactions not of Hugh and his predecessors, but of his tenantry.[82] It might appear here that the monks were keen to establish an association with the local laity of status. So also, the abbey made another arrangement in 1252 with another of the local knights, William III de Pirreho, receiving his body for burial in return for land and rents, but also providing a priest in their conventual church to celebrate mass for his soul.[83]

In a large number of these creations, the integrity of the religious house was perhaps not jeopardized, for no detail about the recruitment of the cantarists is specified, in which case the religious house may have selected the officiants. In some foundations of cantarists, nevertheless, presentation was made by the benefactor, as when Roger de Welton in 1215x1217 secured the right to provide a suitable postulant to celebrate obits for his father and grandfather in Daventry Priory, although the inclusion of the term "suitable" left some discretion with the house.[84] The Basset family was less flexible in its approach, illustrated by the agreement between Alan Basset and Lewes Priory that Alan, as a substantial benefactor of the house, and his heirs, could appoint one monk in perpetuity from 1209x1213.[85] Perhaps even more inimical, although accepted by the canons, was the arrangement conceded by Blackmore Priory to Gilbert Basset who, in 1221x1230, obtained the diversion of thirty acres previously given to the priory, towards the maintenance of a canon in memory of Gilbert's late nephew, Alan de Sanford', son of the priory's patron, John de Sanford. Not only did Gilbert reserve the right of presentation of the canon in perpetuity, but the canon was also to be designated the "Basset canon".[86] The canons thus abandoned some of their control over recruitment to the house.

In many instances, however, the house might have retained control over recruitment, for provision was implicitly made from within the existing complement of canons or monks. Thus Henry *Marescall* only requested Pontefract Priory to find (*ad inveniendum*) a chaplain to celebrate mass, understandable in the context of the slightly meagre nature of his gift of a rood of meadow.[87] The same house, in its arrangement with Ralph de Caprecuria and his sister, Beatrice, undertook to make (*quod facient*) one monk for their mother, one for Beatrice, and one for Ralph when the last two died, who were to pray for them by name. Despite the rule that priests should not celebrate mass more than once each day, it is possible that the resources were found within the conventual number.[88]

Occasionally, however, the acquisitiveness of the beneficiaries became evident, as when Missenden Abbey in 1180x1214 agreed to designate a canon in their church in perpetuity for the salvation of Hugh de Gurney and his *antecessores*, but Hugh's action simply consisted in a confirmation of his parents' benefaction of land in Broughton, whilst the canons were required to pay an annual rent of six marks.[89] It is thus entirely possible that some of these arrangements were, if not prejudicial in terms of recruitment, financially detrimental to the house.[90] What might thus have been more important to the house in such a situation was to attempt to maintain the relationship with the benefactor's family and, by extension, local lay society. That relationship in respect of chantries was maintained as well by local lay society in its apparent preference for chantries associated with religious houses before the later middle ages.

The complexity of the arrangements between parish and priory are demonstrated through the piety of Robert de Sumervyll' who, whilst transferring the advowson of Blackwell parish church to Thurgarton Priory sometime before 1173x1176, yet preferred for his body to be buried at the priory.[91] In many other cases, religious houses took advantage at the expense of the parish, particularly in the provision of services in private oratories or chapels. As late as 1284, Henry de Lacy, earl of Lincoln, enlisted Bradenstoke Priory to supervise his chantry by providing a chaplain to celebrate divine service in his chapel at his manor house at Canford, in perpetuity.[92]

At an earlier time and at lower social levels, the provision of chantries was bypassing the parochial clergy for the benefit of the regulars. In the late twelfth century, Jordan de Escotland' and his family were received into the full fraternity of Southwick Priory, with an anniversary for his father and mother, but equally importantly the regular canons of the priory undertook that, whenever Jordan was resident at Candover for three days in the week, they would celebrate divine service in his chapel there and when he was not resident, they would officiate just once a year.[93] The same canons entered into an agreement with Warin de Plaiz in 1189x1204. As well as receiving his body into the priory after his death and granting full fraternity and an anniversary, they also concurred in serving his chapel of Saint Andrew. Whenever Warin and his wife were resident, a canon of the priory was to celebrate divine service daily in the chapel, but the services were reduced to three days in the week during the absence of the couple.[94] Another house of Austin Canons, Dunstable Priory, engaged in the same process for Sir Alan de Hida and his wife, Alice. Although the priory agreed to inter Sir Alan at the priory, it also undertook to provide a chaplain, regular or secular, to minister in the chapel, the priory to furnish the stipend, Sir Alan to provide food. After the death of Alan and Alice, the chaplain was to celebrate masses at the priory.[95]

Bridlington Priory was involved in the same ambiguous relationship with donors and parish churches, as in this association with the prominent local family, the Constables. William *Nigelli* of that family transferred the advowson of a parish church to the priory in alms for the salvation of his wife's and children's souls, on condition that the parish church be served at least by one canon, for which he was received into the confraternity of the house, the canons to perform the services for him and his wife as a professed canon; it was merely a short step from this general provision of fraternity to a more specific *cantaria*.[96]

If regular canons were not ministering to the laity by instituting regular canons as priests to appropriated parish churches, they were certainly ministering to an influential sector of the local population, but through oratories and chapelries which were exemptions in the parochial structure. Important local notables were more attracted by the regulars than seculars for private ministry to them. It was only very much later that the local laity of this status re-directed its gaze and attention to parish churches as mausolea and chantries for personal salvation. The suggestion has also been advanced that the earliest foundations of chantries within the conventual church of a religious house were a substitute for those without the means to establish their own house.[97]

A stark contrast has been erected between the devotional community before the Reformation in England and religious and social conflict in the late sixteenth century, a transformation of homologous cultures. Late-medieval religion has been portrayed as a reconciling influence, overcoming the fragmentation and hierarchical divisions of society, restoring harmony to social relationships.[98] Taking a long perspective, some issues might be raised about this interpretation of medieval religion and it might help by considering the anterior history of some late-medieval devotional practices.

First, some people's relationship to Christ's body was qualitatively different and superior; they had a closer material relationship with the host in a separate and privileged environment. Second, the foundation of chantries in religious houses did not produce "an increase in divine service" for the generality of the "community", for the performance of the liturgy occurred in seclusion. Whilst it is true that any mass and office for the dead finally remembered all the dead, yet the purpose in this context was a combination of personal salvation through social honor, prestige, and, crudely, disposable income. Donors expected their salvation to be secured through the ministration of a separate, enclosed organization of professed religious rather than depending on the offices of a parochial, secular cleric and the "community" of the parish, in which case the latter must have been deemed inferior, possibly even less effective. By these means, donors were actually marking themselves off from the remainder of their local society for whom such actions were not achievable. Do we then have here (at least) two divergent theodicies, in one of which (immanence) the fortunate needed to confirm that their good fortune was deserved and legitimate?[99]

Notes

[1] *Charters ... Redvers Family*, 123 (no. 83).

[2] *Cartulary of St Augustine's, Bristol*, 87-8 (no. 144).

[3] For recent statements about gifts for specific purposes, Janet Burton, *The Monastic Order in Yorkshire 1069-1215* (Cambridge: Cambridge University Press, 1995), 210: "As the twelfth century progressed, however, benefactors seem to have been more self-confident in their freedom to specify a particular purpose"; and Benjamin Thompson, "Introduction: Monasteries and Medieval Society", in *Monasteries and Society in Medieval Britain*, ed. Benjamin Thompson, Harlaxton Medieval Studies, VI (Stamford: Paul Watkins, 1999), 13.

[4] For the relationship between the laity and religious houses in England at this time, the most recent discussions are: Emma Cownie, *Religious Patronage in Anglo-Norman England* (Woodbridge: Boydell, 1998) and Janet Burton, *Monastic and Religious Orders in England 1000-1300* (Cambridge: Cambridge University Press, 1994), the latter discussing all Orders, the former concentrating on the Benedictine religious houses founded before the Conquest. The concept of associative social bonds between laity and

religious, but before the importance of the parish, is advanced by Megan McLaughlin, *Consorting with Saints: Prayer for the Dead in Early Medieval France* (Ithaca, N.Y.: Cornell University Press, 1994).

[5] For the formation of local networks of knightly families around local religious houses, particularly those of the new Orders introduced into England in the twelfth century, C. J. Wales, "The Knight in Twelfth-century Lincolnshire", unpublished PhD thesis (University of Cambridge, 1983), 235-60. For the development of such knightly relationships at an earlier time and elsewhere, Constance M. Bouchard, *Sword, Miter and Cloister: The Nobility and the Church in Burgundy, 980-1198* (Ithaca, N.Y.: Cornell University Press, 1987)

[6] For pittances, lights, and burial, see the Chapters 2-3, 5.

[7] For the social relationships constituted around land: Barbara Rosenwein, *To be the Neighbor of St Peter: The Social Meaning of Cluny's Property 909-1049* (Ithaca, N.Y.: Cornell University Press, 1989); for a sociological exposition, A. Appadurai, ed., *The Social Life of Things: Commodities in Cultural Perspective* (Cambridge: Cambridge University Press, 1986). For the cost of giving, A. B. Weiner, *Inalienable Possessions: The Paradox of Keeping-while-Giving* (Berkeley, Calif.: University of California Press, 1992). For gift-exchange, there is the classic anthropological examination by Marcel Mauss, *The Gift: The Form and Reason for Exchange in Archaic Societies* trans. W. D. Halls (London: Routledge, 1990)–and here are two points worthy of emphasis: the prescriptive expectation of reciprocity, even demand for it, so that it becomes almost coercive or at least normative, and second, the possibility of competitive developments, as in the N. W. American potlatch. For recent discussions of gift-exchange in the present context, Patrick J. Geary, *Living with the Dead in the Middle Ages* (Ithaca, N.Y.: Cornell University Press, 1994) and Stephen D. White, *Custom, Kinship and Gifts to Saints: The* Laudatio Parentum *in Western France* (Chapel Hill, N.C.: University of North Carolina Press, 1988).

[8] The most recent and lucid examination of free alms is Benjamin Thompson, "Free Alms Tenure in the Twelfth Century", in *Anglo-Norman Studies XVI: Proceedings of the Battle Conference 1993*, ed. Marjorie Chibnall (Woodbridge: Boydell, 1994), 221-43.

[9] See above, Chapter 2.

[10] R. H. Snape, *English Monastic Finances* (Cambridge: Cambridge University Press, 1926); R. A. (Tony) L. Smith, "The *Regimen Scaccarii* in English Monasteries", in *Collected Papers of R. A. L. Smith* (London: Longmands, Green & Co., 1947), 54-73.

[11] Burton, *Monastic Order in Yorkshire*, 210.

[12] Attitudes to these institutional demands might, however, have been ambivalent: Emma Mason, "The Role of the English Parishioner, 1100-1500", *JEH* 27 (1976): 17-29.

¹³ Giles Constable, *Monastic Tithes from their Origins to the Twelfth Century* (Cambridge: Cambridge University Press, 1964); Brian Kemp, "Monastic Possession of Parish Churches in England in the Twelfth Century", *JEH* 31 (1980): 133-60; Christopher Harper-Bill, "The Struggle for Benefices in Twelfth-century East Anglia", in *Anglo-Norman Studies XI: Proceedings of the Battle Conference 1988*, ed. R. Allen Brown (Woodbridge: Boydell, 1989), 113-32; Brian Golding, *St Gilbert of Sempringham and the Gilbertine Order c.1130-c.1300* (Oxford: Oxford University Press, 1995), 353-91.

¹⁴ *Cartulary of Bushmead Priory*, 127-8 (nos. 138-9).

¹⁵ *Cartulary of Blyth Priory*, 194-5 (nos. 303, 305).

¹⁶ *Charters of the Redvers Family*, 203 (no. 39).

¹⁷ For a synoptic, but extended, treatment of these profound changes, Caroline Walker Bynum, *Holy Feast and Holy Fast: The Religious Significance of Food to Medieval Women* (Berkeley, Calif.: University of California Press, 1988 pb. ed.), 31-5, 48-69; Miri Rubin, *Corpus Christi: The Eucharist in Late Medieval Culture* (Oxford: Oxford University Press, 1991), 13-35 (quotation at 13).

¹⁸ Marion Gibbs and Jane Lang, *Bishops and Reform 1215-1272 with Special Reference to the Lateran Council of 1215* (Oxford: Oxford University Press, 1934), 95, 126; Martin Brett, *The English Church under Henry I* (Oxford: Oxford University Press, 1975), 219-21; Anne Williams, *The English and the Norman Conquest* (Woodbridge: Boydell, 1995), 199.

¹⁹ For the ritual precautions in preparing the host in a religious house, Rubin, *Corpus Christi*, 42.

²⁰ For some comments on the notion of a "great rebuilding" of minster and parochial churches between 1050 and 1150, John Blair, "I. Introduction: From Minster to Parish Church", in *Minsters and Parish Churches: The Local Church in Transition 950-1200*, ed. Blair (Oxford: Oxbow, 1988), 9-10.

²¹ For another context: "To be possessed of grain is to hold power; to bestow grain is to enact largesse on the model of divinity or nobility; ... As the seed of adornment grain visibly marks those persons blessed by abundance": A. G. Gold, "Grains of Truth: Shifting Hierarchies of Food and Grace in Three Rajasthani Tales", *History of Religions* 38 (1998): 156. For the "semiotic virtuosity" of some foodstuffs, because associated with elites, Appadurai, "Introduction: Commodities and the Politics of Value", in *The Social Life of Things: Commodities in Cultural Perspective*, ed. Appadurai (Cambridge: Cambridge University Press, 1986), 38; for the extreme symbolism of the host, Bynum, *Holy Feast and Holy Fast*.

²² *Cartulary of Darley Abbey*, II, 427, 448 (nos. I20, I53).

²³ *Cartulary of Darley Abbey*, II, 553 (L1).

²⁴ *Cartulary of Missenden Abbey Part III*, 50 (612).

²⁵ *Sibton Abbey Cartularies*, II, 175-6 (243).

[26] *Cartulary of Darley Abbey*, I, 41 (Axxxiii).

[27] "Charters ... Earldom of Hereford", 21-2 (18).

[28] *Cartulary of Shrewsbury Abbey*, I, 77 (83): *quatinus per illius sacrificii virtutem et per merita beati petri apostoli liberet deus animam meam de perpetue sitis angustia*.

[29] *Early Charters of Waltham Abbey*, 306-7 (448): *ad dominicum corpus et sanguinem conficiendum*.

[30] *Early Charters of Waltham Abbey*, 134 (210).

[31] For the holy loaf, see for example, the custom, perhaps a rota, for its provision in the parish of Chadshunt in 1248: *Magnum Registrum Album*, 85.

[32] Joseph Lynch, *The Medieval Church: A Brief History* (London: Longman, 1992), 282.

[33] *Westminster Abbey Charters*, 201 (355).

[34] Rubin, *Corpus Christi*, 42, 45.

[35] *Early Charters of Waltham Abbey*, 218-19 (327).

[36] *Cartulary of Daventry Priory*, 2-3 (5).

[37] *Rutland MSS IV*, 129.

[38] *Chartulary ... Pontefract*, 419, 424-5 (nos. 313, 321).

[39] For recent revisions of the meanings of the body, historically and contingently, Sarah Beckwith, *Christ's Body: Identity, Culture and Society in Late Medieval Writings* (London: Routledge, 1996), especially 26-7, 32, 35, 37-41; Sarah Kay and Miri Rubin, eds., *Framing Medieval Bodies* (Manchester: Manchester University Press, 1994). For a sociology of the body, Brian S. Turner, *The Body and Society*, 2d. ed. (London: Routledge, 1996). For some comments on the social divisions amongst the laity confirmed through the *practice* of the liturgy in late medieval England, John Craig, "Reformers, Conflict and Revisionism: The Reformation in Sixteenth-century Hadleigh", *Historical Journal* 42 (1992): 2-3.

[40] BL, Add. MS 40,008, fol. 30v.

[41] *Cartulary of Dale Abbey*, 77-8 (no. 60).

[42] BL, Add. MS 40,008, fols. 26r-v.

[43] Bodl., Top Yorks. MS c72, fol. 2r (Drax Priory): *Carta confirmacionis Fulconis Paganell' de ecclesiis de Drax et Calthorp' Sciant presentes et futuri quod ego Fulconneius Paynell' dedi concessi et hac presenti carta mea confirmaui deo et ecclesie beati Nicholai de Drax et canonicis ibidem deo seruientibus Ecclesias de Drax et Garthorp' cum omnibus pertinenciis et libertatibus suis quibus saysyt' erant prefate ecclesie* [sic] *quando hec carta facta fuit ...*

[44] *Thurgarton Cartulary*, 20-1, 43-4, 84-8, 106, 272, 386.

[45] Maurice W. Beresford and H. P. R. Finberg, *English Medieval Boroughs: A Handlist* (Newton Abbot: David & Charles, 1973), 190, for Drax as a borough before ca.1250.

⁴⁶ Bodl., Top Yorks. MS c 72, fols. 8r-33r. The diplomatics are expressed: *et precipue operi eiusdem ecclesie; ad fabricam eiusdem sancti Nicholai; precipue fabrice ecclesie eorundem; precipue operi eiusdem ecclesie;* and in similar style.

⁴⁷ Bodl., Top Yorks. MS c 72, fol. 15r.

⁴⁸ For example, Bodl., Top Yorks. MS c 72, fol. 17r. (Walter *filius Morgani de Draxburgh'*).

⁴⁹ *Cartularium ... Gyseburne,* I, 148-62: *Incipiunt Cartae Fabricae Ecclesiae Gyseburne.* The diplomatics were: *Deo et operi Ecclesiae S. Mariae de G.* or *Deo et fabrice.*

⁵⁰ Christopher R. Cheney, "Church-building in the Middle Ages", *Bulletin of the John Rylands Library* 34 (1951-2): 20-36.

⁵¹ *Charters ... St Bartholomew's,* 85-6 (no. 124)..

⁵² So compare Clive Burgess, "'For the Increase of Divine Service': Chantries in the Parish in Late Medieval Bristol", *JEH* 36 (1985): 48-65.

⁵³ *Cartulary of Dale Abbey,* 122 (no. 139). For a more detailed, but later (1357) specification of the liturgy by the founder of a chantry: *Cartulary ... Wakebridge Chantries,* 52-9 (no. 20).

⁵⁴ BL, Add. MS 40,008, fol. 44v.

⁵⁵ *Cartulary of Bushmead Priory,* 247-8 (no. 302).

⁵⁶ *Thurgarton Cartulary,* 342-3 (no. 561).

⁵⁷ The same concern for the probity of the celebrants is expressed in the *cantaria* established by Stephen Crauncewyk' in the hospital of Saint Giles, Beverley, which was supervised by Warter Priory: Bodl., Fairfax MS 9, fols. 75r-v.: *Ego Stephanus et heredes mei successiue alios present' quos Magister et fratres sine aliqua contradiccione et dilacione recipient qui mihi et heredibus meis inscriptis sacrosanctis fidelitatem facient quod predictum officium plenarie persoluent Si autem dicti Capellani in aliquo fuerint transgressi uel pro aliquo capitali crimine uocati facta eis ammouicione si incorrigibiles extiterunt licet dicto S. et heredibus suis eos amouere et alios in loco eorum constituere.* No doubt Stephen had in mind not only his own salvation, but, in association, the integrity and purity of divine service.

⁵⁸ Kathleen L. Wood-Legh, *Perpetual Chantries in Britain* (Cambridge: Cambridge University Press, 1965), 1-2, 4 (quotation), 8-9, 11, 37-8, 130-54.

⁵⁹ Wood-Legh, *Perpetual Chantries,* 11.

⁶⁰ Wood-Legh, *Perpetual Chantries,* 135.

⁶¹ For supervision of external chantries by religious houses, Wood-Legh, *Perpetual Chantries,* 139-43.

⁶² Wood-Legh, *Perpetual Chantries,* 138-40.

⁶³ Wood-Legh, *Perpetual Chantries,* 135.

⁶⁴ Wood-Legh, *Perpetual Chantries,* 5; the admission about the sources may be very pertinent, since Wood-Legh hardly considered cartularies

with earlier charters, but, for the earlier examples relied on episcopal registers.

[65] For chantries in Gilbertine houses, Golding, *St Gilbert of Sempringham*, 345-9.

[66] *Thurgarton Cartulary*, 373 (no. 601).

[67] *Thurgarton Cartulary*, 342-3 (no. 561).

[68] *Cartulary of Holy Trinity, Aldgate*, 107 no. (534).

[69] *Thurgarton Cartulary*, 6 (no. 5).

[70] *Thurgarton Cartulary*, 186 (no. 318).

[71] *Cartulary of Dale Abbey*, 118 (no. 131).

[72] *Digest of the Charters ... Dunstable*, 119 (no. 357). There was, nonetheless, an alternative recourse in *some* dioceses in which there was a secular cathedral chapter where chantries could be established: *Magnum Registrum Album*, 99 (no. 213) (1246); but the material is complicated throughout this register by the acquisition by purchases for chantries. In Norwich, at a later time, the clerical body was represented in the Corpus Christi Guild, a clerical organization: Norman Tanner, *The Church in Late Medieval Norwich 1370-1532* (Toronto: University of Toronto Press, 1984), 75-6. It has been demonstrated that by the late middle ages the concentration of clergy in some urban centers constituted a "clerical community": Martha Skeeters, *Community and Clergy: Bristol and the Reformation c.1530-c.1570* (Oxford: Oxford University Press, 1993), esp. 11-33.

[73] *Cartulary of Dale Abbey*, 333-4 (no. 491).

[74] *Cartulary of Dale Abbey*, 122 (no. 139).

[75] *Cartulary of Dale Abbey*, 322-3 (no. 489).

[76] *Cartulary of Dale Abbey*, 80-1 (no. 65).

[77] *Cartulary of Dale Abbey*, 186-7 (no. 246).

[78] For analogous connections through benefactions in free alms to religious houses in the twelfth century, Wales, "The Knight in Twelfth-century Lincolnshire", 235-60.

[79] *Chartulary ... Park of Helaugh*, 57-8, 90-1, 92, 202.

[80] *Chartulary ... Pontefract*, 468-9.

[81] *Cartulary of Shrewsbury Abbey*, I, 20-1 (no. 18).

[82] *Sibton Abbey Cartularies*, III, 14-15 (no. 485).

[83] *Sibton Abbey Cartularies*, II, 272 (no. 374).

[84] *Cartulary of Daventry Priory*, 158 (no. 494).

[85] *Basset Charters*, 149 (no. 218): *maximo benefactori nostro*, having given the advowson to Winterbourne Basset: 162-3 (nos. 239-40).

[86] *Basset Charters*, 167-8 (no. 248).

[87] *Chartulary ... Pontefract*, 202.

[88] *Chartulary ... Pontefract*, 468-9 (ca.1150).

[89] *Cartulary of Missenden Abbey Part III*, 14-15 (no. 558).

[90] Golding, *St Gilbert of Sempringham*, 349, refers to the problem of personnel and finance implicit in these arrangements, concluding that, in some cases, "the financial consequences [were] a gamble."

[91] *Thurgarton Cartulary*, 684 (no. 1150).

[92] *Cartulary of Bradenstoke*, 116-17 (nos. 368-9).

[93] *Cartularies of Southwick Priory*, II, 132 (no. III, 373).

[94] *Cartularies of Southwick Priory*, II, 141-2 (no. III, 394).

[95] *Digest of the Charters ... Dunstable*, 173 (no. 577).

[96] BL, Add. MS 40,008, fol. 132r.: *in elemosina pro anima uxoris mee Adeliz et pro me et liberis meis ea condicione ut ipsa ecclesia de Burch' ad minus ab uno deseruietur Canonico. Pro hac ergo elemosina recepi in capitulo eiusdem ecclesie sancte marie hanc fraternitatem ut ipsi Canonici qui modo sunt et qui futuri sunt pro me et pro uxore mea iam defuncta sicut pro canonico professo totum seruicium faceant et liberi mei commune beneficium habeant ...*

[97] Golding, *St Gilbert of Sempringham*, 348.

[98] For a recent re-statement of this interpretation of the late-medieval urban context in particular, Robert Tittler, *The Reformation and the Towns in England: Politics and Political Culture* (Oxford: Oxford University Press, 1998), 13-42; for a mild questioning of it, Craig, "Reformers, Conflict and Revisionism", 2-3.

[99] Malcolm Hamilton, *Sociology and the World's Religions* (London: Macmillan, 1998), 12-13.

5
Pittances and Pittancers

In their original intention, pittances comprised essentially commemoration through food and particularly commemoration through meals.[1] Consumption therefore remained in itself a form of production by adding symbolic value to the substance.[2] Whilst the commemorative meal might thus have served also "to link individuals to the wider social fabric through shared understandings of cultural conventions", it also structured time.[3] Pittances were thus another expression of the semiotic value of food through the form of its consumption, by demarcating time and marking out the consumers and the providers of the foodstuffs. The intention behind pittances had consisted in the associations structured around the foodstuffs, between people, and between people and liturgy. Nevertheless, the symbols were polyvalent, so that the meanings of pittances changed over time and were perceived at different times by different constituencies as having different values. The argument here will explore these different meanings of pittances, suggesting that it was only in the long thirteenth century that the meaning of pittances was anything like homologous.[4] To one extent or another and at one time or another, however, pittances exhibited some of the (unstable) cultural categories of a shared symbolic experience, status symbolism, gift-exchange, and the structuring of time.[5]

First, however, pittances must be defined for the purposes of this paper. Under consideration here are two forms of pittance in the experience of the religious: in the first place are pittances allowed by the religious Order or house on specified feast days, whilst the second form of pittance is that made in benefaction by the laity to a religious house for specific purposes. The first form of pittances consisted of additional dishes at mealtime allowed on holy days within the monastic calendar. More particularly, the second form–provided through benefactions by the laity–is important in the long thirteenth century because these small endowments reveal so much about the proclivities of some of the laity and its association with religious houses, despite and because of the minuscule size of the donations. Moreover, these pittances originating through benefactions by the laity represent an appropriation of the monastic liturgy by the laity in the twelfth, but more particularly the thirteenth century. To some extent, the pittancer was the obedientiary responsible for the management of these pittances, although, as shall be seen, the administration of the finances of religious houses through the system of assignment and offices induced great interference in pittances by other obedientiaries such as the cellarer and sacristan.

By comparison with the greatest offices, such as cellarer, the resources of the pittancer were insubstantial, which makes it paradoxical to place so much emphasis on the significance of pittances.[6] In the case of many Benedictine religious houses, the greatest office in religious houses pertained to the cellarer.[7] From a large Benedictine house, Malmesbury, there survives the cartulary of the pittancer, compiled in the second half of the thirteenth century.[8] The 197 charters relating to the pittancer's property are preceded by a list of the rental income of the office.[9] The pittancer received rents from seventy-nine properties in urban Malmesbury, the mean rent comprising 3s. 6d. and the median 2s. 6d.[10] The section for rents outside Malmesbury (*De Redditu forinseco*) included 13s. 8d. from Southampton, £1 from Minchinhampton, £1 11s. from the vicar of Kemble, and 2s. 6d. from the reeve of Kemble, but additonally 155 rents from rural properties for which the mean rent was 3s. 1d. and the median 2s.[11] The size of the assigned revenues of Malmesbury's pittancer was, however, unusual, and ordinarily the pittancer's income was significantly lower.[12] The account of the pittancer of Osney Abbey in ca.1280 attained a much lower level, comprising £7 in rents of assize and about £1 of miscellaneous income.[13] At Abingdon Abbey, the pittancer in 1322-3 acknowledged receipts of almost £18, but expenses which exceeded that amount.[14] During the fourteenth century, the pittancer of Worcester Cathedral Priory received income of between £74 and £112, although the principal function of the pittancer there was to administer the estates assigned to him rather than provide pittances.[15] At Saint Swithun's Priory, Winchester, the anniversarians, equivalent to the pittancer, recorded annual receipts of over £17 and expenses of over £18 in the years 1394-6; about £16 of the income derived from the lease of the manor of Bishopstone.[16]

From the late twelfth century, two general patterns are evident in benefactions to religious houses, the first of which is a relative decline in the general level of benefactions to the religious in terms of the amount being transferred into religious hands, and the second is a tendency amongst a small proportion of donors to make benefactions for specific purposes: for the provision of alms; burial in the conventual cemetery; *cantarie* within the religious house; and, in an inter-related manner, for anniversaries and pittances. The nature of gift-giving to religious houses was thus transformed. Whereas benefactions to the religious had previously been intended in free alms, that is for unspecified spiritual services–prayers of an undefined nature–and had predominantly consisted of alienations of land, from the late twelfth century that pattern was, in a very general fashion, traduced. Through the thirteenth century, a considerable proportion of gifts to the religious consisted of very small amounts of lands and, significantly, rents. Attached to some of these small benefactions were specific requests by the donor.

It is possible to explain, if only in part, the development of this change through internal financial arrangements within religious houses; they were partly inherent in the introduction of the assignment of revenues to obedientiaries. Inevitably, individual obedientiaries attempted to attract gifts to their offices and, indeed, probably engaged in the acquisition by purchase of these small receipts. A series of contemporary benefactions for a particular purpose might thus represent not only lay piety but also acquisitiveness or good management of a certain obedientiary. Such might have been the case when a flood of benefactions was made in Burghfield in the early thirteenth century to the almoner of Reading Abbey, only some of which were identifiable purchases.[17] The pittancer's cartulary for Malmesbury Abbey includes at least twenty purchases at a total cost exceeding £58.[18] Acquisitions of this nature were important for obedientiaries with limited resources like almoners, infirmarers and pittancers.

For religious houses overall, however, there was a significance to these multitudinous small acquisitions, deriving from a general context. As already mentioned, a general relative decline had occurred in the size of benefactions, concomitant with a reduction of benefactions from significant rural landholders. To some extent it was inevitable that smaller acquisitions would assume more significance. The context was thus a transformation from benefactions by significant actors of seigniorial status to acquisitions from donors of lesser status, down to the free peasantry for rural acquisitions.

Moreover, the context was even more significant, since for some religious houses the source of late-twelfth- and thirteenth-century acquisitions became importantly urban rather than rural. Another aspect of this general context was the increasing importance of the parish as the center of spiritual solace for the laity, if only the lesser laity, as it was enunciated by the Fourth Lateran Council of 1215, and subsequently disseminated in England by the Council of Oxford of 1222 and subsequent synodal decrees. It is, nonetheless, conceivable that the spiritualization of the laity–to employ Vauchez's term from an associated context–within the parish was simply affirmed by Fourth Lateran rather than initiated by it.[19] In contrast, the small benefactions to religious houses can be seen as a perpetuation of a previous pattern which continued to divert some resources, but more importantly some of the laity, from the parish as a center of spiritual devotion and salvation.

Behind these small benefactions, therefore, the intention of the lesser laity was to adopt a strategy for salvation previously reserved to the greater laity. For some of the lesser laity salvation through the parish and the sacramental clergy remained insufficient. Similarly, the expectation of the religious house might have been less the increment of resource–which was hardly significant in real terms and had obligations attached–but an association with the lesser laity at a time of changing patterns of devotion. On both sides, association was an important motive.[20]

For the lesser laity, then, gifts for pittances allowed a spiritual and salvific association with a religious house for an affordable outlay. In some cases, however, the benefits which were allowed to the lesser laity extended further, for pittances permitted flexibility in the expression of devotion through the invocation of the saint's day on which the pittance would be furnished. Flexibility of lay spiritual expression was thus another incentive for pittances to the religious. Yet another incentive was the acknowledgement of an immediate lineage through the orations of the religious house, for many pittances were to be made available on the anniversary of close affines, especially parents.

Superficially, pittances appear to be a very materialistic method of association with the religious and hardly spiritual; indeed, they were prohibited by the Cistercians because of the implication of simony, unless approved by the General Chapter.[21] In most cases, the charters simply record that the grantors provided a rent for the provision of a pittance–a special dish additional to the *generale* or service meal of the religious–on the anniversary of the grantor's death. In return, presumably, it was understood that the religious would incorporate the grantor in their prayers, but most frequently this requirement was never actually stated. Perhaps pittances should be conceived as similar to the lesser gifts which maintain social bonds but which do not impugn the honor of the giver.[22] By not demanding specific reciprocity, the small gifts of food prevented any dishonor and restored time to the "cycle of reciprocity"; the religious were allowed to compensate for the gift in their own time and at their own discretion. The counter-gift was both deferred and different.[23] The grantor of modest benefactions was thus not embarrassed, nor the recipients' honor impugned by the nature of grantor and grant.

Furthermore, although the amount was small, it was transmuted into something symbolically significant, for the rent was used to purchase special food, luxuries restricted to elites, with "semiotic virtuosity".[24] In most of the grants, the content of the pittance is not stated and was presumably left to the discretion of the religious house. At Westminster Abbey, pittances varied according to the liturgical status of the day, so that on major feast days, of which there were sixty to seventy per annum, pittances cost more than the basic dishes and comprised small birds, freshwater fish (especially pike), game and wine instead of ale. "Favourite choices" for pittances provided by special funds on special days consisted of salmon, pike and conger eel; large fish were thus associated with pittances and small fish with usual fare (generals or service meals).[25] This same distinction can be observed in pittances prescribed in the custumal of Bury Saint Edmunds Abbey in 1234.[26] The pittances provided by the sacristan on the feast of Reliquaries consisted of twenty-four pike, each twenty-two inches long with head and tail, and sixty small ones, but also three great pike for the abbot, prior and sacristan (one each). In addition, pike were supplemented by fifty starlings, thirty-six perch, thirty-six roach, sturgeon, bread, wine, ale and wafers.

> Fish consumption none the less continued to carry with it a series of cultural connotations which prevented it from being a truly "popular" food. Preserved fish suggested poverty and social subordination, while fresh fish called up images of wealth, but not an enviable wealth as fish *did not fill one up*; it was "light" food, intended for Lent, and one that could be fully appreciated only by those who did not have to deal with daily hunger.[27]

Montanari's suggestion then implies several points about pittances. Since they consisted of fresh fish, not coarse herring, pittances marked people off. Secondly, the nature of the pittances as a dish was light, not heavy. Partly, that characteristic was the result of the proscription of meat, but light dishes also allow intentions other than socialization.[28] Perhaps also can be elicited from the content of the dish that the purpose was not to replenish the body, which introduces the question of the theological and philosophical issues surrounding food and the body before the middle of the thirteenth century. At the discursive (scholastic) level, debate continued as to the inherent nature of the body in relation to food. In this discourse, food did not add substance to the body—food was not "assimilated"—because the body was an original and discrete organism for the purposes of the Resurrection and through the body's provenance from Adam. That innate character of the body could not be transformed by alimentation.[29] The purpose of pittances might then not have been merely to enable reflection through eating, but to structure ritual time to focus on meditation.

Despite their apparent extravagance at Westminster, however, the pittances furnished by the laity in small benefactions to other houses must have consisted of fare of much less quantity, if not quality. The description of the pittances at that enormous house, however, do assist in addressing a question about pittances for remembrance: why additional indulgence for commemoration? The answer may be that the foodstuffs involved in pittances were those associated with fast rather than feast days. Most fast days in the houses of most religious Orders prescribed not abstinence, but rather limitation, and defined the range of foodstuffs. The pittances consumed were probably fish rather than flesh, so that, although perhaps sumptuous, even lavish, in quality, the foodstuff was associated with fast rather than feast and was thus appropriate for commemoration.[30]

Pittances and small grants were not reserved exclusively to grantors of lower status, as some grantors of higher status indulged in this sort of provision. Thus, Roger Bigod, earl of Norfolk, furnished three marks of rent to Reading Abbey to be used in his lifetime for the repair of shrines and reliquaries before the high altar and after his death for his anniversary. Similarly, William d'Aubigny supplied a mark of rent to the same abbey for a pittance on the anniversary of the death of his uncle. Both these grants of the late twelfth century may have been unusual, however, since both were to a house with royal patronage and both involved grants of rents in places at some considerable remove from the house, as in Norfolk. The grants may thus reflect no more than a slender association between some of the higher nobility and a royal abbey.[31] The same character might be attributed to the pound of rent in London provided to Westminster Abbey by Geoffrey de Mandeville, by his style of earl of Essex, in 1140x1144, for the anniversary of his mother and for the use of the refectory, perhaps two related objectives.[32] A closer association was established by Miles Basset with Selby Abbey, for his body was buried there, but he and his wife Agnes also transferred thirty acres to the abbey for the celebration of mass on their anniversary when the cellarer was to provide a pittance to the convent of wine to the value of 5s.[33] Some of the later benefactions of the Redvers family to its house at Christchurch Priory transferred pittances, such as the salmon as a pittance offered at each of his own and his father's anniversary by Richard de Redvers, earl of Devon, in 1161.[34] More interestingly, the rent of 20s. directed from the fair of Christchurch for the house by William de Redvers, earl of Devon, in 1207x1212, included 6s. 8d. for a pittance on the anniversary of the countess Mabel with the specific exhortation *ad refectionem conventus ut devotius et affectuosius pro ea divinum agant officium*.[35] If, however, these benefactions for pittances were by and large prior and precedent, pittances as a salvific device were later appropriated by lesser laity for the same purpose as expressed in the pittance for the countess Mabel.[36]

Accordingly, the preponderance of grants for pittances comprised rather small amounts, like the rent of 3s. transferred by Emma de Lucy to Missenden Abbey in 1200x1230 to enable pittances on the obits of herself, her brother, Robert, and her lord, Serlo de Marci, specifically allowing 1s. for each pittance.[37] Rarely did the benefaction attain the size of the provision made by Thomas de Twyford to Missenden, conveying *Newmulne* and meadow for two pittances on the anniversaries of his father and mother, or the bovate in Hilton furnished by Henry *persona de Spondon' filius Willelmi de Spondon'* to Darley Abbey in the early thirteenth century for a pittance on his anniversary.[38] What the latter benefaction seems to suggest is, as well as the superior status of these two grantors, the desire of the secular clergy to have commemoration by the religious–in both these cases regular canons–rather than by their secular colleagues, indicating that there was as yet no *communitas* of the secular clergy, and this aspect is perhaps confirmed by the rent of 2s. granted to Darley for a pittance for the convent by Thomas *capellanus filius Simonis clerici* about the same time.[39] The 20s. rent granted by Hugh de Nevill to Waltham for pittances on the anniversaries of himself and his wife in 1224x1230 is explicable as the culmination of his gifts, previously of land, from which he now released the canons of the services except royal service.[40] More typical of the generality of grants for pittances was the rent of 2s. furnished in the early thirteenth century by Adam son of Guy de Cremplesham to Stoke by Clare Priory to provide pittances for the monks there on 23 December (the anniversary of his mother's death) and 22 July (that of Thomas *filius Radulphi*) or the rent of 6d. provided by Geoffrey Patin for another pittance.[41] Comparable grants for pittances to the same house included the 5s. of rent supplied by Richard *filius Simonis* in 1209x1232, 3s. of which was directed to be assigned for a pittance on the anniversary of his mother, an earlier grant of rent of 3s. by the same grantor in 1192x1209 for a pittance for his own anniversary, and a rent of 3s. for a pittance on the anniversary of another grantor's mother (after 1246).[42] Nearby Sibton Abbey, although a Cistercian house, received a rent of 5s. for a pittance on the grantor's anniversary (sometime in the 1220s).[43]

Grants by lay people for pittances for the convent of Thurgarton Priory consisted of a rather more disparate collection. Oliver Deyncourt, the successor of the founder, gave two bovates in 1241x1245 for conventual pittances, so that, although the *largesse* of the patronal family was diminished, the gift for pittances still represented some munificence for this type of benefaction. Another knight, Sir Robert III de Burstall, gave a toft and one bovate for the same purpose to the priory in 1250x1282. Quite large too was the rent of 5s. 6d. granted in 1242x1277 by Thomas de Belew for conventual pittances, as were rents of 6s. from properties in the borough of Nottingham. Only one of the grants for pittances for the convent at Thurgarton was insignificant, that conferring a rent of 1s. from property in the borough.[44] Such grants to the priory were thus of a higher order, two provided by knightly families, but perhaps as significantly these grants were received in the mid to late thirteenth century, between 1241 and 1282, considerably after the canonical requirements confirming the importance of the parish.

Equally adept at attracting pittances was Holy Trinity, Aldgate, and the importance of such endowments was heightened by the nature of its location, in an urban land market, in which rents and services were fragmented.[45] Characteristic transactions in such an environment consisted of rent services and quit rents. In such circumstances, burgesses could participate in the spiritual benefits of the house by making small grants of rents. The house was, however, extremely active in the urban land market, acquisitive for rents, and so it is difficult to know whether, on the regular canons' side, allowing pittances for rents was simply another device for attracting benefactions. Ernald son of Simon the Chaloner provided in 1222x1248 half a mark for pittances in the house on the morrow of Saint Edmund King and Martyr and another half mark for pittances on the anniversary of his death, but the pittance was to be observed during his lifetime on the feast of Saint Leodegarius which suggests that the laity had some initiative in and control over this kind of benefaction.[46] Generally, the levels of the benefactions for pittances seem to have been slightly higher in London, as Simon son of Robert Blund granted a rent of a mark for a pittance on his father's anniversary, William *camerarius* also a mark for the same on his anniversary, William de Mandavill 20s. for the same purpose on his father's and brother's anniversaries, and Thomas de Hauerhill another half mark for his own anniversary.[47] All of these grants for pittances were concentrated in the early thirteenth century, in the 1220s, about the time of the renewed emphasis on parochial conformity.

In the capital also, the nuns of Clerkenwell received benefactions for pittances on the anniversaries of the laity. In 1190x1206, Margaret, widow of Robert *filius Harding*', conveyed land for a pittance at Pentecost, whilst a decade later Matilda de Barrow assigned a rent of 10s. in St Alphege for the commemoration of her anniversary in the refectory.[48] About a dozen rents in all were received for the same purposes–pittances on the anniversaries of the laity–ranging from part of 2s. (which included not only a pittance but also a lamp) to 6s. 8d.[49]

In another urban context, Saint Augustine's, Bristol, was the beneficiary of a number of grants of pittances in the thirteenth century, particularly the first half of the century. The two brothers, Jordan and John *Leveske*, conveyed land in Bristol for the anniversary of their mother, Helen, to be celebrated on the feast of Saint James the Apostle, through the provision of wine for the canons.[50] At a more usual level, a rent of 2s. was committed for the anniversary of a husband and wife.[51] More informatively, the rent of 6s. 8d. from land in Redcliffe Street was furnished in 1240x1260 to the house by David Long, a member of a burgess family, for the purpose of an anniversary for his grandmother, especially for the provision of fish and wine.[52] In another urban context, Southampton, the priory of Saint Denys benefited from separate gifts and grants of 1½ acres of land and rents of 5s. and 1s. for pittances on anniversaries of nominated members of lay families in 1271x1289.[53] Many of these pittances were associated with houses of the new religious Orders which were urban foundations.

Perhaps the Benedictines were less concerned to attract such benefactions than houses of the new religious Orders, but the pittancer of Malmesbury was successful in this endeavor. All his buildings in the suburb of the town, consisting of at least six houses, were directed by Robert Paci to the house, two houses of which were specifically for an annual anniversary for him and his wife.[54] For a pittance for the same purpose, Thomas *le Serclur* and his wife Felicia Dungning transferred to the pittancer a burgage in the high street.[55] A more intimate association was initiated by Christine *la Rower'*, the sister of William *Rot'* chaplain *alias* William *le Rower'* chaplain, for she made a benefaction to Malmesbury of four houses and curtilages for a pittance on her anniversary every year by the direction of the pittancer. The extent of her interest in the house is reflected further in her request to be entered in the martyrology of the house and her further benefaction of two acres to the house in devotion to the rood in the abbey church.[56] Similarly, Henry *le Mareschal'* provided the abbey with a messuage and meadow in three charters for pittances, including his anniversary.[57]

Many of the grants for pittances appear to suggest an initiative by the lay grantors as much as a strategy by the religious house to attract smaller grants, such as urban rents. More complexity might, however, be involved, exemplified by the pittance provided by Alan Gemme at Daventry Priory, for he gave a tenement, a substantial benefaction for a pittance, for a second pittance on the feast of the Transfiguration in memory of Prior James who had instituted the observance of the feast in the priory.[58] Here, then, the initiative belonged to the prior in elevating a feast day and creating a pittance, and it is difficult to ascertain whether the donor's allegiance was primarily to the feast day or the house. What is clear, of course, is that pittances need not always be associated with anniversaries of the specified dead, although they most often were.

Other prelates were involved in establishing pittances, adding to the complexity of the practice. Robert, the first abbot of Malmesbury, assigned substantial amounts of money to the pittancer of the abbey for the weekly Lady Mass.[59] Abbot Robert's constitutions for the house had provided for a pittance of bread and wine, the two symbolic elements, on Saint Stephen's day.[60] Robert had also made provision for a pittance on his own anniversary to the expense of 6s. 8d., as had Robert the second abbot.[61] Abbot William de Culerne assigned substantial funds for the anniversary of his father and mother.⁶² The same abbot directed money for pittances at Christmas, whilst for the feast of Saint Catherine, Abbot John furnished a pittance of fish.⁶³ In similar manner, John *de Cancia*, abbot of Glastonbury, assigned the rents of *bacweremor* to the pittancer for the celebration of John's anniversary, each celebrant monk to receive wine and fish of sufficient portions up to a cost of ten marks.⁶⁴ The significance of these extensions of pittances may be in the inclusion of anniversaries of secular kin, so that prelates were themselves complicit in altering the nature of pittances.

Other heads of religious houses extended the number of feast days for pittances. At Winchcombe, Abbot Robert instituted a *caritas* of wine on Saint Margaret's Day and for the celebration of the Lady Mass on the morrow of Saint Kenelm, symbolising the joint dedication of the house, when geese were to be consumed unless it was a fast day.⁶⁵ At Worcester, Bishop John in 1196x1198 allowed the monks 17s. for a pittance on the feast of Saint Romanus and in 1236 the bishop provided three marks for a pittance on the anniversary of the death of King John.⁶⁶

Despite these different contexts, the profound importance of pittances was located in the twelfth, but more especially the thirteenth century, when the commemorative dish of the religious was appropriated by lay benefactors for their own remembrance. Before that time, pittances had principally been an integral part of the internal liturgical provisions of religious houses to commemorate feast days. Through small benefactions, the laity caused the association of pittances with the anniversaries of selected individuals and families of the laity. At this time, the appropriation of the monastic liturgy by the laity served to perpetuate the importance of religious houses. It was an interesting conjuncture, for this intensity of the association of some of the laity with the religious occurred at the time when the parish was intended to become the focus of lay devotion. In that sense, the continuity of lay benefaction to the religious through pittances can be construed as detraction from the parish. More than that, however, pittances represented an attempt by the lesser laity to obtain the spiritual benefits of the religious, a process which had previously been distant from them. In the nature of their minimal size and cost, benefactions for pittances brought within the realm of the lesser laity–most particularly burgesses and townspeople–an association with local religious houses. Pittances allowed some of the laity to mark themselves off from the rest. The thirteenth century might then have been the apogee of pittances and pittancers.[67]

Notes

[1] That "the meal" has been treated as an analytically distinct category with "a privileged analytical position", see Roy C. Wood, *The Sociology of the Meal* (Edinburgh: Edinburgh University Press, 1995), 47, 116. For an introduction to the theoretical positions on food and meals, Wood is especially helpful. For some of the symbolism of medieval foodstuffs, E. M. Biebel, "Pilgrims to Table: Food Consumption in Chaucer's Canterbury Tales", in *Food and Eating in Medieval Europe,* ed. Martha Carlin and Joel T. Rosenthal (London: Hambledon, 1998), 15-26.

[2] Jean Baudrillard, *Le Système des Objets* (Paris, 1968). How this might work through in an historical context is illustrated by Daniel Roche, *A History of Everyday Things: The Birth of Consumption in France, 1660-1800* (Cambridge: Cambridge University Press, 2000).

[3] Wood, *Sociology of the Meal*, 47.

[4] Only at that time can pittances be examined in the manner of Geertz's "thick description" by taking a single item of culture and from it, through a hermeneutic approach, producing an interpretation of a cultural milieu. At no other time was the culture of the pittance so uniform and synchronic. In the later middle ages, reception of meanings was affected by all those influences which Geertz allegedly did not take into account: power (conflict); diachrony (transformation); and fragmentation (more than heterology) of cultural values. For an evaluation of this critique of Geertz, see Sherri B. Ortner, "Introduction", in *The Fate of Culture: Geertz and Beyond,* ed. Ortner (Berkeley: University of California Press, 1999), 4-9 and William Sewell, "Geertz, Cultural Systems, and History: From Synchrony to Transformation", in *Fate of Culture*, 35-55. Here my argument includes transformation, for the relationship between laity and religious was transformed through appropriation of the commemorative meal by the laity, as in the conclusion below.

[5] For these categories and their instability, see Wood, *Sociology of the Meal*, 47. For a different, "developmental" approach, which has an historical agendum but which was informed by the work of Norbert Elias, see Stephen Mennell, *All Manners of Food: Eating and Taste in England and France from the Middle Ages to the Present* (London: WileyBlackwell, 1985);

for another approach, Jack Goody, *Cooking, Cuisine and Class: A Study in Comparative Sociology* (Cambridge: Cambridge University Press, 1982).

[6] The "system" is described by R. H. Snape, *English Monastic Finances* (Cambridge: Cambridge University Press, 1926), modified by R. A. L. (Tony) Smith, "The 'Regimen Scaccarii' in English Monasteries", in *Collected Papers of R. A. L. Smith*, ed. David Knowles (London: Longman, Green & Co ., 1947), 54-73. Houses of Austin Canons adopted a central reserve fund during the thirteenth century, examples of which are: *Cartulary of Cirencester Abbey*, I, xx-xxi; *Triennial Chapters ... Augustinian Canons*), 22-23; Cambridge University Library MS Dd xiv 2, fol. 128r (Osney Abbey): a payment made *per manus Bursariorum Oseney' qui pro tempore fuerint*.

[7] Compare the offices of cellarer and pittancer in the late middle ages at Saint Benet Holme. In 1511-12 the *officium pietanciarie* was held by Dom John Takylston', prior, whose receipts of £9 17s. 1½d. just exceeded his expenses: Bodl., MS Norfolk Roll 76. By contrast an incomplete cellarer's account of 1373 enumerates expenses exceeding £550, over £44 of which were spent on wine and spices and over £133 on fees and pensions, the last constituting the biggest item of the expense: Bodl., Norfolk Roll 71. For the pre-eminence of the cellarer at Battle Abbey, see *Cellarers' Rolls of Battle Abbey*, 10. Richard Britnell has pointed out to me that, for example, the principal obedientiary at Durham was the bursar.

[8] Bodl., Bodl. MS 191 (iii + 197 leaves).

[9] Bodl., Bodl. MS 191, fols. 2v-11r.

[10] Trimmed mean 3s. 1d.; standard deviation 42.38; minimum 1d.; maximum 16s.; first quartile 7d.; third quartile 5s.

[11] Trimmed mean = 2s. 9d.; standard deviation = 39.43; minimum = 1d.; maximum = 31s.; first quartile = 1s. 6d.; third quartile = 4s. There was some concentration of the rents: 1s. (15 receipts); 1s. 6d. (17); 2s. (25); 4s. (12); and 5s. (18).

[12] The pittancer's cartulary of Fountains Abbey (Bodl., Rawl. MS 449) provides little information about the actual pittances since it consisted of charters of benefactions assigned by the house to the pittancer: *Incipit Compilatio Cartarum Prioris et Conuentus specialiter ad pitanciam dicti Conuentus dat'* (fol. 14r.)

[13] *Cartulary of Oseney Abbey*, VI, 191.

[14] *Accounts ... Obedientiars of Abingdon Abbey*, 1-3.

[15] *Compotus Roll ... Worcester*, 31-40; *Early Compotus Rolls ... of Worcester*, 54-70.

[16] *Compotus Rolls ... Winchester*, 201-7.

[17] *Reading Abbey Cartularies*, II, 41-55 (nos. 710-44).

[18] Bodl., Bodl. MS 191.

[19] André Vauchez, *Sainthood in the Later Middle Ages*, trans. Jean Birrell (Cambridge: Cambridge University Press, 1997), 530-4.

[20] This tradition of association was established much earlier and is best summarized in Megan McLaughlin, *Consorting with Saints: Prayer for the Dead in Early Medieval France* (Ithaca, N.Y.: Cornell University Press, 1994).

[21] Brian Golding, *St Gilbert of Sempringham and the Gilbertine Order c.1130-c.1300* (Oxford: Oxford University Press, 1995), 342-5, especially 343. Compare the pittancer's cartulary of Fountains Abbey: *Carta Ricardi de Percy data Conuentui de Font' specialiter ad pitanciam continens scilicet villam vallem et forestam de Littona*; and the next line: *Confirmacio Abbatis Cist' et tocius Capituli generalis de predicta donacione ad pit'* (Bodl., Rawl. MS 449, fol. 14r). The size of the benefaction for this pittance might have induced this need for corroboration, for the smaller benefaction by Gregory de Flayneburg' of a rent of 1s. *ad pitanciam conuentus* (fol. 18r.) did not receive any comment.

[22] Pierre Bourdieu, *The Logic of Practice*, trans. Richard Nice (Oxford: Blackwell, 1990), 99.

[23] Bourdieu, *Logic of Practice*, 105; Marcel Mauss, *The Gift: The Form and Reason for Exchange in Archaic Societies*, trans. W. D. Halls (London: Routledge, 1990), 59 (gifts of food to Brahmins).

[24] Arjun Appadurai, "Introduction: Commodities and the Politics of Value", in *The Social Life of Things: Commodities in Cultural Perspective*, ed. Appadurai (Cambridge: Cambridge University Press, 1986), 38.

[25] Barbara F. Harvey, *Living and Dying in England 1100-1540: The Monastic Experience* (Oxford: Oxford University Press, 1993), 43-4, 47-50.

[26] *Customary ... Bury St Edmunds*, 54-5.

[27] Massimo Montanari, *The Culture of Food*, trans. C. Ipsen (Oxford: WileyBlackwell, 1996), 82.

[28] An anachronistic comparison would be the heavy family dinner which, at least until recently, structured the family and family time, with the heaviest meal occurring on Sundays to enhance family cohesion.

[29] P. L. Reynolds, *Food and the Body: Some Peculiar Questions in High Medieval Theology* (Leiden: Brill, 1999).

[30] Caroline Walker Bynum, *Holy Feast and Holy Fast: The Religious Significance of Food to Medieval Women* (Berkeley, Calif.: University of California Press, 1987), 31-69, especially 41-2.

[31] *Reading Abbey Cartularies*, I, 221, 369 (nos. 263, 482, 1186x1198).

[32] *Westminster Abbey Charters*, 197 (no. 350).

[33] *Coucher Book of Selby Abbey*, I, 211-12, 240 (nos. 311, 313, 379).

[34] *Charters of the Redvers Family*, 95 (no. 49).

[35] *Charters of the Redvers Family*, 138 (no. 102).

[36] Some benefactions from the laity of higher status were late. A large donation by John Arundel, lord of Sandford Arundel, to Canonsleigh

Priory in 1255x1260 included the rent from a mill for a pittance on the feast of the Invention of the Holy Cross for the souls of his parents and his son, John. It comprised only one of several benefactions by Arundel to the house: *Cartulary of Canonsleigh Abbey*, 44-5.

[37] *Cartulary of Missenden Abbey*, III, 162 (no. 781).

[38] *Cartulary of Missenden Abbey*, III, 75-6 (no. 655); *Cartulary of Darley Abbey*, I, 282 (no. F95).

[39] *Cartulary of Darley Abbey*, II, 360 (no. H32).

[40] *Early Charters of Waltham Abbey*, 142-3 (no. 221).

[41] *Stoke by Clare Cartulary*, II, 380-1 (nos. 590-1).

[42] *Stoke by Clare Cartulary*, II, 368, 370, 378 (nos. 573, 576, 587).

[43] *Sibton Abbey Cartularies*, II, 115 (no. 146).

[44] *Thurgarton Cartulary*, 82, 106, 289, 304, 306, 393 (nos. 129, 169, 489, 507, 510, 649).

[45] Nicola Coldstream commented that it is possible that pittances were cementing a relationship since urban laity frequented religious houses in urban centres and might have left the pittance after their departure.

[46] *Cartulary of Holy Trinity, Aldgate*, 74 (no. 380).

[47] *Cartulary of Holy Trinity, Aldgate*, 90, 109, 137, 210 (nos. 449, 546, 701, 1028).

[48] *Cartulary of St Mary Clerkenwell*, 104-5, 168.

[49] *Cartulary of St Mary Clerkenwell*, 178-9, 183, 207-8, 212-14, 220, 229, 233. Miri Rubin very importantly raised here the question of the extent of grants of pittances to the female religious in the context of the *perceived* administration of their estates and, more significantly, their need to have a priest to conduct their liturgy.

[50] *Cartulary of St Augustine's Abbey, Bristol*, 304 (no. 480).

[51] *Cartulary of St Augustine's, Bristol*, 330 (no. 520); other small benefactions for anniversaries are at 318, 330 (nos. 502, 519).

[52] *Cartulary of St Augustine's, Bristol*, 358 (no. 561).

[53] *Cartulary of St Denys*, 84, 99, 128 (nos. 145, 171, 221). In the late twelfth century, a rent was conveyed for a pittance: 280 (no. 506).

[54] ... *specialiter assignentur ad Anniuersarium meum et Mabilie uxoris mee annuatim in conuentu imperpetuum faciendum*: Bodl., Bodl. MS 191, fol. 29r.

[55] ... *ad pietanciam eisdem die anniuersarii annuali* [sic] *faciendum*: Bodl., Bodl. MS 191, fol. 38v.

[56] One charter specified *ad pietanciam faciendam dicto Conuentui die Anniuersarii mei per manus pitantiarii qui pro tempore fuerit* and *quod cum dies obitus mei uenerit nomen meum eorum martillagio sit scriptum et annuatim secundum morem eorum recitatum Concesserunt et mihi commune beneficium domus eorum et anniuersarium meum in toto conuentu annuatim faciendum;*

a second charter exhibits a devotion to the rood: Bodl., Bodl. MS 191, fol. 49r-v.

[57] ... *ad pitanciam eorum ... ad faciendum anniuersarium meum solempniter singulis annis in pleno conuentu Malm'; ... ad eorum pitantiam pro anniuersario meo annuatim in conuentu solempniter faciendo; ... ad eorum pytantium ... ad emendacionem pytantie eorum*: Bodl., Bodl. MS 191, fols. 68v.-70v.

[58] *Cartulary of Daventry Priory*, 100-1 (no. 329, ca.1217).

[59] ... *ad memoriam faciendam de sancta maria qualibet ebdomada solempniter*: Bodl., Bodl. MS 191, fol. 11r.

[60] *Memorandum quod sacrista die sancti stephani martiris inueniet pitanciam panis et vini de obedientia sua secundum constitucionem Roberti primi abbatis*: Bodl., Bodl. MS 191, fol. 5v.

[61] Bodl., Bodl. MS 191, fol. 5v.

[62] Bodl., Bodl. MS 191, fols. 11r, 12v.

[63] Bodl., Bodl. MS 191, fols. 11v-12r.

[64] ... *pro celebratione sui anniuersarii; unam caritatem boni vini; unum ferculum boni Piscis; per competentes porciones*: Bodl., MS Wood empt. 1, fols 258r-v.

[65] *Landboc ... Winchelcumba*, 167, 242-4.

[66] *Cartulary ... Worcester*, 121, 177 (nos. 229, 332).

[67] One, but not the only, reason for this chronology, might have been a change of allegiance to the mendicants in urban places, a point made to me by Henry Summerson.

6
The Austin Canons in English Towns, ca.1100-1350

The idea of the English medieval town or borough dominated by a religious or ecclesiastical institution is now a familiar one. Indeed, many of these towns and boroughs may have originally developed around and because of the ecclesiastical center. N. M. Trenholme was perhaps the first to offer a wider examination of "monastic boroughs", although Mary Lobel's discussion of a single "monastic borough" at Bury Saint Edmunds is a remarkable piece of work.[1] The relationship between Durham cathedral priory and its borough in the fifteenth century was elucidated by Barrie Dobson, whilst Margaret Bonney more recently elaborated on their co-existence over a longer temporal span.[2] We know so much about twelfth-century Canterbury because of the domination of the borough by the cathedral priory.[3] The role of the Church–that is, the great ecclesiastical institutions–in the towns is currently the theme of broad-ranging research emanating from Birmingham and Oxford.[4] What these studies have in common is that they concentrate on the relationship between the largest ecclesiastical institutions–usually cathedral chapters or older Benedictine houses–and their boroughs, whether boroughs with royal charters or seigniorial boroughs. The power of these ecclesiastical authorities was more or less monolithic within the urban precinct.[5] Recently, moreover, there has been a challenge to Trenholme's original thesis that conflict was necessarily engendered in mesne boroughs. Trenholme had suggested that the restrictions imposed by monastic overlordship became inherently unpalatable to the developing commonality of the burgesses, necessitating conflict. Two very recent studies have suggested, by contrast, that conflict was not inevitable, but co-existence was possible, in the two very different communities which were studied–Westminster and Durham.[6] A new question has therefore been raised: conflict or harmony?

There is another aspect to the role of the Church in the towns. Some towns contained a plurality of religious houses, often of several different Orders. Others were effectively mediatized, but under the authority of a lesser religious house–lesser than the old, large Benedictine houses. In both situations, the Austin Canons were frequently implicated and involved. For example, of the twenty-five monastic boroughs identified by Trenholme, five were controlled by houses of Austin Canons–Bodmin, Cirencester, Dunstable, Hexham and Plympton (Plymouth or Sutton Prior)–and the rest mainly by the Black Monks.[7] All five of these houses of Austin Canons were founded before 1135, in the first phase of foundations of the Order in England.

The suggestions which will be advanced here are as follows: that the involvement of the Austin Canons in English boroughs and towns was an integral part of the original objectives of the Order; and that the first wave of houses of the Order (ca.1100-35) was directed towards towns in southern England. Despite the subsequent withdrawal of several of these houses from the towns, the Austin Canons became inevitably embroiled in conflict with the burgesses on several fronts. These fronts were: constitutional, where the mesne borough was controlled by the Austin Canons; economic, relating to the interest of the houses in urban property and personal tithes; and spiritual, in the sense that the houses controlled urban parish churches. Concentration is therefore on the character of the Order between 1100 and 1135, and the subsequent legacy to ca.1350.[8]

The reason for the involvement of the Black Canons in the towns lies in their origins. The Order was directed at the Lateran Councils of 1059 and 1063 specifically to be a proselytizing Order.[9] By the early twelfth century most colleges of secular canons were largely unreformed, living without a strict rule. The enlarged rule of Chrodegang (and, to a lesser extent, that of Aachen) had been observed sporadically in English cathedral chapters, but had become neglected by the late eleventh and twelfth centuries as territorial prebends developed. Marriage and hereditary prebends persisted.

At a lower level, minster churches continued to have a "collaborative" or communal element, particularly in serving local churches, but it too declined after 1100. Although there was a brief period of patronage of secular minsters–especially castle-chapels–by the Anglo-Norman aristocracy in the late eleventh century, their patronage was short-lived.[10] The ministry of the secular canons thus evoked some criticism from the reform movement. During the later eleventh century, the Austin Canons became established predominantly in urban centres of some (but not all) regions of "France", particularly in cathedral chapters.[11] It was also in the towns that the first wave of Austin Canons settled in England.

It is necessary to distinguish between the north of England and the south–basically delineated by a line from the River Trent at Nottingham eastwards to the Wash and westwards to the Welsh border (but including Darley Abbey by Derby). Most of the earliest houses–those before 1135–were established south of the Trent. These houses had a high level of association with towns and boroughs. Foundations in the north were fewer, especially before 1135. Those houses which were established in the north–both before 1135 and after–had a predominantly rural and contemplative character. There was therefore not only a chronological distinction, but also a geographical difference in the nature of foundations.

The first wave of houses of the Order in England was therefore very closely associated with the towns and boroughs. Before pursuing the Austin Canons in the towns, it might be helpful to review some of the overall characteristics of all the foundations of houses of the Order in England. The first foundations occurred at indeterminate date, perhaps at the very end of the eleventh century, or in the first decade of the twelfth, at Saint Mary's, Huntingdon, Saint Botolph's, Colchester, and Saint Gregory's, Canterbury. The first major wave of foundations, however, occurred during the reign of Henry I (1100-35). Many of the foundations were associated with the *curiales* of Henry and, indeed, with the king himself–although all these benefactors were involved with houses of other Orders to guarantee spiritual insurance.[12] Whilst the principal characteristic of the first wave was their association with the towns, subsequent foundations were largely rural, characterized by very slender endowments, comprising mainly glebe-demesnes and spiritual property.[13] Overall, the houses of the Order were small, rural houses with inadequate estates, some of which were dissolved during the later middle ages because of their insolvency.[14] The overall nature of the houses of the Order, however, has tended to obscure the predominant association of the first houses with English towns and boroughs.

The association was natural given the objectives set out for the Order. The obvious location for missionary work in the twelfth century was in the rapidly expanding towns and boroughs of England. Moreover, many of the colleges of secular canons had already evolved in towns and around castles. The initial settlement of the new Order was thus predominantly in the towns at the expense of the established communities of secular canons. This characteristic is reflected in Table 3, which documents the characteristics of the first houses of Austin Canons established in England before 1135. Most were founded in or adjacent to places which exhibited some form of urban characteristic, although not all were chartered boroughs. This advance guard was, however, small in number and short on enthusiasm for the job in hand. Some houses quickly retreated to the contemplative life in the countryside, away from the towns.

In 1191, the burgesses of Oxford acted communally in placing their common seal to a charter, one of the earliest of any English borough. The burgesses had no formal corporate identity, but came together informally and organically in this particular negotiation. These events are known from the cartulary and charters of Osney Abbey, with whom the burgesses had negotiated. Sixty-three burgesses witnessed the charter, to which the common seal was appended. An earlier dispute among the burgesses, Saint Frideswide's, and Osney over the island of Medley, in 1147, also revealed the incipient communal organization of the burgesses. In the late twelfth century, the community of the burgesses became involved in litigation with Saint Frideswide's over that house's fairs and property in Medley. It is in these reactions to the two houses of Austin Canons with an interest in the borough, that the first glimpses are allowed of the burgesses organizing organically as a community in the late twelfth century, before the grant of the fee-farm placed communal organization on a more formal footing.[15]

Saint Frideswide's had a long existence in Oxford as a college of secular canons, but was re-founded by Henry I in 1122 as a house of Austin Canons. The thesis has recently been ventured that Saint Frideswide's pre-dated the town of Oxford. The minster of Saint Fridewide's may have been erected at important routeways, and the rectilinear burgh of Oxford laid out *de novo* around the minster. By the eleventh century, there were three minster churches in Oxford– Saint Peter's and Saint Michael's as well as Saint Frideswide's–but the last may have held precedence. The other, parish churches in the town proliferated only after 1050. After a period when the minster was in the possession of Abingdon Abbey, the secular canons were reinstalled in 1049. On this evidence, Saint Frideswide's was extremely important in the genesis of the borough.[16]

Osney was founded in 1129 as a priory of Austin Canons by Robert II d'Oilly, through the intercession of his wife, Edith Forne, a former concubine of Henry I. Robert, although of baronial descent and not a new man of Henry, had strong connections with the *curia*. The first tenant in chief of the barony, Robert I, had become patron of the secular college of Saint George in the Castle, when the castle was erected in 1074, although it seems likely that the college had an earlier existence. The college had been substantially responsible for the spiritual life of Oxford: some of the archdeacons were prebendaries. In 1149, the college was appropriated to Osney.[17]

A consistent pattern thus emerges. Oxford had been served spiritually not only by its numerous parish churches, but also by two colleges of secular canons, located within the walls. The two colleges were effectively replaced by houses of Austin Canons in the reign of Henry I, through a connection with the royal *curia*. Although one of the re-foundations–Saint Frideswide's–was intramural, Osney was established outside the walls. Both new houses then proceeded, by and large, to ignore the spiritual needs of the borough, although the Order had originally been charged with the mission in the boroughs. It was only when the friars re-entered the burghal community and physically stayed in the urban precinct that the missionary work in the town was effectively established.

Some wider patterns can be elicited from the example of Oxford. The first is the pattern of involvement of these houses with the borough. The second is the timing of the advent of the houses to the borough. The timing is particularly important. The Austin Canons came to the boroughs at precisely the time when the communal aspirations of the burgesses were developing in quite a pronounced way. During the late twelfth century, the burgesses increasingly acted and thought as an informal corporate community. Their relationship with the houses often involved the nascent communal identity of the burgesses.

Returning to the first theme, several other houses of Austin Canons in the original nucleus exhibited the same pattern–appropriating an intra-mural college of secular canons, ostensibly for a more effective ministry, but then migrating outside the walls of the borough. Only a small number of houses actually remained inside the town–such as Cirencester and Saint Frideswide's. At Derby, Austin Canons were first established in the chapel or oratory of Saint Helen's, on the fringe of the borough, possibly about 1137. By the eleven-fifties, the house had migrated outside the borough to Darley.[18] In 1092, the Black Canons had been abortively established in the chapel of Saint Giles in Cambridge, but in 1112 the house was re-founded outside the borough at Barnwell.[19] Newnham Priory had originally been sited inside the borough of Bedford.[20]

The origins of Southwick Priory lay in Portchester, where the house had been originally founded in the eleven-twenties. The initial site was adjacent to the castle, within the old Roman walls. By 1150, the house had moved to Southwick, allegedly because of the restrictive conditions in the precinct in Portchester. The urban association of the house did not end in 1150, however, as the house was closely involved in the development of the new town of Portsmouth from the end of the twelfth century.[21] Saint Augustine's, Bristol, was founded after the first wave of houses, probably about 1148. The first settlement was at Saint Augustine the Less, in the borough. When the house expanded, and became an abbey, it moved from these cramped quarters to a new site on the fringe of the borough. It has recently been suggested that the site of Saint Augustine the Less had a long association with a religious place–a *locus* or stow. Indeed, the place-name *-stow* in Bristol may relate to this site, although there was only a cemetery there.[22] When Llanthony II was founded in 1135, the site was located outside the borough of Gloucester at Hyde.[23] One of the earliest convents, established at Saint Mary's, Huntingdon, soon also migrated outside the walls.[24]

Derek Keene has pointed out that there is nothing unusual about religious houses being founded in the suburbs of towns from the twelfth century. By that time, the urban centre was already crowded, not conducive to religious houses, nor even to new parish churches. By contrast, the suburbs were already developing rapidly, although still containing large, open spaces.[25] The re-planting of these houses of Austin Canons outside the borough was possibly sensible on these terms. Saint Frideswide's was pressed hard up against the walls of Oxford. In terms of the original mission of the Order, however, the re-location outside the walls was not auspicious, and in some cases quite inappropriate. The re-foundation of Portchester–from a possibly constricting site–at Southwick was several miles distant from the town; Darley was a similar distance from Derby. To some extent, the site of re-foundation depended on the size and geographical distribution of endowments of each house. Nevertheless, moves of such distance were symbolically an impediment to the mission in the towns.

Other houses were actually founded outside the walls, but appropriated colleges of secular canons inside the borough. Osney belonged to this category, as above. Leicester Abbey is another example, founded outside the walls of the borough by Robert, earl of Leicester in ca.1138-39.[26] The house had, however, an original endowment largely based on the appropriation of the college of secular canons at Saint Mary de Castro, another castle-chapel (comprising a dean and twelve canons), which had been founded in the borough in 1107 by Robert's father, Robert de Meulan.[27]

By and large, Austin Canons did not become established in the highest ranking boroughs within the urban hierarchy. There the Benedictine cathedral priories and monasteries mainly continued as the dominant force. Although many minsters and colleges of secular canons succumbed to the Austin Canons, the secular cathedral chapters continued in existence in, for example, Lincoln, York, Exeter, Salisbury, Chichester, Wells, Lichfield and London.[28] The Austin Canons made little headway in these diocesan urban centres. Carlisle, of course, was the exception, a new foundation with a cathedral chapter of Austin Canons. Few of the first wave of houses were thus established in cathedral cities, except for Saint Gregory in Canterbury and Aldgate in London.[29] Failure to become established in these centers may have partly ensued from the pattern of benefactions: the laity there may have continued to patronize the cathedrals and parish churches rather than new religious houses.

The first wave of foundations was thus concentrated in some of the county towns of southern England, such as Oxford, Cambridge, Huntingdon, Derby, Taunton and Colchester. Secondly, they became established in some of those places which Professor Everitt has designated "primary towns", which were expanding organically in the early twelfth century–such as Dunstable and Cirencester, which became, to all intents and purposes, monastic boroughs.[30] Thirdly, the early houses were established in places which probably had by this time some urban characteristics, and where a convenient and inexpensive convent could be endowed by the appropriation of an existing college of secular canons. These colleges and minsters may indeed have been partly responsible for the urban characteristics, at such centres as Plympton.

Another aspect of this urban connection is the colonization of several of these urban convents from Holy Trinity, Aldgate, the premier of houses of Austin Canons dependent on urban siting and economy. Thus, Bishop Warelwast of Exeter invited Aldgate to be instrumental in the re-foundation of the colleges of secular canons at Plympton and Launceston as houses of regular canons in 1121 and 1127. Henry I similarly used Aldgate for his foundation and re-foundation respectively at Dunstable and Saint Frideswide's.[31]

The ultimate effect was that these houses became significant economically and jurisdictionally within the borough, without, in many cases, being part of it. Several spheres of interaction and, in some cases, conflict, were thus occasioned between burgesses and canons. In some boroughs, there was a jurisdictional conflict, in those monastic boroughs such as Dunstable and Cirencester. Secondly, all these houses of Austin Canons acquired significant burgage property, and thus had an interventionist role in the urban land market, and consequently came into direct conflict with burgesses and borough.

The second point can be illustrated by the example of Darley Abbey.[32] Darley's first acquisitions of property were concentrated in the borough of Derby. According to R. R. Darlington, burgage tenure *stricto sensu*–that is, as defined by Hemmeon–did not exist in Derby, where tenure of land, with some feudal incidents, resembled more pure feefarm: reliefs and fealty had to be proffered and performed and land was often held *in feudo et hereditate*.[33] To this extent, the urban land market was already different from that in other boroughs. It was further compromised by the control which Darley exercised over its own burgage property. Firstly, Darley introduced restraint on alienation. Covenants with this restriction appeared in grants by Darley from 1200, although sporadically. Thus, when Abbot Walter granted to Robert son of Richard de Sallowe a toft and shop in Derby in ca.1200, the grantee was not allowed to alienate without the prior consent of the abbot.[34] Abbot Henry (1214-37) made at least two other agreements which contained this restraint on alienation. This restrictive covenant was consistently applied in all the grants by Abbot Ralph (1233-48) and by all subsequent abbots in the thirteenth century.

A second covenant, however, was also inserted in the grants of burgage property. This clause appeared initially ca.1200, although inconsistently until the third decade of the thirteenth century. The abbey insisted on the right of pre-emption, should the grantee wish to sell. This covenant first occurred in the same grant to Robert son of Richard de Sallowe. The abbey's pre-emption was to include a remission or discount stipulated in advance in the covenant. Thus, in the grant to de Sallowe, the abbey could re-purchase the toft and shop at two shillings below the current value or asking price. For this property, de Sallowe was paying ten shillings annual rent. The price of urban property in thirteenth-century Derby was probably ten years' purchase.[35] Such a price would concur with the rate in London, where, according to Hodgett, Holy Trinity, Aldgate, was purchasing quit rents at nine to ten years' purchase.[36] The price of rural land in the thirteenth century may also have been ten years' purchase.[37] The remission on the price for the abbey would thus have constituted about two per cent in this specific case. In other covenants, the remission, on the same calculation, amounted to between one and five per cent.

A further covenant in grants by the abbey allowed for a more specific distraint for arrears of rent. At first, the distraint was only a general clause; from the time of Abbot Ralph (1233-48), however, the distraint was specific. The abbey could distrain on the goods and chattels of the tenant four pence for every term in arrears. The rate per term was fixed regardless of the size of the annual rent. Distraint would be operative as soon as the rent fell in arrears by fifteen days.

In most cases, the annual rent amounted only to between ten and twenty pence. The level of distraint for each term in arrears could thus have comprised a considerable portion or even multiple of the rent. Whether the abbey ever distrained in this way is not known, but symbolically the covenants were against the spirit of the urban land market.

The effect of these covenants must have been to distort the normal working of the urban land market, which in other circumstances would have been fairly fluid, since burgage tenure allowed freedom of devise.[38] Seigniorial and familial restraints on alienation had been effectively removed from feudal tenures by ca.1200–replaced by a notion of property.[39] By contrast, Darley introduced a restraint of alienation and other covenants to modify the nature of the urban land market in Derby, which was supposed to be more fluid–at least in theory.

In Derby, Darley controlled not only a large part of the burgage tenements, but also more than a third of the estimated mills in and around the borough: Mershmulne and Twigrist mill from ca.1176; Prestesmilne from the late twelfth century; Sirreuesmilne from ca.1151; and Copecastle mills from 1263.[40] In several other towns, the intrusion of the Austin Canons into the urban land market was marked by the extensive accumulation of property.

A vast proportion of the property of both Osney and particularly Saint Frideswide's lay within the walls of Oxford. Indeed, the southern part of the town was dominated by the precinct of Saint Frideswide's, not only spiritually, but also economically.[41] The income from Saint Frideswide's derived almost exclusively from its urban holdings there, since it held precious little property in rural Oxfordshire.[42] More importantly, perhaps, was the franchise of Saint Frideswide's to hold extensive fairs in Oxford, during which the prior had significant privileges in the borough. The liberty of the fair had been granted by Henry I in his charter of re-foundation. Accordingly, Saint Frideswide's had the equivalent of the liberty of the verge, during the fair, which lasted for a whole week from the eve of the feast of their saint.[43]

Even that house's holdings in the borough, however, were eclipsed by those of Osney Abbey. Indeed, the example of Osney was used by Charles Gross to demonstrate the growing resentment of some borough communities to the accumulation of urban property–potentially in mortmain–by religious houses. Gross recited the claim by the burgesses of Oxford to the commissioners of the *Rotuli Hundredorum* that the value of Osney's property in the borough was £300.[44] Their claim was undoubtedly an exaggeration, which, however, reflected their concern. The rentals of Osney's urban property suggest a gross income of between £150 and £197 at various points over the later middle ages.[45] In ca.1280, the account of the manciple or kitchener (*coquinarius*) comprised a gross receipt of £151 9s. 11d. from rents of assize in the borough and in the suburb.[46] In the manciple's account of 1359-60, the gross rents from Oxford (presumably including the suburbs) amounted to £181 8s. 11d.[47] Although the burgesses had exaggerated the level of the abbey's interest in burgage property, yet these amounts were still enormous. For example, the gross receipts from Osney's urban property exceeded the total gross income of very many religious houses (see Table 4).

Moreover, the burgage property of Osney–as well as Saint Frideswide's, Eynsham and Godstow–was exempt from taxation, which engendered numerous disputes between the burgage community and the religious house. In 1269, Osney was assessed by the burgesses to contribute £20 to the tallage, which led to conflict.[48] The dispute was resolved by the Crown which confirmed the abbey's exempt status. Further disputes periodically erupted, however, over the same issue.[49] The mere accumulation of property in the borough resulted in conflict between the community of the borough and Osney.

From the thirteenth century, Osney invested little in the improvement of this urban property, acting as scarcely more than a *rentier* landlord. One of the reasons in the later middle ages was the relative decline in the value of its property.[50] The rentals of the house's urban holdings were punctuated with vacant tenements.[51] On the other hand, the house was the chief lord of large numbers of *aule* and *camere* which were the basic foundation of the university.[52] In terms of investment, however, the abbey's main period of activity had been in the late twelfth century, shortly after the acquisition of much of its urban property from benefactors who were burgesses. In particular, the abbey then constructed selds in the parish of Saint Michael at Northgate, which became the basis of the precinct of the cordwainers. The investment probably occurred during the abbacy of Hugh (1184-98). The grants and leases of these selds included covenants for maintenance and good condition.[53] It was probably about this time too that Osney invested in the development of the quasi-suburban area which became the parish of Saint Thomas (see below). After ca.1200, however, there is little evidence of investment by Osney in its urban property other than at the level of necessity.

The pattern and extent of urban property of Leicester Abbey can be very clearly obtained from the rental of 1341, commonly called Geryn's rental.[54] The abbey held tenements or rents in all parishes, but with very strong concentrations in Saint Martin's, All Saints and, in particular, Saint Leonard's. In the last parish, for example, the abbey had an interest in ninety-five tenements in 1341. Charyte's rental of 1477 adds further detail.[55] It reveals the abbey's extensive interest in the Swinemarket, the *vicus Fullonum, le Schepismarket* and the Saturday market: in the last, the abbey had rights in eleven shops as well as *le Pulturhows*. The property in Saint Leonard's was known as the *vicus abbathie*, such was the overriding interest of the abbey there.

Despite having quit Portchester, Southwick retained an association with an urban community. The house had received lands in Portsea Island, at Stubbington, Buckland and adjacent vills around which Portsmouth developed in the late twelfth century. The real stimulus for urban growth occurred when the vill of Portsmouth escheated to the Crown in 1194, but most of what is known of the earlier planning of the borough derives from the charters and cartularies of Southwick. Throughout the middle ages, Southwick remained closely involved with the town and its leading burgesses and acquired substantial urban property. It was rivalled only by God's House, Portsmouth, according to the rent rolls of the liberty of Portsmouth in 1469. In ca.1248, the house collected rent from over seventy burgesses in Portsmouth.[56]

Barnwell Priory, although re-founded outside Cambridge in 1112, retained a substantial economic interest in the borough. The priory's midsummer fair–over four days in June–took place inside the walls and occasioned disputes, notably in 1293-4. These difficulties had rumbled since 1232. In 1295, the house collected rents from at least eighty tenements in Cambridge, although the total value amounted to only £25 6s. 11¾d. As a consequence, there were constant disputes in the thirteenth century over taxation of the priory and its tenants.[57]

The most urban of the houses of the Austin Canons were by definition those founded in the capital. Holy Trinity, Aldgate, was founded in the City in 1107-8, by Matilda, queen of Henry I, on the site where Syred had begun to establish a college of secular canons. As their original endowment, the regular canons received the soke of Aldgate, and, later (in 1125), the soke of the *Cnihtengild* (the Portsoken). About sixty per cent of the income of the house was derived from property within the City, which was valued in 1288-91 at over £125. In the administration of its urban property, Prior Richard (1233-48) adopted the same strategy as Darley was contemporaneously implementing. Grants included a covenant with the right of pre-emption by the house at 2s. (a gold bezant) below the market value. As in Derby, the nature of the urban land market was manipulated and, possibly, rendered less liquid.[58] The canons of Southwark were even more dependent on income from urban property in the borough. In 1535, over ninety per cent of the *valor* of Southwark comprised urban rents.[59]

In some towns and boroughs, there is an association between the Austin Canons and suburban growth. Since the canons had in many cases located just outside the walls of the borough, it is perhaps not surprising that they had a role in this suburban development. Suburbs grew organically outside towns and boroughs from an early time.[60] The Austin Canons were not the initiators of this change, but they were sometimes strongly implicated because of their location. At Derby, the development of the New Land outside the borough owed a great deal to Darley Abbey. The New Land seems to have been just outside the borough walls and not subject to the jurisdiction of the borough, since the tenants of Darley there owed suit twice a year to the abbey's court. Nor was the land simply newly assarted agricultural land. The New Land was primarily divided into tofts, but it might be suspected that many of them were suburban tenements. In many charters, there are references to buildings on the tofts. The annual rent for a toft was frequently twelve pence, which is redolent of the laws of Breteuil–although there was probably no direct relationship with those laws.[61]

The development of the new parish of Saint Thomas in Oxford owed more to Osney Abbey. Osney had appropriated the castle-chapel of Saint George in 1149. Saint George was the original parish church for this area outside the walls. Between ca.1187 and 1191, Osney provided the chapel of ease of Saint Thomas, a fairly justifiable act since the castle-chapel was often inaccessible because of its location within Oxford castle. In a complementary move, the construction of Hythe bridge allowed parishioners easy access to Saint Thomas from across the river. Soon after its provision, Saint Thomas became the real parish church, as Saint George became more or less redundant. Although outside the walls, the suburb of Saint Thomas was, however, subject to the jurisdiction of the borough. Suburban growth here was strongly prosecuted by Osney. In 1279-80, there were about two hundred properties in the parish of Saint Thomas, comprising 125 cottages and sixty-three tenements, houses or messuages. The high proportion of cottages reflects the nature of suburban development. By contrast, there were only thirty-two cottages in the rest of the borough inside the walls, compared with 605 tenements, houses or messuages and 148 selds. Osney was the largest property-holder in Saint Thomas in 1279-80, being chief lord of twenty-five tenements, nineteen cottages and four vacant plots–that is, holding almost forty per cent of the tenements and fifteen per cent of the cottages. Additionally, the abbey, as mesne lord, received rents of £3 10s. 10d. from seventeen other holdings, as well as income from the islands of Medley and Osney, which lay within the parish. There is every reason to suspect that Osney promoted suburban growth from the borough towards the abbey in Saint Thomas's parish, even if suburban growth was a natural and organic development. It seems also reasonable to predicate that these suburbs had become as crowded and densely inhabited as the intra-mural areas.[62]

There are clear signs too in 1477 of the development of the suburbs of Leicester under the auspices of Leicester Abbey. The abbey had an interest in two messuages, four cottages and thirteen tenements in Humberstonegate, the eastward expansion of the borough. Whereas the manor outside the western walls of the borough had been called Bromkinthorpe in 1341, in 1477 it had been transformed into Braunstonegate.[63]

One of the effects of the intrusion of the first wave of houses of Austin Canons into the boroughs was thus to engender conflict over urban property. Disputes were not confined to economic matters. In all boroughs in which the regular canons held property, there were also problems of jurisdiction, if only minor ones in some cases. The major disputes over jurisdiction occurred in those boroughs which developed as seigniorial boroughs under the lordship of houses of Black Canons. The two principal examples are Dunstable and Cirencester. Neither was one of the great cities of England, but they represented important primary and organic towns which proliferated.

Dunstable Priory had been founded by Henry I and under its tutelage the borough was mediatized. From the early thirteenth century, through that century, the burgesses were involved in almost constant dispute with the priory, although our evidence is entirely *parti pris*, from the annals of the house. In 1221, the town had been almost destroyed by fire and had to be rebuilt. At this time, Prior Richard de Morins issued new customs of the borough, which caused some resentment amongst the burgesses. The customs were relatively harmless, but were restrictive. The first dispute happened in 1221, over personal tithes, particularly from commerce. The dispute was resolved in the court of the archdeacon of Bedford, before whom the burgesses were required to pledge their faith. It was not long before conflict arose again, in 1227, over a range of issues: that fines on burgesses should be defined by a standard rate of 4d.; that the prior should not implead any burgess in King's Bench in London (i.e. outside the borough of Dunstable); that no inquisitions in the town should include foreigners; that the prior should not distrain on burgesses in public streets; and that the old customs of the burgesses should be restored. These demands had been occasioned by the confirmation of the liberties of the priory in 1227, on the petition of the prior, after the Crown had incarcerated burgesses implicated by a robber. The prior had paid £100 for the confirmation and attempted to recover one hundred marks from the burgesses by an aid. The dispute was immediately sparked by distraint on one of the burgesses, Martin Duke.[64]

In the following year, the burgesses came into dispute with the prior over oblations, the bishop of Lincoln excommunicating ten burgesses. A further dispute in 1229 was initially resolved by Henry III, but, as soon as he left the town, the problem was resurrected. Henry had to summon two of the most influential burgesses before the Bench. The grievances were still ostensibly those of 1227. The town refused to comply without a special order from the Crown. The king's mandate confirmed that the prior could tallage the burgesses as the king himself might have done; fines of burgesses were to be standardized at 4d. before damages; and those living within the walls owed suit of court, but those outside did not. The burgesses, however, were allowed to tax only the prior's tenants *in capite*; other tenants holding lower down the scale were to be exempt. The twelve burgesses appointed to collect the tax used this remission as a subterfuge for their own exemption, upon which the burgesses revolted and withdrew their tithes and oblations. The entire body of burgesses threatened to leave the town for a new site of forty acres offered by William de Cantilupe. Agreement was reached only after the intervention of the archdeacon of Bedford, whose compromise included that there should be no new aid or tallage and that fines of burgesses should not exceed 4d. A further minor dispute occurred in 1247. A century later, in 1350-8, there was an overt constitutional clash, with the commune of burgesses resisting the prior.[65]

The main crisis at Cirencester occurred also at a later time. Although this major conflict did not arise until 1342, the seeds had been sown much earlier, indeed at the foundation of Cirencester by Henry I. The main endowment of the abbey was the town and it was from the town and the immediate environs that the abbey principally drew its revenue. The importance of the urban revenue was paramount and accounted for the abbey's being the largest and wealthiest of all the houses of Austin Canons (Table 5). Earlier disputes can be inferred. Henry II had to issue a writ ordering the abbey not to vex the townspeople. Richard I fined the burgesses for excessive zeal–about what is not clear. Inquisitions after disputes in 1225 placed the burgesses in the abbot's mercy. There were further disputes in 1232 and 1312.[66]

The crisis in 1342 revolved around the petition of the townspeople to the Crown that the abbey had suppressed the status of the town as a borough. Finberg was inclined to accept burghal status, although the most recent commentator, the late Charles Ross, saw no reason to believe that the town had ever achieved the formal or informal status of a borough, by any criterion of burghality. It is clear, however, that the abbey had itself presumed burghal status in a dispute with the Crown in 1221. The town had also frequently, but not consistently, been assessed as a taxation borough in the lay subsidies of the late thirteenth and early fourteenth century. Whether the town had achieved the status of a borough, however, is really immaterial. Cirencester certainly exhibited distinct urban characteristics. The conflict between town and abbey ensued from the self-consciousness of the community of an expanding and important wool town attempting to divest itself of the jurisdiction of a seigniorial overlord, in the hope of achieving self-government. In this, it nevertheless failed in 1342.[67]

The evolution of the communal identity of the burgesses of Plymouth was slower than that of Dunstable or Cirencester. The town evolved out of the manor of Sutton Prior, controlled by Plympton Priory. By the early fourteenth century, however, overlordship was becoming restrictive to the burgesses. In 1311, a dispute occurred over the provisions of stalls in the market, when the burgesses challenged the prior's control. The prior relented and allowed eighteen stalls to be rented at 1d. per annum. Since the burgesses had no common seal, the reeve sealed on their behalf. In 1317, the townspeople appealed over the head of the prior to the king, in an attempt to lease waste in the town. This action was probably an implicit challenge to the overlordship of the prior. The imputation was that the Crown owned the waste in the borough, which signified that the town was a *liber burgus*. The priory successfully resisted this challenge. The constitutional challenge was, however, deferred only until the thirteen-eighties, when the townspeople attempted to institute a mayor and become a self-governing community.[68]

Bodmin had developed urban characteristics earlier. In 1086, the town had sixty-eight houses and a market. In 1179, the burgesses claimed a gild without warrant and were fined 100s. The privileges of the town, however, were augmented at the instance of Prior Richard (1225-72), who acquired the right to have a gild merchant and the confirmation of Bodmin as a stannary town. The burgesses attempted to divest themselves of the prior's control in 1345.[69]

In these disputes over jurisdiction between burgesses and their monastic lords, the specific causes were incidental. Behind all the situations is the conflict engendered by the organic development of a community meeting the ostensible restrictions of an overlord. Such a constitutional conflict was almost inevitable. The specific points at issue related to the needs of a trading community to preserve its commerce without restrictions and to achieve some degree of self-regulation. The disputes in Dunstable were precipitated in the early thirteenth century, at the time of nascent self-awareness of the community of burgesses, although the first major dispute in Cirencester and elsewhere occurred later.[70] The seeds of both disputes lay in the distant past, inadvertently in the foundation of houses, some by Henry I, who endowed them with jurisdiction over those types of towns which were archetypal in English commercial organization. At the time of their foundation and endowment, the formal and legal differences between towns and boroughs had not crystallized. As the towns developed, the townspeople found seigniorial overlordship restricting and aspired towards self-government.

In addition to the economic and jurisdictional restrictions, these houses of Austin Canons had an impact on the spiritual life of towns, despite their retreat from the urban precinct. The endowment of most houses of Austin Canons depended greatly on the return of the advowsons of parish churches from the laity to the religious. The appropriation of these churches to the Augustinians included urban no less than rural parishes. Thus, Holy Trinity, Aldgate, acquired the advowson of some six parish churches in London.[71] The interest of Osney Abbey in Oxford extended to Saint Peter in the East as well as Saint Thomas.[72] In Oxford too, Saint Frideswide's held the advowson of two other parish churches–Saint Michael Northgate and All Saints.[73] The site of Saint Frideswide's, as noted above, had been and would continue to be a focal point of religion in Oxford.[74] In Cambridge, Barnwell retained the advowson of Saint Giles, its original site, and also appropriated All Saints by the castle and Saint Clement.[75] Saint Augustine, Bristol, controlled three urban parish churches: Saint Leonard, Saint Nicholas, and the important All Saints, the last described in the mid twelfth century, when it was appropriated to Saint Augustine, as *in medio burgi*. The site of Saint Augustine may itself have been of deep religious significance.[76]

The parish church of Portchester had been rebuilt by the Austin Canons, who later moved to Southwick. The church was rebuilt about 1130 in the south-east quarter of the outer bailey. Southwick Priory retained the advowson and instituted a vicarage. The spiritual life of Portsmouth was also served by Southwick Priory, which had received permission from John de Gisors to erect the chapel of Saint Thomas the Martyr, before his lands escheated to the Crown. In 1196, at the instance of the king and the bishop of Winchester, the chapel acquired rights of burial, so that the dead of the borough need not be carried to the mother church at Portsea. The chapel developed into the parish church and, later, cathedral, of Portsmouth.[77]

Like Saint Frideswide's at Oxford, Cirencester Abbey was founded within a minster church inside the urban precinct. The site may have been the endowment of an Anglo-Saxon minster on a royal manor, possibly rebuilt in the tenth century. The church may also thus be "an evident candidate for a key position in the early ecclesiastical organization of the region", in a re-planned royal town. The endowment of the church was augmented in the late eleventh century. Rebuilding took place in 1117 and the institution of regular canons by 1130. Thenceforth, the conventual church dominated the town.[78]

Darley Abbey controlled about half the parish churches in Derby by 1154-9. The house held the advowson of Saint Helen, Saint Michael, Saint Werburgh and Saint Peter, with the rights of a rural dean over the churches and the clergy. Between 1215 and 1223, almost all these livings were appropriated to the house, so that it had a direct interest in personal tithes on the commerce of the borough.[79] Apart from affecting religious life in the towns, the control of these parish churches thus impinged on the economic life of the burgesses, in the exaction of personal tithes on trade–although there are few intimations as to the consequences, except at Dunstable.

Was there then conflict or accommodation between burgesses or townspeople and the Church in the medieval town? Experiences obviously differed from one town or borough to the next. Many houses of Austin Canons came directly and frequently into conflict with the urban community. Even where there is no direct evidence of conflict, there is a sense of latent discord. In the case of the Austin houses, the simple acquisition of (to the burgesses) a disproportionate interest in urban property inevitably led to resentment. In a place like Oxford, dispute was unavoidable. A multitude of corporate institutions–the university and its chancellor as well as half a dozen religious houses–established an interest in the borough which threatened to rival that of the premier corporation, the borough community. Oxford was an extreme situation.

The other variable was that respect for the Austin Canons may have rapidly evaporated: this goes back to the nature of their presence in the borough. The Black Canons came to the towns initially as missionaries, but abandoned that role. In effect, they simply became urban property owners, with their house, in many cases, located on the periphery or outside the town. Symbolically, then, some houses were outsiders–physically and visibly outside the walls–and yet they had an overwhelming control of large amounts of property. The arrival of the friars in the towns highlighted the otiose position of the Austin Canons. The respect that might have been accorded to a cathedral priory or chapter, such as Durham, could not be attributed to the regular canons. By 1300, burgesses were thinking in terms not only of their own corporate identity, but also of new types of benefaction for the well-being of their souls– chantries and fraternities within the parish churches in the town.[80] In Oxford, for example, the wills registered in the *Liber Albus* show the beginnings of this process of foundation of chantries and lights in parish churches rather than at the numerous altars at Osney.[81] And yet, the rectors of very many of those urban parishes were Osney and Saint Frideswide's. The presence of the Austin Canons in the towns was thus a constant irritant. Well before 1350, they had outstayed their welcome.

Table 3 Characteristics of Austin Canon Houses Founded Before 1135

Date	Urban houses (by date of foundation)	Rural houses (alphabetical order)
	Colchester *	Beckford
	(Huntingdon)	Blythburgh *
	Canterbury *	Breamore
1092	[Cambridge]	Breedon *?
c.1107	ALDGATE *	Caldwell
1112	(Cambridge): BARNWELL	Calke, Calwich
	MERTON	[Embsay]
	BODMIN *	Great Bricett
	SOUTHWARK *	Great Paxton
1120	TAUNTON *	HAUGHMOND
1121	PLYMPTON *♦	Hempton
1122	ST FRIDESWIDE'S *♦	Ivychurch
1123	SMITHFIELD	LAUNDE
1125	KENILWORTH	LEEDS
1127	Southampton *, LAUNCESTON *♦	Leonard Stanley
c.1129	(Portchester): SOUTHWICK	MISSENDEN
1129	[OSNEY] *	PENTNEY
1130	CIRENCESTER *, Cambridge	ST OSYTH
1130		Wombridge
1131	Dover *	
1131-2	DUNSTABLE ♦	
c.1135	Ipswich	
1135	(Gloucester): LLANTHONY II, Warwick	
Significant houses after 1135:		
1137	(Derby): DARLEY *	
1138-9	{LEICESTER} *	
1148	BRISTOL	

Notes to Table 3: [] abortive   () change of site from urban to extra-mural ♦ new houses colonized from Aldgate
{} appropriation of intra-mural community of secular canons
* Re-foundation or appropriation of a college or community of secular canons
OSNEY house with a *valor* in 1535 > £500   BODMIN house of which the *valor* in 1535 was above the mean

The dates are derived from Knowles and Hadcock, *Medieval Religious Houses in England and Wales*; J. C. Dickinson, *Origins of the Austin Canons*; Robinson, *Geography of Augustinian Settlement*; but modified where necessary by more recent research which is noted in the footnotes to the main text. By and large, it seems that Knowles and Hadcock took the date of foundation as that of the foundation charter, but the actual foundation may have taken place at an earlier time by oral disposition (Vivian H. Galbraith, "Monastic foundation charters of the 11th and 12th centuries," *Cambridge Historical Journal* 4 (1934): 205-22).

Table 4 *Valor* of Houses of Austin Canons in 1535

To the nearest £1.   All houses irrespective of date of foundation

	All houses	Urban houses
Number of houses	198	23
Mean	168	441
Standard deviation	198.7	311.4
Median	98	344
Maximum	1051	1051
Q1	44	220
Q3	212	654

Table 5 Rank-order of Houses in the 1535 *Valor* (Above £500)

House	*Valor* (£s)
Cirencester *	£1,051.00
Merton	960
Leicester *	951
Waltham	900
Smithfield *	693
St Osyth	677
Bristol *	670
Osney *	654
Llanthony II *	648
Guisborough N	628
Southwark *	626
Thornton N	591
Bridlington * N ♦	547
Kenilworth *	538

Notes to Table 5 Irrespective of date of foundation
♦ Not originally founded as a house of the Order
* urban foundation
N= north of the R. Trent

Notes

[1] N. M. Trenholme, *The English Monastic Boroughs* (Columbia, Mo.: University of Missouri Press, 1927); Mary D. Lobel, *The Borough of Bury St Edmunds* (Oxford: Oxford University Press, 1935).

[2] R. Barrie Dobson, *Durham Priory 1400-50* (Cambridge: Cambridge University Press, 1973), 33-50; Margaret Bonney, *Lordship and the Urban Community: Durham and Its Overlords, 1250-1540* (Cambridge: Cambridge University Press, 1990).

[3] William Urry, *Canterbury under the Angevin Kings* (London: Athlone, 1967).

[4] "The Church in the Towns" project.

[5] Thus David Knowles had a brief chapter on monastic boroughs in *The Religious Orders in England* I (Cambridge: Cambridge University Press, 1948), 261-9, which, because of the state of research at that date, concentrated largely on either the great Benedictine houses or the revolts of 1327 and 1381. Since then, further research has also tended to concentrate on those great houses, probably because the sources are so much better than for the interest of other houses in towns.

[6] Bonney, *Lordship and the Urban Community*, 231-3; Gervase Rosser, "The Essence of Medieval Urban Communities: the Vill of Westminster, 1200-1540", in *The Mediaeval Town: A Reader in English Urban History, 1200-1540*, ed. Richard Holt and Rosser (London: Longmans, 1990), 218.

[7] Trenholme, *English Monastic Boroughs*, 95.

[8] For general discussions of the Order in England, see J. C. Dickinson, *The Origins of the Austin Canons and their Introduction into England* (London: SPCK 1950); David M. Robinson, *The Geography of Augustinian Settlements in Medieval England and Wales*, British Archaeological Reports, British Series, vol. 80, 2 vols. (Oxford, 1980); Robinson, "Site Changes of Augustinian Communities in Medieval England and Wales", *Mediaeval Studies* 43 (1981): 425-44.

[9] Dickinson, *Origins of the Austin Canons*, 29-35.

[10] Kathleen Edwards, *The English Secular Cathedrals in the Middle Ages* (Manchester: Manchester University Press, 2d ed. 1967), 3-12; Dickinson, *Origins of the Austin Canons*, 15-25, 92-6; Julia Barrow, "Cathedrals, Provosts and Prebends: A Comparison of Twelfth-century German and English Practice", *JEH* 37 (1986): 538, 552-64, discusses the impact of the earlier rules on secular cathedral chapters and the decline of communal life; D. Blake, "The Development of the Chapter of the Diocese of Exeter, 1050-1161", *Journal of Medieval History* 8 (1982): 1-11, explains the longer persistence of communal life at Exeter. For minster churches, see John Blair, "Local Churches in Domesday Book and Before", in *Domesday Studies*, ed. James C. Holt (Woodbridge: Boydell, 1987), 271, 275; Blair, "Introduction:

From Minster to Parish Church", in *Minsters and Parish Churches: The Local Church in Transition 950-1200*, ed. Blair (Oxford: Oxbow, 1988), 2, 7 ("The bias of our post-Gregorian sources obscures the fact that the minster community survived great social changes to remain, until the late 11th century, a normal and accepted branch of the religious life", but the Gregorian reform left the seculars "in despised and friendless isolation"); Blair, "Secular Minster Churches in Domesday Book", in *Domesday Book: A Reassessment*, ed. Peter Sawyer (London: Arnold, 1985), 116-17, 123, 125-6, 137-8; Gervase Rosser, "The Cure of Souls in English Towns before 1000", in *Pastoral Care before the Parish*, ed. Blair and Richard Sharpe (Leicester: Leicester University Press, 1992), 267-84.

[11] Dickinson, *Origins of the Austin Canons*, 47-8.

[12] Richard W. Southern, "The Place of Henry I in English History", repr. in his *Medieval Humanism and Other Studies* (Oxford: Oxford University Press, 1970), 206-33; Martin Brett, *The English Church under Henry I* (Oxford: Oxford University Press, 1975), 138-40 for episcopal founders and re-founders.

[13] Ian Kershaw, *Bolton Priory: The Economy of a Northern Monastery, 1286-1325* (Oxford: Oxford University Press, 1973); Rodney H. Hilton, *The Economic Development of Some Leicestershire Estates in the Fourteenth and Fifteenth Centuries* (Oxford: Oxford University Press, 1947).

[14] J. C. Dickinson, "Early Suppressions of English Houses of Austin Canons", in *Medieval Studies Presented to Rose Graham*, ed. V. Ruffer and A. J. Taylor (Oxford: Oxford University Press, 1950), 54-77.

[15] Ralph H. C. Davis, "An Oxford Charter of 1191 and the Beginnings of Municipal Freedom", *Oxoniensia* 33 (1968): 53-65.

[16] John Blair, "St Frideswide's Monastery: Problems and Possibilities", *Oxoniensia* 53 (1988): 221-8; Blair, "St Frideswide's Reconsidered", *Oxoniensia* 52 (1987): 71-127. Blair argues for an earlier date for the re-foundation, certainly before 1120, and possibly as early as 1111 ("St Frideswide's Monastery", 227, n. 45).

[17] Janet Cooper, "The Church of St George's in the Castle", *Oxoniensia* 41 (1976): 306-8.

[18] *Cartulary of Darley Abbey*, I, ii-vi.

[19] *Liber Memorandum ... Bernewell* (Cambridge: Cambridge University Press, 1907), xxxiv-xxxvi, 46.

[20] Dickinson, *Origins of the Austin Canons*.

[21] *Cartularies of Southwick Priory*, II, xii-xiii.

[22] J. C. Dickinson, "The Origins of St Augustine's, Bristol", in *Essays in Bristol and Gloucestershire History*, ed. Patrick McGrath and John Cannon (Bristol: Bristol and Gloucestershire Archaeological Society, 1976).

[23] The site is illustrated in David Knowles and J. K. S. St Joseph, *Mo-*

nastic Sites from the Air (Cambridge: Cambridge University Press, 1952), 210-11 (no. 96).

[24] Dickinson, *Origins of the Austin Canons*, 103-4.

[25] Derek Keene, "Suburban Growth", in *The Mediaeval Town*, ed. Holt and Rosser, 97-119.

[26] For the date, David Crouch, *The Beaumont Twins: The Roots and Branches of Power in the Twelfth Century* (Cambridge: Cambridge University Press, 1986), 201-2; Crouch, "The Foundation of Leicester Abbey, and Other Problems", *Midland History* 12 (1987): 2-4.

[27] A. Hamilton Thompson, *The Abbey of St Mary of the Meadows* (Leicester: Edgar Backus, 1949).

[28] Edwards, *English Secular Cathedrals*, 3-12.

[29] *Cartulary of the Priory of St Gregory*, ix-xvi; Dickinson, *Origins of the Austin Canons*, 104-5.

[30] Alan Everitt, "The Banburys of England", *Urban History Yearbook* 1 (Leicester, 1974): 28-38; Everitt, "The Primary Towns of England", in his *Landscape and Community* (London: Hambledon 1985), 93-107.

[31] *Cartulary of Holy Trinity, Aldgate*, 2, 228.

[32] The following is based on *Cartulary of Darley Abbey*, I, 66-237.

[33] *Cartulary of Darley Abbey* I, lxvii.

[34] *Cartulary of Darley Abbey*, I, 114.

[35] *Cartulary of Darley Abbey* I, passim.

[36] *Cartulary of Holy Trinity, Aldgate*, xviii; Blair, "St Frideswide's Monastery", 227.

[37] Carole Rawcliffe, "Introduction", in *Derbyshire Feet of Fines, 1323-1546*, ed. H. J. H. Garrett, Derbyshire Record Society vol. 11 (Chesterfield, 1985), vi; Sandra Raban, "The Land Market and the Aristocracy in the Thirteenth Century", in *Tradition and Change: Essays in Honour of Marjorie Chibnall*, ed. Diana Greenway, Christopher Holdsworth, and Jane Sayers (Cambridge: Cambridge University Press, 1985), 239-61; Barbara F. Harvey, *Westminster Abbey and its Estates in the Middle Ages* (Oxford: Oxford University Press, 1977), 196-8.

[38] Maurice de W. Hemmeon, *Burgage Tenure in Medieval England* (Cambridge, Mass.: Harvard University Press, 1914).

[39] S. F. C. (Toby) Milson, *The Legal Framework of English Feudalism* (Cambridge: Cambridge University Press, 1976); Samuel E. Thorne, "English Feudalism and Estates in Land", repr. in his *Essays in English Legal History* (London: Hambledon, 1985), 13-30; Robert Palmer, "The Origin of Property", *Law and History Review* 3 (1985): 1-50.

[40] *Cartulary of Darley Abbey*, I, lvii-lviii.

[41] Blair, "St Frideswide's Monastery", 235-7.

[42] *Cartulary of St Frideswide's*.

[43] Janet Cooper, "Markets and Fairs", in *Victoria History of the County*

of Oxford IV (Oxford: Oxford University Press, 1979), 310-11. There were numerous disputes between Saint Frideswide's and the borough concerning cases arising from the fair, especially between 1292 and 1346.

⁴⁴ Charles Gross, "Mortmain in Medieval Boroughs", *American Historical Review* 12 (1906-7): 737.

⁴⁵ *Cartulary of Oseney Abbey*, III, 145, 161, 286.

⁴⁶ *Cartulary of Oseney Abbey*, VI, 195.

⁴⁷ Bodl., MS Roll Oxon. Oseney 27.

⁴⁸ *Cartulary of Oseney Abbey*, III, 84-5; *Cartulary of Eynsham Abbey*, II, 277-8; Herbert E. Salter, ed., *Medieval Archives of the University of Oxford*, Oxford Historical Society vols. 70, 73, 2 vols. (Oxford, 1920-1), I, 193-201; *Munimenta Civitatis Oxonie*, 150-1.

⁴⁹ Dave Postles, "Conflict Between Oseney and the Borough in the Early Fifteenth Century", *Oxoniensia* 41 (1976): 356-7.

⁵⁰ Andrew F. Butcher, "Rent and the Urban Economy: Oxford and Canterbury in the Later Middle Ages", *Southern History* I (1979): 12-18.

⁵¹ *Cartulary of Oseney Abbey*, III, passim.

⁵² Jeremy I. Catto, "Citizens, Scholars and Masters", in *The History of the University of Oxford I: The Early Oxford Schools*, ed. Catto (Oxford: Oxford University Press, 1984), 176, 187. The abbey rebuilt its schools in the fifteenth century to form a consolidated block.

⁵³ *Cartulary of Oseney Abbey*, I, 28-30.

⁵⁴ Bodl., MS Laud Misc. 625, fols. 186-9.

⁵⁵ Bodl., MS Laud Misc. 625, fols. 82v-102v.

⁵⁶ *Cartularies of Southwick Priory*, xxii-xxv, 149-51; Maurice W. Beresford, *New Towns of the Middle Ages* (London: Lutterworth Press, 1967), 447-9.

⁵⁷ *Liber Memorandum ... Bernewell*, xxxvi-xxxvii, xxxix-xl, xlii, xlix, 88-92, 282-90.

⁵⁸ *Cartulary of Holy Trinity, Aldgate*, xvi-xix.

⁵⁹ Robinson, "Site Changes of Augustinian Communities in Medieval England and Wales".

⁶⁰ Keene, "Suburban Growth"; Christopher Dyer, "Towns and Cottages in Eleventh-century England", in *Studies in Medieval History Presented to R. H. C. Davis*, ed. Henry Mayr-Harting and Robert I. Moore (London: Hambledon Continuum 1985), 91-106.

⁶¹ *Cartulary of Darley Abbey*, I, lx-lxii and passim.

⁶² Janet Cooper, "The Hundred Rolls for the Parish of St Thomas, Oxford", *Oxoniensia* 37 (1972): 165-76.

⁶³ Bodl., MS Laud Misc. 625, fols. 92, 96, 100-102v.

⁶⁴ Trenholme, *English Monastic Boroughs*, 12-18, 48-9; *Annales Monastici*, III, 105-7, 110-11, 118-24.

⁶⁵ Trenholme, *English Monastic Boroughs*, 50.

[66] Trenholme, *English Monastic Boroughs*, 50-2; *Cartulary of Cirencester Abbey*, I, introduction where Ross discussed his and Finberg's different views.

[67] *Cartulary of Cirencester Abbey*, introduction.

[68] Trenholme, *English Monastic Boroughs*, 46-8.

[69] Trenholme, *English Monastic Boroughs*, 52-4.

[70] Geoffrey H. Martin, "The English Borough in the Thirteenth Century", repr. in *The Mediaeval Town* ed. Holt and Rosser, 29-48.

[71] *Cartulary of Holy Trinity, Aldgate*, xvii.

[72] Herbert E. Salter, *Medieval Oxford*, Oxford Historical Society vol. 100 (Oxford, 1936), 116-17. There were twenty churches ca.1200, but the number declined thereafter. Henry I had originally intended Saint Frideswide's to have nine churches in the borough.

[73] Salter, *Medieval Oxford*, 116-17. The parish altar of Saint Frideswide's may have been suppressed in 1298 (Blair, "St Frideswide's Monastery", 256).

[74] See above, n. 41.

[75] *Liber Memorandum ... Bernewell*, xxxiv-xxxviii.

[76] See above, n. 22.

[77] *Cartularies of Southwick Priory*, xii-xiii, xxiii-xxiv.

[78] A. K. Babette Evans, "Cirencester's Early Church", *Transactions of the Bristol and Gloucestershire Archaeological Society* 107 (1989): 107-22; Evans, "Cirencester Abbey: The First Hundred Years", *TBGAS* 109 (1991): 99-100.

[79] *Cartulary of Darley Abbey*, I, ii, vii, liii-lv; II, 595-600, 602-11. Similarly Saint Gregory held the advowson of parish churches in Canterbury, which had been given by Lanfranc (*Cartulary of the Priory of St Gregory*, xiii).

[80] Kathleen L. Wood-Legh, *Perpetual Chantries in Britain* (Cambridge: Cambridge University Press, 1965); Helen M. Chew, "Mortmain in Medieval London", *EHR* 60 (1945): 1-15; A. Gervase Rosser, "Communities of Parish and Guild in the Late Middle Ages", in *Parish, Church and People: Local Studies in Lay Religion, 1350-1750*, ed. Susan J. Wright (London: HarperCollins, 1988), 29-55; Caroline M. Barron, "The Parish Fraternities of Medieval London", in *The Church in Pre-Reformation Society*, ed. Barron and Christopher Harper-Bill (Woodbridge: Boydell, 1985), 13-37; Clive Burgess, "'For the Increase of Divine Service': Chantries in the Parish in Late-medieval Bristol", *JEH* 36 (1985): 46-65; Burgess, "'By Quick and by Dead': Wills and Pious Provision in Late Medieval Bristol", *EHR* 102 (1987): 837-58; R. Barrie Dobson, "The Foundation of Perpetual Chantries by the Citizens of Medieval York", in *Studies in Church History* IV, ed. G. J. Cuming (Leiden: Brill, 1967), 22-38. For the development of chantries and fraternities in parish churches in Oxford, Salter, *Medieval Oxford*, 122-9.

[81] *Liber Albus ... Oxoniensis*.

7
Heads of Religious Houses as Administrators

In 1257, 366 *homines* were manumitted in a single charter by Geoffrey, abbot of Sens. The abbot received a total of 6,000 *livres parisis* to be paid over twelve years, in annual instalments of five hundred *livres*. The manumission was the final episode in a long period of tension as the abbot attempted to reimpose servile conditions on his tenantry. Previous explanations of such manumissions have emphasized the realization by lords of the inefficiency of customary services. Recently, however, William Jordan has suggested that the main reason for the manumission *en masse* in the Senonais was the financial difficulty of the abbey. Abbot Geoffrey de Montigny was elected in 1240 and was head of the house for forty-two years. His principal enthusiasm (Frank Pegues describes it as an "obsession"), was the rebuilding of the church of the abbey. In this instance, the abbot had embarked on the programme of building which in turn determined the financial policy of his house.[1]

The ability of the religious to undertake ambitious architectural programmes, rebuilding and patronage of the plastic arts, depended, in part, on their financial aptitude and acumen. There is, indeed, a converse correlation. Their expenditure on such conspicuous consumption and the glory of God and their patronal saint could be construed as disinvestment from their agrarian enterprises. In a sense, such expenditure was unproductive compared with productive investment in their estates, both in width and in depth, an issue which will be developed further below.[2]

In the late thirteenth century, a considerable number of heads of religious houses are judged to have succeeded in revitalizing the financial position of their houses. There is equally a significant historiography of these abbots and priors. The precedent was perhaps established by the late Tony Smith, who elevated Henry de Eastry, prior of Canterbury Cathedral Priory from 1285 to 1331, to something of a mythical position.[3] Subsequent historians have found contemporaries of similar stature. Postan and Hatcher wrote thus:

> Historians could easily cite the case of progressive landlords busily improving their estates–Henry of Eastry of Christ Church Priory, Richard of London and one or two other abbots of Peterborough, Michael of Amesbury of Glastonbury and the Earl of Lacy. (although they qualify this statement by reference to the relatively low technology of the age).[4]

Knowles accepted Smith's conclusions about Eastry, although with a little circumspection.[5] A kindred spirit was perceived by Ian Kershaw in John de Laund, prior of Bolton Priory from ca.1286 to January 1331:

> For Bolton, the Priorate of John of Laund was as important as that of Henry of Eastry, his exact contemporary for Christ Church Canterbury or the abbacy of Geoffrey of Crowland for Peterborough.[6]

In a review, the late Charles Ross remarked on the phenomenon of these administrator-prelates and suggested that a wider study should be made of them.[7]

Although there have been biographies of individual heads of houses within estate studies, there remain some questions which need further consideration. Here, they can perhaps only be outlined. First, there is the question of context. In particular, how did contemporaries such as annalists and chroniclers perceive these reformers, and were their perceptions objective? For example, did annalists writing in the thirteenth century about heads of houses have the same conceptual framework as the annalists of the twelfth century? Did they expect different qualities of their heads? How sympathetic were they to other qualities? Did they exaggerate the qualities with which they were associated?

Heads of Religious Houses as Administrators   161

The second question of context surrounds the actual achievements of the heads of religious houses. Basically, the actions of the reformers can be defined in three categories. First, there was financial reform: the reorganization of the procedures for accountancy in the house. Second and third were related questions of investment. Investment in width comprised the expansion of the estate through purchase and acquisition of land. Investment in depth consisted of capital investment to increase the productivity of the estate.[8] In the case of financial reform, how far was the reform entirely independent and free of external compulsion or example? How did reform of finances relate to the general predicament of religious houses in the thirteenth century? In the case of acquisition of land, how did the expansion of the estates in the thirteenth century compare with the accumulation of the estates in the twelfth? Were the comments of the annalists about acquisition in the thirteenth century colored by the context of the increasing difficulty of attracting endowments? Was productive investment in depth as much as could be achieved? Was it satisfactory? How did it compare with unproductive investment in buildings and devotional expenditure?

A specific example may provide an initial framework for a response to this stream of questions. The case is that of the priors and abbots of Osney, a house founded in 1129 and elevated to the status of an abbey in 1154. The purpose is simply to compare the comments of the writers of the Annals of Osney. The Annals make little comment on the earlier heads of the house. We know, however, that Prior Ralph (1129-38) had been a canon of Saint Frideswide's and confessor to Edith Forne, the wife of the founder of Osney and herself a prime mover in the house's foundation. Wigod (1138-68) had a widespread reputation as a scholar during the pre-history of the Oxford schools. Between 1168 and 1184, Abbot Edward was significant for his exploitation of the property of the house in the borough of Oxford, enhancing its commercial value through the development of selds and shops. The exploitation of the burgage property was continued by Abbot Hugh (1184-1205), in particular the construction of the cordwainery. John de Leche (1235-49) devoted his regime to the expansion of the conventual buildings. Apparently, Adam de Berners (1249-54) marked a return to scholarly interests in the house: *Cuius predicationes solebant scolares*

Universitatis aliquotiens interesse. The annalists provide only cursory remarks about these heads. In contrast, Richard de Apeltree (1254-67) and William de Suttton (1267-84) were almost eulogized by the annalists because of their proficiency in estate administration. Sutton, evidently a protégé of Apeltree, having served as proctor under him for thirteen years, represented the house in the *Quo Warranto* proceedings of 1255-9 and acted as steward of the estates from 1263. Apeltree concluded the difficult litigation with Amory over Weston-on-the-Green, one of the principal assets of the house, which had been rumbling since 1227, and contested the allegedly extortionate taxation of the borough property in 1254-5. The Annals were profuse in their praise of Sutton, *columbinae simplicitatis et prudentiae serpentinae*, and commented on the estates *quin etiam ... non mediocriter augmentauit*. The Annals were quite extraordinarily verbose about these two by comparison with previous heads.[9]

Sutton's administration was, indeed, important. He had caused the compilation of the new cartulary of ca.1280-4; he may have been responsible for the introduction of the *proficuum* calculation and for the enrolled account of ca.1280. Other significant reforms, however, had been introduced before his time, although he may have extended and developed them: these included the exercise of control over a central reserve by the bursary and the organization of the estates into *custodia* or bailiwicks. The claim that Sutton significantly expanded the estates of the house must be colored by the annalist's interpretation. The major expansion of the estates after the original foundation had occurred in the late twelfth century with some isolated but large additions in the first three decades of the thirteenth (for example, the acquisition of Weston-on-the-Green in 1227). Sutton's prelacy, by contrast, saw no major accessions of land).[10]

The imputation is that the annalist knew more about the prelates who were closer in time and also respected more the qualities which they seemingly brought to the house. He also shared the same priorities: the successful exploitation of the estates in very difficult times. The values of the twelfth century, in comparison, were spiritual and contemplative. The reputation of the house had been high in scholarly circles, both in the time of Wigod in the early twelfth century and in the late twelfth century, if in a traditional vein.[11] The estates, nonetheless, had still been vastly expanded at that earlier time. In the thirteenth century, the changes in patterns of piety and the relative drying-up of gifts from the laity to the religious made the annalist more sensitive to the qualities exercised by Apeltree and Sutton, and perhaps therefore somewhat prone to exaggerate their achievements.

There seems little doubt that the heavy rebuilding programme undertaken by Leche strained the financial resources of the house. He added to the nave, chapel of the Virgin Mary, refectory, infirmary and its chapel, abbot's chamber and hall. The building work had, however, commenced before Leche's accession, for the body of Henry II d'Oilly had been interred in the *novum opus* in 1232. An extract from a *liber rationalis*, moreover, made by Bodley's librarian, James, reveals that the principal work on the church extended from at least 1201 to 1269. Eleven minor altars were dedicated from 1201 to 1243 and the high altar by Gravesend in 1269. The work on the church possibly continued even later for it was customary to dedicate altars before the completion of the work. This strenuous programme must have placed a heavy burden on the financial administration of the convent.[12]

Inevitably, the house resorted to raising short-term loans to finance the building. As the house was also a lender of money at this time, it seems that a distinct and separate building fund must have been maintained which was inviolable. A minimum of £740 5s. 4d. was borrowed in at least twenty-one transactions between 1227 and 1271. Of these loans to the abbey, twelve were to be liquidated within a year and seven within a specific period after the obligee's request. The twelve loans for a year involved £642 of the total, illustrating that the borrowing was predominantly short-term.[13]

The abbey managed to devolve much of the expense onto lay benefactors, particularly the cost of the church. The inducement for contributions from the laity was a customary device of the religious to finance their building. The abbey was perhaps precocious in its institution of a *confraria novi operis* (a confraternity of the fabric) before or about 1230, which offered contributors a more impressive spiritual return. The confraternity was undoubtedly aimed towards the burgesses of Oxford. Abbot Richard de Apeltree had an equally acute notion for inducing oblations from the parishioners of the churches in Osney's gift. He despatched itinerant collectors to these parish churches: *nuncii ad vos accedentes pro collectis faciendis oblationum uestrarum ad pia opera aliqua construenda*.... Benefactors were to receive a specified number of masses, psalters and paternosters for five years. Copies of Apeltree's letter were, moreover, retained in each church as a constant prick to the conscience, with a roll of oblations made. The names of the donors would be subscribed on the roll by the incumbent *ut cum defuncti fuerint nomina eorum ad nos deferantur et in capitulo nostro absoluantur*. The listing of indulgences pronounced by prominent ecclesiastics was also useful in inducing gifts. Walerand, bishop of Beirut, who stayed at the abbey in 1245, promulgated an indulgence of thirty days for general benefactions. Indulgence of forty days specifically for contributions towards the fabric was pronounced by the bishop of Sabina when he rested at the convent in 1247. By all these means, the abbey avoided some of the burden of the cost of new buildings of the thirteenth century, but in many houses the expansion of buildings in the thirteenth and early fourteenth centuries resulted in significant financial problems.[14]

The initial prerequisite of reform was reorganization of the financial procedures in the house. First, this change involved the reduction of debt. Innumerable houses had become involved in financial difficulty during the thirteenth century.[15] The second phase was the introduction of some central control over finances. The original arrangement in houses of most Orders was assignment of receipts to individual obedientiaries. Assignation originally had as its purpose the funding of the offices without double counting; subsequently it allowed benefactors to give for specific purposes. As Snape and Smith have shown, during the thirteenth century the assignment of receipts became unsatisfactory. More centralized forms of accountancy and reserve funds became necessary. Smith illustrated how, in many large Benedictine houses, particularly Canterbury and Rochester cathedral priories, a treasury was introduced to exercise central control.[16] The lesser option was a bursary which exercised supervision over the obedientiaries and controlled a reserve fund of unassigned receipts. The additional advantage of the bursary was that it allowed the accumulation of large reserve funds for the purchase of land. In the houses of the newer Orders, with their smaller endowments, it was almost (but not totally) impossible for the individual obedientiaries to raise enough cash to purchase additional lands.[17]

The difficulties of some houses can be illustrated through the example of Bolton Priory. There, John de Laund inherited substantial debts in ca.1286. By 1310, these debts had become more manageable. He introduced more regular accountancy, as reflected in the Bolton *compotus* or ledger of accounts. This initiative has, however, to be placed in context. There had been considerable external pressure from the archbishops of York. When Gifford exercised his right of visitation in 1267, the house had debts of £324 5s. 7d., more than its annual income. There was no proper estate accountancy and there were irregularities in the accounting by obedientiaries. In his visitation of 1280, Wickwane issued two injunctions for the proper rendering of accounts using rolls and tallies and for a proper inventory of the possessions of the house and the extent of its debts. Romeyn in 1286 criticised the level of debt. The role of the Ordinary *cum* Metropolitan had thus been a considerable influence.[18] The question, of course, which emerges is what level of debt a religious house could service and sustain with impunity. The implication is that the equivalent of one year's income was the limit, represented in episcopal attitudes towards monastic indebtedness. Some other smaller houses of Austin Canons experienced similar problems about the same time. At his visitation in 1298, Bishop Sutton found Brooke Priory, a dependency of Kenilworth Priory, almost wasted, with the consequence that the prior of Kenilworth suggested deferring the election of a new prior at Brooke because of the financial difficulty. In this case, the economic problems may well have resulted from the slender endowment, characteristic of houses of the Black Canons.[19]

The same external pressures can be detected behind the introduction of some central financial controls in other houses. In particular, the Chapters General of the Austin Canons in England at an early date issued precepts for the proper keeping of accounts and for the installation of bursaries or central control. The *diffinitores* of the Chapter General of 1220 required a central bursary. A number of houses thereafter adopted one: Osney Abbey by 1247; Newstead Priory by 1261; Leicester Abbey (a treasury) by 1286; Bicester Priory by 1277; Dunstable by the late thirteenth century; and Bolton Priory by 1286. In some cases, however, further compulsion was necessary. Cirencester Abbey had intermittent treasuries between ca.1205 and 1230 through the intervention of the Ordinary and the

Metropolitan, because of the recalcitrance of the obedientiaries. Waltham Abbey had three treasurers by 1191, if not from its refoundation by Henry II in 1177, and royal influence may have been significant in this arrangement. Similar action by the Ordinary can be detected in injunctions issued by Archbishop Pecham to thirteen religious houses in 1283, regulations for Norwich Cathedral Priory by Bishop Bateman in 1346, and visitations of Huntingdon, Elstow and Saint Frideswide's priories. Even the king might intervene to reorganize financial procedures, as happened at Glastonbury Abbey, represented by a fragment of a receiver's roll. The reform of the financial procedures of religious houses did not then occur in a vacuum. Precedents were established by external intervention and there was already a context for their introduction. Heads of religious houses who introduced reforms by their own initiative had an already-established framework in which to work.[20]

When discussing the Benedictines, Knowles adopted a rather different approach. He identified two aspects of the reforms: the introduction of proper audit; and the imposition of a central treasury with control over all finances. He regarded the audit as an innovation of the Papal *curia*, which had proselytized for its introduction into Benedictine houses throughout the thirteenth century.[21] The central audit was belatedly required by the Chapter General of the English Black Monks in 1277.[22] As far as the central treasury was concerned, Knowles perceived it as the initiative of the priors of about four cathedral priories of regular monks, regarding the critical influence as being the relationship of the prior to the chapter, the prior being in a less paternalist relationship to the house than an abbot. In its introduction he thus discerned a "democratic" element, in which he closely followed Smith. There are, however, other aspects to the Benedictine reform. The Chapter General did little to impress the need for central control, by contrast with the Chapters of the Austin Canons, although Peterborough Abbey had adopted a central treasury in 1247.

An interesting example of the financial problems and reform in Black Monk houses is provided by Luffield Priory, a smaller house, founded in the early twelfth century by the earl of Leicester, but with a slender endowment hardly larger than the demesne at Luffield. From the 1230s to the 1260s, the prior invested heavily in the land market, purchasing estates in three villages in south Buckinghamshire which, by the end of the thirteenth century, provided more than half the house's income. From the 1260s, nonetheless, the house fell into increasing financial disarray. Such was the crisis that the king was compelled to intervene in 1286 and again at the turn of the century, as the house descended more deeply into the relentless grip of its creditors.[23] In the winter of 1304-5, the house ran out of victuals and had to borrow on the security of its most valuable possessions, the advowson and glebe of the church of Dodford, which was finally sacrificed to amortize the house's debts. The interesting aspects of the financial difficulties of the house are its own inability to solve them, the failure of the Order to take specific action, and the need for the intervention of the Crown in 1286 to impose central financial control.

Investment in width–the continuous acquisition of land and rents–must really be seen in terms merely of consolidation in the thirteenth and fourteenth centuries. By the end of the twelfth century, the liberality of lay benefactors had evaporated. By that time, the laity was mainly restoring to the religious orders what had previously pertained to the Church but which had been appropriated into lay hands. Instead of returning these benefits to the secular clergy, the laity transferred them to monastic houses or the newer Orders of regular canons. The late twelfth century was thus the main era for the acquisition of spiritual property and the temporalities of parish churches–advowsons, glebes and tithes–by religious houses. In particular, the estates of Austin and Premonstratensian Canons were augmented by the return of glebe-demesnes. As for land and real property, the benefactions of the laity came to be replaced by the early thirteenth century by their concern about the unfettered alienation of land to the religious. This concern was succeeded by the long process of events leading to the Statute of Mortmain in 1279. In the first half of the thirteenth century, this concern was aggravated by the decline of some knights' estates at the hands of some religious houses. Whilst some of the knights of Peterborough Abbey, like the Hotots, survived, others succumbed to the abbey's re-acquisition of their land. Osney Abbey acquired manorial estates at the expense of the Gay family of Hampton Gay and its patrons, the Oillys of the barony of Oilly. Having descended into heavy financial difficulty by the reign of John, the Oillys were finally plunged into total insolvency in 1227, when the abbey acquired the family's manor of Weston-on-the-Green. Although there was no general crisis of the knightly families in Oxfordshire, the scale of benefactions to the religious had contracted to insignificance. The acquisition of land by religious houses in the thirteenth century was thus at a very much lower level than before. Houses such as Crowland and Thorney continued to engage in the land market, but with increasing difficulty.[24]

In this respect, the role of Henry of Eastry in the acquisition of land for Canterbury Cathedral Priory from 1285 to 1331 has recently been reappraised. Smith and Knowles assumed that Eastry entered into the land market in a much greater way than the prior's predecessors. It has now been revealed that Eastry's activity was simply a continuation of previous policy. During the early part of the thirteenth century, particularly from the 1230s to the 1250s, the treasurers of the priory invested in the purchase of land just as extensively as Eastry later did. Their task was relatively easy, since there was less resistance to sales and the price of land was lower, at seven to nine years' purchase–that is, the price established at seven to nine times the estimated annual value of the land. By the end of the century, the task was harder and the price higher. In the first twenty years of the fourteenth century, there was, moreover, a major disinvestment from land in favour of new building, at the same time as Abbot William Compton of Thorney (1305-22) was also diverting funds from investment in land to expenditure on building. This dislocation was partly caused by the temporary difficulties in the administration of the Statute of Mortmain, before general licences to acquire in mortmain removed the problem of specific licensing. Mavis Mate perceptively explains that this investment in land was perhaps less committed to real investment than doing what was expected. "What was the prime motivating factor behind these acquisitions? If the main purpose was to buttress falling revenues, then the monks were often to be disappointed. But to some extent the monks augmented their property because it was expected of them." In other words, it was the purpose of the religious to augment the patrimony of the saint, just as it was their intention to give glory to the saint and God through their buildings. When their role is perceived in this light, investment in land and expenditure in building are not exclusive, but complementary. Indeed, when the large-scale acquisition of land became more difficult in the later thirteenth century, then expenditure on building could be seen as an alternative and successful way of augmenting the status of the saint and God.[25]

Such an argument, however, ignores the question of investment in depth–capital investment in improvement. As the ability to acquire new estates receded, so it should have become more important to maximise the productivity of existing land. The question which has been discussed with some vigour is whether the religious (and lay landowners too) invested sufficiently in their estates, or whether social consumption was a form of disinvestment. Investment in improvement has been calculated to have been little more than five percent of income. On the other hand, it has been suggested that, given the technological limitations which existed, investment was circumscribed at this level by external factors. On the estates of Isabella de Forz, it has been suggested that such a level was sufficient for an increase in productivity. Research into north-east Norfolk, however, has demonstrated that productivity could be substantially further increased through more intensive capital and labour inputs.[26]

This last view is, however, slightly inconsistent with the alternative contention that the level of intensiveness of agriculture was primarily influenced by local custom and usage. In north-east Norfolk, the importance of seigniorial policy and the *pays* or region have been identified as significant determinants. Mate, conversely, considering the estates of Canterbury Cathedral Priory, remarks on the differences in intensiveness in different parts of the estate according to local usage and customary knowledge. This proposition extends her view of the continuity of development on the estates of the cathedral priory rather than radical changes in seignorial policy.

More recently, the emphasis on investment has been directed to the first half of the thirteenth century. Whereas the previous discussions of prelate-administrators had concentrated on the late thirteenth century, intensification of practice is now being discerned on some estates in the earlier thirteenth century. In particular, there seems to have been an enhancement of efforts on royal estates in the 1230s and 1240s and possibly too on the Winchester episcopal estates.[27]

The traditional picture of radical seigniorial change in policy in the later thirteenth century is therefore being somewhat diffused. Higher levels of intensive exploitation in the early thirteenth century antedate the compilation of the treatises on husbandry, except perhaps the perfunctory *Rules* of Robert Grosseteste. According to the most recent elucidation, using the evidence of the Exchequer Pipe Rolls, demesnes which had been leased to *firmarii* were resumed in hand for direct cultivation during the late twelfth and early thirteenth century.[28] The question also arises about what was happening on the estates of the new religious Orders–the Cistercians and Black and White Canons–during the twelfth century. These estates were only being formed at that time. Every indication is that the White Monks retained their estates in hand, particularly through their formation of granges. The regular canons received benefactions of land in a particular condition and may have had to respect that condition–leased or in hand. A principal part of their endowments consisted, however, of appropriated rectories, the glebe-demesnes becoming an important part of their estates. The evidence is that the regular canons instituted vicarages in the late twelfth century; the reforming bishops, such as Welles and Grosseteste, intervened to regulate this process only when it was already well advanced.[29] The regular canons may thus have had more flexibility through the management of glebe-demesnes.

The picture of investment which is emerging, therefore, consists of a patchy mosaic of region and time. Investment related to the appropriateness of the *pays* and seigniorial responses. Whilst north-east Norfolk and parts of the estate of Canterbury Cathedral Priory were managed at a more intensive level, most of Oxfordshire conformed to a conventional husbandry, with the possible exception of some idiosyncratic places such as the Merton College manor of Holywell, hard by Oxford. Seigniorial attitudes and resources were equally important, varying by religious house and, indeed, Order. The concept of a cohort of administrator-heads of the late thirteenth century is therefore much too simplistic; the reality was considerably more complicated.

Heads of Religious Houses as Administrators 171

Notes

¹ William Chester Jordan, *From Servitude to Freedom: Manumission in the Senonais in the Thirteenth Century* (Philadelphia, Pa.: University of Pennsylvania Press, 1986); the quotation is from Frank Pegues, review of Jordan's book in *Speculum* 63 (1988): 948-9.

² Rodney H. Hilton, *The English Peasantry in the Later Middle Ages* (Oxford: Oxford University Press, 1975), 174-214; Michael M. Postan, "Investment in Medieval Agriculture", *The Journal of Economic History* 27 (1967): 576-87, especially 578-81; Ian Kershaw, *Bolton Priory: The Economy of a Northern Monastery 1286-1325* (Oxford: Oxford University Press, 1973), 117-31; Jan Z. Titow, *English Rural Society* (London: Allen & Unwin, 1969), 49-50; Mavis Mate, "Profit and Productivity on the Estates of Isabella de Forz (1260-92)", *EcHR* 2^d ser., 33 (1980): 326-34.

³ Variously in R. A. (Tony) L. Smith, *Canterbury Cathedral Priory* (Cambridge: Cambridge University Press, 1943) and *Collected Papers of R. A. L. Smith* (London: Longman, Green & Co., 1947). David Knowles subsequently devoted a chapter to Eastry: *The Religious Orders in England*, 3 vols. (Cambridge: Cambridge University Press, 1948-59), I, 49-54.

⁴ Michael M. Postan and John Hatcher, "Population and Class Relations in Feudal Society", in *The Benner Debate: Agrarian Class Structure and Economic Development in Pre-Industrial Europe*, ed. Trevor H. Aston and C. H. E. Philpin (Cambridge: Cambridge University Press, 1987), 73.

⁵ Knowles, *Religious Orders in England*, I, 42-51, 322.

⁶ Kershaw, *Bolton Priory*, 13-14.

⁷ Review of *Cartulary of Bradenstoke* in *The Journal of the Society of Archivists* 7 (1982): 36-7, although the editor of the cartulary described the rather modest consolidation of the priory's estates by Priors Simon and William (II) in the early thirteenth century (*Cartulary of Bradenstoke*, 14-15).

⁸ Postan and Hatcher, "Population and Class Relations", 77-8.

⁹ A comparable narrative is contained in Bodl., MS Top. Devon d 5, fols. 3v-6r (cartulary of Newenham Priory, Devon): *De regimine Abbatum huius domus et per quot annos rexerunt* which is almost completely concerned with the material acquisitions of the abbots, but also records the extent of indebtedness on the demise of Abbot Richard Chichester (1293): *Memorandum quod cum domus de Nyweham die cessionis Dompni Ricardi Cicestr' Abbatis eiusdem domus fuisset indebitata in CCiiij^{xx}li. xl.s.* [sic] *v.d.ob. que debita acquietauit successor eius sine distracione mobilium et terrarum ac onerosis corrodiis.*

¹⁰ *Annales Monasterii de Oseneia* in *Annales Monastici*, IV, 1-352; *Cartulary of Oseney Abbey*.

Missed Opportunities?

[11] Dave Postles, "The Learning of Austin Canons: The Case of Oseney Abbey", *Nottingham Medieval Studies* 24 (1985): 32-43.

[12] Bodl., Twyne MS xxi, fol. 264r; *Annales de Oseneia*, 73; Bodl., James MS 26, fol. 159r; *Cartulary of Oseney Abbey*, III, xviii-xix.

[13] *Cartulary of Oseney Abbey*, III, 66-74.

[14] *Cartulary of Oseney Abbey*, I, 136; III, 22-74. For confraternities of the fabric, Christopher R. Cheney, "Church-building in the Middle Ages", *Bulletin of the John Rylands Library* 34 (1951-2): 20-36, especially 33-6;

[15] Eileen Power illustrated from the example of Pipewell Abbey how easily religious houses could descend into deep indebtedness through "high farming" and "improvident wool contracts": *The Wool Trade in English Medieval History* (Oxford: Oxford University Press, 1941), 43-4.

[16] R. H. Snape, *English Monastic Finances in the Later Middle Ages* (Cambridge: Cambridge University Press, 1926); Smith, "The *Regimen Scaccarii* in English Monasteries", in *Collected Papers of R. A. L. Smith*, 54-73; despite Pecham's injunctions, doubt has been expressed as to whether the treasurers were ever installed at Rochester: A. Brown, "The Financial System of Rochester Cathedral Priory: A Reconsideration", *Bulletin of the Institute of Historical Research* 1 (1977): 115-20. For the overwhelming power of the cellarer, *Cellarers' Rolls of Battle Abbey*, 8-14.

[17] For examples of those who did, however, *Digest of the Charters ... Dunstable*, 216 (ca.1225).

[18] Kershaw, *Bolton Priory*, 7-9, 170-1 (Table XXIV and graph).

[19] *Rolls and Registers ... Sutton*, II, 145-6.

[20] W. Holtzmann, *Papsturkunden in England* (Berlin, 1930-52), I, 583-4; *Cartulary of Cirencester Abbey*, I, xx-xxi, and no. 327; *Triennial Chapters ... Augustinian Canons*, 22-3; Cambridge University Library MS Dd xiv 2, fol. 128r. (Osney); *Cartulary of Oseney Abbey*, III, 39-40; "Annales Prioratus de Dunstaplia", in *Annales Monastici*, III, 316, 409-10; J. C. Blomfield, *History of the Deanery of Bicester* (Oxford, 1882), 135; The National Archives, London, SC6/1257/11-12 (Leicester); Kershaw, *Bolton Priory*, 2; Snape, *English Monastic Finances*, 40 (Pecham); John Rylands University Library, Manchester, Lat. MS 226, fols. 4r, 7v-8r (Norwich); Christopher R. Cheney, "Norwich Cathedral Priory in the Fourteenth Century", *Bulletin of the John Rylands Library* 20 (1936): 93-120; H. W. Saunders, *An Introduction to the Obedientiary and Manor Rolls of Norwich Cathedral Priory* (Norwich, 1930), 17.

[21] Knowles, *Religious Orders*, I, 55-63, especially 59-60; Smith, "The *Regimen Scaccarii*"; Christopher R. Cheney, "The Papal Legate and English Monasteries in 1206", *EHR* 46 (1936): 443-52.

[22] *Documents ... English Black Monks*, 64-92, especially 84.

[23] *Luffield Priory Charters*, I, vii-viii.

[24] Brian R. Kemp, "Monastic Possession of Parish Churches", *JEH* 31

(1980): 133-60; David Carpenter, "Was There a Crisis of the Knightly Class in the Thirteenth Century? The Oxfordshire Evidence", *EHR* 95 (1980): 721-52; Edmund King, *Peterborough Abbey 1086-1310: A Study in the Land Market* (Cambridge: Cambridge University Press, 1973), 35-54; King, "Large and Small Landowners in Thirteenth Century England: The Case of Peterborough Abbey" and Peter R. Coss, "Sir Geoffrey de Langley and the Crisis of the Knightly Class in Thirteenth Century England", both in *Landlords, Peasants and Politics in Medieval England*, ed. Trevor H. Aston (Cambridge: Cambridge University Press, 1987), 141-202; Sandra Raban, *Mortmain Legislation and the English Church* (Cambridge: Cambridge University Press, 1982); Edward Miller, "The State and the Landed Interest in Thirteenth Century France and England", *TRHS* 5th ser., 2 (1952): 124-6; Giles Constable, *Monastic Tithes from their Origins to the Twelfth Century* (Cambridge: Cambridge University Press, 1964), 153-60.

[25] Mavis Mate, "Property Investment by Canterbury Cathedral Priory, 1250-1400", *Journal of British Studies* 23 (1984): 1-21; Sandra Raban, "The Land Market and the Aristocracy in the Thirteenth Century", in *Tradition and Change: Essays in Honour of Marjorie Chibnall*, ed. Diana Greenway, Christopher J. Holdsworth and Jane Sayers (Cambridge: Cambridge University Press, 1985), 239-61.

[26] See n. 2 above; Bruce M. S. Campbell, "Arable Productivity in Medieval England: Some Evidence from Norfolk", *Journal of Economic History* 43 (1983): 379-404, and Campbell, "Agricultural Progress in Medieval England: Some Evidence from Eastern Norfolk", *EcHR* 2d ser., 37 (1983): 26-46.

[27] Mavis Mate, "Medieval Agrarian Practices: The Determining Factors", *Agricultural History Review* 33 (1985): 22-31; Robert C. Stacey, "Agricultural Investment and Management of the Royal Demesne Manors, 1236-1240", *Journal of Economic History* 46 (1986): 919-93; Kathleen Biddick and C. C. J. H. Bijleveld,, "Agrarian Productivity on the Estates of the Bishopric of Winchester in the Early Thirteenth Century: A Managerial Perspective", in *Land, Labour and Livestock: Historical Studies in European Agricultural Productivity*, ed. Bruce M. S. Campbell and Mark Overton (Manchester: Manchester University Press, 1991), 95-123.

[28] Paul D. A. Harvey, "The Pipe Rolls and the Adoption of Demesne Farming in England", *EcHR* 2d ser., 27 (1974): 345-59.

[29] Marion Gibbs and Jane Lang, *Bishops and Reform 1215-72 with Special Reference to the Lateran Council of 1215* (Oxford: Oxford University Press, 1934), 167-70.

Part II

8
Gifts in Frankalmoign, Warranty of Land, and Feudal Society

In recent discussion, gifts to the religious have been perceived as exercising a formative influence in the forging of some norms and customs of feudal tenure during the twelfth century. On the one hand, it has been suggested that gifts to the church assisted the clarification in the mind of lay feudal society of the concept of heritability–that is, the future enjoyment of inheritance–since donors could not alienate in perpetuity that which was not already heritable. This suggestion is extremely important in view of the different perceptions of political and legal historians concerning the development of heritability of tenures and tenant right during the twelfth century, which are seen variously to have existed as social or legal norms from varying times and from different causes.[1] A related argument runs that, whilst the warranty clause in charters (but not warranty *per se*) was initially conceived within the framework of the personal relationship between lord and man, its more widespread diffusion in charters was stimulated largely through the auspices of these religious beneficiaries of gifts in frankalmoign. The introduction of warranty into charters at the instance of religious beneficiaries is thus related to their concern to secure their own perpetual rights in the land at a time of a nascent realization of hereditary tenant right, and the religious were thus foremost in the insertion of warranty clauses in charters which they, as beneficiaries, wrote or influenced, to secure their own unbridled tenure in perpetuity. Lay feudal society, it is implied, seeing the Church securing its tenure in this way, subsequently adopted the warranty clause more widely in its own charters to secure its own hereditary rights and tenant rights against superior lords. Whilst warranty of land may have been concerned *stricto sensu* with the feudal relationship between lay lord and lay tenant, it was the religious, who (it has been suggested) did not acknowledge lordship, who were responsible for the more widespread diffusion of the warranty clause in charters.[2]

Some reservations may, however, be suggested before the full acceptance of these interpretations. Consequently, a further assessment is made here of the relationships between gifts (and tenure) in frankalmoign, the heritability of land in tenures, and the development of the warranty clause in charters. Some questions are raised about how gifts to the religious in free alms might have affected lay tenure of land in return for secular services, in such areas as heritability and tenant right in the form of the warranty clause in charters. In the process, other forms of corroboration of gifts to the religious are examined. An attempt is therefore made to assess how far these notions were informed by tenure for spiritual services and how far they were generated within feudal relations between lord and lay tenant.

One of the principal questions involved here is how far tenure in frankalmoign was regarded as a norm and whether its influence would have rubbed off easily onto tenurial relationships between laymen. The performance of spiritual services in return for tenure was in a sense a tenurial relationship, albeit one demanding unenforceable services. On the other hand, there was something extraordinary about tenure in frankalmoign. For example, lay tenants were required to perform homage, whilst the religious did not. The importance here was that a new tenant, even a presumptive and accepted heir, would have been admitted only after the performance of homage. Homage may therefore have been a technical impediment to automatic succession, tenant right and heritability for lay tenants, until the lord could be compelled to accept homage offered by an heir. The religious were not involved in this sort of ceremony and relationship. Whereas livery of seisin and charters ensured the tenure of the religious, for lay tenants homage was primary and charters secondary. Homage existed as the nexus of the relationship between lord and tenant at the time of the oral disposition, before charters became customary between lord and lay tenant.[3] The questions may therefore remain as to the exact relationship between gifts to the religious and the subinfeudation of laymen.

In later legal exposition, gifts in frankalmoign were to God and the patrimony of the Saint. Bracton expressed the gift as *primo et principaliter* to God.[4] There was therefore no relationship between lord and man. Of course, in the twelfth century, this level of sophistication of the concept had not been reached. Founders and patrons in the early twelfth century still regarded religious houses as their *Eigenkirchen*, their own churches, in the physical sense.[5] Moreover, the largest Benedictine religious houses were tenants in chief responsible for knight service.[6] Of course, as Kimball has demonstrated, not all land held in free alms was quit of all secular services, such as intrinsic rent service. As religious houses became more acquisitive of land, especially by purchase, during the later twelfth century, so the difference between tenure in alms and tenure by other services must have narrowed in lay eyes, as the religious also became liable by this means for payment of rent charges. Tenure in frankalmoign may thus have seemed in some respects just another form of tenure.

Nevertheless, even in the twelfth century, gifts to the religious must have had an exceptional nature within the context of feudal tenure. Tenure in return for services which were both spiritual and undefined or unspecified was extrinsic to the basic terms of feudal tenure. Moreover, the unspecified spiritual services could not be enforced. In this context, the gift of lands to the religious in perpetuity may have also seemed exceptional rather than something which should affect the relationship between lord and lay tenant, and exceptional allowances and provisions may have been fostered for the salvation of men's and women's souls which would not easily or within conscience transfer to secular relationships. Recent scholarship relating to earlier gifts to the religious–for example, to Cluny–has regarded them very much within the context of gift-exchange in the anthropological tradition of Marcel Mauss. Moreover, in these earlier benefactions to Cluny, alms were not necessarily perpetual, although gifts in frankalmoign may have become intrinsically perpetual at a later time.[7] Finally, again as Kimball has shown, there was still some confusion, even in the late twelfth century, as to whether land held by the Church should be declared lay fee or be considered as spiritualities. The introduction of the assize *utrum* from 1164 did not immediately resolve these doubts.[8] Even in the late twelfth century, therefore, tenure in free alms may have seemed something entirely different and outside the terms of feudal tenure.

These gifts required the consent of superior lords, as did many alienations by mesne tenants, although the development of substitution changed the rules of this game. In the case of gifts in frankalmoign, this confirmation from above was necessary because the religious were being absolved of the secular services, but someone had to provide for their performance.[9] The barons thus almost certainly had this situation in mind (as well as, possibly, the *maritagium*) when, in 1217, they proposed that no one should alienate so much of their fee that services could not be properly performed.[10] Perhaps the confirmations had more than one rationale, however. Confirmations by all superior lords might well imply that the donor, the mesne tenant or sub-tenant, had no exclusive hereditary proprietary rights in the land, and that only the superior lords could ultimately convey the right to hold in perpetuity.[11] In the majority of cases, furthermore, the religious house took trouble to elicit a charter of confirmation from the heir, presenting a chicken and egg situation. If the heir is acknowledged already to have an indefeasible right to inherit, and therefore to have potential rights in the land alienated for spiritual services, how far did gifts in frankalmoign influence the development of heritability?

The inchoate nature of gifts in frankalmoign in the early and mid-twelfth century perhaps also extended, however, to the perpetual nature of gifts in frankalmoign. Not all charters, it seems, contained the full diplomatic formula referring to perpetual alms; a proportion referred only to free and pure alms.[12] The vagaries of these expressions may have resulted simply from the inchoate diplomatics rather than a deeper reason. Perhaps perpetuity was always understood as an integral part of gifts in frankalmoign, yet the full diplomatic formula as it evolved *later* took care to invoke perpetuity (*in liberam puram et perpetuam elemosinam*). The expression in some charters in early and the mid-twelfth century seems to be more concerned with free and pure, that is, quit of the secular services, with this exception sometimes declared emphatically.[13] Other charters searched for the expression of perpetuity.[14] It seems possible therefore that perpetuity (that is, the equivalent of heritability) in gifts in frankalmoign became an explicit clause later rather than sooner, and this fact may have a bearing on how far these gifts affected the notion of heritability.

When viewed in the context of gifts in frankalmoign, warranty may seem a protection of the perpetual rights in the land.[15] When seen within the feudal relationship between lord and lay tenant, however, as Professor Milsom has illustrated, it seems more like a bond between lord and tenant, but not necessarily between a lord and his heirs and the tenant and his heirs.[16] The warranty is confirmation of the tenant's right against his lord, conceded by the lord, and against the rights of other claimants to the land. In this relationship, the lord originally offered an exchange of land should his warranty to his tenant fail (such as through action in the king's courts).[17] There are a number of important issues involved here: first, the chronology of the appearance of the warranty clause in charters to religious houses by comparison with its inclusion in charters of subinfeudation; secondly, whether warranty was necessarily the preferred form of surety of the religious or whether they had other–earlier and preferred–forms of insurance. In the latter case, the discussion might involve arbitration by ecclesiastics or other religious and oaths and pledges of faith within a spiritual context, which theoretically might also be referred to ecclesiastical jurisdiction if repudiated (but complicated by the late twelfth century by writs of prohibition).[18] Moreover, the overwhelming proportion of charters of the twelfth century comprise benefactions to the religious. By comparison, the number of charters to laymen is comparatively small. This disproportion can convey the impression that warranty in charters to the religious was predominant, but it may be an illusion. An examination of the development of the warranty clause within charters to laymen in the process of subinfeudation and of the forms of securing the gift employed by religious houses, may help to elucidate these developments, although this may be no more than a starting point. From this examination of corroboration clauses and those few precious warranty clauses before 1154, it is hoped to show the possibility that warranty was introduced as a specific clause in charters during the adversities of Stephen's reign, at a time when good lordship was at a premium, when disinheritance was not unlikely, and protection by lords of baronial status was of vital importance. The later diffusion of warranty clauses by charters to the religious is not discounted. On the other hand, it is suggested that the religious had many other forms of assurance which they may indeed have preferred, whilst warranty clauses would have been crucial to lay tenants.

Before the advent of warranty, a number of devices were employed in charters to both lay and religious to secure the gift. A common diplomatic form was a clause *volo* perhaps modelled on the similar clause which had already become common diplomatic form in royal writ-charters in the early twelfth century, The clause became an almost standard feature of the charters of successive Rogers de Mowbray both in subinfeudation of lay tenants and gifts to the religious, from the mid-twelfth century to the third quarter. Similar, elaborate forms of the clause were constantly employed within the charters of Randle, Earl of Chester. In the charters of Randle, the clause became formalized at an early date (by the 1130s and 1140s) as *Quare (Eapropter) volo et firmiter precipio*. The Mowbray clause also attained this ultimate form. The charters of Miles and Roger, earls of Gloucester, contained the same clause in this final form (ca.1143-55). Geoffrey de Mandeville also employed the clause in charters of ca.1143-8 and 1157-8. When Robert, son of Ralph de Sifregaste, gave land to Waverley Abbey, his charter included the corroboration *Et uolo et precipio* (ca.1130-7). Hugh Poer's charter to Daventry Priory was affirmed *Quapropter volo et firmiter precipio* (ca.1148-66). Robert Foliot conveyed the manor of Sulby (Northamptonshire) to Westminster Abbey with exactly the same affirmation (ca.1148-50). When Richard Basset made a quitclaim to Saint Benet Holme (ca.1127-54), he did so emphasizing *Ideo uolo et precipio*. In another gift to Saint Benet, Albert Gresley used the more refined *Quare uolo et precipio*. More elaborately, Walter de Roumara employed the phrase *Eapropter uolo et firmiter corroboro* in his charter to Crowland Abbey (ca.1151-53). When Gilbert de Gant re-seised Sayer de Arceles (ca.1142), he did so reciting *Quare volo et precipio*. *Quapropter uolo (... et nolo)* was the incipit of the clause included in a charter of Robert son of Godwin to Saint Gregory, Canterbury (ca.1136-50). The gift of Waleran, count of Meulan to Bordesley (1141) concluded *Quare uolo et firmiter precipio*, as did charters to other beneficiaries from Richard de Lucy (ca.1153-4), the earl de Warenne (1154), and Geoffrey Ridel (ca.1155-60). Charters to Shrewsbury Abbey also contain the clause in various forms: from William fitzAlan (*ideo precipio... et volo* (ca.1155-60)); Hamon Peverel and his wife Sybil (*et volumus et firmiter concedimus* (ca.1135)); William Peverel (*et volo atque precipio* (1144)); Roger Corbet (*quare volo et firmiter precipio* (ca.1121-35)); and so also in other charters, such as those of Reginald de Warenne (*quare volo et firmiter precipio* (ca.1153-9)); Gilbert de Ghent (*Quare uolo et firmiter precipio* (ca.1148-56)); Robert, earl of Leicester (*Unde et uolo et firmiter precipio* (ca.1139-47)); and Walter Giffard, earl of Buckingham (*Uolo autem et precipio* (ca.1152-8)).[19]

The development of the clause can be followed in the charters of the earldom of Gloucester, in which it occurred in isolation in ca.1126-41, 1132 and 1135, but much more frequently between ca.1140 and ca.1180 (although some incidences can still be found as late as ca.1200-17). In thirty-two cases, the charter was in favour of a religious house, but the grantees in six charters were laymen. In all cases, the clause was to ensure peaceful possession, usually expressing the lord's will with the subjunctive forms of verbs for possession: *habeant, teneant, possideant*. The open address of some of the charters, to the earl's "friends" or kin (*amici*) and ministers, is perhaps indicative of the origins of the clause as a precept or writ. The clause was also included, however, in charters where the address was restricted to the beneficiary.[20]

This clause was first incorporated into the charters of the great baronial donors soon after the early years of Stephen's reign. The fashion may have diffused downwards through imitation of royal writ-charters. It is also possible to regard this clause simply as a notification, in combining a writ within the charter. Whereas a writ *may* (in theory at least) have been supplemental to a charter to notify the intent of the charter, it seems in practice that this two-fold provision rarely happened in the twelfth century, since the charter was itself both evidentiary and a notification. This imitation may have been, on the other hand, a form of rivalry to royal power, reflecting the territorial power wielded by the baronage during the troubles of Stephen's reign, upon which Professor King has recently commented.[21] Although the clause filtered down into the charters of a few lesser donors in the later twelfth century, such as Robert, son of Baldwin, who gave a few acres to Stoke by Clare, the clause was mainly transient, particularly associated with the mid-twelfth century, significantly with baronial donors or benefactors, and especially with the period of civil disturbance and regional baronial power.[22] Its disappearance from charters seems to be incipient from the 1160s. The clause emphasized that the especial will of the donor was that the donee enjoy a free and peaceful possession of the land. In a few cases, the clause claimed to ensure that possession against legal action.[23] In the case of subinfeudation, the free and peaceful enjoyment of the land was linked to the performance of services; but in gifts in frankalmoign, there was no allusion to services or specific exemption from the secular services. The latter stipulation was included in a charter of Roger Corbet in favor of Shrewsbury Abbey (ca.1121-35):

> *Quare volo et firmiter precipio ... quod nullus successorum meorum requirat ab eis inde aliquod servicium nisi orationes.*[24]

The same emphasis appeared in a charter of Roger de Bray to Newington Longeville Priory, in which the donor binds himself and his heirs not to vex the monks or exact anything from them, and to warrant against all men as his pure alms. The description of the gifts simply as pure alms suggests that the primary concern, even in the warranty, was the freedom from secular services. In a further charter of confirmation, however, the warranty clause specifically referred to pure, free and perpetual alms. Both these charters relate to ca.1167-73. About the same time, gifts by several others to the same priory were secured by a pledge of faith or oath on the altar or gospels, that neither the donor nor his heirs would vex the monks nor make any exactions from the house (ca. 1175).[25]

The inclusion of this diplomatic form in many charters of these baronial donors has several implications. First, the donor was unequivocally stating his emphatic will that the seisin of the donee should not be disturbed. The donor emphatically supported the tenant right against third parties. In the case of lay recipients, however, it was also only a commitment to the tenant right provided the services were performed, reflecting the discretionary and disciplinary rights of lords. Consequently, there seems little doubt that this clause was introduced at the instance of the donor as an affirmation of the donor's will. The clause therefore reflected in written form the "good lordship" remarked upon by Professor Milsom.[26] Moreover, the clause seems to have first appeared in charters at the time of maximum insecurity of tenants, during the vicissitudes of Stephen's reign. The clause may therefore not only have been modelled on royal practice, but specifically related to the difficulty of the times. The innate spirit seems to have been the tenurial relationship between lord and lay tenant, the "maintenance" of tenants, and baronial protection within a sphere of influence and affinity.

A second implication of the diffusion of this clause is that some of the baronage may have had their own *scriptores* and were not entirely dependent on religious beneficiaries for the production of charters. The clause *volo* appeared simultaneously in baronial charters to laymen as well as the religious. The imputation is thus that at least some of the charters produced for them at the time of the initial introduction of this clause, were compiled from within the baronial household. Of course, the compilation of some of these charters does not preclude the production of many more in a *scriptorium* of the beneficiaries as well.

Other forms of surety antedated both warranty and the *volo* clause. One alternative method of securing the gift was propagated at the instance of the religious, and had, indeed, a long history. The pledge of faith or oath, especially symbolically on the altar of the religious house, occurred in charters to the religious from their inception. There seems some ground for supposing that some religious houses continued to regard it as a primary way of ensuring the permanence of a gift. This method obviously relied on spiritual sanctions and appealed to men's consciences rather than to the feudal bond or tenurial relationship. Many charters to religious houses continued to contain this form of expression, sometimes to the exclusion of warranty, sometimes reinforcing warranty, well into the thirteenth century.[27] An earlier form of the oath or pledge of faith was the symbolic livery on the altar of the religious house. The symbolic liveries to Durham Cathedral Priory have been fully explored.[28] Symbolic livery was an integral part of all gifts in the early twelfth century, both to lay and religious, but the occurrence of the event on the altar of the religious house induced spiritual confirmation of the gift. Ivo de Clacston confirmed the gift and grant to Belvoir Priory by his father of the advowson, tithes and land in Long Clawson by placing a knife on the altar of Saint Mary. Iwein de Albineio granted the advowson of Plungar to Belvoir by passing a rod (baculum) on the altar of Saint Mary. When Robert Dispenser gave the manor of Cumberton to Westminster Abbey (ca. 1095-8), his wife and brother proffered symbolic items on the altar, including two silver candle holders (and thus committing his wife with right of dower and the potential heir to the gift). When Elias Gifford endowed Gloucester Abbey, he did so by placing a text on the altar of Saint Peter (1121); slightly later (ca.1139-48) an unidentified Philip and his wife made their livery in the chapter house:

> ... et iterum posuimus eam (sc. hanc autem terram) super altare liberam et ab omni servitio et consuetudine quietam...

presumably by placing a sod on the altar. Many of the gifts of the early twelfth century recorded in the *Chronicon* of Abingdon Abbey involved a symbolic livery on the altar of the conventual church. William fitzAudoeni made his before the prior and convent of Saint Denys, Southampton, with a knife (*per hunc cultellum confirmavi*), perhaps, as putatively in the case of the Durham knife-hafts, the one which cut the sod of soil. Hamon Peverel and his wife Sybil endowed Shrewsbury Abbey with the vill of Kinnersley (ca.1136-9) by placing a copy of the bible on the altar (*per textum evangelii eam super altare ... obtulimus*). When Ranulf de Belneis restored to the same house the manor of Betton, of which he had unjustly disseised the house during the civil war, he did so not only before the county court, but also on the altar of the house by symbolic livery. A number of gifts were conveyed to Stoke by Clare symbolically by placing a *candelabrum* on the altar of Saint John the Baptist in the late twelfth century, as well as by the donor and his heirs in one transfer placing their right hands on the same altar. Even grants of jurisdiction over men (*homines*) to Stoke by Clare by the Chievre (Capra) family were sustained by symbolic livery on that altar in the mid-twelfth century.[29] In these symbolic liveries, the act was witnessed by the whole convent or chapter, sometimes afforced with witnesses from outside, and, of course, by God, with spiritual sanctions. Indeed, in some charters of the twelfth century, an anathema, similar to the one in Anglo-Saxon diplomas, was developed against third parties, such as in the charter of Hervey de Wilbrighton in favour of Shrewsbury Abbey in the mid-twelfth century, giving half a virgate and a meadow, and the anathema added by Walter *capellanus* to the foot of the charter which he wrote for Adeliz, wife of Gilbert fitzRichard, in favor of Thorney Abbey (ca.1136-8).[30]

The pledge may have developed more widely in charters in the early twelfth century. A charter of William de Insula to Holy Trinity, London, has the pledge in the notification.

> *Sciatis quod habeo in conventione canonicis Sancte Trinitatis Lundonie per fidem quam feci eis affidare Willelmum Ulculf hominem meum in capitulo ipsorum...* (early twelfth century).[31]

The pledge of faith and oath developed during the twelfth century to become one of the principal devices by which religious houses secured gifts. The pledge and oath were usually performed in the convent or chapter house and specifically recorded in the charters. It seems that some of the older Benedictine houses tended to rely on a pledge or an oath more than on any other form of device until well into the thirteenth century. The majority of charters to Eynsham Abbey have the pledge or oath as the main form of assurance, often to the exclusion of warranty even in the late twelfth century.[32] The pledge had not been exclusively the preserve of religious houses, as it may well have been employed in charters between lay parties, especially the pledge in hand (hand-fast). Its importance in some regions of the Danelaw has been attested, involving charters between laymen. During the twelfth century, however, it became the principal method of security for some religious houses. Thus, Holdsworth, referring to the practice of the pledge of faith in hand in charters to Rufford Abbey, commented: " ... there is sufficient evidence to show that charters which refer to this procedure do not normally have warranty clauses, and that they all precede c1200".[33] The pledge and oath became increasingly associated with spiritual sanctions and enforcement, so that it was not unusual that religious houses may have tended towards this device as at least one mode of assurance. During the late twelfth century, after the more general diffusion of the warranty clause into charters, some charters to religious houses contained both warranty and pledge or oath, sometimes combined in the same clause, as mutual corroboration.

The *laudatio parentum*, corroboration by the prospective heirs (and the wife of the donor to bar dower), was also developed within a secular environment, but became increasingly used to corroborate and secure gifts to the religious.[34] Initially, the *laudatio* comprised only the specific prospective heirs (the eldest son, the brother of the donor), but subsequently developed into a more general commitment of the contingent heirs. That phase, however, was probably not attained until ca.1200. By that time, the *laudatio* was declining, although it continued to feature in many charters in Oxfordshire through to ca.1230.[35] The *laudatio* was also included in charters which contained warranty or oath. In some charters of Newington Longeville Priory, those implicated in the *laudatio* also jointly pledged their faith or made an oath on the gospels or the high altar.[36] The *laudatio* had also developed in an environment where heritability was being recognized as a principle, from the early and middle twelfth century. In practice, it seems to have become increasingly applied in charters to the religious, although its employment in charters between lay parties would not have been excluded.

Religious houses therefore had at their disposal several devices by which they could secure the gift in frankalmoign, a gift sometimes implicitly, sometimes explicitly, in perpetuity. Perhaps not surprisingly, religious houses placed some emphasis on those forms of security assured by spiritual sanctions. Warranty undoubtedly became a further option during the late twelfth century, but it was not consistently used, reflected, for example, in its omission from charters of some religious houses in Oxfordshire before the end of the twelfth century.[37] A large proportion of charters continued to omit warranty even in the late twelfth century. Yet these alternative forms may not have contained the wider enforcement inherent in warranty. Pledge, oath, *laudatio*, and symbolic livery were all specifically concerned to ensure the integrity of the donor, his or her family and heirs, but were not good more widely against third parties. By contrast, warranty ultimately developed as an emphatic assurance against the actions of third parties, in that the donor would provide compensation (by exchange) should the gift be lost by the actions of a third party. Even so, it seems that a number of religious houses preferred to rely on conscience and spiritual sanction until at least the end of the twelfth century, sometimes to the exclusion of warranty.

A few charters suggest that warranty may have been closely related to tenure in frankalmoign. In ca.1150, Gilbert, son of Herbert de Rigsby, endowed Greenfield Priory with a very specific warranty clause in his charter:

> *ego et heredes mei warantizabimus ut puram elemosinam et liberam ab omni seculari seruitio...*[38]

About the same time (ca.1150-60), Hugh, son of Pinceon, gave land to Kirkstead Abbey and promised to warrant *sicut puram et perpetuam elemosinam nostram inperpetuum*. Geoffrey de Turs gave land to Newhouse Abbey, also ca.1150-60, committing himself to warrant *sicut nostram liberam et puram elemosinam*.[39] This association does not necessarily reflect cause. The warranty presumably related to freedom from secular services as well as tenure in perpetuity. In the case of the charter of Herbert de Rigsby, no mention is made of perpetual tenure, although this may have been implicit in free and pure alms. The emphasis of warranty is on the exemption from secular services, with the implication that Herbert would be responsible for them. Neither does the charter of Geoffrey de Turs mention perpetual tenure explicitly. Moreover, none of these early warranty clauses for religious houses referred to exchange in case of failure of the warranty. Moreover, warranty clauses may even have been introduced into charters earlier, in charters to which both parties were laymen.

The origins of warranty may therefore be sought elsewhere. In some cases, the diffusion of the warranty clause in charters may have been expedited by its adoption by some religious houses, but the explanation of the initial impetus to the development of warranty clauses may reside in the secular relationship between lord and man.

Some early warranty clauses have been discovered in charters of the 1130s of York, Ramsey Abbey and Worcester Cathedral Priory, but they occurred in isolation.[40] Some charters from the Mowbrays for Byland Abbey have been discounted as not authentic because of their inclusion of sophisticated warranty clauses more appropriate to a later time.[41] Other charters of the Mowbrays of ca.1141-8 also contain warranty clauses, significantly with the promise of exchange or *escambium*.[42] Warranty with exchange was included in a charter of Simon de St Liz to the Abbey of Saint James, Northampton (ca.1145-50). William fitzAlan included warranty in one of his charters to Shrewsbury Abbey in ca.1144-55, relating to half a fee in Droitwich and a salt mine there, but not in his other charters in favor of the abbey, which were afforced by the *volo* clause. Adam de Neufmarché included a warranty clause in favor of Blyth Priory (ca.1130-61).[43]

Slightly earlier, in the early 1140s, several charters of Randle, earl of Chester, to his lay mesne tenants provide a different insight into the origins of warranty clauses. Randle gave Weekley to William the falconer in ca.1141-3 and his charter included both the formula *Eapropter volo et precipio* and a warranty with exchange, in embryonic form. In ca.1142-6, Randle subinfeudated Hugh Bardulf in the manor of Waddington (Lincolnshire). This charter contains again both the warranty (with exchange) and the *volo* clauses. Randle, in ca.1144-5, enfeoffed Hugh son of Pinceon in one hundred solidates of land in Lincolnshire; the charter contained warranty with exchange and the clause *volo*.[44] In ca.1147-8, Randle enfeoffed Robert fitzHarding in Fifehead (Dorset), a charter again characterized by the *volo* clause and warranty with exchange. In this charter the warranty is more explicit:

> *Et nisi eis* (Robert, his son and their heirs) *istam tenuram de Fifhida warrentizare possem, escambium ad valens et ad eius warandum donarem, priusquam de predicta Fifhida dissaisirentur.*[45]

As Barraclough remarked in his edition of this charter, the explicitness of this clause may have reflected the decline in fortunes of the rebels against Stephen in this region.[46] A similar context surrounded an embryonic warranty clause in a slightly later charter of William, earl of Gloucester, to Ranulf FitzGerold. In ca.1150-9,

William enfeoffed Ranulf in twelve librates of land in addition to land previously transferred to Ranulf, to comprise one knight's fee. William professed that if there was any challenge to the tenure (from a third party) and an exchange could not be procured, William would provide satisfaction for Ranulf from his own demesne, before Ranulf may be disseised (*antequam de sua terra dissaisiatur*). This embryonic warranty is closely related to the fear of disseisin in troubled times and the duty of good lordship.[47]

Herein, perhaps, lies the immediate reason for the introduction of warranty clauses into charters during this precise period–the vicissitudes of Stephen's reign. Warranty clauses had apparently existed in Normandy ca.1100.[48] Their diffusion into charters on this side of the Channel and in these lands of the Anglo-Norman baronage may have been simply a question of time. Nevertheless, it seems more than fortuitous that they were actually introduced at the time of maximum insecurity of tenure and seisin. Other charters of the earl of Chester reveal the re-seisin of several tenants who had probably been disseised.[49] The simultaneous widespread use of the *Quare volo* formula by many baronial donors as well as the incipience of the warranty clause at this time suggests that the impetus to both lay in the uncertainty of the time, in a purely secular world.

Considerations of the nature of feudal tenure in England during the twelfth century differ between political, constitutional and legal historians. Some perceive inheritance in practice sooner rather than later after the Conquest, some attach importance to the Coronation Oath of Henry I in 1100, others the stability of inheritance by the end of the reign of Henry I (at least at the level of baronial families), some the critical importance of Stephen's reign and the compromise of Westminster in 1153-4, others a movement from social norms to legal norms of inheritance (and "property") during the late twelfth century.[50]

It seems certain that political disruption resulted in discontinuity of inheritances during the twelfth century, both in the early years of Henry I, in his establishment of his own *novi homines*, and in the vicissitudes of Stephen's reign, as the country was divided in political allegiances and affinities. Henry had disinherited some families with whose lands he elevated his own *curiales*, during his earlier years.[51] Perhaps other lords, at that time, exhibited a similar mentality. The *Chronicon* of Abingdon Abbey recorded that Abbot Faritius made Henry son of Oini heir of all the lands which his father had held whilst his father was alive provided Henry performed the service of one knight's fee, ca.1104.[52] In this case, it seems, it was the abbot who made the heir within the norms of the time, not God or any unequivocal right of inheritance, so that Faritius seems to be exercising that discretionary right of lordship in a "truly seigniorial world". During the civil war, many of the knights of the abbey encroached on the abbey's own *dominicum* and withdrew their services, which were only restored after Henry II's succession. Similar depredations occurred on the estates of Ramsey Abbey during the civil war. Immediately after the Conquest, subinfeudation had been achieved largely through oral disposition of the land.[53] Charters for subinfeudation and gifts of land were only becoming more widespread by the 1140s. The first generation of tenants had passed by the early twelfth century, and the second generation had, by and large, in practice inherited. All these variables in the 1140s conspired towards the introduction of the warranty clause in charters between lay parties at that time. If, as Tabuteau has suggested, warranty was evident in charters in Normandy in ca.1100, and related there to heritability, the question remains whether its absence from England until some thirty to forty years later reflects on the nature of inheritance in England. A further implication is the timing of the development of "good lordship". It has been suggested that "good lordship" was enforced when the Crown in the reign of Henry II intervened to supervise lords doing right to their tenants, in the process inadvertently removing the judicial process into the royal courts, from the 1160s.[54] The introduction of warranty in the 1130s and 1140s, however, may reflect an earlier enhancement of the relationship between lord and tenant, within the context of the extension of the territorial power of barons, their power in relationship to the Crown, and the "maintenance" of affinities and undertenants.

Notes

[1] James C. Holt, "Feudal Society and the Family in Early Medieval England: II. Notions of Patrimony," *TRHS* 5th ser., 33 (1983): 200-4; Emily Z. Tabuteau, *Transfers of Property in Eleventh-Century Norman Law* (Chapel Hill, N.C.: University of North Carolina Press, 1988), 102-3. For the debate about heritability, see below.

[2] Paul R. Hyams,"Warranty and Good Lordship in Twelfth Century England," *Law and History Review* 5 (1987): 474-476.

[3] Elizabeth Kimball, "Tenure in Frank Almoign and Secular Services," *EHR* 43 (1928): 341-53. I am grateful to Professor Milsom for indicating to me the significance of homage; see also S.F.C. (Toby) Milsom, *The Legal Framework of English Feudalism* (Cambridge: Cambridge University Press, 1976), 172-3.

[4] *Bracton On the Laws and Customs of England*, III, 127.

[5] For political consideration in the foundation of some religious houses during Stephen's reign see Edmund King, "The Anarchy of King Stephen's Reign," *TRHS* 5th ser., 34 (1984): 133-54; Marjorie Chibnall, "The Empress Matilda and Church Reform," *TRHS* 5th ser., 38 (1988): 108-113.

[6] Helen M. Chew, *The Ecclesiastical Tenants-in-Chief and Knight Service* (Oxford: Oxford University Press, 1932).

[7] Barbara H. Rosenwein, *To be the Neighbor of St Peter: The Social Meaning of Cluny's Property, 909-1049* (Ithaca, N. Y.: Cornell University Press, 1989).

[8] Elizabeth Kimball, "The Judicial Aspects of Frank-almoign Tenure," *EHR* 47 (1932): 1-11; Samuel E. Thorne, "The Assize *Utrum* and the Canon Law in England," in his *Essays in English Legal History* (London: Hambledon, 1985), 51-9.

[9] Milsom, *Legal Framework of English Feudalism*, 152-3. In this respect a charter of Robert de Langeport to Luffield Priory (ca.1150-8), assumes some significance. Robert sold to the Priory half his land for eight marks, for the service of half a knight. The corroboration was intended *ut teneant eam in feudo et hereditate*. Here, a house founded in the twelfth century acquired land in return for secular services, not frankalmoign; the vocabulary referred to an hereditary fee rather than to perpetuity. By contrast, see the gift of William de Couele of two acres, specifically exempted of secular services, with the assent of William's lord, Walter, and made in Walter's court at Westbury (before 1198). *Luffield Priory Charters*, II, 100 and 105 (nos. 405 and 411).

[10] Theodore F. T. Plucknett, *The Legislation of Edward I* (Oxford: Oxford University Press, 1970), 94-5; Sandra Raban, *Mortmain Legislation and the English Church* (Cambridge: Cambridge University Press, 1982), 14-15,

who cites Paul A. Brand, "The Control of Mortmain Alienation in England 1200-1300," in *Legal Records and the Historian*, ed. John H. Baker (London: Royal Historical Society, 1978), 29-40, and J. M. W. Bean, *The Decline of English Feudalism 1215-1540* (Manchester: Manchester University Press, 1968), 50.

[11] As note 10.

[12] Kimball, "Tenure in Frank Almoign".

[13] *Reading Abbey Cartularies,* I, 402-3 (no. 533); *Danelaw Documents,* 79 and 119 (nos. 121 and 176); *Cartulary of Shrewsbury Abbey,* I, 272-3 (no. 288); *Cartulary ... Worcester,* 113 and 180 (nos. 213 and 338).

[14] *Reading Abbey Cartularies,* I, 431-2 (no. 577); *Cartulary ... Worcester,* 96 (no. 179).

[15] Tabuteau, *Transfers of Property,* 204.

[16] Milsom, *Legal Framework of English Feudalism,* 42, associates warranty with heritability, but it may be that warranty was no more than an obligation to the tenant and not his heirs by analogy with Robert Palmer, "The Origins of Property in England," *Law and History Review* 5 (1985): 5-6.

[17] Milsom, *Legal Framework of English Feudalism,* 42.

[18] G. B. Flahiff, "The Writ of Prohibition to Court Christian in the Thirteenth Century," *Mediaeval Studies* 6 (1944): 261-313, and 7 (1945): 229-90; *Rufford Charters,* I, lxi-lxii; *Transcripts ... Charters of Gilbertine Houses,* xxx.

[19] *Charters of the Honour of Mowbray,* 212-13, 217, 228, 231, 244, 246, 249, 253 (nos. 334, 336, 343, 354, 360, 379, 383-4, 390, 396); *Charters of the ... Earls of Chester,* 28, 50-1, 68, 73, 78, 80, 82, 84, 86, 97-100 (nos. 16, 35-6, 56, 60, 65-7, 71-3, 84-7); "Charters ... Earldom Hereford", 14, 20-1, 26-7, 29, 31, 34-5, (nos. 5, 7, 16, 29, 33, 39, 43, 52-3, 55); *Ancient Charters,* Pipe Roll Society 10 (London, 1888), 48-9 (no. 28); *Thame Cartulary,* I, 65 (no. 79); *Cartulary of Daventry Priory,* 217 (no. 667); *Westminster Abbey Charters,* 310 (no. 479); *St Benet of Holme,* 88-9, 109, 111 (nos. 196, 200); *Danelaw Documents,* 375 (no. 516); Frank M. Stenton, *The First Century of English Feudalism* (Oxford: Oxford University Press, 1932), 271 (no. 25); *Cartulary of the Priory of St Gregory,* 27 (no. 34); *Facsimiles of Royal and Other Charters,* 15, 34, 37, 42-3; *Cartulary of Shrewsbury Abbey,* I, 16, 24-6, 272-3, 290 (nos. 12, 24-5, 288, 310, 314); *Reading Abbey Cartularies,* I, 426, 432-3 (nos. 567 and 578); *Registrum Antiquissimum,* II, 6, 16-17: Gilbert de Gant, (ca.1148-56); Robert, earl of Leicester (ca.1139-47); Simon, earl of Northampton (ca.1148-66); *Newington Longeville Charters,* 1-2 (no. 1).

[20] *Earldom of Gloucester Charters,* 38, 40, 42-8, 54, 63-4, 68-9, 71-3, 78, 80, 86-8, 93-4, 100-5, 134-5, 141-2, 146-7, 152-4, 163 (nos. 11, 15, 18, 21-6, 29-30, 36, 49-50, 59, 61, 66-7, 71, 74, 83-5, 94, 100-4, 107, 144, 149, 156-8, 167-9, 182). Slightly later, ca.1160-66, Conan, Duke of Brittany to Henry *filius Herueii*: *Facsimiles ... Early Northamptonshire Charters,* 22 (no. 5).

[21] King, "The Anarchy of King Stephen's Reign".
[22] *Reading Abbey Cartularies*, I, 232, 248, 314-15 (nos. 267, 303, 387); *Stoke by Clare Cartulary*, II, 363-4 (nos. 564-6).
[23] *Chronicon Monasterii de Abingdon*, II, 54-5.
[24] *Cartulary of Shrewsbury Abbey*, 272-3 (no. 288).
[25] *Newington Longeville Charters*, 23-5 (nos. 19, 21-2), 62 (nos. 71-2).
[26] Milson, *Legal Framework of English Feudalism*.
[27] *Cartulary of the Abbey of Eynsham*.
[28] Michael T. Clanchy, *From Memory to Written Record* (London: Arnold, 1979), 24-5, and Clanchy, "Some Remarkable Durham Charters," unpublished paper presented to the Harlaxton Symposium on England in the Twelfth Century in 1988.
[29] *Rutland MSS IV*, 101, 129; *Westminster Abbey Charters*, 318 (no. 488); *Historia et Cartularium ... Gloucestriae*, I, 205 (no. CIV), 235 (no. CXLI); *Chronicon Monasterii de Abingdon*, for example 124; *Facsimiles of Royal and Other Charters*, 31; *Cartulary of Shrewsbury Abbey*, 28 (no. 32), 275 (no. 294); *Stoke by Clare Cartulary*, II, 188-9, 222-3, 230-1, 346-7, 351, (nos. 249, 251, 321, 335, 532, 540). See also, *Facsimiles... Early Northamptonshire Charters*, 62 (no. XXII) (1149) (to St Neot's Priory).
[30] *Cartulary of Shrewsbury Abbey*, 294-5 (no. 324); *Chronicon Monasterii de Abingdon*, 54-5, 74; *Facsimiles ... Early Northamptonshire Charters*, 52 (no. XVIII).
[31] *Rutland MSS IV*, 59.
[32] *Cartulary of the Abbey of Eynsham*; *Cartulary of God's House*, I, *passim*, in which warranty was unusual, pledge more usual: *e.g.* I, 174-5 (ca.1198); warranty fails to appear in charters to Stoke by Clare before ca.1180-98, and then only infrequently: *Stoke by Clare Cartulary*, II, 360 (no. 557); the charters of the earldom of Hereford to religious houses do not include warranty, but those to the laity do: "Charters of the Earldom of Hereford" 49-50, 66-7, 71 (nos. 89, 109, 117) (from ca.1160). The charters to Blyth Priory have warranty clauses inconsistently by the late twelfth century; a charter in favor of the house in ca.1189-94 could still, however, include a pledge of faith tantamount to warranty: *quia eas sicut liberam et perpetuam elemosinam fide interposita erga omnes homines ego et heredes mei defendere debemus*. This clause may have related simply to exonerating the house from secular services. *Cartulary of Blyth Priory*, 260 (no. 404).
[33] *Gilbertine Charters*, xxx and 3, 126-8, 340 (nos. 2, 186, 461); *Rufford Charters*, I, lxii; see also, *Cartulary of Worcester Cathedral Priory*, 96 (no. 198). *Rufford Charters* include examples of hand-fast between lay men. A charter of three sisters to William *telarius* in the late twelfth century intermixes pledge of faith and warranty between lay parties, although the gender of the donors may have been the reason for the spiritual sanctions: *Facsimiles*

... *Early Northamptonshire Charters*, 114 (no. XLII). The gift of Gerard de Stirap to Blyth Priory of a wood was secured by a warranty against all men, but which (the warranty) Gerard swore to uphold (*et hoc affidaui tenendum*): *Blyth Priory Cartulary*, 82 (no. 107).

[34] Stephen D. White, *Custom, Kinship and Gifts to Saints: The* Laudatio Parentum *in Western France 1050-1150* (Chapel Hill, N. C.: University of North Carolina, 1988).

[35] David Postles, "Securing the Gift in Oxfordshire Charters in the Twelfth and Early Thirteenth Centuries," in Postles, *Oseney Abbey Studies* (Leicester: University of Leicester, 2008), 25-33.

[36] *Newington Longeville Charters*, 23-5 (nos. 19, 21-2).

[37] *Newington Longeville Charters*. Charters to Newington Longeville Priory had either oaths or warranty and occasionally both. Charters of ca.1175 had oaths on the gospels or the altar, those of ca.1167-73 warranty, and one of ca.1184-97 warranty *pro posse nostro* (the latter at 48, no. 52). Postles, "Securing the Gift".

[38] *Danelaw Documents*, 79 (no. 121).

[39] *Danelaw Documents*, 119-20, 191 (nos. 176 and 256). See also the warranty in the charter of Richard son of John de Hemminctona to Saint Neot's Priory in 1185, *sicut meam et antecessorum meorum propriam elemosinam*: *Facsimiles ... Early Northamptonshire Charters*, 72 (no. XXV).

[40] Hyams, "Warranty and Good Lordship," 456 (and n. 75) and 474 (and n. 159).

[41] *Charters of the Honour of Mowbray*, 29-38 (nos. 35-49).

[42] *Charters of the Honour of Mowbray*, 68-9, 78-9, 84, 99-100.

[43] *Facsimiles of Royal and Other Charters*, 26; *Cartulary of Shrewsbury Abbey*, 77 (no. 84); *Cartulary of Blyth Priory*, 96-7 (no. 135). See also the slightly later charter (ca.1154-69) of Robert de Furnellis to Robert son of Ailric de Twiwell, which includes warranty against all men: *Facsimiles ... Northamptonshire Charters*, 94 (no. XXXIV).

[44] *Charters of ... the Earls of Chester*, 68-9, 78-9, 84 (nos. 56, 66, 71) (all with the promise of exchange, *escambium*).

[45] *Charters of ... the Earls of Chester*, 99-100 (no. 86).

[46] *Charters of ... the Earls of Chester*, 100.

[47] *Earldom of Gloucester Charters*, 78 (no. 71). Moreover, it is known in these cases that the charters were predominantly not written by the beneficiaries, but by *scriptores* employed by the earls, however casually: *Earldom of Gloucester Charters*, 25-30. I am also grateful to Michael Clanchy, who has pointed out to me the possibility that some charters may have been written in the county court where they were proclaimed, rather than by the beneficiaries or a baronial *scriptor*..

[48] Tabuteau, *Transfers of Property*, 245 (document 746) and 376 (no. 1).

[49] *Charters of ... the Earls of Chester*, for example, 27, 68-9 (nos. 15 and 56).

[50] For earlier statements about empirical inheritance, F. R. H. DuBoulay, *The Lordship of Canterbury: An Essay on Medieval Society* (London: Nelson, 1966), 60-1, and Edmund King, *Peterborough Abbey: A Study in the Land Market 1086-1310* (Cambridge: Cambridge University Press, 1973), 27-30; for a recent restatement of unbroken inheritance for tenants in chief by the end of the reign of Henry I, RaGena De Aragon, "The Growth of Secure Inheritance in Anglo-Norman England," *Journal of Medieval History* 8 (1982): 381-91, and Charlotte A. Newman, *The Anglo-Norman Nobility in the Reign of Henry I: The Second Generation* (Pennsylvania, Pa.: University of Pennsylvania Press, 1989); Holt, "Feudal Society and the Family in Early Medieval England: II. Notions of Patrimony," especially 210-11; by contrast, Samuel E. Thorne, "English Feudalism and Estates in Land," in his *Essays in English Legal History*, 13-29; Milsom, *Legal Framework of English Feudalism*, especially 154-86; more recently, Robert Palmer. "The Feudal Framework of English Law," *Michigan Law Review* 79 (1981): 1130-64; Palmer, "The Origins of Property in England," *Law and History Review* 3 (1985): 1-50; Palmer, "The Economic and Cultural Impact of the Origins of Property," *Law and History Review* 3 (1985): 375-96; for a recent restatement of the importance of Stephen's reign, Ralph H. C. Davis, *King Stephen*, revised edn. (London: Longman, 1990), 150-3.

[51] Judith Green, *The Government of England under Henry I* (Cambridge: Cambridge University Press, 1989), 139-57; Marjorie Chibnall, *Anglo-Norman England* (Oxford: Blackwell, 1986), 73-81; but the discretionary exercise of lordship by Henry I may have been more characteristic of his reign than bureaucratic government. See also Thomas N. Bisson, review of Green in (1989) *Speculum* 64 (1989): 437-8, and also James C. Holt, "Politics and Property in Early Medieval England" and "Rejoinder", Edmund King, "The Tenurial Crisis of the Early Twelfth Century", and Stephen D. White, "Succession to Fiefs in Early Medieval England", all reprinted in *Landlords, Peasants and Politics in Medieval England*, ed. Trevor H. Aston (Cambridge: Cambridge University Press, 1987), 65-140.

[52] *Chronicon Monasterii de Abingdon*, 138; see also *Charters of the Honour of Mowbray*, 241-2 and 245-6, which seem to imply discretionary lordship.

[53] James C. Holt, "1086", in *Domesday Studies*, ed. Holt (Woodbridge: Boydell, 1987), 41-64, especially 57-9.

[54] Milsom, *Legal Framework of English Feudalism*, especially 36-7.

9
Seeking the Language of Warranty of Land in Twelfth-Century England

Introduction

Hanc donationem et venditionem ego Willelmus de Haruecurt et Yvo frater meus propriis manibus super altare sancte Marie de Geroldonia obtulimus presente [sic] omni conventu et aliis quam plurimis militibus et clericis francis et anglis Quicunque diebus posteris diabolica ammonitione predictos monachos super hac conventione qualicunque modo infestare contendit ego Willelmus de Haruecurt et Yvo frater meus ceterique amici mei coram regibus principibus in omnibus curiis manutenendo et causam eorum defendendo secundum posse nostrum sicut pro nostro patrimonio et propria hereditate prompti defensores astabimus[1]

Recent research has emphasized that during much of the twelfth century, charters remained *privatae conventiones*, narratives of agreements made between two private parties which were not secured or protected in royal courts, but by their own internal devices and the social, spiritual and political relationships between the parties, dependent on detailed negotiation (*prelocucio*) before the final transaction.[2] Those protracted prior discussions are most evident in arrangements made between lay parties of baronial status during the "Anarchy".[3] Until the action *de warrantia carte* the protection of beneficiaries was imperfectly incorporated in the king's courts.[4] It was consequently vital that modes of authentication, corroboration and especially assurance and security were contained within the charter, as evidence of an event which had taken place and which could be substantiated against challenges.

These modes of assurance are well known: the "consents" clause (*laudatio parentum*), which committed kin and, sometimes, even lords; conjoining significant actors in the dispositive clause (most frequently wives and sons and prospective heirs); an anathema or expression of power/will in the case firstly of religious houses and secondly those of baronial status; attestation clauses, including significant actors (wives, lords, and prospective heirs) amongst the first witnesses; warranty; and confirmation charters (by lords, heirs and the Ordinary).[5] Some of these devices were multivocal and may have served more than one purpose. The *laudatio*, for example, conjoined the actor in the spiritual benefits and in the kinship, so that it was not only a mode of assurance but also a form of participation.[6] These instruments and clauses might, moreover, be perceived to be prudent rather than normative.[7] The essential difference between warranty and other modes of assurance is that the other methods were retrospective–they were constituted around the event which had taken place, even if participation at that event implied (but no more) a future action–whereas warranty was prospective, in that it was an explicit promise of some future action. The other modes might also rely on a wide range of people (again, say, witnesses), but, by contrast, warranty was restricted to a narrow range of actors, the donor or the grantor (and his or her heirs). Responsibility for assurance was thus shifted exclusively to the parties to the negotiations rather than relying on the presence of third parties. Whereas the emphasis in other methods of assurance had been public–ritualized action to communicate and impress knowledge–warranty was an internal arrangement, first of conscience, and then of law. Although it might have been announced (either orally or when the charter was read out), warranty was unlikely to have been a ritualized performance like homage or hand-fast.

Homage, for example, was performative ritual, marked by formalism, restricted language, and prescribed bodily posture.[8] The modes of assurance which were performed through ritual, such as symbolic livery before witnesses, were perhaps slightly less circumscribed linguistically, although it is difficult to recover the language consistently. These occasions might best be placed in the category of "performative actions" or "performative memory", intended to produce group memory of the occasion.[9] Warranty did not depend on "performative memory", but was, in a sense and perhaps anachronistically, promissory or contractual; it inhered in the action of the gift.

Further points concern the introduction and inclusion of devices for security in charters. Some clauses or modes were prior to others; some disappeared from charters, perhaps as a result of the insertion of new modes of assurance; others were, nevertheless, coincidental in the same charter. Both, nonetheless, occurred together in some charters. A range of devices might then be deployed in the same charter as mechanisms of assurance during the twelfth century. Of these, however, warranty came to offer the most efficacious security to the beneficiary because it ultimately, although not initially, became enforceable in royal courts. The common law's competence over warranty, however, was a later development, and warranty had a long prehistory before it became an action at common law.

The origins and overall development of specific warranty in charters have been elucidated by Paul Hyams.[10] The most germane part of his interpretation for the purpose here is his clarification of the paradox that although warranty was in a sense inappropriate for religious beneficiaries, since they could not recognize any secular lord, yet it was precisely religious houses which were responsible for the wider dissemination of the warranty clause in charters, particularly from the 1160s, although some form of warranty clause (even if in the negative) had existed in some charters by and to the religious in the 1130s. Hyams also suggests that warranty developed as a generic category of assurance, perhaps from chattel warranty, rather than as specific to land, while Tabuteau notes that the warranty clause had appeared in private transactions in Normandy by the first decade of the twelfth century.[11]

To this understanding it might now be added that an argument has been advanced that, in one of its purposes, Domesday Book was a form of "warrant[y]" of the oral distribution of land after the conquest, in return for the Salisbury Oath, which may also raise the prospect of some comprehension of some notion of "warranty" in 1086 ("'warranty' in the simple eleventh-century sense which it enjoyed in Domesday, namely authority for tenure"), even if we do not admit of Domesday Book as a great *pancarte*.[12] In this case, warranty intended confirmation or authorization for tenure, but it is possible that the intention in contemporary Normandy was to defend as well as to "demonstrate rightful possession".[13] It has also been suggested that warranty briefly occurred in some form in the 1130s, as noted above, and furthermore that it temporarily resurfaced in arrangements about lay tenurial relationships in the "Anarchy" from the 1140s.[14] Opened too then is the intriguing notion of oral warranty, derived, say, from oral chattel warranty, which might not have been incorporated in written expression in charters because of their inchoateness, their position outside royal justice and thus no impetus from that direction towards uniformity of protocol.[15] It is this last issue which is addressed here by attempting to show that there does not generally appear to have been an earlier precise form of warranty, but that what we can detect from some charters is an experimentation with forms of drafting and irregular expression of some cognate notion. The diversity of expression confirms notions about the local drafting of charters, the potential (but not an inevitable and comprehensive) influence of the beneficiary on the drafting, and tending to suggest that the variety of forms resulted also from exclusion from royal courts at this time.[16]

Evidence for Warranty: Domesday Book

The first section of this paper, however, returns to the evidence of Domesday Book for warranty, material which has now been made more accessible by Robin Fleming.[17] In the *clamores* and *invasiones* in Domesday Book, linguistic variety was used to indicate warrantor and warranty: *advocatus; dator; defensor; protector; tutor; warant'; ad defensorem; ad liberatorem; ad protectorem; ad tutorem;* and *ad warant'*.[18] It might be tedious to recite all the evidence, but some examples will be necessary to establish the import of the variety of lexis. Ketilbert seized two and a half virgates for which he could find neither livery nor *advocatus*.[19] William *homo* of William Gernon, called his lord to warrant against the king (*reclamat ... ad protectorem*).[20] *Ad protectorem* was evinced in four other *clamores* in similar manner.[21] In another five *clamores*, the instrumental term was *tutor*.[22] Thus Oda acquired ten acres and invoked his lord *ad tutorem* (*inde vocat dominum suum ad tutorem*).²³ Although Leodmær of Hempstead held land which he had annexed from Richard FitzGilbert's fee, Richard, it was ascertained, was not his *tutor*.²⁴ When Warner called Ilbold *ad tutorem* in another land plea, he nevertheless failed to bring his warrantor (*non adduxit tutorem*).²⁵ In the *invasiones* against the king, Æthelmær requested warranty from his lord, Richard (*revocavit eum ad tutorem*), but Richard failed to appear and Æthelmær was required to find a pledge.²⁶ Finally, in terms of *tutor*, William de Bouville also vouched his lord, Geoffrey de Mandeville, to warranty (*revocat ad tutorem*) concerning a carucate in Hoo.²⁷ *Defensor* was employed in three *clamores*, when Count Eustace was vouched to warranty (*revocat eum ad defensorem*) by a knight to whom he had subinfeudated, when the king was called to warrant for land in Trowse in Norfolk (*revocat ... regem ad defensorem*) and in Rendenhall in the same county.²⁸

The interest of this Domesday terminology here is its replication in some twelfth-century charters in favour of Garendon Abbey. The subsequent sections of this paper discuss those charters of Garendon and compare their implications for the introduction of written warranty in charters, with the employment of warranty in charters of other Cistercian houses, to evoke three points: first, a line of continuity for warranty of land from the late eleventh century into the twelfth; second, the continuing variety of language which constituted warranty-type actions, as warranty was developing in England; and third, the widely different approach to the adoption of written warranty in charters, even when the beneficiaries belonged to the same religious order.

Evidence for Warranty: Charters from Cistercian Houses

One way of perceiving these influences is to compare charters from houses of the same religious Order. Of particular interest in this respect are the Cistercians, for they are the most likely to have had some form of central influence exerted over the houses. Forms of central organization are evident in the *Carta Caritatis* and in the early development of the Chapter General, in the Order's proscription of the possession of certain forms of property, and in the regulation of foundations of houses. Certain forms of property–advowsons, tithes, mortuaries and obventions to altars–were excluded by c. IX of the *Carta*, whilst the statutes of 1184 regulated involvement in gages.[29] In 1188, the statutes prevented indebted houses from acquiring more property by purchase, and priors and cellarers who complied with abbots in any infraction were to be placed on bread and water.[30] There is no evidence, nonetheless, of central interference in the diplomatics of charters to Cistercian houses.

The Order was also new in England, arriving in the third decade of the twelfth century, so that, unlike Benedictine houses (for example), houses would have no earlier prescriptive tradition of modes of assurance. The material discussed here is consequently derived from some of the earliest cartularies of English Cistercian houses. There seems to have been an early development of cartularies in Cistercian houses.[31] The Cistercians are also interesting because their Order had the strongest strictures to avoid secular relationships, of which warranty might be construed as one.[32] It might therefore be expected that Cistercian houses might have adopted warranty in an equivocal manner.[33]

Unlike transactions between the laity, those to religious houses inherently invoked an external protection, a spiritual sanction, whether explicit (an anathema) or left implicit. Although gifts in free alms were still constructed in inchoate language in the early twelfth century, it might still be surmised that the spiritual element of protection was involved. Thus, although some patrons and founders might have considered their benefactions to be made to their *Eigenkirchen*, other benefactors, despite inchoate phrasing of the charter, presumably recognized that the gift was at least to the honor of God and the patronal saint, even if the intention was not always or consistently expressed. That understanding must have obtained because benefactions were made for salvific purposes, for a reciprocity of spiritual welfare through intercession by the religious and the saints with God. The gift expected and anticipated, indeed perhaps demanded, this reciprocal exchange.[34] The paradox of the adoption of warranty by the religious is thus confirmed.

Garendon Abbey was founded in 1133 in north-west Leicestershire, by the earl of Leicester, as one of the earliest of the Cistercian houses in England. Before Stephen's accession (1135), only a few Cistercian houses had been established in England.[35] The cartulary as it is now extant comprises several discrete redactions compiled within a short time-span, probably all completed by the very early thirteenth century.[36] The property of the house was confined to north Leicestershire and south Nottinghamshire.[37] Rufford Abbey, in central Nottinghamshire, was founded by Gilbert de Gant in 1146, its property concentrated in that county and in north Derbyshire. Its cartulary was produced in the late thirteenth century.[38] In Northamptonshire, Pipewell Abbey was founded by William de Batevileyn in 1141x1143.[39] Although originally endowed by Robert Gait in 1137 with land at Otley in Oxfordshire, Thame Abbey was only satisfactorily founded after the intervention of Alexander, bishop of Lincoln in 1139x1141, providing the alternative site at Thame Park; its cartulary is of the early thirteenth century.[40] Further south, in Bedfordshire, Warden Abbey was founded by Walter Espec in 1135x1136, its cartulary composed predominantly in the first quarter of the thirteenth century.[41] Sibton Abbey was founded later, in 1150, by William de Cainito; its twelve granges were dispersed in Suffolk, Norfolk and Cambridgeshire, whilst the nucleus of its cartulary is of the thirteenth century.[42] All these houses were located in central England and all were modest in their endowments and temporalities. The *Valor* of the houses in 1535 ranged from £159 (Garendon) to £389 (Warden).[43]

The question of the influence of the filiation of houses on the diplomatics of their charters is a real one, but one which is difficult to address.[44] The genealogy of Garendon had its stem at L'Aumône, as did Thame, both houses established as daughters of Waverley. Sibton, Warden, Rufford and Pipewell were affiliated through Fountains or Rievaulx to Clairvaux, Warden, Pipewell and Rufford all daughter houses of Rievaulx.[45] At this juncture, we encounter the problem of materials not surviving or not available to pursue the potential influence. As will be revealed below, however, there remain differences in the diplomatics of charters between houses with the same affiliation.

Garendon Abbey

In 1148/9 William de Haruecurt conveyed to Garendon Abbey a manor at Stanton under Bardon in Leicestershire, some fifteen years after the foundation of the house.[46] One-third was transferred in free alms, for the soul of his father and deceased kin and for the remission of his own sins and those of his "friends" (probably kin). The other two-thirds, however, were an explicit sale and purchase, specifically identified as such in the charter.[47] As well as a consideration of twenty marks and three horses to the donor, counter-gifts were made to his brother, Ivo (a horse) and to his mother, Agnes (one mark and ten acres of corn). By this means, then, the potential challengers to the transaction were committed to it.[48] Ivo was further encompassed by his enlistment as the first witness to the transaction. Both Ivo and Agnes were included also in the *laudatio parentum* or consents clause. The transaction was more widely secured by a symbolic livery on the Lady altar, the altar of the patronal saint of Cistercian houses, and her "presence" no doubt was important in commitment to securing the transfer. A battery of modes of security was thus employed in the charter.

The charter, nonetheless, searched for another mode of assurance, which combines the language of anathema in the term *diabolica ammonitione* with a tentative attempt at some form of "warranty", for, if anyone, presumably then a third party, contested the conveyance, both William and Ivo would stand as much as they could as defenders to maintain and defend the monks' cause "before kings and princes and in all courts". What must be expressed here then is a notion of warranty of the land in any legal forum, even unto the royal courts (or before the king). Although the formula of warranty had not been discovered, yet the intention must be there, most particularly in the explicit language of maintaining and defending the monks' cause in courts.

We might extrapolate from the circumstances and environment of the transaction. It was a time of general insecurity during the "Anarchy". In such circumstances, there might well be anxiety that the transaction would be challenged, not only by the donor's kin, but by third parties. Indeed, the monks might have remembered the circumstances of the foundation of their house in 1133 by the earl of Leicester with the appropriated lands of a tenant of the earl of Chester in the region contested by the two comital antagonists for territorial lordship.[49]

This search for a notion of warranty occurred in other charters to the house. In the gift of William *filius Gilberti de Colevile* is contained the clause:

> *et ego et heredes mei pro predictis monachis contra omnes homines sicut pro nostra propria elemosina defensores astabimus*

In this case, general heirs are specifically bound to maintain the gift and the implication is against third parties.[50]

In these charters there is consistent use of the phrase *defensores astabimus* to express the function of warranty, presumably largely influenced by the religious house. The language was not, however, prescriptive, so that some other donors or grantors attempted to find a more elaborate method of assurance which incorporated the phrase. Thus when, in 1160x1183, Asketil de Berges made a benefaction on the high altar before witnesses, the charter still deployed a lengthy combination of anathema, expression of will, and standing to as defender, but, moreover, invoking the assistance of the witnesses in this last capacity:

> *Unde volo ut omnes amici mei et vicini franci et anglici sciant et intelligant quod ego Asketillus contra omnes qui hanc conventionem temptaverunt infringere ... cum eisdem monachis defensurum astabo et illos precor quatinus huius conventionis sint testes et mecum assistant defensores ut illibate prenominatam terram in perpetuam possessionem conservetur ecclesie Gerold'*[51]

The charter of Serlo de Pleseleia deviates from the pattern in not containing the phrase *defensores astabimus*, but it too exhibits an attempt to find a language of warranty:

> *et si quis forte eis in futuro aliquam calumpniam vel iniuriam inferre voluerit ego eos sicuti fratres meos pro salute anime mee et antecessorum meorum manutenebo et secundum rationabile possibile meum adiuvabo*

Here Serlo was simply confirming a gift of a carucate in Burton on the Wolds by Henry Putrel, but he offered his influence in maintaining and helping the monks against challenges. The clause resembles the anathema, but it significantly employs the language of maintaining and helping rather than simply forbidding.[52] Similar language is contained in charters from Roger de Burtun and Robert de Cheverecurt, with the emphasis on maintaining the monks:

> et si quis de ipsa terra quam tenent de feudo meo in futuro tempore aliquid gravamen vel calumpniam eis inferre voluerit ego et heredes mei pro posse nostro manutenebimus eos[53]

In similar language, Arnold de Bosco, sometime after 1143, and again probably in the context of the uncertainties and vicissitudes of the "Anarchy", assured his transfer of a manor at Stanton under Bardon in which, significantly, he had recently been subinfeudated by Geoffrey de Clinton.

> volo ut predicta ecclesia et monachi bene et in pace et honorifice teneant solutum et liberum et quietum ab omni servitio et exaccione seculari et erga me et heredes meos defendendum [sic] etiam fideliter et pro posse meo manutenendum [sic] contra omnes qui aliquam violentiam vel iniuriam predicte ecclesie vel monachis inferre temptaverint[54]

Although couched in terms of an expression of power, the language sought is that of defending and maintaining.

The cartulary of the house comprises charters prior to the early thirteenth century, in which the phrase *defensores astabimus* consistently recurs. Initially, it appeared on its own in a charter, but when the explicit language of warranty is engaged it is combined with *defensores astabimus* and in some cases also with maintaining. Thus, when in 1163x1189, John *Constabularius* of Chester provided ten bovates with tofts and crofts in Costock, his assurance was simply *ego et heredes mei defensores astabimus*.[55] The next stage of the development is reflected in a charter of Ralph de Queniburc before 1168 in which assurance is extended by this clause:

> et ego et heredes mei sicut propriam elemosinam nostram utrique warantizabimus et manutenebimus et contra omnes calumpnias defensores astabimus[56]

This formula recurred in a charter of Thomas *Dispensator* in 1168x1190, when he proclaimed that:

> *ego et heredes mei manutenebimus et warantizabimus hanc donationem sicut nostram propriam elemosinam et contra omnes homines defensores astabimus*[57]

Two more examples which can be dated represent this tendency towards a consistent association of the verb to warrant and the phrase to stand as defenders. The first is contained in a complex negotiation between the abbey and the earl of Warwick about 1155x1166 in which the earl's obligation for assurance is stated thus:

> *et si quis hoc servicio aliquam eis vexationem in futuro ferre voluerit ego et heredes mei in omnibus locis hanc elemosinam eis warantizabimus et defensores astabimus*[58]

The second obtains in a charter of William de Evermu who sold four carucates in Eastwell in 1162x1170:

> *ego et heredes mei terram prenominatam monachis Geroud' warantizabimus et adquietabimus et contra omnes homines defensores astabimus*[59]

There is then a consistent use of warranty and standing as a defender of the monks' rights, whether in land or (more ambiguously) alms, up to the third quarter of the twelfth century, but in the next phase the term *defensores astabimus* was relinquished in favour of simply to warrant and maintain.[60] What seems evident, therefore, and probably under the influence of this Cistercian house, is a progressive search towards a language of warranty which began in the 1140s. A further question at issue, however, is how the standing to as defender and later warranty is directed towards the free alms status of the benefaction, perhaps a matter of particular concern to a Cistercian house which was required to maintain a distance from secular society. Even if there was such a restriction of sense, there is still an evolution of warranty-type language form the 1140s.

Pipewell Abbey

By comparison, the charters in the cartulary of another Cistercian house, Pipewell Abbey, compiled in the mid-thirteenth century, reflect no such evolution of language. Warranty appears without any precursor in a standardized formula *warantizabimus contra omnes calumnias et calumpniatores* before settling into the normative pattern of *warantizabimus contra omnes homines*. At least fifteen instruments in the short cartulary contain the phrase *warantizabimus contra omnes calumnias et calumpniatores*.[61] The form is reflected in the charter by which Alice Launcelin conveyed to the house two acres:

> *Has predictas acras ego et heredes mei waratizabimus prefatis monachis contra omnes calumnias et calumpniatores*[62]

Here the concern for warranty was not with the status of free alms but directly with the land. Although precise warranty language appeared in the charters to the abbey with no precursor, it assumed a very specific form in *contra omnes calumnias et calumpniatores*. Here is evidence again of the particular influence of the religious house and perhaps also of the emphasis on warranty against third parties.

Rufford Abbey

Moving now to a third Cistercian house, Rufford Abbey, yet another pattern emerges. "But there is sufficient evidence in this collection to show that charters which refer to this procedure [pledge of faith or hand-fast] do not normally have warranty clauses and that they all preceded c1200"; "Pledging of faith then emerges as an archaic practice which occurs alongside warranty in exceptional circumstances, and charters in which it occurs in the absence of a warranty clause are almost certainly to be placed in the twelfth century".[63] The Cistercian house and its benefactors thus conformed to some extent to a local custom, but warranty was also deployed.[64] Occasionally, circumstances dictated the inclusion of warranty, as when William de Tulc made a benefaction in 1146x1154 which he and his heirs would warrant to the monks against all men.[65] Others might sometimes search for a similar language, as Walter de Mundevill' in 1146x1168 when he confirmed the gift of twenty-four acres by his tenant, Maurice, *quas ego tutabor et defendam eis in omni loco*.[66] These exceptions might relate to difficult local political circumstances, as in the case of Garendon. It is probable, moreover, that hand-fast or pledge of faith was not appropriate for larger benefactors, as opposed to the free peasantry, and those of higher status employed other methods of assurance than the pledge.

Thame Abbey

In the case of Thame Abbey, warranty did not intrude into charters to the house until the 1190s. In the first two decades of its existence, the house received some substantial benefactions, but none of the charters incorporated warranty. Edith, daughter of Forne, wife of Robert II d'Oilly, substantially assisted the foundation of the house with her gift of thirty-seven acres in Weston-on-the-Green in 1137, consisting of her *maritagium* during her husband's lifetime. Assurance was provided by the consents of her husband, two sons and her daughters.[67] Security for the benefaction of Geoffrey son of Osmund de Mortone of one and a half hides in Morton in 1152 consisted of similar consents.[68] Warranty was introduced into the charters to the house in seemingly exceptional circumstances, as when the house received the meadow *de la Dene* from Hugh *Pauper* in ca.1190 in return for ten marks for relief for his land and for acquitting debts to the Jews. Included in this charter was warranty with exchange.[69] The initial introduction of warranty may have occurred in 1185 in the charter of Rainburga, who, with her brother's consent, transferred to the house a virgate in Norton, with the promise of exchange if she could not warrant the land.[70] Another early inclusion of warranty occurred in the charter of Milicent, daughter of Eustace de Freschevile, in 1187, who provided a virgate in Norton in her widowhood with the assent of her guardian. "And since the said monks have helped us with thirty-five marks of silver to acquit our land in Norton against Bernard *de sancto Walerico* we should warrant to them this virgate."[71] Undoubtedly, such circumstances were exceptional and problematic–for example, a widow in wardship transferring property–which might have propelled the house to seek stronger and (for the house) new kinds of modes of security. By the 1190s, warranty was more consistently included in charters to the house, but occasional warranty clauses thereafter hint at the association between warranty and exceptional circumstance. Thus in 1190x1200, when Laurence de Stoke made a benefaction, the warranty was associated with the consideration: "And because the said monks have remitted to me three and a half marks which I owed them, I and my heirs should warrant the said three half acres to them."[72] Slightly later, in 1202, the same sort of association was intimated in the charter of Hamund *de sancta Fide* for his provision of a virgate: "And because the said monks have helped me with six marks I and my heirs should warrant all the said land to them."[73]

Warden Abbey

By the early thirteenth century, a standard warranty clause was incorporated in charters to Warden Abbey in Bedfordshire. That standard clause is evident in a small number of charters by the 1180s. The difficulty with this cartulary is the paucity of charters between foundation and the 1170s. What is interesting, however, is the combination of pledge of faith and warranty in charters in the 1160s to 1180s. This phrasing may be exemplified in the charter of Robert *Camerarius* of Dunton providing a benefaction of ten acres in 1165x1176:

> *Hanc elemosinam tenendam et warantizandam affidavit idem Robertus in manu Baldewini Buelot apud Wardon in die Omnium Sanctorum*[74]

The promise of warranty was apparently insufficient of its own and was afforced by an oath or pledge of faith.[75] In a very substantial number of charters of the 1180s and 1190s, a pledge was involved with the warranty, frequently in the form:

> *Et ego affidavi pro me et heredibus meis quod hec omnia supradicta fideliter warantizabimus ... contra omnes homines et feminas in perpetuum*[76]

It appears then that warranty was introduced in the last twenty years of the twelfth century, but circumspectly, as if insufficient in itself, and afforced by a pledge to perform, perhaps influenced by a local tradition of hand-fast which occasionally surfaces in the cartulary.

Sibton Abbey

That same incorporation of pledge with warranty occurred in charters to Sibton Abbey in East Anglia at about the same time. Thus when Drew de Chedestan' provided two acres in the 1170s, the protocol consisted of *affidavimus* plus warranty.[77] Hand-fast is evident, for before 1178 Ranulph *Walensis*, who gave land, pledged his faith in the hand of Robert de Beannei firmly to uphold the *conventio*.[78] Straight warranty thus occurred alongside warranty afforced by the pledge in the last quarter of the twelfth century in charters to Sibton.[79] Although there is a paucity of charters in the 1150s and 1160s, warranty seems to have been introduced in the charter of 1165x1173 of Geoffrey Black and his sons, who sold land to Sibton for twelve and a half marks, with warranty but excluding exchange or cash compensation.[80] The inclusion of oath or pledge to afforce warranty in some cases reflects perhaps in this case too a tentative introduction.

Byland Abbey

A question of status of the benefactor can be perceived perhaps in the relationship between Byland Abbey (founded in 1138 as a Savignac house, but integrated with the Cistercians in 1147 as the Savignac Order was absorbed) and its patronal family, the Mowbrays. In a charter of 1140, explicit warranty is already the mode of assurance, for Mowbray and his heirs are committed forever to maintain and warrant the gift to the monks against all men and women.[81] Three more charters of the patrons to the house in the 1140s invoke the same formulary of to maintain and to warrant.[82] Why warranty was employed in these cases may be a confusion of the benefactor's status and the vicissitudes of the time.

Conclusion

What is perceptible in these charters to Cistercian houses during the twelfth century is, therefore, a diversity of arrangements for securing the gift or purchase. No uniformity of protocol is visible and warranty was adopted in different forms at different times and in different circumstances. In the case of Garendon, an attempt was made towards a proto-language of warranty from an earlier date than its reception at some other houses. For Pipewell, warranty suddenly appeared in precise language, but with a distinctive category of *[contra] calumpnias* and *calumpniatores*. Charters to Thame exhibited no language of warranty until the 1190s, when the precise term was introduced, but sometimes associated with exceptional and problematic circumstances. For some other houses, warranty was introduced tentatively, afforced by an oath or a pledge to observe it.

In the case of Garendon, there is interestingly some continuity of the language employed in the late eleventh century in Domesday Book, particularly of the notion of a *defensor* who was the donor, but also, although exceptionally, *tutor*. It may be that the application of this language reveals something further about the development of warranty-type obligations in the twelfth century.

The insecurity of the 1140s was a stimulus in some cases to seek a language of warranty, which confirms the transient use of the clause in lay tenurial relationships at that time. There was, nevertheless, no consistent employment of the clause in the *tempus guerrae*. The proposition receives confirmation then that some religious houses paradoxically propagated warranty as a device in charters.[83] Complicit in that dissemination of practice were some Cistercian houses, which is interesting since the precepts of the Order exhorted distance from the secular world and especial avoidance of lay tenurial relationships. As interestingly, the Chapter General exerted no central influence over the houses in matters of drafting and specification of charters and different practices thus resulted during the twelfth century.

Notes

[1] BL, Lansdowne MS 415, fol. 15v. For the specific background, David Crouch, *The Beaumont Twins: The Roots and Branches of Power in the Twelfth Century* (Cambridge: Cambridge University Press, 1986), 123-37.

[2] Paul R. Hyams, "The Charter as a Source for the Early Common Law", *The Journal of Legal History* 12 (1991): 173-89, especially 174.

[3] Edmund King, "Dispute Settlement in Anglo-Norman England", in *Anglo-Norman Studies XIV: Proceedings of the Battle Conference 1991*, ed. R. Allen Brown (Woodbridge: Boydell, 1992), 115-30.

[4] R. C. Van Caenigem, *Royal Writs in England from the Conquest to Glanvill: Studies in the Early History of the Common Law*, Selden Society vol. 77 (London, 1958-9), 480-1 (nos. 127-8) has discovered two writs of summons to warrant a gift, one to Reading Abbey (1156x1157) and the other to Biddlesden Abbey (1170x1183), both employing the verb *warantizare*; "Glanvill" entered into a long discussion of warranty of land, including a writ of summons: G. Derek G. Hall, ed., and trans., *The Treatise on the Laws and Customs of the Realm of England Commonly Called Glanvill* (Oxford: Oxford University Press, repr. 1998), 37-41 (Book III, [1]-[5], with a writ of summons to warrant at 39 III, [3]); Maitland may have believed that the fully-formed writ of *warantia carte* as a "contractual" instrument, was not deployed until after "Glanvill" and before the two earliest registers of writs in the early years of Henry III: "The History of the Register of Original Writs", in *The Collected Papers of Frederic William Maitland*, ed. H. A. L. Fisher (Cambridge: Cambridge University Press, 1911), II, 141; for the importance of the writ in the present context, S. F. C. (Toby) Milsom, *The Legal Framework of English Feudalism* (Cambridge: Cambridge University Press, 1976), 63-4.

[5] For England, John Hudson, *Land, Law and Lordship in Anglo-Norman England* (Oxford: Oxford University Press, 1994), 157-229, who maintains that the *laudatio* was less influential in England than in "France", perhaps operative in only a third of early-twelfth-century charters, which is consistent with the Garendon cartulary, as discussed below; Hudson, *Land, Law and Lordship*, 188, n. 65, for the figure of one third in a collection of charters, but he also demonstrates that the proportion fluctuated, mainly below that level; for a European perspective, Emily Z. Tabuteau, *Transfers of Property in Eleventh-century Norman Law* (Chapel Hill, N.C.: University of North Carolina Press, 1988), 113-210, and Constance B. Bouchard, *Holy Entrepreneurs: Cistercians, Knights and Economic Exchange in Twelfth-century Burgundy* (Ithaca, N.Y.: Cornell University Press, 1991), 66-94; for lordship and the cultural aspects of power, Thomas Bisson, ed., *Cultures of Power:*

Lordship, Status and Process in Twelfth-century Europe (Philadelphia, Pa.: University of Pennsylvania Press, 1995).

[6] Stephen D. White, *Custom, Kinship and Gifts to Saints: The Laudatio Parentum in Western France, 1050-1150* (Chapel Hill, N.C.: University of North Carolina Press, 1988), passim; Hudson, *Land, Law and Lordship*, 173-83. The *laudatio* or participation had probably declined in England by the 1170s, if not before: Hudson, *Land, Law and Lordship*, 184-8, especially 187 and n. 62, which is an interesting juxtaposition with warranty.

[7] Hudson, *Land, Law and Lordship*, 181.

[8] For this characteristic of ritual, Maurice Bloch, "Symbols, Song, Dance and Features of Articulation: Is Religion an Extreme Form of Traditional Authority?", in Bloch, *Ritual, History and Power: Selected Papers in Anthropology* (London: Athlone, 1989), 20: "Ritual is an occasion where syntactic and other linguistic freedoms are reduced because ritual makes special use of language" (and, for Bloch, is an integral part of the relationship of power). The same point is made, from a different perspective, by Paul Connerton, *How Societies Remember* (Cambridge: Cambridge University Press, 1989), 58-9.

[9] Connerton, *How Societies Remember*, 36-40 (here I dispense with the term "social memory", which is used by Connerton and also by James Fentress and Christopher Wickham, *Social Memory* (Oxford: Blackwell, 1988), since what is at issue is the event for a selected group rather than a social group or society.

[10] Paul R. Hyams, "Warranty and Good Lordship in Twelfth Century England", *Law and History Review* 5 (1987): 437-503; the apparent paradox is explained at 474-6.

[11] Tabuteau, *Transfers of Property*, 196-210, 245, 376 (n. 1); at 196, she notes that some form of "warrant" had appeared in four charters in the eleventh century.

[12] James C. Holt, "1066", in *Domesday Studies: Papers Read at the Novocentenary Conference of the Royal Historical Society and the Institute of British Geographers*, ed. Holt (Woodbridge: Boydell, 1987), 41-64; the quotation is at 57; see now also Robin Fleming, *Domesday Book and the Law* (Cambridge: Cambridge University Press, 1998) as well as Paul R. Hyams, "'No Register of Title': The Domesday Inquest and Land Adjudication", in *Anglo-Norman Studies IX: Proceedings of the Battle Conference 1985*, ed. R. Allen Brown (Woodbridge: Boydell, 1986), 127-41.

[13] Tabuteau, *Transfers of Property*, 196. See also Milsom, *Legal Framework*, 42: "But the root idea was probably that of warrant with its connotations of authority and protection."

[14] Hudson, *Land, Law and Lordship*, 55-7.

[15] Compare Tabuteau, *Transfers of Property*, 198-200.

[16] For the relationship between written and oral authority, see now Mary Carruthers, *The Book of Memory: A Study of Memory in Medieval Culture* (Cambridge: Cambridge University Press, 1990), 10-11, discarding the stark contrast between "orality" and "literacy", and David Rolson, *The World on Paper: The Conceptual and Cognitive Implications of Writing and Reading* (Cambridge: Cambridge University Press, 1994).
[17] Fleming, *Domesday Book and the Law*.
[18] Fleming, *Domesday Book and the Law*, 535 [index].
[19] Fleming, *Domesday Book and the Law*, 97 [DB, I, 218v].
[20] Fleming, *Domesday Book and the Law*, 172 (no. 794) [DB, I, 137v].
[21] Fleming, *Domesday Book and the Law*, 125, 174-5, 181, 183 (nos. 331, 794, 811, 875, 896).
[22] Fleming, *Domesday Book and the Law*, 282, 307, 309 (*bis*), 410 (nos. 1844, 2100, 2125, 2126, 2995).
[23] Fleming, *Domesday Book and the Law*, 282 (no. 1844) [DB, I, 18b].
[24] Fleming, *Domesday Book and the Law*, 307 (no. 2100) [DB, II, 101b].
[25] Fleming, *Domesday Book and the Law*, 309 (no. 2125) [DB, II, 103a].
[26] Fleming, *Domesday Book and the Law*, 309 (no. 2126) [DB, II, 103a].
[27] Fleming, *Domesday Book and the Law*, 410 (no. 2995) [DB, II. 388a-b].
[28] Fleming, *Domesday Book and the Law*, 287, 319 (nos. 1891, 2203, 2207).
[29] *Statuta Capitulorum ... Ordinis Cisterciensis*, 14-15, 96 (1184, c. 88). See also the comments of Christopher J. Holdsworth, "The Chronology and Character of Early Cistercian Legislation on Art and Architecture", in *Cistercian Art and Architecture in the British Isles*, ed. Christopher Norton and David Park (Cambridge: Cambridge University Press, repr. 1988), 40-55.
[30] *Statuta Capitulorum ... Ordinis Cisterciensis*, 109 (c. 10).
[31] Dave Postles, "The Garendon Cartulary in BL, Lansdowne 415", *British Library Journal* 22 (1996): 162-3.
[32] For proscription of homage and oaths, *Statuta Capitulorum ... Ordinis Cisterciensis*, 57 (1154x1156, cc. 8-9), 68 (1157, c. 70).
[33] But compare J. R. Sommerfeldt, ed., *Cistercian Ideals and Reality*, Cistercian Studies Series 60 (Kalamazoo, Mich., 1978).
[34] In general, Marcel Mauss, *The Gift: The Form and Reason for Exchange in Archaic Societies*, trans. W. D. Halls (London: Routledge, 1980), but further Pierre Bourdieu, *The Logic of Practice*, trans. Richard Nice (Oxford: Polity, 1990), 98-111, especially for the suspension of time between gift and reciprocal action, producing the element of uncertainty as to whether the gift will indeed be reciprocated even if it is expected; the suspension of time is all the more pertinent in the case of gifts for salvific purposes, for the welfare of souls after death. For a certain lack of differentiation

in the language used in benefactions to the religious in the early twelfth century, James C. Holt, "Feudal Society and the Family in Early Medieval England: II, Notions of Patrimony", *TRHS* 5th ser., 33 (1983): 199-200. For relationships of the laity with their saints in the early middle ages, Patrick J. Geary, "Coercion of Saints in Medieval Religious Practice", in his *Living with the Dead in the Middle Ages* (Ithaca, N.Y.: Cornell University Press, 1994), 116-24, and Aron Gurevich, *Medieval Popular Culture: Problems of Belief and Perception* (Cambridge: Cambridge University Press, 1988), 37-77.

[35] Janet Burton, "The Foundation of British Cistercian Houses", in *Cistercian Art and Architecture*, 24-39; Edmund King, "Mountsorrel and its Region in King Stephen's Reign", *Huntington Library Quarterly* 44 (1980): 1-10; Benet D. Hill, *English Cistercian Monasteries and their Patrons in the Twelfth Century* (Urbana, Ill.: University of Chicago Press, 1968).

[36] Godfrey R. C. Davis, *Medieval Cartularies of Great Britain* (London: Longmans, Green & Co., 1958), 49 (no. 431); Postles, "The Garendon Cartularies", 161-71, especially 165.

[37] Dave Postles, *"Defensores Astabimus*: Garendon Abbey and its Early Benefactors", in *Monasteries and Society*, ed. Benjamin Thompson, Harlaxton Medieval Studies, VI (Stamford: Paul Watkins, 1999), 97-116.

[38] *Rufford Charters*, I, xv, xx.

[39] David Knowles and Neil Hadcock, *Medieval Religious Houses: England and Wales* (London, 1971), 113, 123; Edmund King, "The Foundation of Pipewell Abbey, Northamptonshire", *Haskins Society Journal* 2 (1990): 168-77.

[40] Knowles and Hadcock, *Medieval Religious Houses*, 114, 126.

[41] Knowles and Hadcock, *Medieval Religious Houses*, 114; "Cartulary ... Old Wardon", 2, 7.

[42] Knowles and Hadcock, *Medieval Religious Houses*, 114; *Sibton Abbey Cartularies*, I, 116, 150.

[43] Knowles and Hadcock, *Medieval Religious Houses*, 113, 114.

[44] A question posed by Paul Hyams.

[45] Janet Burton and R. Stalley, "Tables of Cistercian Affiliations", in *Cistercian Art and Architecture*, 394-401.

[46] BL, Lansdowne MS 415, fol. 15v.

[47] Bouchard, *Holy Entrepreneurs*, 56-65.

[48] For an analysis of counter-gifts, Henk B. Teunis, "The Countergift *In Caritate* According to the Cartulary of Noyers", *Haskins Society Journal* 7 (1997): 83-8.

[49] King, "Mountsorrel and its Region".

[50] BL, Lansdowne MS 415, fol. 8r.

[51] BL, Lansdowne MS 415, fols. 20r-v. The date is assigned by reference to confirmation by Roger de Mowbray: *Charters of the Honour of Mowbray*, 117-18 (no. 159).

Seeking the Language of Warranty 219

⁵² BL, Lansdowne MS 415, fol. 9v.

⁵³ BL, Lansdowne MS 415, fols. 6r-v.

⁵⁴ BL, Lansdowne MS 415, fol. 16v. It is after 1143 as it is attested by Richard, abbot of Leicester: David Knowles, Christopher N. L. Brooke, and Vera C. M. London, eds., *The Heads of Religious Houses: England and Wales 940-1216* (Cambridge: Cambridge University Press, 1972), 170.

⁵⁵ BL, Lansdowne MS 415, fol. 7r. The date is assigned by reference to *Charters of ... Earls of Chester*, 159, 171-2, 176, 206.

⁵⁶ BL, Lansdowne MS 415, fols. 8r-v.; the date is assigned by reference to Crouch, *The Beaumont Twins*, 16, 220.

⁵⁷ BL, Lansdowne MS 415, fol. 8v.; the date is attributed by reference to William Farrer, ed., *Honors and Knights Fees*, 3 vols. (Manchester: Manchester University Press, 1925), II, 58-9, and since the charter is attested by Robert, earl of Leicester and his wife, Petronilla: Edmund B. Fryde, Diana E. Greenway, Stephen Porter, and Ian Roy, eds., *Handbook of British Chronology*, Royal Historical Society Guides and Handbooks vol. 2 (London, 1986), 468.

⁵⁸ BL, Lansdowne MS 415, fol. 5v.; dated by reference to *Beauchamp Cartulary*, 163-4 (no. 286).

⁵⁹ BL, Lansdowne MS 415, fol. 10r.; dated by reference to *Rutland MSS IV*, 5 (no. 16c), and, for the attestation by W. Basset as sheriff, *Lists of Sheriffs in England and Wales*, List and Index Society vol. 9 (London, 1963), 75, 144.

⁶⁰ *Warantizabimus et manutenebimus* at BL, Lansdowne MS 415, fols. 5v (1163x1189 and n.d., but before 1208), 6v, 7v, 10r, 11r (for example).

⁶¹ BL Add. MS 37,022 and Stow MS 937 (Davis, *Medieval Cartularies*, 88 (nos. 774-775))

⁶² BL Add. MS 37,022, fo. 1v.

⁶³ *Rufford Charters*, I, lxi-lxii.

⁶⁴ *Rufford Charters*, I, 110 (no. 196, 1166x1187), 111 (no. 197, 1170x1187) are some examples of warranty among several in the volume. For the convention of pledge in charters in the Danelaw, *Transcripts of Charters ... Gilbertine Houses*, xxx.

⁶⁵ *Rufford Charters*, I, 150-1.

⁶⁶ *Rufford Charters*, I, 141 (no. 247).

⁶⁷ *Thame Cartulary*, I, 2-3 (no. 1).

⁶⁸ *Thame Cartulary*, I, 41 (no. 41).

⁶⁹ *Thame Cartulary*, I, 6-7 (no. 9).

⁷⁰ *Thame Cartulary*, I, 65-7 (no. 81).

⁷¹ *Thame Cartulary*, I, 67-8 (no. 85).

⁷² *Thame Cartulary*, I, 99 (no. 133).

⁷³ *Thame Cartulary*, II, 132-3 (no. 188).

[74] "Cartulary ... of Old Wardon", 66-7 (no. 88).

[75] Paul Hyams indicated to me that the afforcement was the promise to warrant.

[76] "Cartulary ... of Old Wardon", 24-5 (no. 22). The formula is also visible at 26-9, 32, 38-9, 48, 62-3, 73, 119-20, 122, 126, 133, 226, 229, all belonging to the last quarter of the twelfth century.

[77] *Sibton Abbey Cartularies*, II, 119-20 (no. 152).

[78] *Sibton Abbey Cartularies*, III, 12-13 (no. 483).

[79] For other examples of pledge and warranty, *Sibton Abbey Cartularies*, III, 128-9, IV, 38, 90-1.

[80] *Sibton Abbey Cartularies*, III, 10-11 (no. 480).

[81] *Charters of the Honour of Mowbray*, 29 (no. 35): *Et ego et heredes mei totam hanc donationem eisdem monachis et successoribus suis semper debemus manutenere et warantizare contra omnes homines et feminas.*

[82] *Charters of the Honour of Mowbray*, 33-4, 37-8 (nos. 42-3, 49).

[83] Hyams, "Warranty and Good Lordship".

10
Tenure in Frankalmoign and Knight Service in Twelfth-Century England:
Interpretation of the Charters

In 1217, the barons determined that no one should alienate so much of their fee that the services could not be properly performed. This formal restriction seems mainly to have been directed against the acquisition of lay fee in free alms by religious houses, for which secular services (including knight service) were owed. This decree can be seen as the start of legislation on mortmain in the thirteenth century.[1] It can also be viewed as the culmination of the pragmatic working through of the relationship between free alms and knight service, the most intractable of secular services in this context. This latter aspect is investigated here through charters, which occasionally reveal the thinking of all the parties involved in alienations in free alms or with an interest in the performance of knight service. The evidence is drawn from a wide body of charters–wider than has been considered previously for this purpose–but the emphasis is placed on those with diplomatic forms which are revealing because they are unusual. It is suggested that these unusual forms represent more searching attempts to define the problem.

There has been some debate about the exact nature of the socio-economic changes which precipitated the ordinance of 1217. There was certainly a general sentiment that the balance between lay fee and alms (that is, land held by the religious) had become distorted.[2] Some historians have suggested that the knightly class experienced a "crisis" which had multiple causes, but of which an important one was the acquisition under duress of land by the religious from the hard-pressed knightly families.[3] In Oxfordshire, however, there may not have been a general crisis of the knights, although the evidence is not without some difficulty.[4] Amongst the knights holding of Peterborough Abbey, some experienced a resurgence in fortunes, but others a decline to the benefit of the abbey's entry into the land market.[5] Whatever the precise socio-economic consequences, religious houses were heavily involved in the acquisition of lay fee during the twelfth and early thirteenth centuries.

Gifts to religious houses were expected to be in alms, in return for unspecified spiritual services.[6] When Roger Corbet granted the vill of Winsley to Shrewsbury Abbey in ca.1121-35, he exempted the house from any service *nisi orationes*.[7] In another sense, alms conformed to notions of gift-exchange, if viewed from an anthropological rather than a legal perspective. Not only was some form of service required, but social honor was also attached to the gift and the donor.[8] The diplomatic and legal implications of gifts in alms developed from being inchoate in the twelfth century to a more precise definition by the time of the treatise, customarily attributed to Bracton, which was compiled in the mid thirteenth century. In the fullest diplomatic formula (in free, pure and perpetual alms) these gifts were theoretically free from all secular services, providing in return unspecified spiritual services. In fact, such complete exemption was rarely the case. Shortly after 1152, Roger, earl of Clare, issued a writ to his men conveying his displeasure that Stoke by Clare Priory was being subjected to exactions other than those which had existed in the time of his grandfather or could be asked of free alms (*quam oportet interrogare libere elemosine*); by implication some secular demands could legitimately be made of land held in frankalmoign.[9]

Notions of free alms changed during the course of the twelfth century. One of the influences was the changing judicial competence and jurisdiction over lands held by the Church, which has been explored by, for example, Kimball, Thorne and Douglas. The tenurial aspects were affected accordingly by these judicial changes. Tenurial relationships were also informed by some underlying social and political processes, and it is these variables which are treated here. The emphasis is on those pragmatic considerations which, in the course of their working through, altered notions of free alms, by nuance. Towards the end of the twelfth century, the treatise attributed to Glanvill, but possibly compiled by another contemporary, could classify alms amongst other tenures. It is suggested here that such an interpretation would not have been possible earlier in the century. Glanvill's discussion was mainly informed by judicial considerations (procedure on writs and the competence of royal courts), but by his time social and political considerations had also become effective. Consideration is thus given here to the charters and pragmatic transactions by which religious houses acquired land encumbered with knight service (or, by the late twelfth century, more customarily, its commutation in the form of scutage).[10]

The great Benedictine houses (as well as the episcopacy) had been required to provide a quota of knight service from shortly after the Conquest (having been constituted as ecclesiastical tenants in chief by knight service), but other religious houses had not been allocated a quota nor were they tenants in chief.[11] These other religious houses came under the obligation to provide secular services through the piecemeal acquisition of land encumbered with military service. Gifts in frankalmoign to these religious houses were theoretically to be free of all secular services. In practice, the religious did assume some secular service–most often the service of rent, which presented few problems. Knight service, however, could have been an entirely different matter. The obligation to perform knight service (even through commuted scutage) implied the recognition of a superior lordship and a feudal relationship. This relationship depended on homage–a physical act–and allegiance (through fealty), which may have gone against the spirit of reform behind the new religious Orders which arrived in England in the twelfth century.[12] Some arrangement, moreover, had to be made for the performance of knight service. This decision inevitably involved not only the mesne tenants, but all superior lords up to the tenant in chief (but rarely as far as the Crown). All tenants in the "feudal chain" were affected by the non-performance of knight service by a religious house. Their interest thus reinforced notions of restrictions on alienation. These restrictions might come from the family (which had apparent future rights in the land) (*the retrait lignager*) or from the lord (who had an interest in the nature of subinfeudations and the performance of services). These restrictions on alienation were one of the causes of the deferment of "property" or "estates".[13] The emphasis here is on the seigniorial interest. By the late twelfth century, it was possible in some few cases for gifts to be made by substitution rather than subinfeudation, but these seem to have been isolated occurrences. In cases of substitution, there seems to have been little that a lord could do.[14]

Most gifts in the twelfth century were, however, achieved through subinfeudation. When these subinfeudations involved religious houses, negotiations ensued as to who was to perform knight service, in what way and at what level. In most cases, these discussions are hidden from our view and have to be inferred from the documents. In some few cases, the negotiations are more evident. These examples provide an insight into the nature of feudal relations in the twelfth century. Services attached to land were basically of two types: intrinsec and forinsec.[15] Intrinsec services involved only the donor and the beneficiary. Forinsec services were owed outside the immediate tenure, that is to lords superior to the donor. Knight service was such a forinsec service. Donors could therefore either assume the services themselves so that they became detached from that specific piece of land (effectively transferring the services from the alienated land to other land); or donors could seek permission of the superior lord for the remission of the service. Negotiations about the performance of services come to light in a small number of the transactions between religious houses and mesne tenants.

Some Benedictine houses founded after the Conquest and which were not ecclesiastical tenants in chief were compelled to acquire land without exemption from knight service. In 1150x1158, Robert de Lancport sold to Luffield Priory half his land in Lamport for eight marks. Luffield was to hold the land in a formula usually reserved for lay feudal tenures (*in feudo et hereditate*). The house was, moreover, to perform the knight service attached to the land, providing (the cost of) a quarter of a knight (*pro servicio quarte partis militis*). The charters of confirmation by Robert's son, Jordan (1175x1181) and by their successor, Ralph, son of Ralph de Lancport, in the early thirteenth century, confirmed the nature of the tenure. The land consisted of five virgates, to which Robert I added a half virgate in frankalmoign. The tenure specified in the charter of confirmation was:

liberam et quietam ab omni servitio michi uel heredibus meis pertinente per servicium quarte partis unius militis

Although free of service to the donor's heirs, the forinsec service–knight service–had to be performed. Thus, in acquiring land by purchase, not by gift in frankalmoign, Luffield assumed the responsibility for knight service.[16]

In this case, the priory was to hold in fee and heredity, a formula which differed quite markedly from a gift in frankalmoign, which, in the final diplomatics, was in free, pure and perpetual alms. The term perpetuity was more appropriate for a religious house, which suffered no interruptions of tenure through mortality, but persisted as a corporation sole. Heritability, heredity and inheritance were infelicitous terms for a religious house in this respect. In addition, the term "fee" was unsuitable, since it implied feudal tenure and lordship. Although the great Benedictine houses were constituted tenants in chief responsible for quotas of knight service, houses such as Luffield were a different proposition. Nevertheless, William FitzAlan could, in ca.1155, convey to Shrewsbury Abbey *dimidium feudi mei* [sic] in Droitwich.[17] A charter of 1237-8 could refer simply to the conveyance of *feodum unius militis* by Thomas Fossard to Byland Abbey, without any other description of the land.[18]

An entirely different turn of events happened earlier in the century, when Robert de Burtun endowed the newly-founded Cistercian house at Garendon. Cistercian houses were expected to be exempt from all forms of secular (and some spiritual) exactions.[19] Burtun wished to give to Garendon three carucates in Ibstock (Leicestershire). He had to seek the consent of his immediate lord, Geoffrey de Clinton. Geoffrey's charter of confirmation implied that his consent had been received before Robert's gift, since the notification recited Robert's benefaction. Geoffrey's charter exempted the house from the knight service owed by the land (a third of a knight). The negotiations over the performance of knight service extended further. The earl of Warwick had to agree to the remission of the service, as superior lord. The first charter from him copied into the cartulary of the house was a simple quitclaim, but the service was specified as half a knight. A subsequent charter (in the order in the cartulary), probably of 1155x1166, however, reflects more detailed negotiation. The service from Ibstock was quitclaimed in exchange for the return of the manor of Baddesley (Ensor) which had been given to the house by Henry de Cald' with consent of the earl's father; additionally, the earl gave a consideration of ten marks. The remission of half a knight seems to have been more accurate.[20] In 1086, the mesne tenant, Ingenwulf, had held six carucates in Ibstock.[21] The three carucates in the gift should consequently have answered for half a fee, if the manor and vill had comprised one fee. In order to achieve the exempt status associated with free alms, the house had become involved in quite detailed discussions about the performance of the service.

The motives of tenants in chief towards gifts by mesne tenants varied with circumstances. When tenants in chief were founders and patrons (or, possibly, advocates) of a house, they might encourage gifts by their honorial baronage and mesne tenants to that house, not least because the continued endowment of the house helped to ensure their and their heirs' salvation. Roger de Mowbray accordingly encouraged his tenants to give to Newburgh Priory in one of his own charters of endowment (1145x1157).[22] In these circumstances, the tenant in chief might well tend to remit the service. If, however, the mesne tenant intended to make a benefaction to a house unconnected with the tenant in chief, the services might well be reserved.

Some of these different attitudes can be inferred from charters of William, earl of Gloucester (1153-84). When, in 1153, he confirmed the sale of the manor of Cameley (Somerset) by Alexander *de Alnoio* and members of his family to Saint Peter's, Bath, William permitted the alienation as superior lord, but his charter noted that the abbey would owe the service of a sixth part of a knight's fee, which the monks were to perform to him and his heirs. The definition of tenure thus described the land as being *in elemosinam et feodo* [sic] *totum liberum et quietum in perpetuo*. In the same vein, earl William confirmed the gift of Osbert de Pennard to Saint Augustine, Bristol. Osbert had given to the abbey 124 acres held by the service of a fifth of a knight and thirty acres held by the service of castle guard. In a first charter of confirmation as chief lord, William reserved the services, but in a further, later, confirmation, the earl remitted the service. A different solution obtained when Roger Sturmy granted land in fee-farm to Margam Abbey. The earl of Gloucester's confirmation recited an agreement about the performance of services. Service to the earl was reserved, since the abbey was exempt from secular services *salvo meo servitio*. If this service was deficient, the earl would not distrain against the abbey for more than the half mark of silver which was the fee-farm rent owed by the abbey to Sturmy. Roger was to perform the service which was owed by him and by his father before him. In other words, the whole service had been reserved to that part of the land which Roger retained to himself. The mesne tenant was thus responsible for all the service, including that from the alienated land. The negotiations here looked forward to the provisions of 1217. The earl was attempting to make sure that he was not the loser by any failure to perform service through alienation of part of a fee. In another case, the earl allowed purchase of the remission of services.[23]

Thus also, Saint Albans Abbey paid thirty marks of silver for the remission of the service of half a knight owed from land previously held by William *Camerarius*, even though this house was a tenant in chief by knight service. When Hugh the constable of the bishop of Lincoln confirmed the gift of his under-tenant to a religious house, he specifically provided that the service due to him and his heirs should not be lost (*hac uidelicet conditione ut ego et heredes nostri seruitium inde non amittamus*). By contrast, Robert, earl Ferrers, as superior lord, remitted the service of a knight owed from a hide of land given by his tenant, William Fitz-Otho, to Thame Abbey in ca.1141-8.[24]

The Cistercian houses, such as Garendon, should have avoided becoming entrammelled in military service by the nature of their Order and their general exemption from other obligations. The acquisition of land encumbered with military service contravened the spirit of the *Carta Caritatis*, which formed the basis of the rule of the Order.[25] The intent of the Order was for a contemplative, religious existence, removed from contact with the lay world. Their estates were consequently converted to granges, administered by lay brethren.[26] Villages were, indeed, depopulated to achieve this end.[27] It has sometimes been assumed that the Cistercians received predominantly "waste" and marginal land (although this was certainly not always the case).[28] Had this been the case, it would presumably have been easier for donors to absorb the services from marginal land to other, more profitable, land which they retained.[29] Cistercian houses should, therefore, have been at the forefront of establishing pure alms without attendant knight service.

In practice, however, houses of the Order had to assume knight service with the acquisition of land. A notable example is Fountains Abbey. By several large acquisitions in Kirby Wiske in the late twelfth century, the abbey became responsible for the acquittance of knight service (or its equivalent commutation). When Eudo son of William de Kyrkeby conveyed three bovates there, the monks were to perform knight service in the proportion seven carucates for the service of one knight. Walter Dinant's transfer of half a carucate in the same vill involved the abbey in performing military service on the basis that nine carucates equalled one fee. Two bovates there received from Richard *filius Gleu* required the monks to perform knight service according to the equation that nine carucates made up one fee. Richard de Holetorp's charter to Fountains was professedly in pure and perpetual alms, but he not only reserved an intrinsec rent of 4d. at Pentecost, but also specified that the monks should perform the forinsec service for the carucate which he gave in Moor Monkton, on the basis that eighteen carucates made one knight's fee. The acquisition of half a carucate in Kilnsey from Edulf de Kilnesei had the same consequences. By the charter, the monks were required to perform the forinsec service (where fourteen carucates made up a fee), and this arrangement was confirmed by the charter of the superior lord, Gerard de Glanvill'.[30]

Other religious houses in Yorkshire became entrammelled in knight service in the same way at about the same time. In acquiring half a carucate in Downholme from Gilbert son of Alan de Dunum, Marrick Priory also assumed the obligation of performing the attendant knight service, so much as pertained to half a carucate where fifteen carucates provide the service of one knight. When the same priory received two bovates in Brompton from Thomas son of Robert de Barton, it also assumed the knight service attached to the land on the understanding that twelve carucates performed the service due from one fee. Robert's additional transfer of a carucate in Scotton brought upon the priory further knight service on the same basis.[31] Osbert de Haward's gift of a bovate to Drax Priory in the late twelfth century involved the house in the acquittance of knight service or scutage at the rate of ten carucates to the fee.[32] Similarly, Malton Priory's acquisition of one and a half bovates in Amotherby required knight service from the house, at the appropriate level when thirteen carucates made a fee. The charter from Hugh son of Richard de Aimundreby provided the land in pure and perpetual alms free from all earthly service and secular exaction, but forinsec service was reserved.[33]

In the same way, Kirkstall Abbey became obliged to perform knight service (or its equivalent commutation in scutage) by its acquisition of eight bovates from Robert son of Peter Scot in 1174-91 (*monachi eciam facient forinse servitium*). When Roger Mustel transferred three carucates in 1172-4, however, his superior lord (Paynel) exempted the abbey from services due to the King, including knight service (at the rate of ten carucates to the fee). The charter of confirmation did not specify who should perform the service.[34] At a much earlier time, Kirkstall Abbey received sixty acres from William de Stret, but the inchoate diplomatics of the charter included the terms *in feudo et perpetuam elemosinam* [sic]. Here and elsewhere, the terms seem ostensibly to be inappropriate and incompatible, but they illustrate that there was no clear distinction in people's minds between how far alms should be exempt from fee (that is, implicitly, secular tenure, by knight service).[35]

By contrast, Saint Peter's (later Saint Leonard's) Hospital, York, was exonerated from knight service incumbent on land in Heslington provided by Robert *filius Copesi* and his son, Torfin, shortly before 1148. These joint benefactors passed twenty-four bovates free from all exactions (geld, customary payments and aids) and quit of all service to the King or to the donor's superior lord, the earl of Richmond. The benefactors specifically undertook to perform the services themselves (*sic eciam quod ego et heredes mei omne seruicium quod ad eandem terram pertinet semper faciemus* ...). Their charters, nevertheless, had an inchoate form, since the first gift was made in alms in fee forever (*et eas habeant in elemosinam in feudum et imperpetuum*). The second charter had a similar formula: *et eas habeant in feudum et elemosinam perpetuam*. Since the gift involved land from which knight service was owed, frankalmoign was not fully distinguished from lay fee, even though the monks were exempted from the services. The gifts were confirmed some time afterwards by charters of Henry II and Roger de Mowbray to Robert *filius Copesi*.[36]

By 1166, a small number of religious houses had already acquired land encumbered with knight service and were consequently listed in the returns of the barons (*Carte Baronum*) amongst the subinfeudated knights. For example, the abbot of Saint Osyth held half a fee; Launde Priory held a fee; Huntingdon Priory held one and a half fees; and at least three other houses held fees or parts of fees.[37] It seems likely, however, that most land acquired by religious houses before 1166 was exempted from knight service. Charters before this date are so inchoate, however, that it is impossible to be entirely certain on this point. This mirrors the uncertainty of contemporaries before the processes had been worked through.[38] About 1123x1126, some doubt arose as to whether Shrewsbury Abbey might have become liable to contribute to scutage (*auxilium militis*). An inquest held by the bishop of London, Richard de Belmeis, found that the abbey was exempt, since the house had not previously contributed and had a writ-charter of the king exempting the monks.[39] The lack of definition is reflected in those charters which describe the land as held in both fee and perpetual alms. Although fee may have been intended to imply heredity, the term also had the implication of military tenure.

By the time of John, numerous religious houses owed small amounts of scutage for lands which they had acquired. In 1204, for example, the following still owed debts for scutage for the preceding years: Ford Abbey one mark for the first; Furness Abbey (Cistercian) owed 40s. *de dono* towards John's second scutage; Stratford Abbey five marks for the third; Grimsby Priory 2s. 4d. and half a mark, and Taunton Priory three marks *de dono* for the fourth. The abbot of Bruern had been acquitted by royal charter from four marks owed to the second scutage. The fifth scutage was levied in 1204. At least twenty religious houses which were not tenants in chief were required to give fines or aids (*dona*) towards this scutage. The fines and aids were raised arbitrarily at very high levels, regardless of what fees the houses had acquired. Although included under the heading of the scutage on the Pipe Rolls, the exactions were thus really a levy on those houses which had not previously paid scutage, on the slightest pretext of their holding some land to which knight service was attached. This political action by John was perhaps the first marked extension of scutage to religious houses which were not ecclesiastical tenants in chief. The fines and aids provided by these houses for the fifth scutage were disproportionate to the small amount of land held by them which was encumbered with knight service. Exactions were made in 1204 from houses of Austin Canons such as Waltham (thirty marks), Merton (twenty marks), Osney (fifteen marks), Saint Augustine, Bristol (ten marks), Cirencester (thirty marks), Keynsham (ten marks), Bridlington (fifteen marks), and Nostell (ten marks). Crowland Abbey was one of the Benedictine houses founded before the Conquest which did not become an ecclesiastical tenant in chief responsible for knight service. In 1204, however, whilst indicating this status (*et nullum tenent militem*), the abbey still proffered thirty marks *de fine suo*. John, at least, was prepared to subject religious houses to scutage in an extensive manner.[40]

Table 6 Descriptive Statistics of Fines and Aids Levied on Religious Houses (Including Those Which Were Not Ecclesiastical Tenants in Chief) Towards the Fifth Scutage of John in 1204

Number of houses	Mean (marks)	Standard deviation	Median (marks)	Minimum (marks)	Maximum (marks)	First quartile (marks)	Third quartile (marks)
29	31.48	28.66	20	2	100	10	40

In normal circumstances, however, religious houses could transfer scutage to their own tenants. Barnwell Priory, required to pay scutage for one fee in Barton in the late thirteenth century, thus had a formal record of its devolution onto its tenants there, nineteen tenants being assessed at rates from a penny halfpenny to five shillings.[41]

Towards the end of the twelfth century, it became more difficult to acquire land without the attached services. By this time, however, knight service was commonly commuted for scutage and so the performance of the service was less inappropriate. To some extent it was hardly distinguishable from rents and taxation.[42] The forinsec service incumbent on Guisborough Priory on its acquisition of half a carucate from Roger de Cava before 1219 was thus specifically described as scutage, on the basis of six and a half carucates comprising half a fee.[43] Forinsec service in charters to houses in Yorkshire in the late twelfth century was constantly described in terms of so much service pertaining to the amount of land transferred when so many carucates composed a fee. It seems fairly clear that this computation of standard service and fee was related to the payment of scutage from fragmented fees and the realization that military service would not be elicited. Religious houses may have felt less compunction about rendering what was effectively taxation in money than providing actual military service. On the other hand, it was becoming more usual for the religious to be taxed separately from laymen, by assessment specifically granted by ecclesiastical authority.[44]

Other types of military service may have required performance rather than commutation. On the acquisition of land in ca.1180, Shrewsbury Abbey assumed the obligation of providing forinsec service to the chief lord of that fee, that is, a bowman for fifteen days of castle guard at Ludlow and a man to lead a horse when the chief lord was in Wales with the army. It is unclear whether the service was commuted or exacted in kind from the abbey's tenants.[45]

Even in cases of scutage, there were sometimes negotiations, not about who should perform the service, but its level. The Gay family increasingly passed land to Osney Abbey from ca.1195. Reginald made two separate benefactions of a virgate, whilst Robert transferred three virgates and fourteen acres. In all transfers, Osney was responsible for the forinsec service. Finally, in 1220x1222, Robert alienated the entire manor of Hampton Gay to the abbey, but the abbey was to perform the military service, which was defined as half a fee held from each of the honors of Champernulf and St Walery. St Walery and his successor, Richard, earl of Cornwall, allowed no remission of the service. Champernulf, however, remitted half the service for a consideration of four marks of silver. For the half fee held of Champernulf, therefore, the abbey was obliged to pay scutage for only a quarter of a fee, whilst the Champernulfs acquitted scutage for the other quarter. This remission of the service may have been inspired partly as a benefaction to the religious and partly as a commutation by sale.⁴⁶

Another effect of the replacement of actual service by scutage may have been the loss of definition between intrinsec and forinsec service. For example, when William *filius Helte* granted to Fountains Abbey a carucate in Hawkswick in 1175/6, he specified that the land would be free of all service and custom, *ita quod ipsi [monachi] dabunt mihi et heredibus meis annuatim dimidiam marcam* [at each of two terms].⁴⁷ This annual payment would appear to be an intrinsec arrangement. On the other hand, it might be that with this rent (or part of it), William defrayed the cost of the forinsec service. The distinction between intrinsec and forinsec service may thus have become blurred as commutation and taxation replaced actual military service. Charters relating to gifts in frankalmoign might thus have no reference to forinsec service, not because it was not due, but because it was accounted for by an intrinsec payment in cash. This transaction may have been delayed for some time after scutage became normal, as superior lords may have wished for the distinction to be preserved.

The accumulation of land encumbered with both intrinsec and forinsec services had far-reaching consequences. Religious houses, even the Cistercians, were drawn into secular and tenurial relationships, not only in the provision of the services (through aids and *dona*), but also because of the possibility of distraint for non-provision of services. One interpretation which has been posited is that there was therefore no practical difference between tenure in alms and "socage" (in the sense of free tenures), but that the essence of tenure in frankalmoign was simply the provision of undefined spiritual services amongst other services.⁴⁸ Although such may have been the pragmatic result, a slightly different emphasis can be suggested. In theory, gifts in free alms were notionally different from lay tenures, but they became debased by practical circumstances. Despite the wish that frankalmoign should be different from lay fee and exempt from secular services, it became impossible to circumvent those services. Especially was this so as the twelfth century proceeded, as the number of religious houses proliferated (especially those of the new Orders introduced into England in the twelfth century), as these houses became in a sense "competitors" for benefactions, and as they, consequently, entered into the land market as purchasers rather than passive beneficiaries. As the amount of land available for transfer to religious houses declined, and as the imbalance between lay fees and free alms was perceived by the laity, so the remission of services from land became less possible.

Another perception of the problem is the evolution of custom, norms and law in the eleventh and twelfth centuries. Although frankalmoign developed into a specific form of tenure by the end of the twelfth century, gifts in alms may have had a more inchoate nature at an earlier time. Referring to Normandy, both Yver and Tabuteau have suggested that giving land in alms did not involve a tenure, only an intention: that alms denoted mainly the intention of the donor.[49] Thus donors need in all conscience only waive those secular services which it was possible for them to waive. References to a *ius elemosinae* and to a statement attributed to William the Conqueror that alms ought to be given "pure", however, suggest some notion of an ideal gift in frankalmoign before the middle of the twelfth century.[50] When William Peverel gave the vill of Cutsdean to Worcester Priory (1149x1157), his charter thus also included the phrase *ecclesiastico iure perpetualiter possidendam*.[51] Such phrases might have hearkened back to the jurisdiction exercised by ecclesiastical courts over alms at an earlier time, especially in the reign of Stephen, and also to an earlier understanding of "pure" alms.[52] Kimball suggested that a greater *quantum* of secular services was likely to be remitted when the gift was in "pure" alms.[53] There are some cases, however, in which in twelfth-century England alms were made "pure" but forinsec service was required from the beneficiary. Pure alms may not inevitably imply a greater freedom from secular services at all times.[54]

Nor does the expression of some of the gifts in frankalmoign suggest a uniform perception of which services should be remitted in the twelfth century. In his gift to Saint Mary's Abbey, York, in ca.1115-35, Geoffrey Murdac allowed the land to be free of all earthly service *sicut tenent melius et honorificencius alias elemosinas baronum benefactorum suorum*.[55] Although he may have had a notion of an ideal gift in frankalmoign, Geoffrey equated the nature of his gift with those made by others to that house. By the end of the twelfth and early thirteenth century, this ideal was mentioned in numerous charters in which the land was to be free of secular services: *Sicut ulla elemosina liberius potest dari* (1190-1210); *prout aliqua elemosina potest liberius melius et quietius dari alicui domui religiose* (1226); *sicut aliqua elemosina liberius et melius dari potest* (1208-25).⁵⁶ These expressions recognized the comparative nature of gifts in frankalmoign–that some would be freer of secular services than others.⁵⁷ Thus when Nigel de Stockeld made a benefaction to the hospital of Saint Peter (later Saint Leonard), York, he exempted the house from all secular services *et ECIAM a forinseco seruicio regis* … [my capitals], realizing that such an exemption was unusual.⁵⁸ Bracton, however, accorded only a limited exemption to phrases such as *sicut aliquam liberius aut quiecius teneri debet aut potest*. For him, in the mid-thirteenth century, such expressions related only to intrinsec service.⁵⁹ It is possible, however, that in the early twelfth century, something more expansive was intended, related to a notion of the *ius elemosinae*.

Some charters which recorded gifts to religious houses (though by no means all) contained warranty clauses. Such clauses usually warranted the actual land, particularly in transactions between the laity. In charters to the religious, however, there is an implication that warranty may also have related to freedom from secular services. A common formula for warranty in charters to the religious was warranty *sicut meam puram elemosinam*, which may have placed an emphasis on freedom from services.⁶⁰ If an attempt was made to levy or distrain for services, donors (and their heirs) would warrant the exemption of the religious house (presumably by performing the service or giving compensation). If the intention behind warranty did not include this element of services, then it reflects also on the uncertainty behind exemption from services.

On balance, it seems more reasonable to expect that greater efforts were made to exempt gifts in alms from forinsec service before the middle of the twelfth century. Before the *Carte Baronum* of 1166, attitudes towards knight service may have been less hardened. After that date, the increasing commutation of military service to scutage, the financial problems ensuing from these fiscal exactions, the difficulties experienced by some of the knightly social group, the growing imbalance of the ratio of land held by the laity and the religious, and the increasing entrance into the land market by religious houses as purchasers, may well have contributed to circumstances in which the laity was more reluctant to or could not remit forinsec service any more. The Cistercians accumulated as many of these obligations as any other Order, despite the objectives which had been set forth in their rule.

The specific problem which the clause of 1217 seems to have been addressing had already been resolved in practice. By the early thirteenth century few alienations to the religious were exempt from secular services, knight service or scutage. The clause was probably addressing this issue not because of its immediacy, but as an expression of concern about the perceived changing balance between the lands of the Church and the lands of the laity. Changes in the relationship between tenure and frankalmoign and secular services had already been worked through in practice through social and political processes as well as by those legal and jurisdictional changes effected during the late twelfth century and initiated by Henry II.

Notes

[1] The reissue of Magna Carta 1217, c. 39: Paul A. Brand, "The Control of Mortmain Alienation in England, 1200-1300", in *Legal Records and the Historian*, ed. John H. Baker (London: Royal Historical Society, 1978), 31; Sandra Raban, *Mortmain Legislation and the English Church 1279-1500* (Cambridge: Cambridge University Press, 1982), 14.

[2] Edward Miller, "The State and the Landed Interest in Thirteenth-century France and England", *TRHS* 5th ser., 2 (1952): 109-29.

[3] For example, Peter R. Coss, "Sir Geoffrey de Langley and the Crisis of the Knightly Class in Thirteenth-century England", repr. in *Landlords, Peasants and Politics in Medieval England*, ed. Trevor H. Aston (Cambridge: Cambridge University Press, 1987), 166-202, developing ideas suggested by Rodney H. Hilton and Michael M. Postan.

[4] David A. Carpenter, "Was There a Crisis of the Knightly Class in the Thirteenth Century? The Oxfordshire Evidence", *EHR* 95 (1980): 721-52. It may be, however, that there were more critical times for baronial and knightly families in Oxfordshire in the late twelfth century.

[5] Edmund King, "Large and Small Landowners in Thirteenth-century England: The Case of Peterborough Abbey", repr. in *Landlords, Peasants and Politics*, 141-65; compare, however, Westminster Abbey which rarely purchased subinfeudated fees: Barbara F. Harvey, *Westminster Abbey and its Estates in the Middle Ages* (Oxford: Oxford University Press, 1977), 166.

[6] Elizabeth G. Kimball, "Tenure in Frank Almoign and Secular Services", *EHR* 43 (1928): 341-53.

[7] *Cartulary of Shrewsbury Abbey*, II, 272-73 (no. 228); *Early Yorkshire*

Charters, V, 24 (no. 327) *(exceptis tantummodo oracionibus)* (late twelfth century); *Charters of the ... Earls of Chester*, 39 (no. 27) *(nisi oraciones tantummodo)*; *Cartulary of Darley Abbey*, II, 371 (no. H46, ca.1149-53: *preter orationes*); John Rylands University Library, Manchester, Lat. MS 222, fols. 28r-v *(preter oraciones in domino)*. These words probably occur mainly before ca.1160.

[8] For example, Barbara H. Rosenwein, *To Be the Neighbor of St Peter: The Social Meanings of Cluny's Property, 909-1049* (Ithaca, N.Y.: Cornell University Press, 1989); Joel T. Rosenthal, *Purchase of Paradise: Social Function of Aristocratic Benevolence, 1307-1485* (London: KeganPaul, 1972); Stephen D. White, *Custom, Kinship and Gifts to Saints: The* Laudatio Parentum *in Western Fance 1050-1150* (Chapel Hill, N.C.: University of North Carolina Press, 1988), especially 4-5.

[9] *Stoke by Clare Cartulary*, I, 22 (no. 32).

[10] Samuel E. Thorne, "The Assize *Utrum* and the Canon Law in England", repr. in his *Essays in English Legal History* (London: Hambledon, 1985), 51-9; Elizabeth G. Kimball, "The Judicial Aspects of Frankalmoign Tenure", *EHR* 47 (1932): 1-11; Audrey W. Douglas, "Frankalmoign and Jurisdictional Immunity: Maitland Revisited", *Speculum* 53 (1978): 26-48; G. Derek G. Hall, ed. and trans., *The Treatise on the Laws and Customs of the Realm of England Commonly Called Glanvill* (Oxford: Oxford University Press, 1965), XII, ii, 137.

[11] Helen M. Chew, *The Ecclesiastical Tenants-in-Chief and Knight Service* (Oxford: Oxford University Press, 1932).

[12] For example, Paul R. Hyams, "Warranty and Good Lordship in Twelfth Century England", *Law and History Review* 5 (1987): 442; for the importance of homage, S. F. C. (Toby) Milsom, *The Legal Framework of English Feudalism* (Cambridge: Cambridge University Press, 1976), 172-3; Thorne, "English Feudalism and Estates in Land", repr. in *Essays in English Legal History*, 16-24.

[13] Thorne, "English Feudalism and Estates in Land"; Milsom, *Legal Framework of English Feudalism*; Robert Palmer, "The Origins of Property in England", *Law and History Review* 3 (1985): 1-50.

[14] Milsom, *Legal Framework of English Feudalism*, 151-3, but contrast with Harvey, *Westminster Abbey and its Estates*, 165, the abbey trying to prevent substitutions without licence.

[15] Kimball, "Tenure in Frank Almoign", 341-3; Audrey W. Douglas, "Tenure *In Elemosina*: Origins and Establishment in Twelfth-century England", *American Journal of Legal History* 24 (1980): 97.

[16] *Luffield Priory Charters*, 105-7 (nos. 411-13). For other lands, acquired *in feudum et hereditatem* and *in pheudo et hereditate*, by a Cistercian house, *Rufford Charters*, I, 52-3, 100-1, 235 (nos. 95, 179-80, 431).

[17] *Cartulary of Shrewsbury Abbey*, I, 77 (no. 84).

[18] *Early Yorkshire Charters*, IX, 159 (no. 88).

[19] Benet D. Hill, *English Cistercian Monasteries and their Patrons in the Twelfth Century* (Urbana, Ill.: University of Chicago Press, 1968), 56-62; perhaps thus also the reason for the caution in the confirmation of a gift to the Templars, which allowed alienation to any religious house except the Cistercians (*exceptis albis monachis*): *Early Yorkshire Charters*, V, 338-9.

[20] BL, Lansdowne MS 415, fols. 5r-v; see also *Beauchamp Cartulary Charters*, 163-4 (no. 286).

[21] DB, I, fol. 237b.

[22] *Early Yorkshire Charters*, IX, 245-6.

[23] *Earldom of Gloucester Charters*, 33, 42-3, 47-9, 118-19, 123 (nos. 5, 19, 29-30, 126, 134); see also Douglas, "Tenure *In Elemosina*", 118, n. 74.

[24] *Earldom of Gloucester Charters*, 153 (no. 168); *Thame Cartulary*, I, 43-4, 78 (nos. 46, 101).

[25] Hill, *English Cistercian Monasteries*, 56-62.

[26] Colin Platt, *The Monastic Grange in Medieval England: A Reassessment* (New York and London: Fordham University Press, 1969); Robert A. Donkin, "The Cistercian Grange in England in the Twelfth and Thirteenth centuries, With Special Reference to Yorkshire", *Studia Monastica* 6 (1964): 95-144.

[27] Robert A. Donkin, "Settlement and Depopulation on Cistercian Estates During the Twelfth and Thirteenth Centuries", *Bulletin of the Institute of Historical Research* 33 (1960): 141-65.

[28] Constance H. Berman, *Medieval Agriculture, the Southern French Countryside, and the Early Cistercians*, Transactions of the American Philosophical Society vol. 76 (Philadephia, Pa., 1986).

[29] Douglas, "Tenure *In Elemosina*", 115, n. 66.

[30] *Early Yorkshire Charters*, V, 190-2, 218 (nos. 286-8, 310), VI, 112 (no. 31), VII, 72, 145, 188-90 (nos. 27, 83, 120, 122), IX, 144-5 (nos. 73-4), X, 96 (no. 56).

[31] *Early Yorkshire Charters*, V, 29-30, 73 (nos. 127, 170).

[32] *Early Yorkshire Charters*, VI, 160 (no. 71).

[33] *Early Yorkshire Charters*, VI, 106 (no. 26).

[34] *Early Yorkshire Charters*, VI, 255, 258-9 (nos. 152, 157).

[35] *Early Yorkshire Charters*, VI, 133 (no. 51).

[36] *Early Yorkshire Charters*, V, 63-6 (nos. 156, 158-60).

[37] *Red Book of the Exchequer*, Rolls Series vol. 99 (London, 1896), 187, 221, 262, 331, 372, 377.

[38] *Danelaw Documents*, cxx-cxxi.

[39] *English Lawsuits*, I, 209 (no. 243).

[40] *Pipe Roll 6 John*, PRS n.s., vol. 18 (London, 1940), 3, 28, 34-6, 50, 58, 61, 76, 83, 90-1, 101-2, 105, 112, 128, 130, 152, 169, 181-2, 185, 189, 217, 223-4,

226, 229, 232, 241, 245, 252, 254; See also *Pipe Roll 17 John*, PRS n.s. vol. 37 (London, 1964 for 1961), 15-17 (fees held by smaller religious houses from the Honor of Boulogne).

[41] *Liber Memorandum ... Bernewelle*, 306.

[42] S. K. Mitchell, *Taxation in Medieval England* (New Haven, Conn.: Yale University Press, 1951), 4-5, 111-12, 164-6. Scutage existed as a composition from at least the reign of Henry I, but was exacted as a *general* levy only after 1166. As early as ca.1140, however, a gift to a religious house could exclude exemption from scutage, as though the tax was regularly levied: *Thame Cartulary*, I, 67 (no. 84).

[43] *Early Yorkshire Charters*, IX, 190 (104).

[44] William E. Lunt, *The Visitation of Norwich* (Oxford: Oxford University Press, 1926), 7-9; see also Lunt, *Financial Relations of England with the Papacy to 1327* (Cambridge, Mass.: Medieval Academy of America, 1939).

[45] *Cartulary of Shrewsbury Abbey*, I, 252-3; II, 271-2 (no. 286).

[46] *Cartulary of Oseney Abbey*, VI, 41-61 (nos. 962A-K, 96, 967-72).

[47] *Early Yorkshire Charters*, VII, 145 (no. 83).

[48] Kimball, "Tenure in Frank Almoign", 347-8; Douglas, "Tenure *In Elemosina*", 95.

[49] Emily Z. Tabuteau, *Transfers of Property in Eleventh-century Norman Law* (Chapel Hill, N.C.: University of North Carolina Press, 1988), 38-9; J. Yver, "Une Boutade de Guillaume le Conquérant: Note Sur la Génèse de la Tenure en Aumône", in *Études d'Histoire du Droit Canonique Dédiées à Gabriel le Bras* (Paris, 1965): 783-96.

[50] Tabuteau, *Transfers of Property*, 37; Yver, "Une Boutade de Guillaume le Conquérant".

[51] *Cartulary ... Worcester*, 69 (no. 119).

[52] Thorne, "The Assize *Utrum*", 51-9; Kimball, "The Judicial Aspects", 1-11.

[53] Kimball, "Tenure in Frank Almoign", 342-3; Douglas, "Tenure *In Elemosina*", 127-8.

[54] Douglas, "Tenure *In Elemosina*", 127-8.

[55] *Early Yorkshire Charters*, X, 139 (no. 70).

[56] *Early Yorkshire Charters*, IX, 150 (no. 78), X, 40-1, 96-7; *Charters of the ... Earls of Chester*, 140, 155-6 (nos. 126, 148); *Cartulary of Burscough*, 19-20 (no. 1). These are only selected examples.

[57] Compare Douglas, "Tenure *In Elemosina*", 111.

[58] *Early Yorkshire Charters*, X, 66-7 (no. 43) (ca.1194).

[59] *Bracton on the Laws and Customs of England*, II, 93 (Bracton, fol. 27b).

[60] *Early Yorkshire Charters*, VII, 160 (no. 95) (warranty *sicut puram et perpetuam elemosinam*), IX, 193 (no. 105) (warranty of "this our alms" against the King, lords and all men); *Newington Longeville Charters*, 62 (no. 71) (*sicut meam puram elemosinam*).

11
Choosing Witnesses in Twelfth-Century England

The public witnessing of transactions and actions existed in antiquity and was, perhaps, the simplest mode of assurance or corroboration. Sale of goods, consequently, became restricted in large measure to formal markets where transactions were made public. This regulation of exchange and sale of goods in a public forum developed strongly in Anglo-Saxon England. At the same time, formal documents (diplomas) were introduced for the alienation of land (bookland). These documents included a formal attestation of the act through the inclusion of lists of subscriptions or *signa* (crosses) of dignitaries. As diplomas were replaced by charters in the eleventh and twelfth centuries as the medium for recording transactions in land, the *signa* gave way to simple lists of witnesses (although sometimes residual features from diplomas–such as *signa*, arenga and anathema–persisted within charters). Diplomas had mainly been royal instruments, but charters had a wider role embracing private transactions in land.[1] Lists of witnesses thus became an integral part of charters, usually found at their foot, corroborating and assuring the deed. Private transactions needed to be made more public to ensure their integrity. Livery of seisin and attestation were two inter-related methods of achieving this end.[2]

By the late twelfth century, the witness or attestation clause in charters had become formalized and static. The diplomatics were almost invariably *Hiis Testibus* followed by the names of the witnesses in the ablative. In large part, this development reflected the transition from inchoate forms to common diplomatics. By this time also, however, the attestation clause had been supplanted in importance by a number of other forms of corroboration, some of which were coeval with witness clauses. These other methods of ensuring the integrity of gifts included, *inter alia*, the *laudatio parentum*, corroboration and consent of the lord within the charter or by a separate charter of confirmation, pledge of faith and hand-fast, warranty, and other methods external to the charter itself, such as final concords (tripartite from 1195), notification to the Ordinary in the case of gifts to the religious, and other devices.[3] The range of these formulae contributed to the relative decline in the importance of the witness list, even though some of the devices (such as *laudatio parentum*) were effectively transient. Thus, by the third quarter of the twelfth century, *Hiis Testibus* increasingly intruded into charters as the normal form.

At an earlier time, however, witness clauses had been more significant and precise in reflecting the objectives of attestation as a form of surety or security. The clauses were more inventive, flexible and purposive.[4] The vitality of the forms of phrase employed reflected the importance of attestation at that embryonic time in the deployment of charters, before the development of other modes of assurance. Even in the second quarter of the twelfth century, religious houses could be founded and endowed by oral disposition, without charters.[5] Towards the middle of that century, however, it became less conscionable for religious houses not to have charters for their benefactions, leading in some cases to the reconstruction of unauthentic charters of the oral endowment which had taken place at an earlier time.[6] Charters relating to the tenurial and personal relationship between lord and tenant were even less usual, although increasingly in evidence from the 1140s and 1150s. The important features of oral disposition had therefore been to make the transactions public. The wider notification could be achieved through a number of methods: through proclamation (such as in the honorial or county court or to the Ordinary); through symbolic (public) livery; and through formal attestation. These devices were not exclusive, but inter-related, so that attestation might embrace proclamation in a court and ceremonial livery of seisin. In this sense, witnessing of transactions in land preceded the use of charters. Attestation had its origins in the world of oral disposition of land. Witness lists in charters were thus not simply a formal aspect of diplomatics, but a recollection of an event which had been publicly enacted, and thus confirmed the evidentiary nature of charters as against the oral disposition of the livery of seisin. On the other hand, the introduction of charters, authenticated by seals, may have tended *ipso facto* towards the eclipse of the importance of witnessing, if the charters and seals would stand alone (or as primary evidence) as legal and moral corroboration.

Accordingly, earlier witness clauses reflected the nature of the event which was attested. The present tense was more likely to have been used in witness clauses and the witnesses listed in the nominative, with specific references to the act of disposition: *Huius donacionis testes sunt hii; Testes sunt isti; Huius donacionis testes sunt qui afuerunt; universi qui aderant super hiis testes existerent.*[7]

Until ca.1180, virtually all the charters for Saint Benet Holme had one of two introductory phrases for the witness list: *Huius rei testes sunt* or *Huius donationis et concessionis testes sunt*.[8] Some exceptions occurred at an early time. For example, in ca.1126-27 and 1134-40, the clause began: *Testimonio eorum qui affuerunt*. In ca.1134-40 also, a charter to that house referred to the attestors as witnesses to the gift which had been made on the altar of Saint Benedict. Some later charters refer to the witnesses attesting both the gift (*donatio*) and the charter (*cartula*).[9]

In William Achard's charter to Sandford, the witnesses were specifically present: *Huius autem donacionis presentes testes affuerunt*; as also in a charter of Abingdon Abbey: *In horum testium praesentia*. In a charter from John de Port to a preceptory of the Templars, the witness clause was similarly emphatic: *Ut hec donatio mea jugiter inconcussa permaneat adsunt testes*.[10] In this case, the witnesses seem to be specifically charged with protecting the integrity of the gift.

There was then a wide variety of forms employed. Most of these phrases suggest the actual presence of the witnesses and the importance of that presence. The phrases reveal that the presence of the attestors was at the livery of seisin. Symbolic liveries of seisin were thus designed to imprint the event in the memory of the witnesses. Accordingly, when Iwein *de Albineio* and his brother, Geoffrey de Chauenni, made a benefaction to Belvoir Priory, they did so by the symbolic placing of a rod on the altar before witnesses. The clause relating to the symbolic livery elided into the witness list in the charter.

> *Hanc donationem baculo quodam super altare beate marie optulimus Astante conventu eiusdem loci et Willelmo de Albin[eio] et filio eius Willelmo* [with three other named witnesses] *et nonnullis aliis testibus*[11]

Similarly, a candlestick was often the instrument of the symbolic livery on the altar in favour of Stoke by Clare Priory. The clause revealed that the charter recording the livery elided into the witness clause in several cases. William de Musterol placed a candlestick accordingly *rogavi et obtestatus sum quatinus universi qui aderant super hiis testes existerent* (and thus positively requested those present to witness the act). Robert de Watteville's charter revealed that the livery was enacted before named witnesses (... *coram testibus acta sunt*). A more explicit statement occurred in the charter of Ralph Brison to Fountains Abbey: *Isti sunt testes qui presentes fuerunt ubi hanc terram super altare de Fontibus obtuli.*[12] Robert Despenser restored Wick to Westminster Abbey in ca.1095-98. Before the witnesses, his wife and brother placed on the altar of Saint Peter two silver candlesticks, a thurible, altar cloth and tapestry, to which the list of witnesses in the charter bore testimony. The witnesses, therefore, were attesting the symbolic livery rather than the evidentiary charter. The ceremonial use of these memorable articles may have been intended not only to represent the livery of seisin, but also to imprint the occasion in the minds of the witnesses.

Some witness clauses included memoranda, which were probably designed to assist witnesses to recall the event. Thus, the gift to a specific altar in the parish church of Habrough was attested by the parishioners and others on the Sunday when the abbot of Barling celebrated mass at that altar. The witness clause of a charter to Newhouse Abbey recorded that the attestation occurred on the day of the consecration by the bishop of Lincoln of two abbots, both of whom also witnessed the gift. Yet another charter to the same house mentioned that the witnesses were present when the charter was passed from the donor to the bishop and then by him to the abbot. The actual presence of the witnesses at the livery is confirmed by the incremental attestation of a charter from Nigel son of Ralph de Stockeld to Sallay Abbey. The gift was made with the assent of his lord, William de Perci, and William son of Gilbert de Mikelthuait (probably his tenant). Separate witness lists were included for each of the confirmations by lord and tenant, and for the symbolic livery by the donor on the altar of the house, all in the same charter.[13] The witnesses were actually present, and the reference to the events in the witness clause of the charters was intended to stimulate their memories. Consequently, the later, stereotyped incipit *hiis testibus* may have been a contraction of the fuller phrase *coram hiis testibus* found in some charters of Winchcombe Abbey, which implies a real presence at the transaction.[14]

Some unusual attestations confirm the importance of the witnessing of transactions in and before the middle of the twelfth century. For example, Gilbert de Gant had given all his demesne at Eakring to Rufford Abbey. In a separate, and probably later, document, his brother, Robert de Gant, issued a notification, addressed to the royal officials and justices in Nottinghamshire, that he (Robert) had witnessed this act with many others.

> *Huius donationis testis sum ego et paratus sum ubique inde facere quod legitimus testis facere debet et mecum multi alii qui interfuerunt et valete*

The importance of this particular witness probably lay in his being a potential heir of Gilbert, so that attestation is conjoined with the *laudatio parentum*.[15] When Walter son of Miles, earl of Hereford, confirmed the vill of Alvington to Llanthony Secunda in ca.1143-48, he invoked the witnesses to corroborate his gift:

> *Huius donationis mee testem et confirmatorem atque protectorem esse volo et precor te, episcope Hereford' ... cum ceteris testibus qui affuerunt vel a me ipso audierunt et factum meum sine omni calumpnia collaudaverunt ...*

In this case, Walter invited the help not only of the witnesses actually present at the disposition, but also anyone who had heard of the gift in the time between the original gift and the subsequent confirmation.[16] This more active role for witnesses was echoed in a charter in favor of Winchcombe Abbey, where they are described not only as *testes*, present at the transaction, but also as *cooperatores*.

Charters of Cecily and Alice de Rumilly also exhibited this invocation of witnesses. Alice's charter (ca.1152-54) specified that the witnesses attended *peticione mea*, whilst the witnesses in Cecily's (ca.1131-40) were "vouched" to witness (*advocati sunt*).[17] Finally, when Roger, earl of Hereford, issued a general charter of confirmation (ca.1143-45) to Llanthony, he recited his previous, separate gifts, all with their separate witness lists. The general charter was thus not subscribed by one general list of witnesses to the confirmation, but by reciting all the previous separate lists of attestations.[18]

The choice of witnesses was not random, but deliberate, and for specific purposes. Including the donor's wife and potential heirs amongst the witnesses was an alternative to the *laudatio parentum*. The *laudatio* had been related before the end of the twelfth century to prospective heirs and the inclusion of specific kin was related to the life-course of the donor. Thus, if there was no issue at that stage of the donor's life, brothers would be included in the consent; if there were no sons amongst the issue, all daughters (co-parceners) would be contained in the consent. Wives were always included to bar rights of dower. The *laudatio* was thus determined by the donor's life-course and to prevent familial claims.[19]

The alternative was to include the relatives in the list of witnesses, usually in prominent positions. In virtually all the charters of William, earl of Gloucester, for example, the countess Hawise attested in first place (ca.1150-83), because of her potential right of dower. The gift of Ralph de Langetot to Reading Abbey was attested by his mother, Cecily, since it came from her dower.[20] Charters of Robert d'Oilly (II) were often attested, in prominent positions in the list of witnesses, by his wife, Edith, and brother, Fulk.[21] Manasser Arsic's charter for Eynsham Abbey was attested in first and second positions by his wife, Margaret, and son, Alexander.[22] When Robert, earl of Leicester, confirmed the foundation and endowment of Garendon Abbey, his charter was attested first by the Countess Petronilla, then by his son, William, and by the head of the other local house in his patronage, the abbot of Leicester.[23]

Many charters have as their first witnesses the potential heirs. Indeed, copies in cartularies sometimes only transcribed the attestation of those heirs, omitting the other witnesses. Thus some charters in the cartulary of Stoke by Clare have truncated witness lists:

Testes Lambertus frater meus et alii; *Testes huius donacionis Warinus et Hugo filii mei et alii*.[24] The brothers of Ralph Musard, Serlo and Hastulf, attested as first witnesses his charter to Sandford as well as consenting to the gift (*Testibus et concedentibus* …). The charter of Richard de Chaynes in favor of Luffield Priory was attested first by his son, William (ca.1160-3). That of Henry, Count of Eu, to Bec was witnessed first by his brother, William, as was that of Manasser Biset to Eynsham, ca.1154-8.[25] The charter of Ralph son of Robert Puintel to Saint Benet Holme was made by witness (*Testimonio*) of his two brothers. When Faramus made a charter in favor of Bec, the *laudatio parentum* and witness list were elided, so that his brothers, Eustace and Simon, featured at the head of the list of witnesses as *concessores* and *testes* (after 1159). The same elision occurred in a charter of William de Rossendale, to which his son was first witness and consentor (*testante et concedente*). A charter of Henry Putrel to Garendon Abbey was attested significantly by Robert Putrel, Richard Putrel and William Putrel.[26]

Perhaps the most remarkable series of charters attested by close relatives and potential heirs is that of Philip de Kyme, recording his numerous benefactions to religious houses in Lincolnshire. At least fourteen of his charters were attested in first position by one of more of his sons, variously one to four in number (Simon, William, Philip and Walter). A few are witnessed only by Simon, as son and heir, but most are attested by more than one of his male siblings. The number may reflect different stages of the development of the family. Inclusion in the witness list was here an alternative to the *laudatio parentum*.[27] On the other hand, William, son of Hugh FitzRalph, signified his agreement both through a *laudatio* and by witnessing in first position, as double assurance, but at a much earlier time (ca.1123-53). Some later charters in Yorkshire also refer to the son(s) and heir(s) as assenting and witnessing. The prominent witnessing by potential heirs thus performed the same function as the *laudatio parentum*: to commit those heirs to the gift and forestall any familial challenge.[28]

Other categories of witness were obviously desirable. In the "truly seigniorial world" of the early twelfth century, attestation by the honorial baronage was important and equivalent to (and, indeed, probably the same as) a symbolic livery and proclamation in the honorial court.²⁹ Thus, Gilbert, earl of Clare, made a benefaction in ca.1139-43 by a charter, which concluded: *Testes sunt huius rei ...* (named witnesses) ... *et barones ipsius comitis Clare* .... Similarly, the clause in a charter of William, earl of Gloucester, concluded ... *et multi alii barones mei* .... When Ranulph de Belmeis surrendered to Shrewsbury Abbey Belton which he had held unjustly, his charter was attested by his *barones* and the whole county court of Shropshire. A charter of Richard, earl of Chester, of ca.1106, was attested by his honorial baronage (*Hoc autem fecimus testimonio nostrorum baronum*). Many from the affinity of Ranulph, earl of Chester, attested numerous charters of the earl, such as William (de) Colville, Geoffrey Malbusse, and Thurstan Banastre.³⁰

Conversely, gifts by mesne tenants often needed the consent of superior lords, which could be effected by including the lord as first witness: *Huius donacionis testes sunt qui afuerunt Rogerus comes de Clar' et alii* (a charter from Hamo Pecche in ca.1151-73). The first witness in a charter of Hugh de Druval in favour of Bec was his lord, Richard de Belfou (ca.1150-76). Philip de Kyma and his three sons attested in first place the charter from their tenant, William, son of Humphrey de Oxcumbe, to Bullington Priory.³¹

Another category of "natural" witnesses of baronial charters was household retainers. Many of the charters of the earls of Chester–in favor of both lay tenants and the religious–had a number of witnesses from the earl's household. William de Roumare, earl of Lincoln, invoked eleven named witnesses for his charter to Warter Priory in ca.1141-42, but also the rest of his *curiales*. Similarly charters in favour of religious houses were frequently attested by lay servants of the convent, especially, for example, those of Belvoir Priory.³²

Since many gifts and charters were proclaimed in courts, the suitors of that forum sometimes became witnesses to the transaction, although often apparently anonymously and collectively. This process is illustrated by several charters in favour of Winchcombe Abbey. Those from William Russell and William *le Nevu* were attested before the hundred court. Another charter had as its first witness Thomas Smelred, reeve (*prepositus*) of the hundred court. A gift by Smelred's widow and son was attested by nine named witnesses and the hallmoot of Winchcombe, whilst another charter had six named witnesses and the whole hundred court of Winchcombe. The hundred court of Winchcombe witnessed an agreement after a dispute over pasture, which was also attested by six named witnesses and others who witnessed (*qui viderunt*) the perambulation of the bounds, as well as nine officials of the abbey. Important charters were also proclaimed before and attested by the shire court. Thus a gift from William Taillard had a list of witnesses comprising ten named, the whole county court, seven other named, and the rest of the freemen of Enstone, whilst another charter had as its first witness William FitzStephen, sheriff, followed by twenty-four named witnesses, *et coram comitatu*. Other charters were attested by the hallmoot of Enstone. Attestation in private courts may have been more prevalent in the early twelfth century than later. The gift of Bartholomew *Gigator* to Byland Abbey was enacted before his lord, Roger de Mowbray, and Roger's knights (honorial baronage) in Roger's court at Thirsk. The witness clause simply stated: *Testis est hujus rei tota plena curia*. There were many other statements that transactions were made in baronial and private courts. During the late twelfth century, however, the activity of these courts may have declined, as pleas of land were removed more frequently to royal courts. Consequently, attestation by private courts may have accordingly subsided.[33]

Important charters in favor of the religious–such as foundation charters or those providing large benefactions–were usually attested by important ecclesiastical and religious dignitaries. The Ordinary might be a principal witness to a foundation charter or large gift. Thus the bishop of Lincoln attested in first place a charter to Sixle Priory in ca.1150. This attestation might have been equivalent–perhaps even an alternative to–notification of the gift to the Ordinary. Heads of religious houses of the same Order would be prominent witnesses for the early endowments of new religious houses. Thus, the priors of Spalding and Pontefract were witnesses to a charter of Lucy, countess of Chester, in favour of Stixwould Priory in ca.1135. Most frequently, several priests and incumbents from the locality were included in the lists of witnesses in charters in favor of religious houses.[34]

Apart from heirs, wives, honorial baronage, and dignitaries, witnesses at this time may have required other characteristics. At a time when the function of witnessing was so important, it might have been desirable to have potentially longevious witnesses, to attest to the gift for some time to come. Perhaps at the instance of the prior of Belvoir, a charter to that house from Hugh son of Ivo de Clacston was attested *et alii quam plures iuvenes quam senes*. Many elder and younger witnesses were appended to a charter of Saint Benet Holme after twenty-one named witnesses (*et multi alii seniores et juniores de uilla*–Yarmouth) (1168x1175). Similarly, a charter to Abingdon Abbey included in the witnesses some *juvenes* and some *pueri*.

It was equally important to have witnesses drawn from all those interest groups which might be concerned in the transmission of the land. Consequently, when Geoffrey son of Hubert de Bentley gave property in Beverley to the Hospital of Saint Giles, his list of witnesses included specifically priests (*isti presbiteri*), clerks (*clerici*), knights (*milites*) and burgesses (*burgenses*).[35] A charter to Belvoir was attested by fourteen witnesses on behalf of the priory and an equal number on behalf of Hugh and his wife (*Testes ex parte Hugonis et uxoris sue isti ... Et ex parte monachorum ... testes*). Another charter from Robert de Roppesle to the same house had witnesses for Robert and those for the monks.[36] An agreement between Colchester Abbey and Stoke by Clare Priory contained witnesses explicitly on behalf of the two parties. Another agreement between Saint Benet Holme and Fulk Closham was attested *ex parte* the two parties in ca.1168-75. An earlier charter in favour of that house (ca.1127-34) had been witnessed *ex monachis* (seven named monks) and *ex laicis* (fourteen named witnesses).[37] Another agreement between the earl of Gloucester and the Bishop of Bayeux was attested by witnesses representing the two parties. Robert Foliot's charter of ca.1148-50 was attested *ex parte Roberti Foliot* and *ex parte monachorum* (Westminster Abbey).[38] The charter compiled for Eborard, bishop of Norwich, which recorded the enfeoffment of Roger de Valoniis in Bacton, by his nephew, William de Bachetuna, in ca.1121-35, was attested *ex parte mea* (the bishop) with thirty-five witnesses and *ex parte Rogeri* with twenty-three witnesses. A charter between Reading Abbey and Walter de Mans was attested *ex parte* the two parties, in ca.1148-54. As late as 1172, Roger de Hottot, in a charter for Bec, enumerated witnesses *ex parte mea*.[39]

Witnesses aligned in this way were often involved in charters between parties of baronial status, representing their affinities. The concords of Stephen's reign are extraordinary examples. The charter of the earl of Chester to William, earl of Lincoln, was attested by those *ex parte mea* and those *ex parte vero comitis* (that is, Lincoln).[40] Examples of this practice–of separate (sometimes equal) numbers of witnesses for each party–are few, but are perhaps redolent of an earlier stage in witnessing, when it was common practice to include representatives of both interests. Many lists of witnesses, moreover, may implicitly have followed the same principle, without overtly stating the allegiances of the witnesses. Witness lists specifically related to the parties were, however, more prevalent in contemporary Normandy.[41]

Perhaps a variant of this attestation by allegiance to the parties was the witnessing by women for women. Attestation by women was normally associated with their renunciation of right of dower in the alienated land. Most women who attested, consequently, were wives of the donor. Otherwise, women seem not to have attested very frequently. Occasionally, however, charters by women were attested by women. When Acilia (sic, but perhaps Alice), wife of Richard Frumentin, made a benefaction to Garendon Abbey, a first list of witnesses comprised men, but a supplementary list consisted entirely of women: Denise, wife of Asketil; Rohesia, wife of Asketil de Berges; Matilda, wife of Godfrey; and Alice, wife of Ivo of Prestewald. Another charter to the same house, recounting the gift of Quenilda, wife of Ralph *stabularius*, was attested only by women: Petronilla; Edalina; Geva; Emma; Goda; and Agnes.[42]

The charter of Matilda daughter of Roger de Huditoft to Revesby Abbey, ca.1170-98, included two lists of witnesses: the first list of males was appended with Lady Margaret and Helen, wife of Roger *clericus*; the second list of ten males was followed by an additional list (*Testes sunt etiam*) of Christine, wife of Henry de Claxeb', and Eda, wife of Richard *clericus de Mar'*. Another charter relating to land in Lincolnshire, that of Beatrice, widow of Joslan de Engelbi, had a list of ten male witnesses, followed at the end by three women. Two lists of attestations were appended to the charter of Alexandria, widow of Robert de Herierbi, when she gave twelve bovates in frankalmoign in Honington (Lincolnshire) in ca.1172-

80–one list witnessing the gift at Lincoln and the other attesting the gift at Honington. Both lists consisted firstly of males, with shorter lists of female attestors which followed. In all, thirty males and nine females attested this charter. When five sisters made a benefaction to Stixwould Priory, their lists of attestations comprised forty-three men and twenty women, the female witnesses always appearing after the men in the sequence. The charter of Aaleis de Craft, however, was attested by only one female witness, her sister, Amice de Craft, again at the end of the list, possibly, however, as an heir presumptive.[43]

The charter of Helen de Hastinges to Egglestone Abbey (ca.1201-4) was mainly attested by men, but also by one woman, her namesake, Helen de Bindona. When Walter Dinant and his wife, Emma, made a benefaction to Fountains, both engaged in hand-fast and pledge of faith, Walter in the hand of Richard, the priest of Kirby Wiske, and Emma in the hand of another woman, Raisant, wife of William *filius Eudonis*. Emma's hand-fast was appended to the charter at the foot, after the main text. The main text was concluded by a list of male witnesses. There followed the memorandum of Emma's hand-fast, with a list of female witnesses of that event.[44]

Such instances of women attesting for women are rare, but possibly reflect a social convention. Women did not normally attest charters, except as wives (implicitly renouncing rights of dower). When they attested as wives, they could appear anywhere in the list, even at the head. Otherwise, women rarely appeared in the capacity of witness, except when they attested for female donors. In many charters of female donors, the witnesses were exclusively male, but in some, particularly in the Northern Danelaw, women attested for women. Invariably, the female witnesses were listed after the males. Very often, the female witnesses were wives or sisters of the male witnesses.[45]

One category of "witnesses" which was extremely unusual, but significant, was saints. Saints "attested" only in exceptional circumstances. At the instance of Robert *Mauduit* and his wife, Ralph, abbot of Westminster, issued a confirmation that certain assigned revenues would only be used to provide lights at the Lady altar in the abbey (1210x1214). The sole witnesses to this charter were God, the blessed Mary (whose patrimony was involved), and all the saints of God, but curiously not specifically Saint Peter, the patron saint of the abbey. Although this list is ostensibly in the form of a witness list commencing *Teste*, it probably acted also as an invocation for protection similar to the anathema clause. The further implications are that the saints had a physical and actual as well as a spiritual presence, and that they were prepared to exact retribution–divine punishment–against any infraction, even the diversion of assigned revenues. The clause thus portrayed the saints in the same light as some of the penitentials, although not so crudely.[46] Another charter of ca.1200, which involved a lease of seven acres by Christ Church, Canterbury, to Conan, son of Ellis, was attested firstly by Jesus, the Virgin Mary, Saint Thomas the Martyr, Saint Dunstan, Saint Ælfæg *et omnibus sanctis ecclesie nostre*. Saints, thus, when they were invoked as witnesses, attested gifts and grants *by* religious houses, which involved attestation by those saints associated with their house. The religious grantors believed in the actual presence of these spiritual witnesses.[47]

The length of witness lists was determined by a number of variables. By and large, gifts to the religious tended to have longer lists than subinfeudations of lay tenants. Gifts to the religious were attested by both ecclesiastical dignitaries and lay witnesses, but subinfeudations only by the laity, often the honorial baronage. The significance of the gift also influenced the length of the list. Thus, charters granting quittance from toll from the earls of Gloucester had very truncated lists, as did their charters of their confirmation. In essence, however, charters of confirmation increased the the number of witnesses, as the new ones in the confirmation augmented those in the original charter. The serious business of agreements between great dignitaries warranted very long lists of witnesses. The concord between the earl of Gloucester and the Abbot of Fécamp (1128), consequently, had a quadripartite witness clause: dignitaries (six witnesses); witnesses *ex parte* the abbot (six more *et toto conventu*); lay people (*laici*) (five); and those *ex parte* the earl (eleven).[48] At any date, therefore, the length of witness lists might vary with the circumstances of the gift, charter or agreement.

There does, on the other hand, seem to have been an overall decline in the length of these lists towards the very end of the twelfth century. Some statistical evidence of the length of lists in the twelfth century is presented below (Table 7). The data are mainly drawn from original charters; evidence has only been accepted from copies in cartularies if it is fairly certain that the list has not been truncated. Charters which finish *et multis aliis* (or a similar phrase) have been excluded, except when at least ten named witnesses have been listed. The data thus reveal that lists of witnesses were long in the twelfth century. Occasionally, circumstances produced longer lists at a later date, particularly in charters of foundation of new religious houses in the late twelfth century and in charters recording initial gifts to them. In the late 1160s, for example, five charters to Keynsham Abbey from the earl of Gloucester, including the charter of foundation, described twenty-nine witnesses (*et aliis pluribus*), sixteen, twenty-nine, nineteen and sixteen witnesses. These attestations were afforced by many ecclesiastical dignitaries as well as laity. Charters tended, nevertheless, to have longer lists of witnesses in the earlier twelfth century because attestation was one of the primary methods of corroboration and enforcement of the integrity of the gift. By the end of the century, other forms of assurance had become more important, and lists of witnesses had become accordingly rather stereotyped. During the thirteenth century, lists probably became, in general, shorter.[49]

Table 7 Length of Some Lists of Witnesses in the Twelfth Century

Source	Number	Mean	Standard deviation	Median	Minimum	Maximum	1st quartile	3rd quartile
Belvoir Priory	25	13	7	12	5	30	8	16
Gloucester I	33	13	7	10	3	30	8	18
Gloucester II	29	14	6	13	6	29	10	17
Rufford I	47	11	4	11	4	21	7	14
Rufford II	93	10	4	9	3	23	7	12

Notes to Table 7 *Belvoir Priory*: to ca1200; *Gloucester I*: earldom of Gloucester to ca1160; *Gloucester II*: earldom of Gloucester ca1160-1200; Rufford I: to ca1160; *Rufford II*: ca1160-1200.
Sources as above.
Number= number of charters; all other figures relate to the number of witnesses per charter.

This displacement of the witness clause may have been one of the reasons–amongst several–why *scriptores* who transcribed the charters into cartularies, severely truncated the list of witnesses, often recording no more than three or four of the most important attestors. The list of witnesses was no longer regarded as of primary significance in charters. The *scriptor* of the cartulary of the preceptory of Sandford (Templars) thus abruptly abrogated the list of witnesses in a charter of ca.1164-74 because of the tedium of transcription:

> *multi et alii ad hanc rem testificandam ... fuerunt testes quorum nomina tedio preventi scribere pretermisimus.*[50]

The extent of truncation in cartularies can be illustrated by nine sample charters of Belvoir Priory, which were transcribed into the house's cartulary, the charters ranging from the twelfth century to 1310. In the cartulary, the charters have a total of twenty-eight witnesses–a mean of three witnesses per charter. The original nine charters have a total of sixty-two additional witnesses, that is, a mean of seven additional witnesses per charter. In the transcription of the two earliest charters, the *scriptor* of the cartulary omitted twenty and ten witnesses. The transcriber may have omitted these witnesses because the house still held the original charters in its muniments. On the other hand, he was conscientious enough in his transcription of every other clause in the charters.[51] By the time the cartulary was compiled, lists of wtinesses had lost the importance which had obtained in the twelfth century. The cartulary of Blyth Priory, which was commenced in the late thirteenth century, omitted all lists of witnesses, with few exceptions. Some of the royal writs were accorded their attestors, as was the important foundation charter. Scribes D and E, who transcribed the short, final entries in the cartulary, also made the "error" of including the lists of witnesses to a small number of charters.[52] By the 1140s, the witness lists in many of the charters issued by the great baronial families were becoming formulaic, simply *Teste* or *Hiis Testibus*. A small number of their charters still contained more flexible clauses, reflecting back on earlier procedures, when witness clauses had been more important. The essential nature of the clause diminished as other forms and modes of assurance developed. The charter of William, earl of Warenne (ca.1138-47), to the Templars, which included a witness list of eight named men, concluded, however, that the charter had been made at Lewes in the presence of Pain de Mundesonero and Ascelin *Rothomagus*, thus maintaining the distinction between witnesses to the livery and the making of the charter. By the middle of the century, nonetheless, witnesses of the charter instead of the livery were appearing in a small number of charters.[53]

When the lord of Geoffrey son of Hubert de Bentley confirmed the latter's gift to Saint Giles, Beverley, he did so by handing the charter (*cartula*) on the altar of Saint Giles, rather than using some other object for a symbolic livery. At the time of some–but not all–gifts to Sallay Abbey between ca.1147 and 1176, the *charter* was made before, read to, and granted before witnesses.[54] Their intrusion might have reflected a change in understanding, whereby charters and seals were becoming legally acceptable evidence to title without the testimony of witnesses. A doctrine of charters may have been evolving during the twelfth century, but its development may have been curtailed by the emphasis of Henry II's legal reforms by which the pendulum swung back to seisin. By the thirteenth century, some confusion thus surrounded the relative status of charters and seisin, depending on forms of action. The emergence of a doctrine of charters in the twelfth century was thus abated.[55]

The advance of the concept of seisin in the reign of Henry II may have had important repercussions on the status of witness lists in charters. The contemporaneous development of the Grand Assize may have had an equally important influence. In the Grand Assize, the role of the "witnessing" to the truth of the ownership of land rested with the jurors of the assize. The "witnesses" were not therefore the actual witnesses of the charters, but those who knew, by common knowledge, of the ownership of the land. The role of witnesses to the fact was thus abated, in contrast with the role of such witnesses in ecclesiastical courts.[56]

By the middle of the twelfth century, the lists of witnesses in many charters were becoming stereotyped, a process which was completed in the later half of that century. One of the reasons for the change was the development of the common forms as the diplomatics of charters developed. Many other clauses which had appeared in charters of the twelfth century also changed from being inchoate to a common form, and still others disappeared completely. Nevertheless, before the middle of the twelfth century, witness clauses had been both vital and deliberate, as one of the principal modes of assurance. Witnesses had been selected for specific purposes and to meet different circumstances. The lists of witnesses were longer in the twelfth century, as they comprised different categories of attestor. The eclipse of attestation by other forms and modes of assurance was another contributory reason why the witness clause became increasingly stereotyped.

Notes

[1] For witnessing of transactions in antiquity and in "primitive" societies: A. S. Diamond, *Primitive Law Past and Present* (London: Methuen, repr. 1971), 381-3. For diplomas, Simon D. Keynes, *The Diplomas of King Æthelred "the Unready" 978-1016* (Cambridge: Cambridge University Press, 1980); Frank M. Stenton, *Latin Charters of the Anglo-Saxon Period* (Oxford: Oxford University Press, 1955); Pierre Chaplais, "The Origin and Authenticity of the Royal Anglo-Saxon Diploma", "The Anglo-Saxon Chancery: From the Diploma to the Writ", "Who Introduced Charters into England? The Case for Augustine", all in *Prisca Munimenta: Studies in Archives and Administrative History Presented to Dr A. E. J. Hollander*, ed. Felicity Ranger (London: Hodder and Stoughton, 1973), 28-62, 88-109. For witnessing of transactions in Anglo-Saxon England and warranty of chattels, Frederick Pollock and Frederic W. Maitland, *The History of English Law*, with an introduction by S. F. C. Milsom, 2 vols. (Cambridge: Cambridge University Press, 1968), I, 59, and Paul R. Hyams, "Warranty and Good Lordship in Twelfth-century England", *Law and History Review* 5 (1987): 443-6; Henry R. Loyn, *The Governance of Anglo-Saxon England 500-1087* (London: Hodder Arnold, 1984), 129 (*team*). For the change from diplomas to charters, Vivian H. Galbraith, "Monastic Foundation Charters of the Eleventh and Twelfth Centuries", *Cambridge Historical Journal* 4 (1932-4): 205-22, and Galbraith, "The Literacy of the Medieval English Kings", repr. in *Studies in History*, ed. Lucy S. Sutherland (Oxford: Oxford University Press, 1966), 95-102; R. C. Van Caenigem, *Royal Writs in England from the Conquest to Glanvill*, Selden Society vol. 77 (London, 1958-9), 37, suggests that proof by witnesses to the fact was developed first in canon law, but that witnesses to charters were allowed to testify in lay courts. Disputes about property were as likely to go to a technical trial by battle–duel (bilateral ordeal)–(and compromise): see, for example, Robert Bartlett, *Trial by Fire and Water: The Medieval Judicial Ordeal* (Oxford: Oxford University Press, 1988), 27, 108.

258   Missed Opportunities?

² Samuel E. Thorne, "Livery of Seisin," in his *Essays in English Legal History* (London: Hambledon, 1985), 31-50.

³ Samuel E. Thorne, "English Feudalism and Estates in Land", in his *Essays in English Legal History*, 26, 28; S. F. C. (Toby) Milsom, *The Legal Framework of English Feudalism* (Cambridge: Cambridge University Press, 1986), 42-4; Stephen D. White, *Custom, Kinship and Gifts to Saints: The Laudatio Parentum in Western France* (Chapel Hill, N.C.: University of North Carolina Press, 1988); Hyams, "Warranty and Good Lordship", 437ff.; *Rufford Charters*, I, lxi-lxii; *Transcripts ... Charters of Gilbertine Houses*, xxx.

⁴ Emily Z. Tabuteau, *Transfers of Property in Eleventh-century Norman Law* (Chapel Hill, N.C.: University of North Carolina Press,1988), 146-57, for an analysis of witnesses in Normandy. Several of the editors of cartularies and charters have commented on witness clauses in their general discussion of the diplomatics of charters; see, for example, *Feudal Documents ... Bury St Edmunds*, xii. See also the perceptive comments in Michael T. Clanchy, *From Memory to Written Record* (London: Hodder and Stoughton, 1979), especially 101-2, 203-5, 242-4. For a recent analysis of witness clauses to establish the affinity of the Earl Marshal, David Crouch, *William Marshal: Court, Career and Chivalry in the Angevin Empire 1147-1219* (London: Longman, Green & Co., 1990), 134.

⁵ Galbraith, "Monastic Foundation Charters".

⁶ Galbraith, "Monastic Foundation Charters".

⁷ Examples as follows: *Rutland MSS IV*, 100; *Stoke by Clare Cartulary*, I, 20 (no. 28) and II, 226-7, 328, 333, 340, 349-50, 364 (nos. 328-9, 503, 521, 537-8, 566); *Sibton Abbey Cartularies*, IV, 78 (no. 135); *Earldom of Gloucester Charters*, 73-4, 125 (nos. 68, 135); *Rufford Charters*, I, 80 (no. 147), II, 176, 181, 289-90, 380, 393, 395 (nos. 325, 338, 572, 720, 736); "Charters ... Earldom of Hereford", 23-4, 29 (nos. 25-6, 39); *Newington Longeville Charters*, 23-5 (nos. 19, 21-2); *Sandford Cartulary*, II, 216-19, 246, 248 (nos. 312, 314, 316, 318, 368, 371); *Luffield Priory Charters*, 2-3, 72-3, 105, 118-19 (nos. 293-4, 371, 411, 431-2); *Shrewsbury Cartulary*, I, 77 (no. 83); *Westminster Abbey Charters*, 318 (no. 488); *Transcripts ... Charters of Gilbertine Houses* (e.g.. Sixle Priory), 1-3, 8, 13, 16, 21, 30, 33 (nos. 1, 4, 6, 16, 24, 27, 38, 53, 60); *Cartulary of Oseney Abbey*, V, 61 (no. 572A); *Cartulary of Eynsham Abbey*, I, 69-70, 72-3, 97-8, 101-2, 112, 118, 125 (nos. 59, 64, 66, 112, 119, 140, 152-3, 165). For witnesses who *affuerunt, Early Yorkshire Charters*, IV, 3-5 (nos. 2, 4). See also *Early Yorkshire Charters*, IV, 31 (no. 28): *Et hoc factum fuit coram his testibus*.

⁸ *St Benet Holme*, II, 51-2, 73-5, 77-8, 83-6 (nos. 87, 126, 128, 131, 135, 137, 146-50, 153).

⁹ *St Benet Holme*, 72, 76, 79-80, 139 (nos. 124, 132, 139, 141, 256).

¹⁰ *Sandford Cartulary*, II, 219, 225-6 (nos. 318, 329-30); *Chronicon Monasterii de Abingdon*, 109.

¹¹ *Rutland MSS* IV, 101.

[12] *Stoke by Clare Cartulary*, II, 346-7, 361 (nos. 532, 560); *Early Yorkshire Charters*, XI, 342 (no. 271).

[13] *Westminster Abbey Charters*, 318 (no. 488); *Danelaw Documents*, 202-3, 227-9 (nos. 270, 303, 305); *Early Yorkshire Charters*, XI, 258 (no. 204).

[14] For example, *Landboc ... Winchelcumba*, I, 164; see also *Transcripts ... Charters of Gilbertine Houses* (Sixle), 1 (no. 2); *Danelaw Documents*, 199-200 (no. 207).

[15] *Rufford Charters*, II, 409 (no. 758) (after 1156). For similar elisions of *laudatio* and witnessing, *Early Yorkshire Charters*, XI, 236-7, 278 (nos. 186, 216).

[16] "Charters of the Earldom of Hereford", 41-2 (no. 68).

[17] *Landboc ... Winchelcumba*, I, 212; *Early Yorkshire Charters*, VII, 56, 63 (nos. 5, 16). Several examples can be found of witnesses being vouched, such as *Early Yorkshire Charters*, XI, 137 (no. 120) (*Et hos advoco testes*) suggesting perhaps a more active role for witnesses, in the same language as warranty and patronage.

[18] "Charters ... Earldom of Hereford", 16-19 (no. 11).

[19] White, *Custom, Kinship and Gifts to Saints*.

[20] *Earldom of Gloucester Charters*, for example, 62-5, 71, 82, 89-91, 115, 117, 119-20, 153, 167 (nos. 47, 49, 51-2, 65, 77, 88-9, 120, 124, 127-9, 136, 168, 188-9); *Reading Abbey Cartularies*, I, 218-19 (no. 261). So also charters of the earl of Richmond attested by Countess Margaret: *Early Yorkshire Charters*, IV, 61-4 (nos. 64-7).

[21] *Cartulary of Oseney Abbey*, V, 61 (no. 572A); *Cartulary of Eynsham Abbey*, I, 73 (no. 65).

[22] *Cartulary of Eynsham Abbey*, I, 108-9 (no. 132).

[23] BL, Lansdowne MS 415, fol. 5r. See also the charter of Roger de Mowbray attested in first and second places by his mother and wife, both presumably to bar dower, but with the *laudatio* of his son: *Early Yorkshire Charters*, IX, 145-6 (no. 165). The wife of Robert de Stuteville attested his charter in first place: *Early Yorkshire Charters*, IX, 96-7 (before 1166).

[24] *Stoke by Clare Cartulary*, II, 254-5, 304 (nos. 376, 460).

[25] *Sandford Cartulary*, II, 221-2 (no. 324); *Luffield Priory Charters*, I, (no. 292); *Select Documents ... Bec*, 23 (no. xliii); *Cartulary of Eynsham Abbey* II, 108-9 (no. 132).

[26] *St Benet Holme*, II, 110 (no. 198); *Select Documents ... Bec*, 25-6 (no. xlix); BL, Lansdowne MS 415, fol. 18v.

[27] *Danelaw Documents*, 3-4, 15, 32-3, 35, 37-42, 46-7, 57-8, 67 (nos. 3, 20, 48-9, 52, 56, 59-61, 63, 71, 89-90, 103).

[28] *Reading Abbey Cartularies*, I, 431-2 (no. 577). See also *Early Yorkshire Charters*, V, 103-4, 112, 311, 314 (nos. 184A, 196, 363, 367), VI, 156, 229-30 (nos. 67, 125) (sons and heirs attesting first), IX, 198 (no. 108). For some

heirs as witnesses and consenting, *Early Yorkshire Charters*, IV, 112 (no. 196), VI, 156 (no 67), XI, 26, 28-9, 236-7, 278 (nos. 12, 14, 186, 216).

[29] Milsom, *Legal Framework*, passim; Frank M. Stenton, *The First Century of English Feudalism* (Oxford: Oxford University Press, 2ᵈ ed. 1961), passim.

[30] *Stoke by Clare Cartulary*, I, 15 (no. 21); *Earldom of Gloucester Charters*, 153-4 (no. 169); *Shrewsbury Abbey Cartulary*, II, 275 (no. 294); *Charters of the ... Earls of Chester*, 12-13 (no. 6) and passim. See also Donald F. Fleming, "*Milites* as Attestors to Charters in England, 1101-1300", *Albion* 22 (1990): 185-98, where it is argued that the title *miles* was not employed in lists of witnesses in the twelfth century.

[31] *Stoke by Clare Cartulary*, II, 236 (no. 346); *Documents ... Bec*, 13-14 (no. xxiv); *Transcripts ... Charters of Gilbertine Houses*, 97 (no. 16).

[32] *Charters of the ... Earls of Chester*, passim; *Early Yorkshire Charters*, X, 114-15; *Rutland MSS* IV, passim.

[33] *Landboc ... Winchelcumba*, I, 105, 113, 177, 191, 195, 197-8, 216, 246. See also *Early Yorkshire Charters*, VI, 241 (no. 139) (*et wapentac de Strafford*); VIII, 157 (no. 110) (charter made in the court of the earl of Warenne at the honorial *caput*, Conisborough, ca.1147-59); IX, 246-7 (nos. 166-7) (Bartholomew Gigator); XI, 165-6 (no. 141) (which has named witnesses *et comitatus Eboraci*, ca.1175-90); XI, 317 (no. 245) (*et omnis comitatus Ebor'*).

[34] *Transcripts ... Charters of Gilbertine Houses*, 1 (no. 1); *Charters of the ... Earls of Chester*, 29-30 (no. 19).

[35] *Rutland MSS*, IV, 129; *Early Yorkshire Charters*, X, 103 (no. 62); *St Benet Holme*, II, 167-8; *Chronicon Monasterii de Abingdon*, 136-7.

[36] *Rutland MSS* IV, passim.

[37] *Rutland MSS* IV, 131; *Stoke by Clare Cartulary*, II, 409 (no. 636); *St Benet Holme*, II, 74-5, 163 (nos. 130, 304).

[38] *Earldom of Gloucester Charters*, 34 (no. 6); *Westminster Abbey Charters*, 310 (no. 479).

[39] *Select Documents ... Bec*, 18 (no. xxxiii); Barbara Dodwell, "Some Charters Relating to the Honour of Bacton", in *Medieval Miscellany for Doris Mary Stenton*, ed. Patricia M. Barnes and C. F. Slade, PRS n.s., vol. 36 (London, 1962), 148, 158-9; *Reading Abbey Cartularies*, I, 283.

[40] *Charters ... of the Earls of Chester,* 82 (no. 70); Edmund King, "The Anarchy of King Stephen's Reign", *TRHS* 5ᵗʰ ser., 34 (1984): 133-53; Ralph H. C. Davis, *King Stephen* (London: Longman, 3ᵈ ed., 1990), 108-11; Stenton, *First Century of English Feudalism*, 250-6.

[41] Tabuteau, *Transfers of Property*, 153. For other examples, *Chronicon Monasterii de Abingdon*, 137-8, 176-7.

[42] BL, Lansdowne MS 415, fols. 19v-20r, 23r.

[43] *Medieval Miscellany for Doris Mary Stenton*, 232-3; *Danelaw Documents*, 214 (no. 148), 281-2 (no. 378), 285-6 (no. 381), 290 (no. 388).

[44] *Early Yorkshire Charters*, VI, 190-1 (no. 287) (ca.1170-90). See also *Early Yorkshire Charters*, VI, 152, 155 (nos. 62, 66) (charters of Avice de Rumilly, ca.1150-76, attested by her daughter and another woman). For a female attesting the charter of a male donor, *Early Yorkshire Charters*, IV, 67 (no. 161), in which Alice Burdun attested the charter of Conan son of Torfin alongside Conan's wife, Jueta.

[45] For women's rights in property in the twelfth century, S. F. C. Milsom, "Inheritance by Women in the Twelfth and Thirteenth Centuries", in *On the Laws and Customs of England: Essays in Honor of Samuel E. Thorne*, ed. M. S. Arnold et al. (Chapel Hill, N.C.: University of North Carolina Press, 1981), 60-89; James C. Holt, "Feudal Society and the Family in Early Medieval England: IV. The Heiress and the Alien", *TRHS* 5th ser., 35 (1985): 1-28, especially 17; RaGena C. DeAragon, "In Pursuit of Aristocratic Women: A Key to Success in Norman England", *Albion* 14 (1982): 258-66; Scott Waugh, "Women's Inheritance and the Growth of Bureaucratic Monarchy in Twelfth- and Thirteenth-century England", *Nottingham Medieval Studies* 34 (1990): 71-92.

[46] *Westminster Abbey Charters*, 177 (no. 329); see also Aron Gurevich, *Medieval Popular Culture: Problems of Belief and Perception* (Cambridge: Cambridge University Press, 1990), 47-9, although Gurevich is addressing an earlier and less refined time: "The saint zealously saw to the inviolability of his own property ... Saints in need of proving the legality of their rights thought nothing of producing witnesses from the other world ..."

[47] Galbraith, "The Literacy of the Medieval English Kings", 102, cited the charter of ca.1200, which was printed by Kathleen Major, "Some Early Documents Relating to Holbeach", *Associated Architectural and Archaeological Society Reports* 41 (1934): 39-45, a reference provided to me by Michael Clanchy, who also made the point about the actual presence *pace* Galbraith; see also Clanchy, *From Memory to Written Record*, 234, n. 13.

[48] *Charters of the Earldom of Gloucester*, passim. The charters–as well as notifications and writs–of the first earls of Warenne, however, have very cursory lists of witnesses. The reason may be that there was little differentiation between writs and charters, and that they were more or less confined to a single *genus* of writ-charter. The shortness of the lists may also be related to the elevated status of the Warennes, comparable with royal writ-charters having fairly short witness lists (and ultimately simply *Teste me ipso*): *Early Yorkshire Charters*, VIII, 52-100; *Charters of the Earldom of Gloucester*, 75-8 (no. 70).

[49] See, for example, the statement that some formularies required at least five or six witnesses in the late thirteenth century, but that this number

was rarely exceeded in the fourteenth: C. A. F. Meekings and P. Shearman, eds., *Fitznells Cartulary*, Surrey Record Society vol. 26 (Richmond, 1968), cxlvii.

[50] *Sandford Cartulary*, II, 181 (no. 250). See also *Reading Abbey Cartularies*, I, 296 (no. 365): *et pluribus aliis quorum nomina tarde est mihi numerare*; and *Early Yorkshire Charters*, XI, 28-9 (no. 14): *et alii complures tam clerici quam laici quorum nomina seriatim inserere perlongum foret*. In the last case, there was sufficient excuse since the transcriber had already listed forty-two named witnesses.

[51] *Rutland MSS* IV, passim.

[52] *Cartulary of Blyth Priory*, x, 134, 198, 206-9, 334-5, 337-9 (nos. 134, 198, 325, 512-13) and passim.

[53] *Early Yorkshire Charters*, X, 103 (no. 62), XI, 26, 28-9, 122-3, 143 (nos. 12, 14, 107, 124). Also *Early Yorkshire Charters*, VIII, 94 (no. 46): *Hec carta facta [fuit] Lewiis in presencia Pagani de Mundesoreno et fratris Acelyni Rothomagi*.

[54] *Danelaw Documents*, 390-2 (nos. 540-1). See also *Reading Abbey Cartularies*, I, 376-7 (no. 495).

[55] Theodore F. T. Plucknett, "Charters and Seals", in his *Studies in English Legal History* (London: Hambledon, 1983), chapter VII (no revised pagination).

[56] Charles Donahue, "Proof by Witnesses in the Church Courts of Medieval England: An Imperfect Reception of the Learned Law", in *On the Laws and Customs of England*, 127-58.

Bibliography

Manuscript Sources

London, British Library
    Add. MS 40,008 (Bridlington Priory, cartulary)
    Add. MS 37,022 and Stow MS 937 (Pipewell Abbey, cartularies)
    Lansdowne MS 415 (Garendon Abbey, cartulary)
London, The National Archives
    SC6/1257/11-12 (Leicester Abbey, treasurers' accounts)
Cambridge University Library
    MS Dd xiv 2
Manchester, John Rylands University Library
    Lat. MS 226
    Lat. MS 222
Oxford, Bodleian Library
    Bodl. MS 191 (Malmesbury Abbey, pittancer's cartulary, compiled late 13th century)
    Laud MS Misc. 625 (Leicester Abbey, rentals)
    Norfolk Roll 71 St Benet Holme, cellarer's account, 1373)
    Norfolk Roll 76 (St Benet Holme, pittancer's account, 1511-12)
    Rawl. MS 449 (Fountains Abbey, pittancer's cartulary)
    Roll Oxon. Oseney 27 (Osney Abbey, manciple's account)
    Top. Devon MS d 5 (Newenham Priory, cartulary)
    Top Yorks. MS c 72 (Drax Priory, cartulary)
    Wood MS empt. 1

Printed Primary Sources

All such sources are specified in the list of Abbreviations at pp. xi-xxiii.

Secondary Works

Appadurai, Arjun, ed. *The Social Life of Things: Commodities in Cultural Perspective*. Cambridge: Cambridge University Press, 1986.

Appadurai, Arjun. "Introduction: Commodities and the Politics of Value." In *The Social Life of Things: Commodities in Cultural Perspective*, edited by Appadurai, 3-63. Cambridge: Cambridge University Press, 1986.

Ariès, Philippe. *Western Attitudes Towards Death: From the Middle Ages to the Present*. Baltimore: Johns Hopkins University Press, 1974.

Ariès, Philippe. *The Hour of Our Death*. Translated by Helen Weaver. Oxford: Oxford University Press, 1981.

Bainbridge, Virginia. *Gilds in the Medieval Countryside: Social and Religious Change in Cambridgeshire c.1350-1558*. Woodbridge: Boydell, 1996.

Barnes, G. D. *Kirkstall Abbey 1147-1539: A Historical Survey*. Thoresby Society vol. 58, Leeds, 1984.

Barron, Caroline M. "The Parish Fraternities of Medieval London." In *The Church in Pre-Reformation Society*, edited by Barron and Christopher Harper-Bill, 13-37. Woodbridge: Boydell, 1985.

Barrow, Julia. "Cathedrals, Provosts and Prebends: A Comparison of Twelfth-century German and English Practice." *JEH* 37 (1986): 536-64.

Barrow, Julia. "Urban Cemetery Location in the High Middle Ages." In *Death in Towns: Urban Responses to the Dying and the Dead 100-1600*, edited by Steven Bassett, 78-100. Leicester: Leicester University Press, 1992.

Bartlett, Robert. *Trial by Fire and Water: The Medieval Judicial Ordeal*. Oxford: Oxford University Press, 1988.

Baudrillard, Jean. *Le Système des Objets*. Paris: Gallimard, 1968.

Bean, J. M. W. *The Decline of English Feudalism 1215-1540*. Manchester: Manchester University Press, 1968.

Beckwith, Sarah. *Christ's Body: Identity, Culture and Society in Late Medieval Writings*. London: Routledge, 1996.

Bell, Catherine. *Ritual Theory, Ritual Practice*. Oxford: Oxford University Press, 1992.

Bell, Catherine. *Ritual: Perspectives and Dimensions*. Oxford: Oxford University Press, 1997.

Ben-Amos, Ilana K. *The Culture of Giving: Informal Support and Gift-Exchange in Early Modern England*. Cambridge: Cambridge University Press, 2008.

Berman, Constance H. *Medieval Agriculture, the Southern French Countryside, and the Early Cistercians*. Transactions of the American Philosophical Society vol. 76, Philadelphia, Pa., 1986.

Biddick, Kathleen, and C. C. J. H. Bijleveld. "Agrarian Productivity on the

Estates of the Bishopric of Winchester in the Early Thirteenth Century: A Managerial Perspective", in *Land, Labour and Livestock: Historical Studies in European Agricultural Productivity*, ed. Bruce M. S. Campbell and Mark Overton (Manchester: Manchester University Press, 1991), 95-123.
Biebel, E. M. "Pilgrims to Table: Food Consumption in Chaucer's Canterbury Tales." In *Food and Eating in Medieval Europe*, edited by Martha Carlin and Joel T. Rosenthal, 15-26. London: Hambledon, 1998.
Bijsterveld, Arnoud-Jan. "The Medieval Gift as Agent of Social Bonding and Political Power: A Comparative Approach." In *Medieval Transformations: Texts, Power, and Gifts in Context*, ed. Esther Cohen and Mayke B. de Jong, 123-56. Leiden: Brill, 2001.
Bisson, Thomas, ed. *Cultures of Power: Lordship, Status and Process in Twelfth-century Europe*. Philadelphia, Pa.: University of Pennsylvania Press, 1995.
Blair, John. "Secular Minster Churches in Domesday Book." In *Domesday Book: A Reassessment*, edited by Peter Sawyer, 104-42. London: Arnold, 1985.
Blair, John. "Local Churches in Domesday Book and Before." In *Domesday Studies*, edited by James C. Holt, 268-78. Woodbridge: Boydell, 1987.
Blair, John. "St Frideswide's Reconsidered." *Oxoniensia* 52 (1987): 71-127.
Blair, John. "I. Introduction: From Minster to Parish Church." In *Minsters and Parish Churches: The Local Church in Transition 950-1200*, edited by Blair, 1-19. Oxford: Oxbow, 1988.
Blair, John. "St Frideswide's Monastery: Problems and Possibilities." *Oxoniensia* 53 (1988): 221-8.
Blake, D. "The Development of the Chapter of the Diocese of Exeter, 1050-1161." *Journal of Medieval History* 8 (1982): 1-11.
Bloch, Maurice. "Symbols, Song, Dance and Features of Articulation: Is Religion an Extreme Form of Traditional Authority?" In Bloch, *Ritual, History and Power: Selected Papers in Anthropology*, 19-45. London: Athlone, 1989.
Blomfield, J. C. *History of the Deanery of Bicester*. Oxford: 1882.
Boase, T. S. R. *Death in the Middle Ages: Mortality, Judgment and Remembrance*. London: Thames and Hudson, 1972.
Bonney, Margaret. *Lordship and the Urban Community: Durham and Its Overlords, 1250-1540*. Cambridge: Cambridge University Press, 1990.
Bouchard, Constance B. *Sword, Miter, and Cloister: Nobility and the Church in Burgundy, 980-1198*. Ithaca, N.Y.: Cornell University Press, 1987.
Bouchard, Constance B. *Holy Entrepreneurs: Cistercians, Knights and Economic Exchange in Twelfth-century Burgundy*. Ithaca, N.Y.: Cornell University Press, 1991.

Bourdieu Pierre. *The Logic of Practice*. Translated by Richard Nice. Oxford: Blackwell, 1990.
Brand, Paul A. "The Control of Mortmain Alienation in England, 1200-1300." In *Legal Records and the Historian*, edited by John H. Baker, 29-40. London: Royal Historical Society, 1978.
Brentano, Robert. *The Two Churches: England and Italy in the Thirteenth Century*. Berkeley and Los Angeles: University of California Press, pb. ed., 1988.
Brett, Martin.*The Church under Henry I*. Oxford: Oxford University Press, 1975.
Brigden, Susan. *London and the Reformation*. Oxford: Oxford University Press, 1989.
Brooke, Christopher N. L. "The Missionary at Home: The Church in the Towns, 1000-1250." In *Studies in Church History* vol. 6. 59-83. Oxford: Blackwell, 1970.
Brooke, Christopher N. L. Brooke. *The Monastic World 1000-1300*. London: Thames and Hudson, 1974.
Brown, Andrew D. *Popular Piety in Late Medieval England: The Diocese of Salisbury 1250-1550*. Oxford: Oxford University Press, 1995.
Brown, Ann. "The Financial System of Rochester Cathedral Priory: A Reconsideration." *Bulletin of the Institute of Historical Research* 1 (1977): 115-20.
Buc, Philippe. *The Dangers of Ritual: Between Early Medieval Texts and Social Scientific Theory*. English edn., Princeton: Princeton University Press, 2009.
Bull, Marcus. *Knightly Piety and the Lay Response to the First Crusade: The Limousin and Gascony, c.970-1130*. Oxford: Oxford University Press, 1993.
Burgess, Clive. "'For the Increase of Divine Service': Chantries in the Parish in Late Medieval Bristol." *JEH* 36 (1985): 48-65.
Burgess, Clive. "'By Quick and by Dead': Wills and Pious Provision in Late Medieval Bristol." *EHR* 102 (1987): 837-58.
Burton, Janet and R. Stalley. "Tables of Cistercian Affiliations." In *Cistercian Art and Architecture*, edited by Christopher Norton and David Park, 394-401. Cambridge: Cambridge University Press, 1986.
Burton, Janet. "The Foundation of British Cistercian Houses." In *Cistercian Art and Architecture*, 24-39.
Burton, Janet. *Monastic and Religious Orders in Britain, 1000-1300*. Cambridge: Cambridge University Press, 1994.
Burton, Janet. *The Monastic Order in Yorkshire 1069-1215*. Cambridge: Cambridge University Press, 1995.
Butcher, Andrew F. "Rent and the Urban Economy: Oxford and Canterbury in the Late Middle Ages." *Southern History* 1 (1979): 11-43.

Bynum, Caroline Walker. *Holy Feast and Holy Fast: The Religious Significance of Food to Medieval Women*. Berkeley, Calif.: University of California Press, 1987.
Campbell, Bruce M. S. "Arable Productivity in Medieval England: Some Evidence from Norfolk." *Journal of Economic History* 43 (1983): 379-404.
Campbell, Bruce M. S. "Agricultural Progress in Medieval England: Some Evidence from Eastern Norfolk." *EcHR* 2^d ser., 37 (1983): 26-46.
Carpenter, Christine. "The Religion of the Gentry of Fifteenth-century England." In *England in the Fifteenth Century: Proceedings of the 1986 Harlaxton Symposium*, edited by Daniel T. Williams, 53-74. Woodbridge: Boydell, 1987.
Carpenter, David A. "Was There a Crisis of the Knightly Class in the Thirteenth Century? The Oxfordshire evidence." *EHR* 95 (1980): 721-52.
Carpenter, David A. "The Second Century of English Feudalism." *Past and Present* 168 (2000): 30-71.
Carruthers, Mary. *The Book of Memory: A Study of Memory in Medieval Culture*. Cambridge: Cambridge University Press, 1990.
Catto, Jeremy I. "Citizens, Scholars and Masters." In *The History of the University of Oxford I: The Early Oxford Schools*, edited by Catto, 151-92. Oxford: Oxford University Press, 1984.
Chaplais, Pierre. "The Origin and Authenticity of the Royal Anglo-Saxon Diploma." In *Prisca Munimenta: Studies in Archives and Administrative History Presented to Dr A. E. J. Hollander*, edited Felicity Ranger, 28-42. London: Hodder and Stoughton, 1973.
Chaplais, Pierre. "The Anglo-Saxon Chancery: From the Diploma to the Writ." In *Prisca Munimenta: Studies in Archives and Administrative History Presented to Dr A. E. J. Hollander*, edited Felicity Ranger, 43-62. London: Hodder and Stoughton, 1973.
Chaplais, Pierre. "Who Introduced Charters into England? The Case for Augustine." In *Prisca Munimenta: Studies in Archives and Administrative History Presented to Dr A. E. J. Hollander*, edited Felicity Ranger, 88-107. London: Hodder and Stoughton, 1973.
Cheney, Christopher R. "Norwich Cathedral Priory in the Fourteenth Century." *Bulletin of the John Rylands Library* 20 (1936): 93-120.
Cheney, Christopher R. "The Papal Legate and English Monasteries in 1206." *EHR* 46 (1936): 443-52.
Cheney, Christopher. "Church-building in the Middle Ages." *Bulletin of the John Rylands Library* 34 (1951-2): 20-36.
Cheney, Mary. "Inalienability in Mid-twelfth Century England: Enforcement and Consequences." In *Proceedings of the Sixth International Congress on Medieval Canon Law*, edited by Stephen Kuttner and K. Pennington, 467-78. Vatican City, 1985.

Chew, Helen M. T*he Ecclesiastical Tenants in Chief and Knight Service.* Oxford: Oxford University Press, 1932.
Chew, Helen M. "Mortmain in Medieval London." *EHR* 60 (1945): 1-15.
Chibnall, Marjorie. "Monks and Pastoral Work: A Problem in Anglo-Norman History." *JEH* 18 (1967): 165-72.
Chibnall, Marjorie. "L'Ordre de Fontrevault en Angleterre au xiiie S." *Cahiers de Civilisation Médiévale* 29 (1986): 41-7
Chibnall, Marjorie. *Anglo-Norman England.* Oxford: Blackwell, 1986.
Chibnall, Marjorie, "The Empress Matilda and Church Reform." *TRHS* 5th ser., 38 (1988): 107-30.
Clanchy, Michael T. *From Memory to Written Record.* London: Arnold, 1979.
Clark, James G. *A Monastic Renaissance at St Albans: Thomas Walsingham and his Circle, c.1350-1440.* Oxford: Oxford University Press, 2004.
Colvin, Howard M. *The White Canons in England.* Oxford: Oxford University Press, 1951.
Colvin, Howard M. "The Origin of Chantries." *Journal of Medieval History* 26 (2000): 163-73.
Connerton, Paul. *How Societies Remember.* Cambridge: Cambridge University Press, 1989.
Constable, Giles. *Monastic Tithes from their Origins to the Twelfth Century.* Cambridge: Cambridge University Press, 1964.
Cooper, Janet. "The Hundred Rolls for the Parish of St Thomas, Oxford." *Oxoniensia* 37 (1972): 165-76.
Cooper, Janet. "The Church of St George's in the Castle." *Oxoniensia* 41 (1976): 306-8.
Cooper, Janet. "Markets and Fairs." In *Victoria History of the County of Oxford* IV, 305-12. Oxford: Oxford University Press, 1979.
Coss, Peter R. "Sir Geoffrey de Langley and the Crisis of the Knightly Class in Thirteenth Century England." In *Landlords, Peasants and Politics in Medieval England,* edited by Trevor H. Aston, 141-202. Cambridge: Cambridge University Press, 1987
Coss, Peter R. "Knighthood and the Early Thirteenth-century County Court." In *Thirteenth Century England II,* edited by Coss and Simon D. Lloyd, 45-58. Woodbridge: Boydell, 1988.
Coss, Peter R. *Lordship, Knighthood and Locality: A Study in English Society c.1180-c.1280.* Cambridge: Cambridge University Press, 1991.
Cownie, Emma. *Religious Patronage in Anglo-Norman England.* Woodbridge: Boydell 1998.
Craig, John. "Reformers, Conflict and Revisionism: The Reformation in Sixteenth-century Hadleigh." *Historical Journal* 42 (1992): 1-23.
Crouch, David. *The Beaumont Twins: The Roots and Branches of Power in the Twelfth Century.* Cambridge: Cambridge University Press, 1986.

Crouch, David. "The Foundation of Leicester Abbey, and Other Problems." *Midland History* 12 (1987): 1-13.
Crouch, David. *William Marshal: Court, Career and Chivalry in the Angevin Empire 1147-1219*. London: Longman, Green & Co., 1990.
Crouch, David. *The Image of the Aristocracy in Britain 1000-1300*. London: Routledge, 1992.
Crouch, David. "The Origins of Chantries: Some Further Anglo-Norman Evidence." *Journal of Medieval History* 27 (2001): 159-80.
Davis, Godfrey R. C. *Medieval Cartularies of Great Britain*. London: Longmans, Green & Co., 1958.
Davis, Ralph H. C. "An Oxford Charter of 1191 and the Beginnings of Municipal Freedom." *Oxoniensia* 33 (1968): 53-65.
Davis, Ralph H. C. *King Stephen*. London: Longman, 3^d ed., 1990.
DeAragon, RaGena. "The Growth of Secure Inheritance in Anglo-Norman England." *Journal of Medieval History* 8 (1982): 381-91.
DeAragon, RaGena. "In Pursuit of Aristocratic Women: A Key to Success in Norman England." *Albion* 14 (1982): 258-66.
Dendy, D. R. *The Use of Lights in Christian Worship*. Alcuin Club Collections vol. 41. London, 1959.
Diamond, A. S. *Primitive Law Past and Present*. London: Methuen, repr. 1971.
Dickinson, J. C. "Early Suppressions of English Houses of Austin Canons." In *Medieval Studies Presented to Rose Graham*, edited by V. Ruffer and A. J. Taylor, 54-77. Oxford: Oxford University Press, 1950.
Dickinson, J. C. *The Origins of the Austin Canons and their Introduction into England*. London: SPCK, 1950.
Dickinson, J. C. "The Origins of St Augustine's, Bristol." In *Essays in Bristol and Gloucestershire History*, edited by Patrick McGrath and John Cannon. Bristol: Bristol and Gloucestershire Archaeological Society, 1976.
Dobson, R. Barrie. "The Foundation of Perpetual Chantries by the Citizens of Medieval York." In *Studies in Church History* IV, edited by G. J. Cuming, 22-38. Leiden: Brill, 1967.
Dobson, R. Barrie. *Durham Priory 1400-50*. Cambridge: Cambridge University Press, 1973.
Donahue, Charles. "Proof by Witnesses in the Church Courts of Medieval England: An Imperfect Reception of the Learned Law." In *On the Laws and Customs of England*, edited by M. S. Arnold et al., 127-58. Chapel Hill, N. C.: University of North Carolina Press, 1982.
Donkin, Robert A. "Settlement and Depopulation on Cistercian Estates During the Twelfth and Thirteenth Centuries." *Bulletin of the Institute of Historical Research* 33 (1960): 141-65.
Donkin, Robert A. "The Cistercian Grange in England in the Twelfth and

Thirteenth Centuries, With Special Reference to Yorkshire." *Studia Monastica* 6 (1964): 95-144.

Douglas, Audrey W. "Frankalmoign and Jurisdictional Immunity: Maitland Revisited." *Speculum* 53 (1978): 26-48.

Douglas, Audrey W. "Tenure *In Elemosina*: Origins and Establishment in Twelfth-century England." *American Journal of Legal History* 24 (1980): 95-132.

Douglas, Mary. *Purity and Danger: An Analysis of the Concepts of Pollution and Taboo*. London: Routledge, repr. 1995.

DuBoulay, F. R. H. *The Lordship of Canterbury*. London: Nelson, 1966.

Duffy, Eamon. *The Stripping of the Altars: Traditional Religion in England 1400-1580*. New Haven, Conn., and London: Yale University Press, 1992.

Dyer, Christopher C. *Standards of Living in the Middle Ages: Social Change in England c.1200-1520*. Cambridge: Cambridge University Press, new edn., 1994.

Dyer, Christopher C. "Towns and Cottages in Twelfth-century England." In *Studies in Medieval History Presented to R. H. C. Davis*, edited by Henry Mayr-Harting and Robert I. Moore, 91-106. London: Hambledon Continuum, 1985.

Edwards, Kathleen. *The English Secular Cathedrals in the Middle Ages*. Manchester: Manchester University Press, 2^d. ed. 1967.

Elkins, Sharon. *Holy Women of Twelfth-Century England*. Chapel Hill, N.C.: University of North Carolina Press, 1988.

Evans, A. K. Babette. "Cirencester's Early Church." *Transactions of the Bristol and Gloucestershire Archaeological Society* 107 (1989): 107-22.

Evans, A. K. Babette. "Cirencester Abbey: The First Hundred Years." *Transactions of the Bristol and Gloucestershire Archaeological Society* 109 (1991): 99-116.

Everitt, Alan. "The Banburys of England." *Urban History Yearbook* 1 (1974): 28-38.

Everitt, Alan. "The Primary Towns of England." In his *Landscape and Community*, 93-107. London: Hambledon 1985.

Fentress, James, and Christopher Wickham. *Social Memory*. Oxford: Blackwell, 1988.

Finucane, Ronald W. "Sacred Corpse, Profane Carrion: Social Ideals and Death Rituals in the Later Middle Ages." In *Mirrors of Mortality*, edited by Daniel Whaley, 40-60. London: Europa Publications Ltd., 1981.

Finucane, Ronald W. *Miracles and Pilgrims: Popular Belief in Medieval England*. London: Palgrave Macmillan, repr. 1995.

Flahiff, G. B. "The Writ of Prohibition to Court Christian in the Thirteenth Century". *Mediaeval Studies* 6 (1944): 261-313 and 7 (1945): 229-90.

Fleming, Donald. "*Milites* as Attestors to Charters in England, 1101-1300." *Albion* 32 (1990): 185-98.

Fleming, Peter. "Charity, Faith and the Gentry of Kent, 1422-1529." In *Property and Politics: Essays in Later Medieval History*, edited by A. (Tony) J. Pollard, 36-58. Gloucester: Sutton, 1984.

Fleming, Robin. *Domesday Book and the Law*. Cambridge: Cambridge University Press, 1998.

Franklin, Michael J. "The Cathedral as Parish Church: The Case of Southern England." In *Church and City 1000-1250: Essays in Honour of Christopher Brooke*, edited by David Abulafia, Franklin, and Miri Rubin, 173-98. Cambridge: Cambridge University Press, 1992.

Franklin, Michael J. "Bodies in Medieval Northampton: Legatine Intervention in the Twelfth Century." In *Medieval Ecclesiastical Studies in Honour of Dorothy Owen*, edited by Franklin and Christopher Harper-Bill, 57-81. Woodbridge: Boydell, 1995.

French, Katherine L. *The Good Women of the Parish: Gender and Religion after the Black Death*. Philadelphia, Pa.: University of Pennsylvania Press, 2007.

Fryde, Edmund B., Diana E. Greenway, Stephen Porter and Ian Roy, eds. *Handbook of British Chronology*. Royal Historical Society Guides and Handbooks vol. 2, London, 1986.

Galbraith, Vivian H. "Monastic Foundation Charters of the Eleventh and Twelfth Centuries." *Cambridge Law Journal* 4 (1932-4): 205-22.

Galbraith, Vivian H. "The Literacy of the Medieval English Kings." In *Studies in History*, edited by Lucy S. Sutherland, 95-102. Oxford: Oxford University Press, 1966.

Geary, Patrick J. "Échanges et Relations Entre les Vivants et les Morts dans la Société au Haut Moyen Âge", *Droit et Cultures* 12 (1986): 3-17.

Geary, Patrick. *Living with the Dead in the Middle Ages*. Ithaca, N.Y.: Cornell University Press, 1994.

Geary, Patrick J. "Coercion of Saints in Medieval Religious Practice." In his *Living with the Dead in the Middle Ages*, 116-24. Ithaca, N.Y.: Cornell University Press, 1994.

Gibbs, Marion, and Jane Lang. *Bishops and Reform 1215-1272 with Special Reference to the Lateran Council of 1215*. Oxford: Oxford University Press, 1934.

Gilchrist, Roberta. *Gender and Material Culture: The Archaeology of Women Religious*. London: Routledge, 1994.

Gittings, Clare. *Death, Burial and the Individual in Early Modern England*. London: Routledge, 1984.

Godelier, Maurice. *The Enigma of the Gift*. Translated by Nora Scott. Cambridge: Polity, 1999.

Gold, A. G. "Grains of Truth: Shifting Hierarchies of Food and Grace in Three Rajasthani Tales", *History of Religions* 38 (1998): 150-71.

Golding, Brian. "Burials and Benefactions: An Aspect of Monastic Patronage in Thirteenth-century England." In *England in the Thirteenth Century: Proceedings of the 1984 Harlaxton Symposium*, edited by W. Mark Ormrod, 64-75. Woodbridge: Boydell, 1985.

Golding, Brian. "Anglo-Norman Knightly Burials." In *The Ideals and Practice of Knighthood: Papers from the First and Second Strawberry Hill Conferences*, edited by Christopher Harper-Bill and Ruth Harvey, 35-48. Woodbridge: Boydell, 1986.

Golding, Brian. *St Gilbert of Sempringham and the Gilbertine Order c.1130-c.1300*. Oxford: Oxford University Press, 1995.

Golob, Peter. "The Ferrers Earls of Derby: A Study of the Honour of Tutbury (1066-1279)". PhD dissertation, University of Cambridge, 1984.

Goody, Jack. *Cooking, Cuisine and Class: A Study in Comparative Sociology*. Cambridge: Cambridge University Press, 1982.

Greatrex, Joan. "After Knowles: Recent Perspectives in Monastic History." In *The Religious Orders in Pre-Reformation England*, edited by James G. Clark, 35-47. Woodbridge: Boydell, 2002.

Green, Judith. *The Government of England Under Henry I*. Cambridge: Cambridge University Press, 1989.

Gurevich, Aron. *Medieval Popular Culture: Problems of Belief and Perception*. Cambridge: Cambridge University Press, 1990.

Hamilton, Malcolm. *Sociology and the World's Religions*. London: Macmillan, 1998.

Hanawalt, Barbara. "Keepers of the Lights: Late Medieval English Parish Gilds," *Journal of Medieval and Renaissance Studies* 14 (1984): 21-37

Harper-Bill, Christopher. "The Piety of the Anglo-Norman Knightly Class." In *Proceedings of the Battle Conference II 1979*, edited by R. Allen Brown, 63-77, 173-6. Woodbridge: Boydell, 1980.

Harper-Bill, Christopher. "The Struggle for Benefices in Twelfth-century East Anglia." In *Anglo-Norman Studies XI: Proceedings of the Battle Conference 1988*, edited by R. Allen Brown, 113-32. Woodbridge: Boydell, 1989.

Harvey, Barbara F. *Westminster Abbey and its Estates in the Middle Ages*. Oxford: Oxford University Press, 1977.

Harvey, Barbara F. *Living and Dying in England 1100-1540: The Monastic Experience*. Oxford: Oxford University Press, 1993.

Harvey, Paul D. A. "The Pipe Rolls and the Adoption of Demesne Farming in England", *EcHR* 2^d ser., 27 (1974): 345-59.

Hase, P. H. "The Mother Churches of Hampshire." In *Minsters and Parish Churches*, edited by John Blair, 45-66. Oxford: Oxbow, 1988.

Heath, Peter. "Urban Piety in the Later Middle Ages: The Evidence of

Hull Wills." In *The Church, Politics and Patronage in the Fifteenth Century*, edited by R. Barrie Dobson, 209-34. Gloucester: Sutton, 1984.

Hill, Bennet D. *English Cistercian Monasteries and their Patrons in the Twelfth Century*. Urbana, Ill.: University of Chicago Press, 1968.

Hilton, Rodney H. *The Economic Development of Some Leicestershire Estates in the Fourteenth and Fifteenth Centuries*. Oxford: Oxford University Press, 1947.

Hilton, Rodney H. *The English Peasantry in the Later Middle Ages*. Oxford: Oxford University Press, 1975.

Holdsworth, Christopher J. "The Chronology and Character of Early Cistercian Legislation on Art and Architecture." In *Cistercian Art and Architecture in the British Isles*, edited by Christopher Norton and David Park, 40-55. Cambridge: Cambridge University Press, 1988.

Holdsworth, Christopher. *The Piper and the Tune: Medieval Patrons and Monks*. Reading: University of Reading Stenton Lecture 1990, 1991.

Holt, James C. "Feudal Society and the Family in Early Medieval England: II, Notions of Patrimony." *TRHS* 5th ser., 33 (1983): 193-220.

Holt, James C. "Feudal Society and the Family in Early Medieval England: IV, The Heiress and the Alien." *TRHS* 5th ser., 35 (1985): 1-28,

Holt, James C. "Politics and Property in Early Medieval England." In *Landlords, Peasants and Politics in Medieval England*, edited by Trevor H. Aston, 65-114. Cambridge: Cambridge University Press, 1987.

Holt, James C. "1066." In *Domesday Studies: Papers Read at the Novocentenary Conference of the Royal Historical Society and the Institute of British Geographers*, edited by Holt, 41-64. Woodbridge: Boydell, 1987.

Holt, James C. "Rejoinder." In *Landlords, Peasants and Politics in Medieval England*, edited by Trevor H. Aston, 132-40. Cambridge: Cambridge University Press, 1987.

Houlbrooke, Ralph A. *Death, Ritual and Bereavement*. London: Routledge, 1989.

Hudson, John. *Land, Law and Lordship in Anglo-Norman England*. Oxford: Oxford University Press, 1994.

Humphrey, Caroline, and James Laidlaw. *The Archetypal Actions of Ritual: A Theory of Ritual Illustrated by the Jain Rite of Worship*. Oxford: Oxford University Press, 1994.

Hyams, Paul R. "'No Register of Title': The Domesday Inquest and Land Adjudication." In *Anglo-Norman Studies IX: Proceedings of the Battle Conference 1985*, edited by R. Allen Brown, 127-41. Woodbridge: Boydell, 1986.

Hyams, Paul R. "Warranty and Good Lordship in Twelfth Century England." *Law and History Review* 5 (1987): 437-503.

Hyams, Paul R. "The Charter as a Source for the Early Common Law." *The Journal of Legal History* 12 (1991): 173-89.

Hyams, Paul R. *Rancor and Reconciliation in Medieval England*. Ithaca, N. Y.: Cornell University Press, 2003.

Hyde, Lewis. *The Gift: How the Creative Spirit Transforms the World*. Edinburgh: Canongate Books, 2006.

Jordan, William Chester. *From Servitude to Freedom: Manumission in the Senonais in the Thirteenth Century*. Philadelphia, Pa.: University of Pennsylvania Press, 1986.

Kay, Sarah, and Miri Rubin, eds. *Framing Medieval Bodies*. Manchester: Manchester University Press, 1994.

Keene, Derek. "Suburban Growth." In *The Mediaeval Town*, edited by Holt and Rosser, 97-119.

Kemp, Brian. "Monastic Possession of Parish Churches in England in the Twelfth Century." *JEH* 31 (1980): 133-60.

Kemp, Brian. "Some Aspects of the *Parochia* of Leominster in the Twelfth Century." In *Minsters and Parish Churches: The Local Church in Transition 950-1200*, edited by John Blair, 83-95. Oxford: Oxbow, 1988.

Kempers, B. "Icons, Altarpieces and Civic Ritual in Siena Cathedral, 1100-1530." In *City and Spectacle in Medieval Europe*, edited by Barbara A. Hanawalt and Kathryn Reyerson, xx-xx. Minneapolis, Minn., University of Minnesota Press, 1994.

Kershaw, Ian. *Bolton Priory: The Economy of a Northern Monastery, 1286-1325*. Oxford: Oxford University Press, 1973.

Keynes, Simon D. *The Diplomas of King Æthelred "the Unready" 978-1016*. Cambridge: Cambridge University Press, 1980.

Kimball, Elizabeth G. "Tenure in Frank Almoign and Secular Services." *EHR* 43 (1928): 341-53

Kimball, Elizabeth G. "The Judicial Aspects of Frankalmoign Tenure." *EHR* 47 (1932): 1-11

King, Edmund. *Peterborough Abbey 1086-1310: A Study in the Land Market*. Cambridge: Cambridge University Press, 1973.

King, Edmund. "Mountsorrel and its Region in King Stephen's Reign." *Huntington Library Quarterly* 44 (1980): 1-10.

King, Edmund. "The Anarchy of King Stephen's Reign.", TRHS 5th ser., 34 (1984): 133-53.

King, Edmund. "The Tenurial Crisis of the Early Twelfth Century." In *Landlords, Peasants and Politics in Medieval England*, edited by Trevor H. Aston, 115-22. Cambridge: Cambridge University Press, 1987.

King, Edmund. "Large and Small Landowners in Thirteenth-century England: The Case of Peterborough Abbey." In *Landlords, Peasants and Politics*, edited by Trevor H. Aston, 141-65.

King, Edmund. "The Foundation of Pipewell Abbey, Northamptonshire." *Haskins Society Journal* 2 (1990): 168-77.
King, Edmund. "Dispute Settlement in Anglo-Norman England." In *Anglo-Norman Studies XIV: Proceedings of the Battle Conference 1991*, edited by R. Allen Brown, 115-30. Woodbridge: Boydell, 1992.
Knowles, David. *The Religious Orders in England*. Cambridge: Cambridge University Press, 1948.
Knowles, David, and J. K. S. St Joseph. *Monastic Sites from the Air*. Cambridge: Cambridge University Press, 1952.
Knowles, David, and Neil Hadcock. *Medieval Religious Houses: England and Wales*. London: Longman, 1971.
Knowles, David, Christopher N. L. Brooke and Vera C. M. London, eds. *The Heads of Religious Houses: England and Wales 940-1216*. Cambridge: Cambridge University Press, 1972.
Koziol, Geoffrey. *Begging Pardon and Favor: Ritual and Political Order in France*. Ithaca, N. Y.: Cornell University Press, 1992.
Kümin, Beat A. *The Shaping of a Community: The Rise and Reformation of the English Parish c.1400-1560*. Aldershot: Scolar Press, 1996.
Levett, Elizabeth A. *Studies in Manorial History*. Edited by Helen M. Cam, M. Coate and Lucy S. Sutherland. Oxford: Oxford University Press, 1963 ed.
Lists of Sheriffs in England and Wales. List and Index Society vol. 9, London: HMSO, 1963.
Lobel, Mary D. *The Borough of Bury St Edmunds*. Oxford: Oxford University Press, 1935.
Loyn, Henry R. *The Governance of Anglo-Saxon England 500-1087*. London: Hodder Arnold, 1984.
Lunt, William E. *The Visitation of Norwich*. Oxford: Oxford University Press, 1926.
Lunt, William E. *Financial Relations of the Papacy with England to 1327*. Cambridge, Mass.: Medieval Academy of America, 1939.
Lynch, Joseph H. *The Medieval Church: A Brief History*. London and New York: Longman, 1992.
McLaughlin, Megan. *Consorting with Saints: Prayer for the Dead in Early Medieval France*. Ithaca, N.Y.: Cornell University Press, 1994.
Maitland, Frederic William. "The History of the Register of Original Writs." In *The Collected Papers of Frederic William Maitland*, edited by H. A. L. Fisher, 110-73. Cambridge: Cambridge University Press, 1970.
Mansfield, Mary C. *The Humiliation of Sinners: Public Penance in Thirteenth-century France*. Ithaca, N.Y.: Cornell University Press, 1995.
Martin, Geoffrey H. "The English Borough in the 13th Century." In *The Mediaeval Town*, edited by Holt and Rosser, 29-48.

Mason, Emma. "The Role of the English Parishioner 1100-1500." *JEH* 27 (1976): 17-29.

Mate, Mavis. "Profit and Productivity on the Estates of Isabella de Forz (1260-92)." *EcHR* 2^d ser., 33 (1980): 326-34.

Mate, Mavis. "Property Investment by Canterbury Cathedral Priory, 1250-1400." *Journal of British Studies* 23 (1984): 1-21.

Mate, Mavis. "Medieval Agrarian Practices: The Determining Factors." *Agricultural History Review* 33 (1985): 22-31.

Mauss, Marcel. *The Gift: The Form and Reason for Exchange in Archaic Societies*. Translated by W. D. Halls. London: Routledge, 1990.

Mennell, Stephen. *All Manner of Food: Eating and Taste in England and France from the Middle Ages to the Present*. London: WileyBlackwell, 1985.

Miller, Edward. "The State and the Landed Interest in Thirteenth Century France and England." *TRHS* 5th ser., 2 (1952): 109-29.

Milsom, S. F. C. (Toby). *The Legal Framework of English Feudalism*. Cambridge: Cambridge University Press, 1976.

Milsom, S. F. C. (Toby). "Inheritance by Women in the Twelfth and Thirteenth Centuries." In *On the Laws and Customs of England: Essays in Honor of Samuel E. Thorne*, edited by M. S. Arnold et al., 60-89. Chapel Hill, N.C.: University of North Carolina Press, 1981.

Mitchell, S. K. *Taxation in Medieval England*. New Haven, Conn.: Yale University Press, 1951.

Montanari, Massimo. *The Culture of Food*. Translated by C. Ipsen. Oxford: WileyBlackwell, 1996.

Morgan, Nigel. "Texts and Images of Marian Devotion." In *England in the Thirteenth Century*, edited W. Mark Ormrod, 69-103. Harlaxton Medieval Studies I, Stamford, 1991.

Newman, Charlotte E. *The Anglo-Norman Nobility in the Reign of Henry I: The Second Generation*. Philadelphia, Pa.: University of Pennsylvania Press, 1989.

Nightingale, Pamela. *A Medieval Mercantile Community: The Grocers' Company and the Politics and Trade of London 1000-1485*. New Haven, Conn., and London: Yale University Press, 1995.

Oliva, Marilyn. *The Convent and the Community in Late Medieval England: Female Monasticism in the Diocese of Norwich, 1350-1540*. Woodbridge: Boydell, 1998.

Ortner, Sherri B. "Introduction." In *The Fate of Culture: Geertz and Beyond*, edited by Ortner, 1-13. Berkeley, Calif.: University of California Press, 1999.

Owen, Dorothy M. "Two Manorial Parish Books from the Diocese of Ely: New College MS 98 and Wisbech Museum MS 1." In *East Anglian and Other Studies Presented to Barbara Dodwell*, edited by Malcolm Barber,

P. McNulty and P. Noble, 121-32. Reading Medieval Studies vol. 11, Reading, 1985.
Palmer, Robert. "The Feudal Framework of English Law." *Michigan Law Review* 79 (1981): 1130-64.
Palmer, Robert. "The Economic and Cultural Impact of the Origins of Property." *Law and History Review* 3 (1985): 375-96.
Palmer, Robert. "The Origin of Property in England." *Law and History Review* 3 (1985): 1-50.
Paxton, Frederick S. *Christianizing Death: The Creation of a Ritual Process in Early Medieval Europe*. Ithaca, N.Y., and London: Cornell University Press, 1990.
Platt, Colin. *The Monastic Grange in Medieval England: A Reassessment*. New York and London: Fordham University Press, 1969.
Plucknett, Theodore F. T. *The Legislation of Edward I.* Oxford: Oxford University Press, 1970.
Plucknett, Theodore F. T. "Charters and Seals." In his *Studies in English Legal History*, chapter VII (no revised pagination). London: Hambledon, 1983.
Pollock, Frederick, and Frederic W. Maitland. *The History of English Law.* With an Introduction by S. F. C. Milsom. 2 vols., Cambridge: Cambridge University Press, 1968.
Postan, Michael M. "Investment in Medieval Agriculture." *The Journal of Economic History* 27 (1967): 576-87.
Postan, Michael M., and John Hatcher. "Population and Class Relations in Feudal Society." In *The Brenner Debate: Agrarian Class Structure and Economic Development in Pre-Industrial Europe*, edited by Trevor H. Aston and C. H. E. Philpin, 64-78. Cambridge: Cambridge University Press, 1987.
Postles, Dave. "Conflict Between Oseney and the Borough in the Early Fifteenth century." *Oxoniensia* 41 (1976): 356-7.
Postles, Dave. "The Learning of Austin Canons: The Case of Oseney Abbey." *Nottingham Medieval Studies* 24 (1985): 32-43.
Postles, Dave. "Garendon Abbey and its Early Benefactors." In *Monasteries and Society*, edited by Benjamin Thompson, 97-116. Harlaxton Medieval Studies 6, Stamford, 1999.
Postles, Dave. "The Garendon Cartulary in BL, Lansdowne 415." *British Library Journal* 22 (1996): 161-71.
Potts, Cassandra. *Monastic Revival and Regional Identity in Early Normandy*. Woodbridge: Boydell, 1997.
Power, Eileen. *The Wool Trade in English Medieval History*. Oxford: Oxford University Press, 1941.
Raban, Sandra. *Mortmain Legislation and the English Church, 1279-1500*. Cambridge: Cambridge University Press, 1982.

Raban, Sandra. "The Land Market and the Aristocracy in the Thirteenth Century." In *Tradition and Change: Essays in Honour of Marjorie Chibnall*, edited by Diana Greenway, Christopher Holdsworth and Jane Sayers, 239-61. Cambridge: Cambridge University Press, 1985.

Rappaport, Roy. *Ritual and Religion in the Making of Humanity.* Oxford: Oxford University Press, 1999.

Rawcliffe, Carole. "Introduction." In *Derbyshire Feet of Fines, 1323-1546*, edited by H. J. H. Garrett. Derbyshire Record Society vol. 11, Chesterfield, 1985.

Reynolds, P. L. *Food and the Body: Some Peculiar Questions in High Medieval Theology.* Leiden: Brill, 1999.

Reynolds, Susan. *Fiefs and Vassals: The Medieval Evidence Reinterpreted.* Oxford: Oxford University Press, 1994.

Robinson, David M. *The Geography of Augustinian Settlements in Medieval England and Wales.* 2 vols., British Archaeological Reports, British Series, vol. 80, Oxford, 1980.

Robinson, David M. "Site Changes of Augustinian Communities in Medieval England and Wales." *Mediaeval Studies* 43 (1981): 425-44.

Roche, Daniel. *A History of Everyday Things: The Birth of Consumption in France, 1660-1800.* Cambridge: Cambridge University Press, 2000.

Rolson, David. *The World on Paper: The Conceptual and Cognitive Implications of Writing and Reading.* Cambridge: Cambridge University Press, 1994.

Rosenthal, Joel T. *The Purchase of Paradise: Gift Giving and the Aristocracy 1307-1485.* London: Routledge and K. Paul, 1972.

Rosenwein, Barbara H. *To Be the Neighbor of St Peter: The Social Meanings of Cluny's Property, 909-1049.* Ithaca, N.Y.: Cornell University Press, 1989.

Rosser, A. Gervase. "Communities of Parish and Guild in the Late Middle Ages." In *Parish, Church and People: Local Studies in Lay Religion, 1350-1750*, edited by Susan J. Wright, 29-55. London: HarperCollins, 1988.

Rosser, A. Gervase. *Medieval Westminster 1200-1540.* Oxford: Oxford University Press, 1989.

Rosser, A. Gervase. "The Essence of Medieval Urban Communities: The Vill of Westminster, 1200-1540." In *The Medieval Town: A Reader in English Urban History, 1200-1540*, edited by Richard Holt and Rosser, 216-37. London: Longmans, 1990.

Rosser, A. Gervase. "Parochial Conformity and Popular Religion in Late Mediaeval England." *TRHS* 6th ser., 1 (1991): 173-90.

Rosser, A. Gervase. "The Cure of Souls in English Towns before 1000." In *Pastoral Care before the Parish*, edited by John Blair and Richard Sharpe, 267-84. Leicester: Leicester University Press, 1992.

Rubin, Miri. *Corpus Christi: The Eucharist in Late Medieval Culture.* Oxford: Oxford University Press, 1991.

Salter, Herbert E. *Medieval Oxford*. Oxford Historical Society vol. 100, Oxford, 1936.
Saul, Nigel. "The Religious Sympathies of the Gentry of Gloucestershire, 1200-1500." *Transactions of the Bristol and Gloucestershire Archaeological Society* 98 (1981): 99-112.
Saul, Nigel. *Scenes from Provincial Life: Knightly Families in Sussex, 1280-1400*. Oxford: Oxford University Press, 1986.
Saunders, H. W. *An Introduction to the Obedientiary and Manor Rolls of Norwich Cathedral Priory*. Norwich: Norfolk Record Society, 1930.
Scarisbrick, Jack J. *The Reformation and the English People*. Oxford: Oxford University Press, 1984.
Sewell, William. "Geertz, Cultural Systems, and History: From Synchrony to Transformation." In *Fate of Culture*, edited by Ortner, 35-55. XXX
Silber, Ilana. *Virtuosity, Charisma, and Social Order: A Comparative Sociological Study of Monasticism in Therevada Buddhism and Medieval Catholicism*. Cambridge: Cambridge University Press, 1995.
Silber, Ilana. "Gift-giving in the Great Traditions: The Case of Donations to Monasteries in the Medieval West." *Archives Européennes de Sociologie* 36 (1995): 209-43.
Silber, Ilana, Jeffrey C. Alexander, and Steven Seidman. *Virtuosity, Charisma and Social Order: A Comparative Sociological Study of Monasticism in Thereveda Buddhism and Medieval Catholicism*. Cambridge: Cambridge University Press, 1995.
Skeeters, Martha. *Community and Clergy: Bristol and the Reformation c.1530-c.1570*. Oxford: Oxford University Press, 1993.
Smith, R. A. (Tony) L. *Canterbury Cathedral Priory*. Cambridge: Cambridge University Press, 1943.
Smith, R. A. (Tony) L. *Collected Papers of R. A. L. Smith*, edited by David Knowles. London: Longman, Green & Co., 1947.
Snape, R. H. *English Monastic Finances in the Later Middle Ages*. Oxford: Oxford University Press, 1926.
Sommerfeldt, J. R., ed. *Cistercian Ideals and Reality*. Cistercian Studies Series 60, Kalamazoo, Mich., 1978.
Southern, Richard W. "The Place of Henry I in English History." In his *Medieval Humanism and Other Studies*, 206-33. Oxford: Oxford University Press, 1970.
Spencer, H. Leith. *English Preaching in the Late Middle Ages*. Oxford: Oxford University Press, 1993.
Stacey, Robert C. "Agricultural Investment and Management of the Royal Demesne Manors, 1236-1240." *Journal of Economic History* 46 (1986): 919-93.
Stenton, Frank M. *Latin Charters of the Anglo-Saxon Period*. Oxford: Oxford University Press, 1955.

Stenton, Frank M. *The First Century of English Feudalism*. Oxford: Oxford University Press, 2^d ed. 1961.
Stöber, Karen. *Late Medieval Monasteries and their Patrons: England and Wales, c.1300-1540*. Woodbridge: Boydell, 2007.
Swanson, Heather. *Medieval Artisans: An Urban Class in Late Medieval England*. Oxford: WileyBlackwell, 1989.
Swanson, Robert N. *Religion and Devotion in Europe, c.1215-1515*. Cambridge: Cambridge University Press, 1995.
Tabuteau, Emily J. *Transfers of Property in Eleventh-century Norman Law*. Chapel Hill, N.C.: University of North Carolina Press, 1988.
Tanner, Norman. *The Church in Late Medieval Norwich 1370-1532*. Toronto: University of Toronto Press, 1984.
Teunis, Henk B. "The Countergift *In Caritate* According to the Cartulary of Noyers." *Haskins Society Journal* 7 (1997): 83-8.
Thomas, Hugh. *Vassals, Heiresses, Crusaders, and Thugs: The Gentry of Angevin Yorkshire, 1154-1216*. Philadelphia, Pa.: University of Pennsylvania Press, 1993.
Thompson, A. Hamilton. *The Abbey of St Mary of the Meadows*. Leicester: Edgar Backus, 1949.
Thompson, Benjamin. "Free Alms Tenure in the Twelfth Century." In *Anglo-Norman Studies XVI: Proceedings of the Battle Conference 1993*, edited by Marjorie Chibnall, 221-43. Woodbridge: Boydell 1994.
Thompson, Benjamin. "Monasteries and their Patrons at Foundation and Dissolution." *TRHS* 6th ser., 4 (1994): 103-25.
Thompson, Sally. *Women Religious: The Founding of English Nunneries after the Norman Conquest*. Oxford: Oxford University Press, 1991.
Thorne, Samuel E. "English Feudalism and Estates in Land." In his *Essays in English Legal History*, 13-30. London: Hambledon, 1985.
Thorne, Samuel E. "Livery of seisin." In his *Essays in English Legal History*, 31-50. London: Hambledon, 1985.
Thorne, Samuel E. "The Assize *Utrum* and the Canon Law in England." In his *Essays in English Legal History*, 51-59. London: Hambledon, 1985.
Titow, Jan Z. *English Rural Society*. London: Allen & Unwin, 1969.
Tittler, Robert. *The Reformation and the Towns in England: Politics and Political Culture*. Oxford: Oxford University Press, 1998.
Trenholme, N. M. *The English Monastic Boroughs*. Columbia, Mo.: University of Missouri Press, 1927.
Tsurushima, H. "The Fraternity of Rochester Cathedral Priory about 1100." In *Anglo-Norman Studies XIV. Proceedings of the Battle Conference 1991*, edited by Marjorie Chibnall, 313-37. Woodbridge: Boydell, 1992.
Turner, Brian S. *The Body and Society*. London: Routledge, 2^d ed. 1996.
Urry, William. *Canterbury under the Angevin Kings*. London: Athlone, 1967.

Vale, Malcolm G. A. *Piety, Charity and Literacy Among the Yorkshire Gentry, 1370-1480*. York: Borthwick Papers, 1976.
Vauchez, André, *Sainthood in the Later Middle Ages*. Translated by Jean Birrell. Cambridge: Cambridge University Press, 1997.
Wales, C. J. "The Knight in Twelfth-century Lincolnshire."PhD thesis, University of Cambridge, 1983.
Ward, Janet. "Fashions in Monastic Endowment." *JEH* 32 (1981): 427-51.
Wardrop, Joan. *Fountains Abbey and its Benefactors 1132-1300*. Kalamazoo, Mich.: Medieval Institute Publications, 1987.
Waugh, Scott. "Women's Inheritance and the Growth of Bureaucratic Monarchy in Twelfth- and Thirteenth-century England." *Nottingham Medieval Studies* 34 (1990): 71-92.
Whaley, Joachim, ed., *Mirrors of Mortality: Studies in the Social History of Death*. London: Europa Publications Ltd., 1981.
White, Stephen D. "Succession to Fiefs in Early Medieval England." In *Landlords, Peasants and Politics in Medieval England*, edited by Trevor H. Aston, 123-31. Cambridge: Cambridge University Press, 1987.
White, Stephen D. *Custom, Kinship and Gifts to Saints: The* Laudatio Parentum *in Western Fance 1050-1150*. Chapel Hill, N.C.: University of North Carolina Press, 1988.
Whiting, Robert. *The Blind Devotion of the People: Popular Religion and the English Reformation*. Cambridge: Cambridge University Press, 1989.
Wiener, Annette B. *Inalienable Possessions: The Paradox of Keeping While Giving*. Berkeley: University of California Press, 1992.
Williams, Anne. *The English and the Norman Conquest*. Woodbridge: Boydell, 1995.
Williams, D. H. "Layfolk within Cistercian Precincts." In *Monastic Studies II*, edited by Judith Loades, 87-118. Bangor: Loades, 1991.
Wood, Roy C. *The Sociology of the Meal*. Edinburgh: Edinburgh University Press, 1995.
Wood, Susan. *English Monasteries and Their Patrons in the Thirteenth Century*. Oxford: Oxford University Press, 1955.
Wood-Legh, Kathleen L. *Perpetual Chantries in Britain*. Cambridge: Cambridge University Press, 1965
Wunderli, Richard M. *London Church Courts and Society on the Eve of the Reformation*. Cambridge, Mass.: Medieval Academy of America, 1981.
Yver, J. "Une Boutade de Guillaume le Conquérant: Note Sur la Génèse de la Tenure en Aumône." In *Études d'Histoire du Droit Canonique Dédiées à Gabriel le Bras*, 783-96. Paris: Sirey, 1965).

Index

Abberton (Worcestershire) 52
Abingdon Abbey (Benedictine, Berkshire) 8, 69-70, 92, 114, 135, 186, 192, 243, 250
Achard, William 243
advocatus 23, 33
Alderbury (Wiltshire) 46
Aldgate, see London
Alphamstone (Essex) 91
altars 57, 58
Alvaston (Derbyshire) 99
Alvington (Gloucestershire) 245
Amotherby (Yorkshire) 229
anathema clause 187, 204, 206, 207
Apeltree de, Richard, abbot of Osney 162, 163
Ariès, Philippe, sociologist 61-2, 78
Arsic, Manasser 246
Arundel family (Somerset) 127-8
association (between laity and religious houses) 7, 20-2, 29, 30, 32, 42, 79, 81, 86-8, 91, 93, 100, 101, 106, 113, 116, 125, 127
Aubigny d', Iwein 243
Aubigny d', Nigel 35
Aubigny d'. William 92-3, 119
Aubigny d', family 92-3
Austin (Augustinian) Canons 1, 8, 27-8, 71, 85, 90, 94, 97, 98, 99, 104, 131-58, 165, 167, 231

Bachtuna de, William 250
Bacton (Norfolk) 250
Baddesley Ensor (Warwickshire) 226
Baivel family, lords of Shalstone (Buckinghamshire) 73
Barkeston (Leicestershire) 92
Barnsley (Yorkshire) 101
Barnston (Nottinghamshire) 97, 99
Barnwell Priory (Austin Canons, Cambridgeshire) 136, 142, 148, 151, 231
Basset family 101
Basset, Miles 119
Basset, Ralph 65, 70
Basset, Richard 182
Batevileyn de, William 205
Battle Abbey (Benedictine, Sussex) 126
Bearsted (Kent) 55
Beauchief Abbey (Premonstratensian, Derbyshire) 75
Beaulieu (Hampshire) 64
Beaulieu Abbey (Cistercian, Hampshire) 38, 44, 64
Bedford (Bedfordshire) 136, 151
Bedfordshire 205, 212-13
Belew de, Thomas 121
Belfou de, Richard 248

Belneis de, Ranulf 186
Belvoir Priory (Benedictine, Leicestershire) 8, 29, 92, 186, 243, 248, 250, 254, 255
Berges de, Asketil 207
Berkeley (Gloucestershire) 58, 76
Berkeley, Robert de 85
Beverley, hospital of St Giles (Yorkshire) 109, 250, 256
Bicester (Oxfordshire) 44
Bicester Priory (Austin Canons, Oxfordshire) 44, 165
Bigod, Roger, earl of Norfolk 119
Biset, Manasser 247
bishops, as witnesses 249
Bishopstone (Herefordshire) 115
Blackwell (Derbyshire) 103
Blyth Priory (Benedictine, Nottinghamshire) 8, 44, 57, 89, 190, 195, 196, 255
Blythburgh (Suffolk) 64
Blythburgh Priory (Austin Canons, Suffolk) 8, 64, 73, 151
Bodmin (Cornwall) 132, 147
Bodmin Priory (Austin Canons, Cornwall) 132, 147, 151
Bolton Priory (Austin Canons, Yorkshire) 8, 151 (Embsay), 160, 165
Bordesley Abbey (Cistercian, Worcestershire) 182
Bosco de, Arnold 208
Boston (Lincolnshire) 81
Brackley (Oxfordshire) 56
Bradenstoke Priory (Austin Canons, Wiltshire) 103, 171
Braibroc, family 27
Bray de, Roger 184
Bret le, Simon 91
Bretville, family 27
Bridlington (Yorkshire) 94
Bridlington Priory (Austin Canons, Yorkshire) 8, 19, 25-6, 29-30, 93, 94, 97, 104, 110, 153, 231
Brison, Ralph 244
Bristol (Gloucestershire) 76, 122, 148
Bristol, St Augustine's Abbey (Austin Canons) 85, 122, 136, 148, 151, 153, 226, 231
Brompton (Yorkshire) 228
Brooke Priory (Austin Canons, Rutland) 165
Brus de, Peter 28
Buckinghamshire 167
Buckland (Hampshire) 142
Bucton' de, Arnold 25
building, see fabric
Bullington Priory (Gilbertine, Lincolnshire) 248
Bures (Suffolk) 48
Burghfield (Berkshire) 115
burial (in religious houses) 28, 29, 61-84, 99, 101, 119, 163
Burscough (Lancashire) 64
Burscough Priory (Austin Canons, Lancashire) 8, 64
Burstall de, Robert 121
Burton Abbey (Benedictine, Staffordshire) 8, 67-8
Burton on the Wolds (Leicestershire) 207
Bury Saint Edmunds (Suffolk) 131
Bury Saint Edmunds Abbey (Benedictine, Suffolk) 118
Bushmead Priory (Austin Canons, Bedfordshire) 27-8, 53, 89, 97
Byland Abbey (Cistercian, Yorkshire) 190, 213, 249, 255

Cainito de, William 205
Cambridge (Cambridgeshire) 138, 142, 148, 151
Cambridge, Saint Giles 136, 151

284   Index

Cambridgeshire 205
Cameley (Somerset) 226
Candlemas (the Purification) 52
candles 37-42, 50, 54, 55, 56
candlewekesilver 41
Candover (Hampshire) 103
Canford (Dorset) 103
Canonsleigh Priory (Austin Canons, Devon) 127-8
Canterbury (Kent) 71, 131, 158
Canterbury, cathedral priory (Benedictine, Kent) 160, 164, 168, 169, 170
Canterbury, Saint Gregory's Priory (Austin Canons, Kent) 8, 71, 133, 137, 151, 158, 182
Capra (Chievre) family 73, 186
Caprecuria, family, see also Cheverecurt 102
Carlisle (Cumberland) 137
cartularies, witness lists in 254-5
Caruncewyk', Stephen 109
Chadshunt (Warwickshire) 108
chantries (*cantarie*) 2-3, 7, 27, 28, 29, 34, 62, 86, 89, 96-104, 105, 150, 158
Chauenni de, Geoffrey 243
Chaworth family 75
Chaynes de, Richard 247
Chedestan' de, Drew 213
Chesney de, Alice 73
Chester, earls of 182, 190
Cheverecurt de, Robert, see also Caprecuria 208
Chievre family, see Capra
Christchurch Priory (Benedictine, Hampshire) 89, 119
Cirencester (Gloucestershire) 48, 132, 136, 138, 145, 146-7, 148, 231
Cirencester Abbey (Austin Canons, Gloucestershire) 8, 48, 132, 136, 138, 145, 146-7, 148, 149, 151, 153, 165-6, 231
Cistercians 8, 117, 203-20, 225, 227, 227-8, 233, 235, 237, 238
Clare 'Priory' (Friars, Suffolk) 75, 80
Clare (Suffolk) 80
clergy (secular) 1-3, 4, 7, 30, 55, 62, 76, 89, 96, 97, 98, 99, 100, 103, 104, 105, 120, 132
clergy, as witnesses 249, 250
Clerkenwell Priory, see London
Clinton de, Geoffrey 208, 225
Cockersand Abbey (Premonstratensian, Lancashire) 8, 64
Colchester (Essex) 138, 151
Colchester Priory (Austin Canons, Essex) 138, 151
Colchester, Saint Botolph's (Essex) 133, 151
Cold Ashby (Northamptonshire) 55
confession 88
confraternity, see fraternity
Conisborough (Yorkshire) 260
Constable family 104
Corbet, Roger 184
Cornehell de, Ralph 44
Costock (Nottinghamshire) 208
Cotheridge (Worcestershire) 66
Cound (Salop) 91
county court, as witness 248
Cranham (Gloucestershire) 72
Cremplesham de, family 120
Cressy de, Margaret 91
Croftuna de, Helewise 73, 74
Crowland Abbey (Benedictine, Lincolnshire) 182, 231
Cuxham (Oxfordshire), 37

Dale Abbey (Premonstratensian, Derbyshire) 8, 44, 64, 93, 96, 99-101

Index 285

Danelaw 219
Daneys le, family 27
Darlaston (Staffordshire) 68
Darley (Derbyshire) 64
Darley Abbey (Austin Canons, Derbyshire) 36, 48, 64, 90, 91, 120, 136-7, 138-9, 143, 149
Daventry (Northamptonshire) 64
Daventry Priory (Benedictine, Northamptonshire) 39, 43, 45, 49, 55, 64, 68-9, 92, 101, 123-4, 182
Derby (Derbyshire) 44, 48, 136, 137, 138-40, 143, 149, 151
Derbyshire 205
Deyncourt, Oliver 121
Dinant, Walter 228
dishes, see pittances
Domesday Book 201, 202-3
Downholme (Yorkshire) 228
Drax (Yorkshire) 108
Drax Priory (Austin Canons, Yorkshire) 8, 29, 94-5, 108, 228-9
Droitwich (Worcestershire) 190, 225
Druval de, Hugh 248
Dunstable (Bedfordshire) 132, 138, 145-6, 148, 149, 151
Dunstable Priory (Austin Canons, Bedfordshire) 100, 104, 132, 138, 145-6, 148, 149, 151, 165
Durham (Durham) 131-2
Durham, cathedral priory (Benedictine) 185, 186

Eakring (Nottinghamshire) 245
East Anglia 4
Easter wax 41, 46-7
Eastwell (Leicestershire) 209
Elmstead (Essex) 48
Ely, Isle of (Cambridgeshire) 41
Escotland de, Jordan 103

Espec, Walter 205
Esseburn' de, Robert 90, 93
estate administration 168-70
Etchingham (Sussex) 76
Etchingham, William 75
Evermu de, William 209
excommunication 55
Eynsham (Oxfordshire) 64
Eynsham Abbey (Benedictine, Oxfordshire) 8, 64, 141, 187, 246, 247

fabric (of religious houses) 28, 29, 57, 89, 94-6, 109, 159, 163-4, 172
famuli (estate labourers) 37
Ferrers de, Henry 74
Field (Staffordshire) 68
Fifehead (Dorset) 190
finances, monastic 115, 159-72
fish 28-9, 117-18, 124
FitzAlan, William 91, 190, 225
FitzGerald, Ranulf 190
FitzHarding, Robert 190
FitzHerbert, Walter 92
Flamborough (Yorkshire) 30
Foliot, Robert 182, 250
food, see pittances
Fossard, Thomas 225
founders, of religious houses, 3, 63, 179
Fountains Abbey (Cistercian, Yorkshire) 126, 127, 228, 233, 244, 252
Foxton (Leicestershire) 45
Fraisthorpe (Yorkshire) 26
frankalmoign, see free alms
fraternity (confraternity) 28, 57, 64, 66, 70, 80, 96, 103-4, 110
free alms 177-239
Furness Abbey (Cistercian, Lancashire) 230
Gait (Gay) family 232
Gait, Robert 205

Gant, Gilbert de, earl of Lincoln 19, 182, 205
Garendon (Leicestershire) 64
Garendon Abbey (Cistercian, Leicestershire) 8, 22-3, 59, 64, 199, 204, 205-9, 214, 215, 225, 227, 246, 247, 251
Garsington (Oxfordshire) 70
Geertz, Clifford, anthropologist 125
Gifford, Elias 72, 186
gifts (and gift-exchange) 9-12, 21, 24, 26, 50, 53, 57, 64, 69, 71, 73, 74, 75, 79, 85-111, 113, 115, 117, 177-97, 199-200, 204, 222, 244-5, 253, 254
Glapwell (Derbyshire) 49
Glastonbury Abbey (Benedictine, Somerset) 166
Gloucester Abbey (Benedictine, Gloucestershire) 72, 136, 186
Gloucester, earls of 182, 190-1, 226, 246, 248, 253-4
Godstow Abbey (Benedictine, Oxfordshire) 141
Goverton (Nottinghamshire) 94
Guisborough Priory (Austin Canons, Yorkshire) 28-9, 94, 95, 153, 232

Habrough (Lincolnshire) 244
Haddenham (Buckinghamshire) 55
Haddon (Derbyshire) 68
Hampton Gay (Oxfordshire) 167, 232
hand-fast 187, 195, 210-11, 213, 252
Haruecurt de, William 205
Hauerhill de, Thomas 122
Haverhulle de, William 92
Haveringtona de, family 26
Hawkswick (Yorkshire) 233
Hawton (Nottinghamshire) 71, 99

Headington (Oxfordshire) 48
Helaugh Park, Priory (Austin Canons, Yorkshire) 98, 101
Hereford (Herefordshire) 91
Hereford, earls of 91, 245, 246
Hereford, Saint Guthlac 91
Hertford (Hertfordshire) 48, 92
Heslington (Yorkshire) 229
Hexham (Northumberland) 132
Heybridge (Essex) 46
Hida de, Alan 104
Hilton (Derbyshire) 120
Holetorp' de, Richard 228
Holywell (Oxfordshire) 170
homage 178, 200, 223, 237
Honington (Lincolnshire) 251
honorial baronage, as witnesses 248, 249, 253
Hottot de, Roger 250
Houton' de, Roger 99
hundred court, as witness 248-9
Hungerford (Berkshire) 44
Huntingdon (Huntingdonshire) 55, 138
Huntingdon Priory (Austin Canons, Huntingdonshire) 230
Huntingdon, Saint Mary's (Huntingdonshire) 133, 136, 151

Ibstock (Leicestershire) 225, 226
indebtedness, of religious houses 164-7, 171
indulgences 66-7, 75, 96, 164
investment (estate) 168-70

Kaynes de, William 89
Kemble (Wiltshire) 114
Kenilworth Priory (Austin Canons, Warwickshire) 165
Kilnesei de, Edulf 228
Kilnsey (Yorkshire) 228
kin, as witnesses 246-7

Kinnersley (Salop) 186
Kirby Wiske (Yorkshire) 228
Kirkby Green (Lincolnshire) 49
Kirkstall Abbey (Cistercian, Yorkshire) 59, 229
Kirkstead Abbey (Cistercian, Yorkshire) 189
knight service 221-39
knight's fee 225, 226, 227-30, 232
knightly families 6, 23, 99, 100-1, 106, 121, 167-8, 221-2, 236
Knowles, David, historian 3, 4
Kyme, family 247, 248

Lamplogh de, Robert 26
Lamport (Northamptonshire) 224
land (land market) 21, 167-8, 177-97, 233-4
Langetot de, Ralph 246
Langliver de, John 26
Lateran Council, Fourth 2, 5, 50, 88, 116, 132
Lateran Council, Third 132
laudatio parentum 188, 215, 216, 246, 247
Launcelevey, John 43
Launcelin, Alice 210
Launceston (Cornwall) 138, 151
Launceston Priory (Austin Canons, Cornwall) 138, 151
Launde Priory (Austin Canons, Leicestershire) 230
Leake Newland (Lincolnshire) 91
legitim (custom) 63, 67-70, 77, 79
Leicester (Leicestershire) 64, 137, 142, 144
Leicester Abbey (Austin Canons, Leicestershire) 64, 137, 142, 144, 151, 153, 165
Leicester, earls of 20, 22, 204, 246
Leicestershire 205
Leigh (Staffordshire) 68

Lenham (Kent) 39
Lestrange, family 101
Leveske, family, of Bristol 122
Lewes Priory (Benedictine, Sussex) 101
Lichfield (Staffordshire) 45
Lichfield, cathedral chapter 45
liege men 63, 67-8, 77
lights (in churches and religious houses) 28, 35-60
lights (in parish churches) 45-8
lightscot 39, 41
Lincoln, cathedral chapter 50
Lincoln, earls of 248 (see also Roumara and Gant)
Lincolnshire 7, 24, 33, 91, 106, 190, 247, 251
Little Hallam (Derbyshire) 100
liturgy (monastic; in religious houses) 27, 29, 30-1, 32, 36, 51, 54, 88, 96, 108, 113, 124
livery of seisin, see seisin
Llanthony II (Austin Canons, Gloucestershire) 136, 151, 245-6
London 119, 122, 143, 148
London, Aldgate, Holy Trinity Priory (Austin Canons) 8, 99, 121, 137, 138, 139-40, 143, 148, 151
London, Clerkenwell Priory (Austin Canons) 122
London, Saint Paul's cathedral chapter 46-7, 52
Long Clawson (Leicestershire) 186
lordship, territorial 11, 20, 183-5, 192, 206
Loudham (Nottinghamshire) 49
Lucy de, Emma 120
Lucy de, Richard 182
Ludlow (Salop) 232
Luffield (Buckinghamshire) 64
Luffield Priory (Benedictine,

288 *Index*

Buckinghamshire) 64, 73, 166-7, 193, 224, 225

Malchenceio de, Geoffrey 69
Malesours, Geoffrey 69
Malmesbury Abbey (Benedictine, Wiltshire) 8, 114, 115, 123
Mandavill de, William 122
Mandeville de, Geoffrey, earl of Essex 119, 182
Mans de, Roger 250
manumission 159
Marton' de, family, 25
mass 85, 88, 89, 90-4, 97, 99, 100, 101, 102, 103, 104, 107, 109
mausolea 76
meals, see pittances
Meulan, count of 182
mills 140
Minchinhampton (Gloucestershire) 114
Missenden Abbey (Austin Canons, Buckinghamshire) 8, 90, 102-3, 120
Moor Monkton (Yorkshire) 228
Moriceby de, family 26
Mowbray family 189-90, 213, 226, 249
Moyne le, family 27
Murdac, Geoffrey 234
Musard, family 247
Mustel, Roger 229

Navestock (Essex) 47
neighborhood 23, 30, 72, 86, 106
Newenham Priory (Cistercian, Devon) 171
Newington Longeville Priory (Cluniac, Oxfordshire) 184, 188, 196
Newnham Priory (Austin Canons, Bedfordshire) 136, 171

Newstead Priory (Austin Canons, Nottinghamshire) 165
Niger, Roger 43
Norfolk 119, 169, 170, 205
Northamptonshire 205
Nortohft de, Edmund 75
Norwich (Norfolk) 110
Norwich, cathedral priory 80
Nostell Priory (Austin Canons, Yorkshire) 231
Nottingham (Nottinghamshire) 121, 205
Nottinghamshire 245

Oakover (Staffordshire) 68
oaths 184, 185, 187, 188, 195, 196, 210-11, 212-13, 219, 252
obedientiaries 87, 113-14, 115, 126, 164-6
Oddington (Gloucestershire) 73
Oilly d', family 246
Oilly d', Henry 163
Oilly d', Robert 69
Osney Abbey (Austin Canons, Oxfordshire) 45, 95, 114, 126, 134, 135, 137, 140-2, 144, 148, 151, 153, 161-4, 165, 167-8, 231, 232
Otley (Oxfordshire) 205
Owthorpe (Nottinghamshire) 44, 98
Oxford (Oxfordshire) 45, 49, 134-6, 137, 138, 140-2, 144, 148, 150, 158, 161
Oxford, Council of 2, 5, 88, 116
Oxford, Saint Frideswide's Priory (Austin Canons) 44, 134-5, 136, 137, 138, 140, 141, 148 151, 155, 158, 161, 166
Oxfordshire 170, 188, 221-2, 236

Paris candle 54
parish and parish churches 1-3,

4-5, 35, 42-3, 45-8, 50-1, 55, 56, 62-3, 70-1, 75, 76, 79, 86-8, 89, 91, 92, 95-6, 97, 98, 99, 103, 116, 121, 124, 132, 144, 148, 150, 167, 244
parish cemeteries 76-7
parish churches, appropriated 148-9, 163-4
parish churches, visitations of 46-7
parish, burial rights 66
Paschal candle 52, 55
patrons (of religious houses) 3, 63, 70, 101, 121, 163, 179, 213, 259
Paynell, Fulk 108
peasantry, free 49
Pennard de, Osbert 226
Pentecostal oblations 39
Percy de, Richard 127
Percy de, Walter 101
Pertesoil, family 27
Peterborough Abbey (Benedictine) 41, 166, 222
Peverel, Hamon 186
Peverel, William 234
Pincent, Robert 69, 72
Pipewell Abbey (Cistercian, Northamptonshire) 172, 205, 210, 214
Pirre(ho) de, William III 72, 102
pittances 28-9, 57, 59, 113-29
Plaiz de, Warin 103
pledge of faith, see oaths
Pleseleia de, Serlo 207
Plungar (Leicestershire) 186
Plymouth (Devon) 132, 147, 151
Plympton (Devon) 132, 138, 147, 151
Plympton Priory (Austin Canons, Devon) 85, 132, 138, 147, 151
Pontefract Priory (Benedictine, Yorkshire) 93, 101, 102
Port de, John 243
Portchester (Hampshire) 136, 137, 142, 148-9

Portsea (Hampshire) 149
Portsea Island (Hampshire) 142
Portsmouth (Hampshire) 44, 136, 142, 149
Potter Heigham (Norfolk) 68
purgatory 53
Purification, feast of the (see also Candlemas) 55, 56
Putrel family 23
Putrel, Henry 207-8, 247
Putrel, Robert 23

Queniburc de, Ralph 208-9
Quincy de, Saer 92

Ramsey Abbey (Benedictine, Huntingdonshire) 41, 55, 189, 192
Reading (Berkshire) 64
Reading Abbey (Benedictine, Berkshire) 8, 39, 64, 69, 74, 115, 119, 215, 246, 250
Redenesse, Robert de 25
Redvers family 119
Ridel, Geoffrey 183
Rieboc de, Theodore 101
Rigsby de, Herbert 189
ritual 12-13, 37, 39, 40, 54-5, 78, 87, 89, 90, 107, 118, 200, 216
Robertsbridge Abbey (Benedictine, Sussex) 76
Rochester, cathedral priory (Benedictine, Kent) 55, 66, 164
rood, devotion to the 129
Ros de, Robert, lord of Belvoir 33
Rothwell (Northamptonshire) 48
Roumara de, Walter 182
Rowington (Warwickshire) 39
Rufford (Nottinghamshire) 64
Rufford Abbey (Cistercian, Nottinghamshire) 8, 64, 74, 187, 205, 210-11, 245, 254

Rumilly de, Alice 246
Rumilly de, Cecily 246
Rushton (Northamptonshire) 48
Ruyton (Salop) 101

Saint Albans Abbey (Benedictine, Hertfordshire) 3-4, 82, 227
Saint Bees Priory (Benedictine, Cumberland) 26
Saint Benet Holme (Benedictine, Norfolk) 68, 126, 182, 243, 247, 250
Saint Denys Priory, see Southampton
Saint Frideswide's Priory, see Oxford
Saint Liz de, Simon 190
Saint Neot's Priory (Benedictine, Huntingdonshire) 196
Saint Osyth's Priory (Austin Canons, Essex) 230
saints, as witnesses 244, 252-3
Salisbury, cathedral chapter (Wiltshire) 36
Sandford (preceptory of Templars, Oxfordshire) 243, 247, 255
Sawbridgeworth (Hertfordshire) 74
Scarcliffe (Derbyshire) 48
Scopwick (Lincolnshire) 49
Scotton (Yorkshire) 228
scutage 230-3, 235, 236, 239
seisin (livery of) 206, 243, 244, 256
Selby Abbey (Benedictine, Yorkshire) 35, 119
Senlis de, Matilda 92
Sewerby (Yorkshire) 26
Shiplake (Oxfordshire) 44, 48
shire court, as witness 249
Shrewsbury (Salop) 45
Shrewsbury Abbey (Benedictine, Salop) 8, 43, 44, 45, 91, 101, 184,
186, 187, 190, 222, 225, 230, 232, 248
shrine 56
Shropshire 248
Sibton Abbey (Cistercian, Suffolk) 64, 71-2, 91, 101, 121, 205, 213
Silver family, of Bridlington 25, 93
Sixle Priory (Gilbertine, Lincolnshire) 249
Southampton (Hampshire) 114, 122
Southampton, Saint Denys Priory (Hampshire) 8, 50, 64, 122, 151, 186
Southwark Priory (Austin Canons, London) 143, 151
Southwick (Hampshire) 43, 44, 64
Southwick Priory (Austin Canons, Hampshire) 8, 43, 44, 64, 73, 74, 103, 136, 137, 142, 148-9
Speeton (Yorkshire) 26
Spetona de, family 25
Stanmere (Sussex) 82
Stanton under Bardon (Leicestershire) 205-6, 208
statutes, diocesan 36-7
Steane (Northamptonshire) 56
Stirap de, Gerard 196
Stixwould Priory (Gilbertine, Lincolnshire) 249, 252
Stockeld de, Nigel 235
Stoke (Berkshire) 69
Stoke by Clare Priory (Benedictine, Suffolk) 8, 48, 63-4, 69, 120, 184, 186, 222, 244, 246-7, 250
Stret de, William 229
Stretleg' de, family 100
Stubbington (Hampshire) 142
substitution (tenure) 237
suburbs 136-7, 144
Sudbury, Saint Bartholomew's Priory (Benedictine, Suffolk) 96

Suffolk 205
Sulby (Northamptonshire) 182
Sulhampstead (Berkshire) 74
Sumervyll' de, Robert 103
Sutton de, William, abbot of Osney 162
Sutton Prior (Devon) 132, 147
Sutton, Oliver, bishop of Lincoln 40, 67
Sywardby de, John 26

Tadcaster (Yorkshire) 101
Tadmarton (Oxfordshire) 70
Talebot, family 74
tallow 38, 54
Tamerton de, William 29
Tarrant Keynston (Dorset) 89
Taunton (Somerset) 138
Taunton Priory (Austin Canons, Somerset) 230
tenebrae (lights) 36, 53
tenure 177-220, 221-39
Tewkesbury Abbey (Benedictine, Gloucestershire) 64
Thame (Oxfordshire) 64
Thame Abbey (Cistercian, Oxfordshire) 8, 40, 64, 73, 205, 211-12, 214, 227
Thetford (Norfolk) 80
Thetford Priory (Benedictine, Norfolk) 64
Thorney Abbey (Benedictine, Lincolnshire) 168, 187
Thurgarton (Nottinghamshire) 64
Thurgarton Priory (Austin Canons, Nottinghamshire) 8, 43, 49, 57, 64, 71, 94, 97, 98-9, 103, 121
Tillingham (Essex) 46
Tilly de, Ralph 89
Tithby (Nottinghamshire) 49
torches 53
towns 121-2, 124-5, 131-58

Turs de, Geoffrey 189
Tutbury Priory (Benedictine, Staffordshire) 8, 64, 74
Twyford de, Thomas 120

Valoniis de, Roger 250
Vilers de, Robert 98-9
volo clause in charters 182-5

Waddington (Lincolnshire) 190
Waltham Abbey (Austin Canons, Essex) 8, 48, 91, 92, 120, 153, 166, 231
Warden Abbey (Cistercian, Bedfordshire) 64, 205, 212-13
Warenne de, earls of 183, 255-6
warranty 177-220, 235, 239
Warter Priory (Austin Canons, Yorkshire) 33, 109, 248
Warwick, earls of 209
Waverley Abbey (Cistercian, Surrey) 182
wax 37, 38, 39, 40, 41, 46, 55
Weekley (Northamptonshire) 190
Weldeboef, family 27, 97
Wellow Abbey (Austin Canons, Lincolnshire) 7, 24
Wells, cathedral chapter (Somerset) 36
Welton (Northamptonshire) 68
West Haddon (Northamptonshire) 55
Westminster 132
Westminster Abbey (Benedictine) 44, 92, 96, 117, 119, 182, 186, 236, 244, 250, 252-3
Westminster, Council of 66
Weston-on-the-Green (Oxfordshire) 162, 168, 211
Wilbrighton de, Hervey 187
Willerby (Yorkshire) 26
Winchcombe Abbey (Benedictine, Gloucestershire) 124, 245, 248-9

Winchester (Hampshire) 50, 74
Winchester, cathedral priory (Benedictine) 115
Windlesor' de, family 74
wine 90-4
Winterbourne Basset (Wiltshire) 110
Winwick (Huntingdonshire) 55
Wirksworth (Derbyshire) 90
witnesses, in charters 24-5, 241-62
Wiverton (Nottinghamshire) 97, 99
women, as witnesses (in charters) 251-2
women, gifts by 44, 45, 48, 73, 74, 89, 91, 92, 102, 120, 122, 210, 211-12, 246, 249
women, land transactions by 95, 195
Woodborough (Nottinghamshire) 99
Wootton-under-Edge (Gloucestershire) 76
Worcester, cathedral priory (Benedictine, Worcestershire) 66, 114, 124, 189, 234
Wrangle (Lincolnshire) 91
Wyverton' de, Richard 71, 97, 99

York, Saint Mary's Abbey (Benedictine, Yorkshire) 234
Yorkshire 228-30, 247

www.ingramcontent.com/pod-product-compliance
Lightning Source LLC
Chambersburg PA
CBHW020744160426
43192CB00006B/239